Billy Graham and the Beloved Community

Published Works

Against Us, but for Us: Martin Luther King, Jr. and the State

Martin Luther King, Jr. on Creative Living

God and Country? Diverse Perspectives on Christianity and Patriotism
(Palgrave Macmillan, 2007)

Billy Graham and the Beloved Community

Michael G. Long

First published in 2006 by
PALGRAVE MACMILLAN™
175 Fifth Avenue, New York, N.Y. 10010 and
Houndmills, Basingstoke, Hampshire, England RG21 6XS
Companies and representatives throughout the world.

PALGRAVE MACMILLAN is the global academic imprint of the Palgrave Macmillan division of St. Martin's Press, LLC and of Palgrave Macmillan Ltd. Macmillan® is a registered trademark in the United States, United Kingdom and other countries. Palgrave is a registered trademark in the European Union and other countries.

ISBN-13: 978–1–4039–6869–2
ISBN-10: 1–4039–6869–1

Library of Congress Cataloging-in-Publication Data

Long, Michael G.
    Billy Graham and the beloved community / Michael G. Long.
      p. cm.
    Includes index.
    ISBN 1–4039–6869–1
     1. Graham, Billy, 1918– I. Title.
BV3785.G69L66 2006
269'.2092—dc22   2005058661

A catalogue record for this book is available from the British Library.

Design by Newgen Imaging Systems (P) Ltd., Chennai, India.

First edition: August 2006

10 9 8 7 6 5 4 3 2 1

Printed in the United States of America.

For Karin

CONTENTS

ACKNOWLEDGMENTS

One of the most satisfying parts of my research has been the opportunity to watch film archives of the evangelist squirming this way and that when admiring interviewers would recount all of his achievements. When lauded, Graham would usually become uncomfortable and refuse to take credit for the success of his worldwide ministry, citing instead the contributions of his staff members as well as the major reason behind their incessant work—the triune God they worshipped so enthusiastically. Although I have little personal interest in his Christian theism, I discovered the Billy Graham of those clips to be nothing less than a moral exemplar of humility and gratitude, and it is in his grateful spirit that I offer him my deepest thanks for making this study possible. Had he not jumped so energetically into the public square, even while futilely denying his own central place in American politics, I would most likely have joined the rest of the academy in overlooking the importance of his remarkable ministry.

There are many others who deserve my gratitude, too. The staff members of the Billy Graham Center Archives at Wheaton College were truly extraordinary in their efforts to help me access the requisite materials for this study. They are not to be held responsible for my conclusions, but Paul Ericksen, Bob Shuster, Wayne Weber, and Christian Sawyer deserve special thanks for making their Archives the premier research site in the field of American evangelical thought.

Staff members of the Archives at the Martin Luther King, Jr. Center for Nonviolent Social Change, Inc., and Boston University's Mugar Library also offered precious assistance. I have not visited either institution since my dissertation days at Emory University, but portions of the research I offer in this book are directly traceable to the contributions of the friendly and professional staff at both institutions. Andrea Dowdy of the Martin Luther King, Jr. Papers Project, as well as Michele Rubin and Talia Shalev at the Writers' House in New York City, also provided invaluable assistance.

I owe a debt of gratitude to my home institution, Elizabethtown College in Pennsylvania. Special thanks goes to Donald Kraybill, formerly acting provost, for offering me a generous faculty grant that supported research trips to the Graham Center. In addition, Christina Bucher, an excellent administrator and wonderful colleague, enabled me to devote significant amounts of my professional life to research and writing; her former work as chair of the department of religious studies was a sheer pleasure to behold. My colleague Tracy Sadd, whose analytical abilities are matched by few on campus, kindly read and critiqued the entire manuscript. Two excellent students, Brian Hess and Jason Livermore, offered their sharp eyes and minds for proofreading and critical reactions. Sylvia Tiffany Morra, acting librarian at High Library, shared her investigative abilities as I floated through the black holes of computer databases. And MaryAnn Sluzis, the best administrative assistant on campus, also deserves my appreciation and respect, as does David Eller, the new sturdy chair of religious studies.

I cannot identify them by name, but I extend my gratitude to the overly sharp external reviewers of my manuscript, enlisted by Palgrave Macmillan during the acquisition stages, for the numerous ways in which they unknowingly strengthened my argument. Fortunately, I can name my excellent editor, Amanda Johnson, who deserves thanks upon thanks not only for her early enthusiasm for the project but also for her steady hand in guiding the manuscript through the maze of publication. I am more than fortunate to have such a smart and professional editor.

As usual, I am particularly indebted to my dear friend Sharon Herr, who proofread the manuscript with her typical exactitude and offered encouragement with her typical warmth. Sharon and I occasionally met to discuss her findings at my favorite home away from home—Cornerstone Coffeehouse in Camp Hill. Susan and Al Pera, along with their fun and creative staff, especially Matthew and Kelly, have given our community the best coffeehouse (and the best place to write) in the world.

I reserve my most heartfelt gratitude for Karin Long. She tells me that she is proud of me, and here I must tell her that I love her for that—and for being with me as I search, sometimes vainly, for my own beloved community. The world's best scholars have schooled me in critical thinking, but it is Karin, above all others, who has taught me the meaning of life—a love that endures. Today she and I celebrate not only the completion of this project, but especially the lively family that we have created, including our inquisitive son, Jackson Griffith, and his new baby brother, Nathaniel Finn. It is our family that I love most in life, and it is their hugs and kisses that have sustained me throughout this study.

Thanks, everyone, for all you have been to me. If only I could be the same to you, your life would be as rich as mine.

ABBREVIATIONS IN NOTES

BGCA
: Billy Graham Center Archives
Wheaton College
Wheaton, Illinois

DDEL
: Dwight D. Eisenhower Library
Abilene, Kansas

HSTL
: Harry S. Truman Library
Independence, Missouri

LBJL
: Lyndon Baines Johnson Library
Austin, Texas

MLKA
: Martin Luther King, Jr., Papers
Martin Luther King, Jr., Center for Nonviolent Social Change
Atlanta, Georgia

Papers 1
: *The Papers of Martin Luther King, Jr.*, volume 1, *Called to Serve, January 1929–June 1951*, ed. Clayborne Carson et al. (Berkeley, CA: University of California Press, 1992)

Papers 2
: *The Papers of Martin Luther King, Jr.*, volume 2, *Rediscovering Precious Values, July 1951–November 1955*, ed. Clayborne Carson et al. (Berkeley, CA: University of California Press, 1994)

Papers 3
: *The Papers of Martin Luther King, Jr.*, volume 3, *Birth of a New Age, December 1955–December 1956*, ed. Clayborne Carson et al. (Berkeley, CA: University of California Press, 1997)

Papers 4
: *The Papers of Martin Luther King, Jr.*, volume 4, *Symbol of the Movement, January 1957–December 1958*, ed. Clayborne Carson et al. (Berkeley, CA: University of California Press, 2000)

RMNPM
: Richard M. Nixon Pre-presidential Materials
The Richard Nixon Library Archive
Yorba Linda, California

Introduction: "Bowed in Prayer"—Resurrecting the Assassinated King

"There on the golf course I had all the journalists and the others gathered around, and we bowed in prayer for Dr. King's family, for the United States, and for the healing of the racial divisions of our world." It must have been a jolting feeling for Billy Graham as he bowed his head after finishing a relaxing round of golf in Brisbane, Australia, where he was holding yet another successful crusade. Graham had just received news that Martin Luther King, Jr. had been assassinated, shot while checking the weather from the balcony of his room at the Lorraine Motel in Memphis. The civil rights leader had gone to Memphis at the invitation of his good friend, James Lawson, to help the city's sanitation workers, the lepers of the American workforce, in their battle for economic justice against a belligerent, racist mayor. "I was almost in a state of shock," Graham recalled. "Not only was I losing a friend through a vicious and senseless killing, but America was losing a social leader and a prophet, and I felt his death would be one of the greatest tragedies in our history."[1]

Graham's sense of shock was more than understandable. Like President Kennedy, King had seemed so alive and vivacious, so youthful and invincible, in his whirlwind travels at home and around the globe. Less understandable, however, was the evangelist's lamentation that America had lost a social leader and prophet. After all, by the time of the assassination Graham had vigorously opposed many of King's efforts to dig a foundation for the "beloved community," with its three pillars of racial reconciliation, economic justice, and peace.

The beloved community was the regnant theme of King's public ministry, providing substantive content for both the goal and the means of the movement. Early in his public career, the civil rights leader had described this community as a world in which "men will live together as brothers; a world in which men will no longer take from the masses to give luxuries to the classes. A world in which men will throw down the sword and live by the higher principle of love."[2] In effect, the beloved community was the imaginary world to which King devoted his life and ministry; all of the various parts of his campaigns—the early boycott against Jim Crow, the marches against poverty and slums, and the conscientious objection from the Vietnam War—were designed to transform the broken community of America into an inclusive, just, and peaceable community.

Graham was not an enthusiastic supporter. Although he had denounced segregation as evil, a prophetic move for any white Southerner at that time, the evangelist had publicly dissented from King's plan to require Americans to integrate their social institutions, roles, and practices. Racial reconciliation was for the willing, not the unprepared and resistant. Although he had lobbied for the War on Poverty, partly out of devotion to Lyndon Baines Johnson, Graham had also questioned whether America's poor, when compared to the world's, were really poor at all. Shortly after King's death, he would even ridicule the Poor People's Campaign, King's final push for economic justice in America, on exactly this point. And although he had enthusiastically endorsed nonviolence for African Americans seeking redress for years of slavery and discrimination, Graham had characterized pacifism as naïve and dangerous for a nation teetering on the edge of chaotic disorder and in a world facing the evils of communism. For Graham, the threat of disorder and communism always trumped the mandates of Jesus' nonviolence, and Kennedy and Johnson were right if not righteous in their violent mission to safeguard Western civilization from a demonic political ideology.

By the time of the assassination Graham had also sniffed at King's pie-on-the-earth theology. For example, just after the climactic "I Have a Dream Speech," the evangelist pricked King's growing popularity by saying that only when Jesus comes again would little black children and little white children ever hold hands together. Perhaps even more significantly, Graham had begun to look at the civil rights leader with deep suspicion when he learned of the confidential reports of King's moral failings. The unsuspecting public would learn of the indiscretions in years to follow, but Graham, with easy access to the inner sanctum of J. Edgar Hoover's FBI, knew them so well that by 1968 he had become, in his own words, "mixed up in my thinking about [King]. I became concerned about the people who were around him. I think it was because of Hoover, and all the things he kept warning me about in regard to King."[3] The evangelist would never divulge the exact content of his conversations with the FBI's chief moralist, but it is conceivable, given the impressive scholarship of Taylor Branch and David Garrow, that Hoover might have shared information about King's bacchanalian tendencies—his extramarital sexual encounters and occasional thirst for a good stiff drink—or his unwillingness to sever ties with associates accused of communist leanings.

In spite of all this, Billy Graham bowed his head, right there on the golf course, and offered a prayer for King's family, for America, for the healing of racial divisions. And he would pray again, this time more publicly. A few days after the golf-course prayer, Graham's vigilant public relations team, most likely concerned that the evangelist's image would suffer if he seemed removed from the inner-city riots that had exploded following King's death, put out a press release stating that the evangelist had closed the

Brisbane conference by inviting his audience "to stand for a minute of silent prayer 'for peace in Vietnam, for peace on the streets of America and for the bereaved family of Martin Luther King, Jr.' "[4] Predictably, Graham did not invoke the spirit of King and call for a national march for peace in Vietnam; nor did he suggest local marches to help channel the anger of inner-city blacks frustrated by King's death. This was not the evangelist's style.

It was never his style. If King survived on the margins of American society, where black men and women sat in the rear of segregated buses, where black boys and girls wondered why they could not cool their little bodies in community pools, where poor people of all colors struggled to put food on the table, and where young men feared being killed by communists in faraway Southeast Asia, Graham flourished far above the mainstream, spending numerous nights at the White House, playing countless rounds of golf with industry and entertainment leaders, dining in private quarters with Wall Street's most influential money men, and standing shoulder-to-shoulder with the brass of the U.S. military. To be sure, King enjoyed some access to power, and Graham did take a few side trips to the margins; but the two traveled in widely different directions *ab initio*.

From their different social locations, both men also desperately tried to save the hell-bent soul of America, but in significantly different ways. King sought to pull America from its plunge by directly transforming the nation's institutions, roles, and practices: salvation was largely a social phenomenon to be accomplished through marches, sit-ins, imprisonments, legislation, and executive orders. Graham, however, tried to win America's soul one heart at a time: salvation was mostly an individual event wrought by preaching Christ crucified so that individual Americans would come to the foot of the cross, bow their heads, and accept Jesus Christ as personal Lord and Savior. Steering away from streets and jails, the evangelist preferred this type of soul-saving while ensconced behind stadium pulpits and radio microphones and while beaming in front of television cameras.

Graham was certainly not out of character, then, when he bowed his head on the golf course and later invited the Brisbane audience to pray for peace and the King family; he was simply being himself, a pious evangelist who favored prayer in orderly settings to marches in noisy streets or tactical sessions in dank jail cells. Yet he also was not being himself, or at least the individual he had been for so many years, namely, a would-be obstructionist of King and his beloved community. But this is not wholly surprising: death often reconciles oppositional ideas and the personalities behind them, sometimes against their own will. In the case of the living Graham and the dead King, the former took the occasion of death to transform, as if by mental magic, his difficult relationship with the latter. No longer did Graham envision and depict the civil rights leader as an imminent threat, an opponent in the mission to save America's soul; the dead King had become a social leader and a prophet. Of course, there were characteristic circumlocutions and tergiversations along the way. For example, in his first *Hour of Decision* sermon after King's death, Graham seemed to damn the civil rights leader with the faintest of praise.[5] The absolute best he could say was that "while Dr. King was a controversial figure in America, yet to the world outside he was a moral leader and a hero."[6] Missing was the personal voice, the warmth, the generosity that had marked Graham as America's pastor.

Graham would never praise the slain leader in stentorian tones, but he would continue to work hard at transforming his depiction of King. Like so many other white opponents of the civil rights leader, the evangelist would eventually co-opt King, transform him from an angry African American into a loving leader, and resurrect him as a dear friend of all whites and an unabashed cheerleader for stadium revivals. Why? The final answer to this question lies with Billy Graham, but the context would suggest that part of the reason for the transformation had to do with a rising fear of African Americans out of control. Simply put, at the time of King's death America's white leadership was frightened that African American militants would fill the vacuum by arming the inner cities with strident black nationalism and smoking black steel. Graham, most likely frightened by these violent militants, quickly joined the growing chorus of white leaders who had begun to set their criticisms aside and extol a moderate, white-loving King as the best model for African Americans in desperate search of recognition and a trusted leader.

The white evangelist would present a sanitized view of King in years to follow, too, totally effacing the civil rights leader's militant side—his democratic socialism, his granitic resistance to the Vietnam War, and his advocacy of forced integration. It was as if the dead King had matriculated to middle-class white America. Significantly, Graham's most celebrated and publicized memory of King usually came out in defense of his own actions during the civil rights movement. Obstreperous members of the press would occasionally pummel Graham with questions about his refusal to hit the streets, join the marchers, and stride toward jail, and each time he would invoke what he presented as a precious memory of the slain civil rights leader. "No," Graham would say in defense, "I did not march on the streets, and that came about as a result partially of a conversation I had with Martin Luther King." Graham would remember the conversation so apodictically that he would feel free to quote the dead prophet at considerable length. "He said, 'Billy . . . I think you ought to do just what you're doing—have integrated crusades in these stadiums.' He said, 'That helps prepare the way for me in the South.' And he said, 'You keep doing that, and I'll take to the streets. But if you go to the streets, your people will desert you, and you won't have the opportunity to have these integrated crusades.' I don't think it was a mistake."[7]

But the evangelist's memory was selective and, conveniently, his former opponent was not around to amplify. Graham could have recalled the letter King had written imploring the evangelist to stop granting privileged dais seats to segregationist politicians at the so-called integrated crusades. Or, as this book will show, he could have remembered numerous other substantive conflicts with the slain civil rights leader over such issues as economic justice and the Vietnam War. But he did not, and neither have some Graham interpreters; David L. Chappell, for example, has recently depicted the evangelist's work merely as complementary to King's public ministry and as a necessary ingredient for the success of the civil rights movement in the South.[8] But much more needs to be said about the evangelist in order to clarify the historical record, and this leads to the purpose of my book. In the study before you I will add to Graham's selective memory by using press conference transcripts, taped and written sermons, private correspondence with U.S. presidents, and speeches to present a relatively comprehensive analysis of the evangelist's reaction to King's beloved community. With the bulk of my attention on Graham rather than King, I intend to show that although the evangelist occasionally supported part of King's mission to save America, he largely opposed both the beloved community and the tactics King adopted for leading America into the Promised Land. More fundamentally, I will argue that Graham's commitments to political conservatism, as well as an evangelical theology marked by individualism and otherworldliness, precluded his ministry from ever becoming even a pale imitation of King's. To be sure, the icons occasionally came together on such significant issues as segregation and the War on Poverty, but Billy Graham neither dreamed of nor worked for the beloved community on earth.[9]

Graham Studies

Early in my research at the Billy Graham Archives, I began to realize that my study faced a potentially significant problem: Graham was rarely the sole author of his written and taped works, including his evangelistic sermons. Far from the public stage, staff members on the revivalist's team, including Lee Fisher and Robert O. Ferm, faithfully drafted books, speeches, columns, and sermons for Graham throughout the King years. Curiously, the evangelist, while acknowledging assistance for some of his works, blatantly denied that his staff had ever helped him draft and complete his evangelistic sermons. But the available evidence, as presented in the appendix, suggests otherwise, and this raises a critical question: If Graham did not write his sermons and other public documents, is it academically legitimate to use such sources to explicate his positions as carefully as possible? It is doubtless that the most authentic sources for unpacking Graham's views are the unfiltered statements he offered in discursive press conferences, but I will assume that all texts and sermons that list Graham as author are also valid sources for this study, primarily because the evangelist encouraged and gave approval for such works and because he never disowned any of the published or unpublished documents and tapes. To be sure, themes in Graham's works sometimes sharply conflict with one another—and this may be due to the different authors behind the various sources—but for the most part, the works present a well-rounded if not always coherent evangelical theology.

All of this would be known by now if it were not for the relatively deplorable state of Graham scholarship. Unfortunately, there is no field comparable to the fine academic works gathered together under the umbrella of contemporary King studies, there is no dean of Graham scholarship, and there is no well-organized papers project like the one directed by Clayborne Carson at Stanford. One can find a few credible, critical studies of Graham, most notably by Joe Barnhart and William McLoughlin, but the bulk of writing about the evangelist is little more than hagiography, fluffy reflections on an endearing Protestant saint.[10] My sense is that the literati have dismissed Graham for a number of reasons, including the one captured in William F. Buckley's self-important autobiography. "It has been said," the conservative theorist writes, "there is no theological question Billy Graham cannot vulgarize."[11] Like Buckley, scholars seem to have adopted an elitist view of Graham, depicting him as a theological lightweight, hardly worth a second look, if indeed a first one. But this is a shame, a sham, and a classic case of academic negligence.

The evangelist's written works may seem far less weighty than Buckley's literary tomes, but Graham himself is far more important to American history than Buckley or any other contemporary political philosopher, theologian, or ethicist could ever hope to be. The evangelist preached to millions upon millions of individuals—ordinary and extraordinary, liberal and conservative, Democrat and Republican, rich and poor, black and white—affecting their everyday lives in immeasurable ways, and some of these individuals include American presidents whom Graham counseled during crisis-packed situations in American history, like the Little Rock crisis during the King years. Moreover, some Graham interpreters believe that he not only transformed countless individual lives but also empowered one of the most radical social movements of the twentieth century—not the civil rights movement, of course, but the breathtaking collapse of communism. "Indeed, when the Berlin Wall finally came crashing down," former president Gerald Ford recalled, "I attributed no small part of the credit to Billy for planting seeds of faith in long-neglected soil. It was perhaps the greatest revival of his extraordinary career."[12] To be sure, it is difficult if not impossible to document or assess this claim with any certainty, but at the very least Ford is right to suggest that Graham cracked the Wall when he scaled it, with permission of governments he had once denounced, to preach about a God who offers salvation apart from governments and ideologies. Finally, there is also a notorious American social movement for which Graham cut a wide swath—the powerful rise of conservative Christians in the public square, including the Religious Right, the holy crusaders of the 1980s.

In short, the time has come for academics and others to put aside their elitist dismissal of Graham, recognize the evangelist as one of the most significant figures in the last century, and add to a corpus of writings devoted to explaining and critiquing his mission. This is not an entirely new plea; Mark Noll, for example, made a similar point shortly after publication of Graham's autobiography.[13]

Given the voluminous material that Graham produced, the task before us is enormous, and in this study I cannot even begin to address the evangelist's social thought during all of his public years of ministry. My modest hope here is simply to test Graham's suggestion that his ministry was complementary to King's, and to this end I will explain, clarify, and evaluate the content and evolution of Graham's social thought, especially his views on the interrelated dimensions of King's beloved community—racial reconciliation, economic justice, and peace—during one of the most critical periods of American history. But if this book, even with its limited focus, turns out to be another small step toward the formation of Graham studies, I am pleased to make it and hope that other scholars will journey with me into the peculiar but promising land of Billy Graham and evangelical social thought.

CHAPTER ONE

"The Bible Says": Heart Problems
and the Divine Cure

"Ladies and gentlemen, the problem of the world tonight is sin!"[1] The year was 1958, and the Reverend Billy Graham had returned to his home state of North Carolina for the Charlotte Crusade. The white revivalist preacher, now Southern Baptist but formerly Reformed Presbyterian, felt that the growing southern city had vibrant signs of Christian faithfulness, but he also sensed that something was wrong with the community and that the social world beyond Charlotte was no less troubled: crime rates were soaring, the possibility of nuclear war loomed large, and conflicts between blacks and whites were not dissipating. Racial tension was especially palpable to those gathered for the crusade that September evening in Charlotte. Only a few years earlier, in 1955, the Reverend Martin Luther King, Jr., then pastor of Dexter Avenue Baptist Church in Montgomery, had helped to plan the infamous bus boycott, and now that he had become president of the Southern Christian Leadership Conference, he seemed intent on eliminating segregation throughout the South.

Interestingly, the civil rights leader had penned a letter to Graham shortly before the beginning of the Charlotte Crusade, thanking him for the opportunity to lead a prayer at the 1957 New York Crusade, congratulating him on the success of that crusade, "a literal *tour de force* in the area of evangelism," and encouraging him to address race relations throughout his preaching ministry. "I am sure," King wrote, "you will continue this emphasis in all of your preaching, for you, above any other preacher in America can open the eyes of many persons on this question. Your tremendous personality, your extensive influence and your powerful message give you an opportunity in the area of human rights above almost any other person that we can point to."[2] Clearly, King was practicing flattery, as preachers tend to do for one another, but his glowing assessment of the extent of Graham's influence was quite accurate. By 1958 Graham was a best-selling author, a charismatic preacher who attracted overflowing audiences in massive sports stadiums, and a trusted adviser who shared confidences with business leaders and politicians, all the while preaching Christ crucified.

Graham was also one of the influential founders of an emerging and culturally significant religious group that had carefully labeled itself "neo-evangelical." The neo-evangelicals first emerged in the early 1940s, when Graham and other young moderate fundamentalists, especially John Harold Ockenga and Carl F.H. Henry, began to be troubled by a nagging sense that the judgmental character of conservative fundamentalism had become a barrier to effective evangelism. They also felt that fundamentalism's defiantly defensive posture had precluded serious intellectual engagement with the wider culture, and that its focus on the Second Coming of Christ had virtually undercut the possibility of faithful action in political and economic society. Disenchanted with this asocial fundamentalism, Graham and his colleagues combined forces, foreswore religious parochialism, and began to practice what Christian Smith has aptly called "engaged orthodoxy." While expressing orthodox Protestant theology, the neo-evangelicals also committed themselves to proactive engagement with the wider culture and society.[3]

Graham's particular form of orthodox engagement was especially visible by the time of the Charlotte Crusade in the ecumenical approach he had adopted in organizing his crusades. At the New York Crusade, for example, the evangelist had boldly cooperated with the Protestant Council of the City of New York, effectively decreeing a divorce of sorts from the exclusivist fundamentalists, who were no less outraged by the decision to invite King, whom they saw as a dangerous communist, to lead one of the services in prayer.[4] Beyond the New York Crusade, Graham's social engagement was also evident in his 1954 decision to found *Christianity Today*, an evangelical alternative to the theologically liberal *Christian Century*;[5] in his close relationship with politicians and business leaders, even ones with questionable scruples; and in his social preaching, the type that King encouraged in his fawning letter to Graham.

As Chappell has noted, the civil rights leader was deeply appreciative of Graham's early forms of engaged orthodoxy.[6] "I am delighted," King wrote, "to know that you will be conducting a crusade in Charlotte, North Carolina on a non-segregated basis. This is certainly a great step." But King was not wholly satisfied, and so he gently encouraged the evangelist to deepen his social engagement by conducting similar interracial crusades throughout the Deep South, in Mississippi, Tennessee, and Alabama, where the effects of a crusade "would be immeasurably great."[7] Glaringly absent from King's letter was an invitation for his fellow southerner to join the marches, leave behind the relatively safe confines of the stadium pulpit, and become an active participant in the civil rights movement as it took form in the dangerous streets and jails of the South in the 1950s. The absence of this invitation most likely reflected not only King's social manners, as well as his practical sensibilities about the movement, but also his awareness and acceptance of Graham's particular vocation as a Christian evangelist.

Graham did not believe that God had called him to be a leader of a social movement dedicated to advancing human rights, however Christian such a movement might have been. The unambiguous divine directive from on high was that he become an evangelist who would use any and all means to proclaim the Good News of Jesus Christ and challenge the unconverted to accept Jesus as their personal Lord and Savior.[8] This was not the type of calling that King, a son of the black Baptist Church, had been trained to listen for and discern.[9] Ordained under the pastoral leadership of Reverend Martin Luther King, Sr., who understood direct political action to be part and parcel of his calling as a black Baptist preacher, King, Jr. must have found Graham's calling to be alien, counter-intuitive, and perhaps suspect.[10] But his eventual acceptance of Graham's vocation is suggested both in the 1957 letter and in the evangelist's own reflections on his private meetings with King. In one such discussion, Graham recalled, King "urged me to keep doing what I was doing—preaching the Gospel to integrated audiences and supporting his goals by example—and not to join him in the streets . . . I followed his advice."[11]

But it was not only King's advice that the evangelist considered when he decided time and again to devote his energies to the crusades rather than to boycotts, marches, sit-ins, and freedom rides; he was also abiding by the dictates of the evangelical theology that gave substance to his identity and work as a Christian evangelist.[12] It is true that Graham's neo-evangelicalism called for social engagement, but the primary themes of his orthodox faith—biblicism, individualism, pessimism, and premillenialism—established terms for engagement that were far different from and even opposed to the beliefs and social practices of King and the civil rights movement.[13] In short, these themes flatly rejected the major premises of King's work—that social problems are largely the result of supra-individual social institutions, that one of the most effective methods for eliminating social problems is direct social action, and that significant structural change is historically possible.[14] Rather than supporting King and the beloved community, the primary themes of Graham's neo-evangelicalism actually opposed the civil rights leader's strategy and goals, eventually leading to an unbridgeable chasm that would exist between the two preachers throughout most of the King years.

"The Bible Says . . ."

With the Bible in one hand and the newspaper in the other, Graham would follow part of King's advice, and frequently preach on a wide variety of social issues throughout the King years. Interestingly, Graham's loudest critics at the time, like Union Seminary's Reinhold Niebuhr, complained that the evangelist virtually ignored social issues in his sermons—a criticism that survives even today in Mark Noll's baffling claim that Graham "minimized offense at his preaching by restricting his enumeration of sins mostly to those that received close attention in the evangelical culture: malicious neglect of spouse and children, overindulgences in drink, sexual immorality, and capitulation to anomie."[15] But even the most cursory of glances at Graham's sermons reveals that the evangelist regularly devoted the beginning of his sermons, and often their middle and end, less to the traditional sins of pious Christianity than to such troubling social issues as materialism, race, and crime. The minimization of offense in his preaching was due not to the type of sins he listed but to the solution he recommended for overcoming social problems—a converted heart. Above all else, it was his stereoscopic focus on a clean heart that made his ministry so "benign," as Martin Marty has put it.[16]

Much more helpful than either Niebuhr or Noll for interpreting Graham's preaching is a little-known oral history of Dan Potter on file at the Graham Archives. In his fascinating interview, Potter, a mainstream Protestant who had helped organize the New York Crusade, recalled that Graham's Madison Square Garden sermons were full of "statements in such areas as housing, poverty, race relations, employment. . . . In these sermons the statements that Billy made, and I remember some of them vividly, were stronger and more effective statements than most ministers in the churches of New York City could possibly make from their pulpits."[17] To be sure, the evangelist might not have addressed social issues with the type of depth preferred by the liberal Niebuhr—Graham always subsumed his social commentary under his primary mission of making disciples for Jesus Christ—but it is wholly inaccurate to claim that the evangelist's sermons were largely absent of social themes. Billy Graham was a social preacher who addressed everything from church–state relations and federal deficits to labor relations and tax policies.

Even in Charlotte, still a parochial town in the 1950s, Graham felt compelled to preach that the world was beset with one social problem after another. The evangelist, however, was interested less in the specific dynamics of any particular social issue than in the ultimate reason for the existence and flourishing of social problems, and so with the impeccable skills of an engaging preacher, he set before his Charlotte audience one of the major questions he sought to answer in his evangelistic ministry—What is the cause? What is the cause of the social problems of the world? Could poverty be the driving force behind the rising crime rates? Could the lack of appropriate power in the United Nations be the cause of the nuclear crisis? Could insufficient legislation be the cause of the race problem?[18]

To answer the question of cause Graham consistently turned to his most trusted source for theology and ethics—the Bible, especially stories of the life, death, and resurrection of Jesus. Like Martin Luther King, Jr., Graham had been exposed to biblical fundamentalism at a young age: He was raised in a fundamentalist Presbyterian home, converted to Christianity under the fundamentalist preaching of Mordecai Ham, and practiced his new faith in a culture of Southern fundamentalism.[19] But unlike King, with his degrees from Morehouse College, Crozer Theological Seminary, and Boston University, Graham had never attended educational institutions where modern biblical criticism was taught and encouraged as a viable option for

Christians in the twentieth century. Trained at the Florida Bible Institute, a nondenominational school in the fundamentalist tradition, and at Wheaton College, then the intellectual center of fundamentalism in Middle America, Graham had come to believe, understandably, in the full inspiration of Scriptures—a belief in the Bible, all of the Bible, as inerrant and infallible.

This conviction remained with Graham as he evolved into a neo-evangelical, and it was one of his unshakeable beliefs as he stood before his Charlotte audience in 1958. But earlier in his life, at the age of thirty, Graham had experienced serious questions about biblical authority, primarily because his own readings in contemporary theology, coupled with conversations with a trusted friend familiar with biblical criticism, had heightened a sense of apparent contradictions within the Bible. The questions eventually reached epic proportion in Graham's life, even threatening the continuation of his already successful ministry. But rather than trying to address the crisis by peering further into biblical criticism, Graham did what he knew best—he studied the words of the Bible all the more and then took the matter to God in prayer during a late-night walk. As he strolled through the woods at a retreat center near Los Angeles, the troubled Graham fell to his knees, with the Bible in hand and tears of anguish streaming down his face, and experienced what he remembered as the power of the Holy Spirit liberating his searching heart to trust, finally and wholly, in the absolute authority of the Word of God. With the Holy Spirit as his guide, Graham then offered a simple prayer to the God who had so confounded him: "Father, I am going to accept this as Thy Word—by *faith*. I'm going to allow faith to go beyond my intellectual questions and doubts, and I will believe this to be Your inspired Word."[20]

It is impossible to overstate the importance of this anxiety-ridden moment for the early development of Graham's social thought. From the moment he offered the prayer, Graham believed that the Bible was divinely inspired and therefore the one trustworthy source for analyzing, judging, and solving the social problems of the world. Just so, he consistently sought to develop his theology and ethics in accord with the choice of Martin Luther as he stood against a corrupt tradition of indulgences—*sola scriptura*.

Martin Luther King, Jr., however, was another story. Four years after Graham dropped to his knees, accepting the Bible as God's Word, King wrote a graduate school paper in which he argued for understanding "the Bible as both the Word of God and the Word of Man." The paper reflected King's characteristic attempt to steer a middle course, this time between liberal biblical criticism, which depicted scripture as merely a human product, and orthodox views of scripture as God's self-revelation. "We may wish," he wrote, "to supplement [the orthodox Karl] Barth's exclusive emphasis upon God's self-revelation in Scripture with a corrective emphasis upon tradition, reason or Christian experience, but we must agree that the Christian revelation is classic and normative for Christian thought; it is the central pillar on which the whole structure of Christian theology must rest." Like Graham, King interpreted the Bible as "a personal word from a living God," but unlike the orthodox evangelist, he also understood the Bible to be a product reflective of the social and cultural biases in which it was written—biases best analyzed with the tools of modern biblical criticism.[21]

If King's studies with liberal theologians had encouraged him to understand the Bible as a human product, and to treat extra-biblical material as sources that could call into question time-honored biblical truths, Graham simply sought to ensure that the Bible would trump all other ethical sources. In fact, Graham's social thought was largely biblicist, dismissive of modern biblical criticism in favor of his own fundamentalist interpretation of the ineluctable laws and principles of the Bible. This is not to suggest, even slightly, that Graham's social thought was purely biblicist. On the contrary, his evangelical faith was deeply embedded in the power structures of American society and often reflected American values more than biblical values.[22] Nevertheless, in the rich history of Protestant reformers, Graham tried to align himself more closely with Martin Luther's use of scripture than with John Wesley's broad appeal to scripture, tradition, reason, and experience, an appeal that King understood as altogether normative for modern Christians. With Luther as his ancestor, then, Graham frequently prefaced his theology and ethics with three simple words—"The Bible says."

Of course, the Bible says a lot, and it even says things that conflict with one another. But Graham, hermeneutically rooted in individualistic fundamentalism, dismissed such problems as unproblematic and focused on six biblical texts in particular to form the biblical foundation of his primary response to the social problems of the world.

Heart Problems

What is the cause of the world's problems? "The Bible," Graham preached to his Charlotte audience, "has an answer. Jesus had an answer."[23] The pious appeal to Jesus had given Graham's social critics quite a chuckle during the earlier New York Crusade. Among the most snobbish of his New York critics was Reinhold Niebuhr, who could barely contain himself when he warned America, in an editorial for *Life*, that Graham's ministry was a classic case of "frontier American evangelism," and guilty of "oversimplifying every issue of life."[24] It was the same criticism he had leveled in greater detail in a 1956 issue of *The Christian Century*. In this particular article, the hardnosed theologian had accused Graham of preaching "within the framework of pietistic moralism," which Niebuhr understood as "a source of illusion whenever it interpreted the problems of justice in America's growing industrialism as merely the fruits of a lack of individual discipline," and more seriously, as "particularly dangerous when it interpreted the differences between wealth and poverty as due to diligence on the one hand and sloth on the other."[25]

But Graham was typically inattentive to criticism from heady intellectuals employed by liberal theological seminaries, and so foremost in his mind in Charlotte was not Niebuhr's complex social analysis but the primary text for the evening's sermon: "And he said, 'It is what comes out of a person that defiles. For it is from within, from the human heart, that evil intentions come: fornication, theft, murder, adultery, avarice, wickedness, deceit, licentiousness, envy, slander, pride, folly. All these evil things come from within, and they defile a person'" (Mark 7:20–23). The author of the Gospel of Mark had included this passage not to make a point about the world's social problems but rather to teach that external practices, such as following dietary rules, were not the proper indicators for distinguishing Christians from non-Christians.[26] But Graham also rarely took note of historical criticism, and so he identified the text as the proper starting point for understanding the origin of the world's social ills. He could have highlighted biblical texts that identify unjust social practices as the root of community problems (for example, prophetic writings from Hebrew scripture), but his hermeneutic for selecting and interpreting scripture was essentially individualistic; it tended to focus stereoscopically on passages about the individual heart. And in this case, his individualistic hermeneutic steered him to pinpoint Mark 7:20–23 as the very heart of Christian social ethics.

In Graham's reading of the text, Jesus taught that the world's social problems are really not social at all. Social ills may reflect the material conditions of humanity, the faulty configuration of social institutions, or misdirected public policy, but the root cause of social problems can never rightly be equated with social distortions. Thus, although a primary cause of the soaring crime rate may seem to be an increase in poverty, and although a primary cause of war may seem to be a weak United Nations, and although a primary cause of segregation may seem to be an insufficient structuring of democracy, the real cause of these social problems is entirely something else. "The heart of the problem," Graham preached, "is something deeper, Jesus said. He said our problems originate from within. And he called it S-I-N—sin."[27]

What did the evangelist mean by sin? For King, sin was largely a social phenomenon embedded in anemic yet frighteningly powerful social institutions and the roles and policies that buttressed them—for example, the system of segregation as it assumed form in governmental agencies, offices, and roles throughout the South.[28] King did not lack a notion of sin as residing in the individual heart—just before his assassination he told his Ebenezer congregation that the most important question they would ever have to answer is, "Is your heart right?"—but he rarely emphasized the individual dimension of sin when articulating the mission of the civil rights movement. Graham, on the other hand, rarely characterized sin as social, as transcending the individual heart, or as residing in social institutions, roles, and practices that are much larger than and separate from individual personalities. The evangelist was not foolish enough to deny the existence of social sin—for example, in *The Seven Deadly Sins*, he lambasted a "social pride" that leads to class and racial divisions—but he never understood social sin as separate from the individual human heart.[29] "No matter how much we tend to think of sin as a social something," he stressed time and again, "it will forever remain true that social groups are groups of individuals. The real problem is always with the individual."[30]

It is no surprise, then, that the evangelist criticized social gospel advocates, Marxists, and secular sociologists as altogether wrong in their respective analyses of the cause of the world's problems. At root, social problems resulted not from social structures but from individual vices, the evil intentions found both on the surface of the individual heart and in its deepest chambers. It is envy that causes crime, it is lust that causes war, and it is prejudice that causes segregation. The political was always personal, a matter of individual moral character, in Graham's social ethics.

Standing against liberal social analyses, Graham identified the heart as the root cause of all social problems throughout the King years. Long before Charlotte, for example, he used one of his earliest *Hour of Decision* sermons to rant against theological liberalism's emphasis on social sin. "Systems are wrong," he railed, "only because men are wrong at heart."[31] Three years after Charlotte, he would preach, again on the *Hour of Decision*, that Jesus "wants to deal with the root cause of your difficulty and the world's troubles. He wants to deal with our hearts."[32] Even in Birmingham, a major target of the civil rights movement, the evangelist boldly preached that a "social malady" was not the cause of social problems. "The problem of man is that he is suffering from a moral disease. He has 'heart trouble.' "[33] And in 1967, during the heat of the Vietnam War, Graham stated: "World problems are only an extension of individual problems. Look at the world and you see yourself with all the fear, meaninglessness, hatred, and self-centeredness."[34]

The fundamental problem was not an impersonal social system but a bad heart—a really bad heart. Unlike King, who echoed the optimistic theology of the social gospel by describing the human individual as largely good and therefore capable of playing a significant role in forming the beloved community on earth, Graham joined Augustine and his hordes of theological disciples, Luther among them, in characterizing the heart as depraved in the innermost chambers. In fact, two years before the Charlotte Crusade, the evangelist had clearly stated, in an *Hour of Decision* sermon titled "Christ's Marching Orders," that the Bible had led him to prefer Augustinian pessimism over the optimism of theological liberalism: "There are two conceptions of the condition of man's fallen nature. Some assert that human nature is radically good. . . . However, the Bible asserts that human nature is radically bad."[35]

The depravity of the human heart was thus another constant theme throughout Graham's public ministry during the King years, and it received perhaps its clearest expression in *World Aflame*. A centerpiece of this 1965 bestseller was the second of the most significant biblical verses in Graham's social ethics: "The heart is devious above all else; it is perverse—who can understand it?" (Jeremiah 17:9)[36] Actually, Graham seemed to know it quite well. The pessimistic evangelist explained, no doubt with the help of his more theologically inclined staff writers, that the heart revolts against God by desiring to be independent of God, longing for what God has forbidden, and preferring self over God.[37] Consistent with his fundamentalist training, Graham also held that sin was both inherited from one's parents and consciously chosen by every individual, and that it affects every significant part of the individual—the mind, the will, and the conscience.

But Graham wanted to preserve a small slice of the human heart as capable of hearing and responding to the call of Christian conversion—the trademark of his crusades. Labeling the human individual as irredeemably corrupt, after all, would have given him sufficient reason to terminate his own position as a Christian evangelist. Graham thus argued that depravity "does not mean that man is totally sinful, hopelessly and irreparably bad, without any goodness at all." Still, even with this slight qualification, which separated him from the depressing Calvinists, Graham added: "[Depravity] means that sin has affected the totality of man's life, darkening his intellect, enfeebling his will, and corrupting his emotions. He is alienated from God and in need of restoration. His natural, instinctive inclinations are away from God and toward sin."[38] The evangelist thus maintained that moral character in unredeemed individuals is not moral at all, and that Freud, Marx, Nietzsche, and all liberal social scientists were foolish in their assessment of human nature. "The idea that man is good but that circumstances, environment, and society have made him the undesirable creature he is," Graham argued in 1967, "is a false illusion. Man is rebellious by nature, and the first rebellion was committed in Paradise—where the environment was perfect."[39]

Combined together, these two theological points—the heart as the most fundamental element of society, and the utterly depraved character of the heart—constitute the substance of Graham's theological analysis of the world's social problems. "Individuals that are sinners," he preached in Charlotte, "make up our society, and that causes the tensions and the problems and the wars and the troubles in your life, in the world in which we live. The international problems are only reflections of the individual problems."[40] In this sense, crime, war, and segregation are the results of human vices, symptoms of utterly depraved individual hearts. Just so, pessimistic individualism, with roots extending as far back as the sixteenth-century Reformation, was the hallmark characteristic of Graham's analysis of contemporary social problems.[41]

The Limits of Law

The evangelist did not want to leave his Charlotte audience, or any audience for that matter, simply with a message about the cause of sin, however important that message might have been. On the one hand, he found crime, war, and segregation, among other social problems, to be actively antithetical to the reign of God and therefore in need of remedy, and on the other, he feared for the salvation of individual souls. And so Graham reminded his own Charlotte audience that the wages of sin is death and that, should individuals remain unrepentant in their state of sin, the God of justice would force them to pay for their sin by consigning them to burn in the "everlasting fire" depicted in Matthew 25. Graham thus sought to lead his audience from thinking about the cause of their wrecked lives, individual and social, to experiencing the remedy for their wretched hearts. "How can we do away with sin?" he asked the residents of Charlotte. "How can we deal with human nature that Jesus said is the cause of all the problems and troubles in the world? How can it be changed?"[42] Indeed, how to counter crime, war, and segregation?

Martin Luther King, Jr. thought he knew at least part of the answer. In his first public speech at the beginning of the Montgomery movement, King emphasized that one of the best methods for countering segregation was social protest designed to force the formulation and implementation of legislation that would desegregate racist institutions. During the first public gathering in response to the arrest of Rosa Parks, the young King, inspired by Paul Tillich's logically loose but theologically creative interweaving of the themes of love, power, and justice, announced: "Not only are we using the tools of persuasion, but we've come to see that we've got to use the tools of coercion. Not only is this thing a process of education, but it is also a process of legislation."[43] From this moment on King would consistently emphasize that God is a God of justice, that the persuasive tactics of love are insufficient tools for social transformation, and that the coercive tools of justice—legislation, executive decrees, judicial decisions, and all the street protests that sought social change—are indispensable for transforming broken communities into the beloved community.

Graham, however, chose another point of emphasis when addressing the social problems of the world. Unlike King, the evangelist argued that social institutions, especially political and legal ones, are wholly insufficient as remedies for social problems—a point he explained around the time of the Montgomery boycott. "Today in America," he preached, "there are statesmen who assume that human government is the remedy for the world's dilemma. They assume that inasmuch as vice and crime flow from ignorance and poverty that virtue could arise from knowledge and competency. Yet history proves that this theory is inadequate. Constitutional and statutory law lacks the essential element to purify human nature."[44] Graham would never really set forth a developed theory of law, but as this sermon suggests, he was quick to condemn the use of civil law as "the remedy for the world's dilemma." Law is insufficient as a remedy because it fails to identify and respond to the real cause of social ills—the sinfulness of individual moral character. And just because it misidentifies the root cause of social problems, focusing instead on social conditions such as poverty or a lack of education, human law exercises no real power in combating vice and creating virtue, individual or social. Graham, of course, was not making the case to rid society of civil law. The evangelist was a law-and-order preacher, sometimes *in extremis*, who understood civil law as necessary for guaranteeing human rights and especially for restraining individuals who would break existing laws or violate human rights. Still, however important he found such laws to be, he consistently emphasized that civil laws never adequately address the root of the world's problems and therefore cannot suppress vice and encourage virtue.

This point gets to the core of his argument regarding the inadequacy of all social institutions and their embedded moralities. Consider government alone. Graham held that even if it could properly identify the root cause of social problems, government would still prove wholly insufficient, exactly because "[t]he power to suppress vice and develop virtue is not in man nor of man but outside of man, higher than man."[45] To be sure, government wields an earthly power to restrain the wicked and establish justice, but it is ultimately powerless to remedy the sin-sick hearts of individuals. The human heart is so sick, so sinful, so utterly depraved, that only *divine* power—power far beyond any social institution—can heal the individual, freeing him or her to live a good personal life and change the social order.[46] With his orthodox embrace of sheer depravity, Graham thus parted ranks with King and the civil rights movement by claiming that the best means for social transformation actually transcends the politics in which the civil rights leader had steeped the movement. In Graham's theology, Calvary, not Washington, holds the remedy for a new social order.[47]

Nothing but the Blood

If not social institutions and laws, what is the best remedy for curing the world of its many social problems? Graham once again turned to his most trusted source, the Bible, and there he focused on the third important verse for understanding his social ethics: "But if we walk in the light as he himself is in the light, we have fellowship with one another, and the blood of Jesus his Son cleanses us from all sin" (I John 1:7). Contrary to liberal theologians, the evangelist believed that the blood hymns of traditional Christianity had it right after all. "The only real cure for the spiritual disease that we all have," he preached in Charlotte, "is the blood of Jesus."[48] Unsurprisingly, the evangelist was not speaking metaphorically.

Graham's evangelical Christology located the significance of Jesus not so much in his moral teaching and actions but in the indispensable role he played in salvation history. For Graham, Jesus was less sanctifier, justifier, moral exemplar, or even teacher, than the Redeemer, the Savior, the Christ, the Son of God who had victoriously conquered death on the cross of Calvary, thereby making possible the redemption of human individuals, indeed all of creation, from sin and its deadly wages.[49] In his crusade sermons, Graham only sketched his understanding of the way in which the crucifixion of Jesus could save individuals in the twentieth century from the wages of sin, but he detailed his explanation, in painstaking fashion, in *World Aflame*. In the tradition of St. Anselm of Canterbury, Graham argued that the justice of God actually required the crucifixion of Jesus in order to create clean hearts and reconcile God and humanity. "If the problems of the world could have been resolved in any other way," he wrote, "God would not have allowed Jesus to die."[50] But not only did God allow Jesus to die, God also ordained the crucifixion of Jesus. Because the justice of God demanded atonement for the sins of the individual, and because only the sacrifice of the Son of God could ever satisfy God's thirst for justice, God required that Jesus die by crucifixion. On the cross, the Lamb of God then assumed the sins of the world, and through his sacrificial death, satisfied God's demand for justice, thereby allowing for the possibility of a new heart, a clean heart, for all sinners, and of reconciliation between God and individuals.

Graham's restatement of Anselm's theology of satisfaction sharply diverged from King's liberal theology.[51] Academically trained in a tradition that rejected Anselm wholesale, King would never ground his social thought in a bloodthirsty God or the Lamb that was slain for the sins of the world. Even as a seminary student, King had written a critical reflection on Anselm's satisfaction theories. "Such views taken literally," he argued, "become bizarre." On the one hand, merit and guilt are not transferable from one person to another, and on the other, the practice of human repentance requires a condition in which Jesus Christ has not already "paid the full penalty of sin." But King reserved his greatest displeasure for the type of God reflected in Anselm's theology: "It presents God as a kind of feudal Overlord, or as a stern Judge, or as a Governor of a state. Each of these minimizes the true Christian conception of God as a free personality."[52] Rejecting Anselm, King eventually identified Jesus not as the Lamb slain for the sins of the world but as the Liberator who could free blacks from the oppressive reign of racist pharaohs. Also contradictory to Graham, the civil rights leader held that the cross of the Liberator was never about cleansing blood for individual hearts seeking salvation but about virtues and practices that mark the people of God—forgiveness, love, sacrifice, and nonviolence. The cross was not a nice place to kneel at in quiet prayer; it was rather *the* way of life to take up and bear. It was the locus of reconciliation and healing for the world, not because it cleansed confessing converts, but because it revealed the way, the truth, and the life—the reconciling power of turning the other cheek even while demanding that pharaoh let God's people go.

Throughout the King years, however, Graham remained convinced that the only cure for the problem of sin is the "blood of Jesus," and with this in mind he invited his Charlotte audience to come to "the foot of the cross." Although the evangelist believed that the blood of Jesus is necessary for salvation, he never once claimed that the blood has full salvific power apart from human action: Graham was Armenian, not Calvinist, in his view of salvation, and true to his individualistic piety, he preached personal responsibility, good old-fashioned individual initiative.[53] The evangelist thus stressed the fourth important verse of his social ethics: "You must be born from above" (John 3:7).

Graham had preached born-againism long before 1955 and decades before anti-institutional hippies would organize themselves into the Jesus Movement, strolling through Berkeley in search of anyone who was not yet converted to Jesus. In fact, the evangelist had stylized his call for conversion during his years at the Florida Bible Institute, if not earlier, preaching that the practice of being "born again," or of journeying to "the foot of the cross," requires individuals to (1) acknowledge that God sacrificed Jesus for the sins of the world; (2) repent of their sins, understanding them as defilement before God and deliberately turning away from them; (3) receive and trust in Jesus Christ, by faith, as their personal Lord and Savior; and (4) confess the Lordship of Jesus publicly. "If you haven't been to the foot of that cross and washed in the blood of the Lamb," Graham preached years later in Charlotte, "you cannot say that your sin is forgiven you and that all is right between you and God or that all is right between you and your fellow man."[54] But if individuals do journey to the cross, God will forgive them, adopt them as God's own beloved sons and daughters, and give them a heart cleansed by the blood of Jesus and marked by the enduring presence of the Holy Spirit—the Spirit of Christ—who empowers individuals to resist temptation and sin.

Converting Hearts, Transforming Society

Here, at last, is the seed of social change in Graham's evangelical thought—the Spirit of the living Christ dwelling in the hearts of converted individuals. Among Graham's primary theological convictions was his belief that born-again individuals would take on and develop a new moral character, experiencing the type of radical transformation that Jesus had alluded to when he told Nicodemus that he must be born again. By delivering that ultimate challenge, Graham held, Jesus had acknowledged that converted individuals "can be changed, radically and permanently, from the inside out. There is the possibility of a completely new man."[55] With a twist of Christian mysticism Graham also added: "The new man is actually Christ in the heart, and Christ in the heart means that He is in the center of our being. The Biblical use of the word 'heart' symbolizes the whole realm of the affections, with the result that the things for which we formerly had affection pass away, and the things for which we now have affection are new and of God."[56]

The evangelist would never develop a theory of moral character, but he would suggest throughout the King years that the result of personal conversion is not just a heart "strangely warmed," as Wesley described his Aldersgate moment, but also a heart that would immediately begin to express itself socially. On the one hand, born-again Christians would turn away from the vices of old—hate, lust, greed, and prejudice—thereby eliminating in their own moral characters the ultimate reasons for the world's social problems. On the other hand, they would fully embrace the virtues characteristic of God's salvific work in Christ—joy, peace, gentleness, patience, and perhaps most importantly, love for neighbor.[57] "When you repent of your sins and receive Jesus Christ as your Savior," Graham preached, "he enlarges your capacity and gives you new ability to love your neighbor. He gives you new power, new directions, new strengths, new visions, new dimensions of living when you come to know him."[58] In this sense, individual conversion does not merely assure salvation in heaven; it also inevitably leads one to consider his or her neighbor with a spirit of Christian love and even to undertake good works that help eliminate the social problems that plague our neighbors.

But how should converted Christians love their neighbors and eliminate the social problems that plague them? Contrary to simplistic characterizations of his social thought, Graham set forth more than one model for Christians to adopt in their efforts to change society, but his preferred method was always the interpersonal conversion of individual hearts.[59] Unlike King, the evangelist consistently held that the most important method for turning the world upside down was not to become part of a social institution or a social movement devoted to making structural changes, but to share the good news of Jesus Christ with an individual in his or her home, at the coffee shop, or even on the street: Society is best transformed not en masse—this is impossible—but one heart at a time. And thus the most important social action is not marching or voting or enacting legislation or signing executive decrees or ringing a Salvation Army bell at Christmas, but winning souls for Jesus Christ—the practice of Christian evangelism.[60]

Predictably, Graham grounded this point in his interpretation of the life of Jesus: "Christ came into the world to redeem individuals. . . . Search the scriptures and you will find that the only sequence recognized in the Bible is a transformed society through transformed men."[61] Christ was "more interested in heart change," as he put it in a 1965 sermon in Alabama, "than social change, for he well knew that when the heart is right, then other matters fall into place."[62] The evangelist offered virtually the same point when he was asked to assess the social gospel movement: "There is no doubt that the social gospel has directed its energies toward the release of many of the problems of suffering humanity. I am for it! I believe it is biblical. However . . . There is one Gospel and one Gospel only, and that Gospel is the dynamic of God to change the individual and, through the individual, society."[63] Underlying this core conviction, of course, was the evangelist's individualistic characterization of society. Lacking a significant institutional perspective, the evangelist did not even consider the possibility that institutions have their own moralities and can shape and mold the moral character of individuals. Individuals make institutions, not vice versa;

and just because individuals are the fundamental blocks of the moral universe, any meaningful social change must always begin with their transformation.

Fascinatingly, this point is exactly what Graham preached at the 1957 New York service for which King offered the invocation. After the civil rights leader prayed for expansive understanding of social problems ("And in these days of emotional tension, when the problems of the world are gigantic in extent and chaotic in detail, give us penetrating visions, broad understanding, power of endurance, and abiding faith") and renewed energy for works of peace and justice ("And, O God, we ask Thee to help us work with renewed vigor for a warless world and for a brotherhood that transcends race or color"), Graham preached a sermon that virtually dismissed the structural methods of the civil rights movement in favor of individual conversion. "Almost every great social reform that the English-speaking world has ever had," he emphasized, "was led by men that had great conversion experiences and an encounter with the living God."[64] With a virtually undetectable subtlety, Graham elevated his own evangelical strategy for social change over the civil rights movement's, depicting his conversionist strategy as the most important practice for establishing the good society.

"Be a soul winner!" Graham thus advised in his best-selling *Peace with God*.[65] Opposed to vulgarian fundamentalism, the neo-evangelical recommended a positive, user-friendly evangelism marked by "wholesome living" and loving interpersonal relationships: Be a good person, dress nicely, love the people around you, and tell them about Jesus.[66] This may seem quite basic, but Graham was convinced that with an increase in the number of born-again Christians—individuals who would turn away from their hate, lust, greed, and prejudice, and begin to embrace a love for neighbor—a whole society of love could begin to form. As he put it during the New York Crusade, "Like a powerful leaven, these thousands of changed lives will have their inevitable effect on the community."

The effect could be mind-boggling. "Out of the Wesleyan revivals," Graham often noted, "came the social revolutions of Great Britain that led to social reform in America. Out of them came the emancipation of slaves, an end to child labor, the British labor movement, the YMCA, and many other social and political effects."[67] Prison reform, the prohibition of slave trade, the protection of children, and even the crusade against cruelty to animals were other examples of the tremendous social effects of Christian conversion.[68] In addition, Graham was not too humble to note the potential worldwide effects of his own revivalist preaching. In a March 26, 1955 letter to President Eisenhower, for example, he just happened to mention that his preaching at Glasgow was "the beginning of the greatest religious awakening in history. This could have a profound effect on its future politics and eventually on world events."[69]

At times Graham offered an unqualifiedly optimistic assessment of the social effects of conversion. In New York City, for instance, he preached: "Every human problem can be solved and every hunger satisfied and every potential can be fulfilled when a man encounters Jesus Christ and comes in vital relation to God in him." Seizing on this quotation, Niebuhr portrayed Graham as a Christian perfectionist who naively believed, contrary to "the continual possibilities of good and evil in every advance of civilization," that the world would be perfect if everyone would just accept Jesus in their hearts.[70] In spite of his sniping critics, however, Graham continued to embrace "the miracle motif," the perfectionist notion that if all individuals were converted to Christianity, social problems would simply disappear.[71] In 1964, for example, he suggested that if every citizen would just surrender their lives to Jesus and obey the Bible, Jesus would "solve the race problem, the crime problem, the home problem, the international problems."[72] Massive numbers of converts would indeed lead to "a new Christian order" marked by love and understanding.[73]

To be sure, then, Graham sounded individualistic when he concluded the Charlotte sermon, as well as countless other sermons, by extending a personal invitation to the men and women gathered for the crusade: "I am going to ask you to come and receive Jesus Christ, who died on the cross."[74] To the untrained ears of shallow critics, the invitation sounded like typical evangelical piety, but to Billy Graham, acceptance of this simple invitation was personal and social—the beginning of not only life eternal but also a socially engaged life committed to building a society that would finally confess Jesus Christ and live according to the dictates of Christian love.

Nevertheless, contrary to simplistic interpretations of Graham, the miracle motif was not the enduring motif in his social thought, for when pushed to clarify his position, the evangelist ultimately refused to be overly optimistic about the social effects of individual conversion, even the transformation that resulted from his evangelical preaching. In the end, his perfectionism would collapse, yielding the way to good old-fashioned evangelical pessimism.

Depravity Redux: The Limits of Conversion

Martin Luther King, Jr. never stopped believing in the possibility of miracles. Even near the end of his life, after having endured the murders of little black girls in Birmingham, numerous death threats against his own life, and an increasing resistance among white liberals, King remained mutedly hopeful that the broken communities of the world would one day come together to form the beloved community. The community of reconciliation was not an empty dream that the people of God would never be able to fulfill in their daily lives. With the power of God to make a way out of no way, and with the power of legal, educational, and religious institutions to make lasting social change, the people of God would indeed cross over to the Promised Land.

Graham disagreed, and he vocalized his dissent most pointedly just after King delivered "I Have a Dream" on the steps of the majestic Lincoln Memorial. "Only when Christ comes again," Graham objected, "will the little white children of Alabama walk hand in hand with little black children."[75] Ultimately, Billy Graham embraced an evangelical realism that refused to put great hopes in the historic possibility of a society that would one day be Christian in attitude and action. Among the early Graham interpreters, it was McLoughlin, not Niebuhr, who properly identified this realistic strain in the evangelist's social thought. "Graham," McLoughlin wrote, "is predominately pessimistic: the world is lost beyond redemption and only a few are chosen."[76] To be sure, the evangelist often implied that the social effects of his own method would be dramatically effective; but when pressed to clarify these bold claims, especially in the mid-to late King years, he would allow his perfectionism to take a back seat to traditional evangelical realism. In the final analysis, the miracle motif in Graham's social ethics would collapse under the weight of human depravity, making the evangelist the pessimist of all pessimists.

As the King years progressed, the increasingly realistic Graham emphasized that two complicating factors in particular—the world's ongoing rejection of Jesus, and the incompleteness of the new birth—precluded optimism about social transformation. On the one hand, the evangelist acknowledged that millions of people in the world would continue to reject the only remedy for their sin-sick hearts and that the world would consequently continue to be plagued by social problems. On the other hand, when pressed by members of the media, Graham also held that even if the whole world should turn to Christ, accepting him as Lord and Savior and giving rise to a new social order marked by a spirit of Christian love, social problems would nevertheless remain.[77] The evangelist acknowledged the intransigence of social problems primarily because of his belief that the new birth is far from complete—a realistic conviction he grounded in the writings of the Apostle Paul, specifically Galatians 5:17, the fifth important verse for understanding Graham's social ethics: "For what the flesh desires is opposed to the Spirit, and what the Spirit desires is opposed to the flesh; for these are opposed to each other, to prevent you from doing what you want."

Although he had claimed that being born again results in a "radical" change, Graham was careful to note that the new individual, with a heart cleansed by Christ, can never really attain perfection. "It is true," he wrote, "that the Christian possesses a new nature, but the old nature is still there." Like the famous "realized eschatology" of C.H. Dodd, with its peculiar argument that the reign of God is already here but not in complete form,[78] Graham's theology of the converted heart had a here-but-not-yet dimension: Jesus cleanses the converted heart, but the old heart does not disappear altogether. Even in the heart of the most faithful Christians there is a raging war between the new and old natures, and sometimes Christians simply yield to the old nature, giving life anew to the causes of the world's social problems. The Spirit of Jesus may be the only remedy for a sin-sick heart, then, but the remedy is far from completely effective in transforming the individual, let alone society. The transformation of the heart is therefore not as radical as the word "radical" would seem to suggest.

Contrary to Graham, King envisioned human history as a movement of ongoing process that would one day lead to the beloved community. But the pessimistic Graham scoffed at King's optimism, emphasizing instead that human history was on the road to destruction. Sounding just like Marx on the demise of capitalism, the evangelist put the point this way: "History is not infused with factors and forces that can produce a glorious end. History does not carry its own happy fulfillment. The human equation is too evident. Man is too prone to depravity."[79] Deep in the recesses of his evangelical heart, Graham remained convinced that the beloved community was nothing but a silly dream, never to be realized in human history, especially by a group of individuals with little respect for civil law: The broken community, not the beloved community, was the only possibility within human history.

However, Graham was also apocalyptic. And as an apocalyptic evangelical, he steadfastly refused to grant lasting power to the social problems of the world, preaching instead that the broken community would not endure forever. But Graham believed that the broken community would collapse not because of human effort, but because of the inevitable arrival of the day—"that day"—when Christ would come again. Finally, then, it is impossible to understand the primary theological themes of Graham's social thought without attending to his eschatological convictions.

Apocalypse Soon: Social Reckoning and the Kingdom Society

"Ladies and gentlemen," Graham announced to Charlotte in 1958, "the hope of the Second Advent of Christ has filled the church for centuries."[80] Once again Graham was not speaking metaphorically. Unlike King, who argued that that the Second Coming would not be an event in space and time—"Actually," he wrote, "we celebrate it every time we open our hearts . . . every time we forgive"[81]—Graham believed that Jesus would come again, in person, to complete and fulfill the reign of God on earth. Unsurprisingly, the ascension story in Acts 1:10–11, the sixth key text for understanding his social ethics, formed the basis of his interpretation of the end of history: "While he was going and they were gazing up toward heaven, suddenly two men in white robes stood by them. They said, 'Men of Galilee, why do you stand looking up toward heaven? This Jesus, who has been taken up from you into heaven, will come in the same way as you saw him go into heaven.' " This text was Graham's morning star. "Many times when I go to bed at night," he testified in 1956, "I think to myself that before I awaken Christ may come. Sometimes when I get up and look at the dawn I think that perhaps this is the day He will come."[82]

Contrary to King, Graham claimed that as human history moves into the future, it travels ever closer to the time when sin will become so overwhelming, so unredeemable, so maddening, that God will deem it necessary to intervene directly in the course of human affairs by sending Jesus Christ back to earth. Without this direct intervention of God, the sinful world would plunge itself into a chaos that could result only in the obliteration of the creation.[83] Graham, of course, did not believe that God would ever allow that to happen. With roots in fundamentalist dispensationalism, the evangelist even held that God would soon send Christ back to earth, that the end of the world was so imminent that signs of its arrival were present for all to see. "I believe," he preached in Charlotte, "we see certain signs today which indicate that the climactic point of history is about to be reached." The signs of the times included lawlessness, licentious behavior, widespread persecution of Christians, affluence without conscience, wars and rumors of wars, worldwide evangelism, and false prophets. But however terrible, the signs were no reason to fear the Second Coming. "What a moment that is going to be!" Graham exclaimed. On "that day" Christians from all times and places will be dressed in white robes and elevated to the skies for the coronation of Jesus as King of kings and Lord of all, and all the saints of glory will join angels upon angels in singing "redemption's grand theme song, 'Saved, saved by the blood of the crucified One.' "[84]

Graham's premillenialist convictions, which were entirely foreign to King's liberalism, suggested that the coronation would mark the beginning of a thousand-year reign during which Christ the King would rule all of creation with righteousness and justice, this time entirely transforming the whole individual heart and thus the social order. Significantly, three years before the Charlotte Crusade, in 1955, Graham had suggested that the reign of Christ would usher in a radically just social order. "The inequalities of injustice and life," he preached, "will be removed. . . . The poor, starving people of the earth will have in Christ a true Champion. . . . Men will no longer be rated by what they have, or even by how much they know, but by what they are by the grace of God. That day will be a day of social reckoning. . . ."[85] Noticeably absent in Graham's eschatological vision at this point was the topic of race, but in response to the civil rights movement swirling around him, the evangelist would later expand his vision of the glorious future to include reconciliation between the races. Graham would also later expound on his vision in relation to the Johnson Administration's plans for the great society. In 1965, for example, he began to describe "that day" as the beginning of "the kingdom society."[86]

The substantive content of Graham's kingdom society overlapped significantly with King's beloved community. For example, the kingdom society would be marked by integration, economic justice, and peace— the three interrelated dimensions of the beloved community. As Graham put this in *World Aflame*: "It will be a future in which there will be no war. There will be no poverty. There will be happy peaceful human relations . . . a state of complete reconciliation between man and

God—between race and race—between nation and nation."[87] A year earlier, the evangelist had offered a much more colorful description, far more bourgeois than King's beloved community, at a press conference in San Diego. "There is going to be heaven on earth," he announced. "We are going to have world peace. We are going to have two chickens in every pot, and two cars in every garage, and two television sets in every home." Ever the biblicist, however, Graham felt the need to qualify his colorful description: "Now the Bible doesn't say there'll be two chickens in every pot, but I'm using that only as an illustration of the type of world that it's going to be. It's going to be a tremendously affluent world. A world of peace. By the way, the sentence of death will be gone even."[88] In addition, in a 1967 press conference, this one in King's hometown of Atlanta, Graham used a distinctively political metaphor, perhaps with a bit of irony, when characterizing the future of Christians in the kingdom society. "We are going to have a period of peace and tranquility where every man is going to be a king and every woman is going to be a queen."[89]

Although the social content of his kingdom society overlapped considerably with that of the beloved community, there was an unmistakable point of difference between Graham's and King's futuristic vision—the issue of the means by which the good society would be established. Whereas King believed that humanity could establish the beloved community within human history, Graham argued that no human hands could completely establish the kingdom society. "The fabulous future that we Christians are looking for," he wrote in *World Aflame*, "will not be the natural development of history. It will not come by political restructuring. . . . It will come . . . by God's direct intervention!"[90] The exclamation point, although often overused by an enthusiastic Graham, is quite fitting here, because the consummation of the kingdom society, unlike the arrival of the great society or the beloved community, will be the result of a cataclysmic action that transcends human history and social institutions. The final arrival of the kingdom society does not depend upon any social institutions but actually follows, indeed *requires*, their complete destruction. "But when the Kingdom of God is established . . . it will be established by the hand of God in the midst of the ruins of our social and governmental institutions."[91] However marble-laden they may be, social institutions will finally end in ruins because of one reason— they chose self-interest over the truth of God.[92]

Although he rarely emphasized it when addressing the cause and remedy of social problems, Graham did indeed set forth a notion of social sin embedded in "the world system." He would never offer a clear description of this system, but he vaguely suggested that it includes the world's governments, cultures, and religions, many of which, he believed, are under the influence and power of Satan. "Satan," Graham preached, "is behind the scenes of the present era, calling the moves that are taking place within this world system." And taking cues from the Apostle Paul's writings about "principalities and powers," the evangelist argued that because of the infiltration of Satan, many social institutions are not ultimately benevolent institutions structured for carrying out the will of God on earth, but demonic powers that seek to control the hearts and minds of individuals. "Fallen man," Graham preached, "has always been antagonistic to the will of the sovereign God. Much of human government, culture, and even religion has been contrary to his plan for the world."[93]

Interestingly, Graham never used his theology of world systems to argue that institutions are primary causes of the world's problems; nor did he ever use this theology to identify the restructuring of institutions as one of the most important practices for accomplishing social transformation. Instead, he simply appealed to his theology of world systems when speaking of the judgment that God would bring to bear against existing social, political, economic, cultural, and religious institutions. Because many human institutions have acted contrary to the divine will, God will thunder forth at the time of the Second Coming and judge them so righteously that they will end in a heap of ruins upon which Christ would build the kingdom society.[94] Unlike King, who never understood social institutions to be beyond human redemption—the civil rights leader really did believe that the state could help the beloved community emerge within human history— Graham ultimately surrendered institutions to the dustbin in which God would sweep them at the Second Coming.

According to Graham, then, the arrival of the kingdom society is the result of God's action, not the action of individuals or social institutions. Only God in Jesus could lead humanity to the Promised Land. No institution could establish the kingdom society, and no Lyndon Baines Johnson or Martin Luther King, Jr. could ever see, let alone get to, the Promised Land—unless the apocalyptic return of Jesus had already happened. With this climactic point of history in mind, Graham finally set forth the question of questions for his Charlotte audience: "Are you ready?" In Graham's theology, there was one way to get ready, and it had nothing to do with social protests or social engineering. "If you are not ready to meet Christ," Graham preached, "you . . . can make ready by coming and repenting of your sins and receiving Christ. It's a very simple act. It's a sincere act by which you present yourself to Jesus Christ and say, 'Lord, from this moment on I'm yours. I want to receive you, I want to follow you, I want to live for you.' "[95]

Individualism, at last, trumped collective action. Ultimately, Graham focused on conversion of the individual heart because of his sense that only conversion could adequately prepare individuals for the coming destruction—a time when social institutions, whose demonic possession made them ultimately useless in remedying sin-sick hearts and establishing the kingdom society, would not just wither away but actually be obliterated by the wrath of God.

Beyond Evangelism?

Graham devoted his time and energy to the pulpit during the King years, rather than to the civil rights movement, because he felt that God had uniquely called him to be a Christian evangelist, and because the primary themes of his evangelical theology—biblicism, individualism, pessimism, and premillenialism—largely dismissed King's methods and goals as vacuous and unrealistic. Clinging to orthodox evangelicalism, the evangelist depicted structural methods as wrongheaded in their identification of the cause of social problems and labeled the beloved community as a fanciful dream that ignored the intransigence of human sin. Contrary to King's abiding faith in structural methods, Graham's faith suggested that the conversion of the individual heart is the most effective method for changing society and preparing individuals for the coming destruction. In fact, the primary themes of his evangelicalism drove a mile-high wedge between him and King—a wedge that prevented the evangelist from marching in the streets, sitting at segregated counters, and riding on busses attacked by rabid segregationists. Sheltered in stadium pulpits and radio and television studios, far removed from high-pressure hoses, vicious German shepherds, and the guns of assassins, Graham found the methods and goals of the movement to be alien to the essence of the Christian Gospel. In short, the primary themes of his faith were far more in line with the isolationism of fundamentalism than with the social activism of King and his followers.[96]

Nevertheless, Graham did engage in social action beyond the indirect method of evangelism, and Lee Nash rightly notes that "Graham's theology of social engagement goes much deeper than the simplistic formula that social change automatically follows conversion."[97] The evangelist would never embrace the beloved community as a reachable goal within human history, nor would he ever march in the streets—a decision that also resulted from his understanding of political authority. But Graham would concede the importance of working toward racial reconciliation, economic justice, and peace, and he would lobby Congress, seek to influence the minds of presidents, lend support to social welfare programs, and more generally, call for Christians to support social agencies and become involved in political society at all levels. In order to do this, however, he would have to move beyond the major emphases of his theology, appealing to secondary theological principles, a subtext of sorts, that few Graham followers realized was present in his thought. The subtext would never endear Graham to all of the strident tactics and goals of the civil rights movement, but it would allow him to act as an occasional social moderate—albeit the type of moderate that King would eventually denounce in the harshest of terms.

CHAPTER TWO

"Preaching Nothing but the Bible": Against a Political Church

"I think the church needs to get back to preaching nothing but the Bible." It was 1964, and Billy Graham was at a press conference in Phoenix, Arizona, for the purpose of publicizing his Crusade there. "We're so involved in all of these social programs and organizations and political pressures," he stated, "that we're leaving the Bible [behind]. . . I feel that in this country, with all our problems, that if preachers would stick to the Gospel and preach the Gospel and all of its power, that . . . could turn the world upside down."[1] Curiously, Graham had announced to the press only minutes earlier, and without making any appeal to the Bible, that he strongly supported a legislative effort to counter the 1964 Supreme Court decision that ruled state-sponsored school prayers as unconstitutional (*Engel v. Vitale*). Was it logically coherent for Graham, on the one hand, to announce his opposition to the Supreme Court's decision on school prayer, and on the other, to denounce church involvement in politics?

One did not have to put the same question to Martin Luther King, Jr. in 1964, especially when he stood before a gathering of European Baptists and proclaimed that the time had come for the church "to accept responsibility for the governments which we elect, or allow to be elected through our indifference." For King, the primary obligation of the church is not only to preach the Word of God but also to act as "the conscience of the state." Because the state is so racist, so classist, so violent, it is in desperate need of a catalyst that will push it toward the beloved community, and the church, as the agent of divine reconciliation on earth, has an enduring if largely forgotten responsibility to do exactly this role. As King put it in *Strength to Love*, "The church must be reminded that it is not the master or the servant of the state, but rather the conscience of the state. It must be the guide and critic of the state, and never its tool."[2] The civil rights leader even dared to suggest that social problems such as segregation and war arise largely because the church reneges on its responsibility to act as the conscience of the state—because the church seeks to extract itself and then escape from the political world. "The alternative to escape," he told the Europeans, "is a creative and courageous attempt to enter the world in revolution and there struggle with principalities and powers of this age as though we really believed that Christ has overcome the world, not just our little private world of salvation for my soul, but the world of rockets, steel mills, and hungry, overpopulated nations."[3]

Although Graham had taken a few steps away from the self-imposed isolation of his fundamentalist predecessors, he could never quite bring himself to embrace King's expansive and deeply political vision of the good church. In fact, his neo-evangelical ecclesiology sharply opposed the civil rights leader's strenuous efforts to transform the church from an otherworldly institution into a mastodonic activist in the civil rights movement. In effect, Graham encouraged communities of faith to be little more than what the civil rights leader described as "ready lackeys of the state."[4]

Beyond the issue of the church itself, the evangelist's perspective on the political role of individual Christians also sought to undermine King's earth-bound mission to save America's soul. Contrary to the civil rights leader, Graham depicted the good Christian not as an activist who would practice civil disobedience for the sake of the beloved community, but as a polite accommodationist who would recognize the state as a servant of God, deserving of respect, honor, and obedience. If King's good Christian was a construction worker for the beloved community, Graham's was a foot soldier for the state.

Politics Is Local

Long before postmodern theology began to deconstruct classic ecclesiology, Billy Graham, like many other writers of his day, set forth a notion of "the great universal church." "The New Testament," he wrote in *Peace with God*, "teaches that . . . even though there may be many cleavages and divisions within the structure of the church, yet we have only 'one Lord'. . . Jesus Christ is the head of this great universal church."[5] The evangelist was never specific in his New Testament references, most likely because it is simply impossible to find any biblical texts on a universal church. Far from biblical, the traditionalist Graham was actually communicating ancient creeds ("I believe in the holy catholic church") and common but easily deconstructable Enlightenment beliefs in universals. Nevertheless, the evangelist ascribed to this great universal church an essence (the crucified and risen Jesus, whose Holy Spirit gathered the church at the first Pentecost) and various purposes—glorifying God in worship, providing fellowship for Christians, strengthening the faith of believers, channeling funds for Christian work, and leading in "civic righteousness."[6]

Behind Graham's belief that the church should involve itself in civic matters was a high Christology. "It is important," he preached in 1964 Birmingham, "that the church and state remain separate, but there's another sense in which Christ cannot be separated from anything that pertains to life, for he is all and in all. . . . He's the master of every phase of our lives . . . Christ is king of government." But the great tragedy is that "we've tried to get [Christ] to abdicate from the realm of politics, economics, science, and religion. . . . We have made the mistake of dividing our lives into neat little compartments—politics in one section, economics in another, and religion poked back in a dark little corner for a few minutes on Sunday morning."[7] The challenge is therefore to recognize the sovereignty of Christ in all areas of life, including civil society. So how to act as if Christ is master of our civic lives?

The phrase "civic righteousness," of course, raises the critical issue of Graham's support for church involvement in politics—an issue as slippery as any in the evangelist's social thought. When asked in 1967 whether "the church ought to concern itself with politics, or should it confine itself entirely to a spiritual ministry," the evangelist replied that the answer depends upon what one means by the word "politics." "If we use the word to denote party politics," he wrote, "then clearly the church ought not to interfere in such matters."[8] Graham had stated this rather mundane point a bit more colorfully in a press conference four years earlier: "I don't think the church ought ever to say that 'I'm a Republican church,' or 'I'm a Democrat church.' "[9] Graham's argument against partisanship has been stated *ad nauseum* in Christian political ethics, but it was a bit ill-fitting in his own evangelical system. After all, if Christ is "all and in all," and if party politics is part of "the all" of our lives, on what grounds would the church refuse to "interfere" in party politics? Nevertheless, most important here is Graham's belief that politics, properly understood, "really has reference to the community life of a town or city—and with this, needless to say, Christianity is very deeply concerned."[10]

On the one hand, this narrow definition of politics is important because it reveals his intentional separation from the fundamentalists, who favored withdrawing from depraved political society into a holy enclave marked by their particular version of pious discipleship. Opposed to fundamentalist ghettoes, the evangelist called upon the church to embed itself within the politics of community life, not to get its hands dirty or bloody, but to traverse the dangerous planks crossing the quicksand of local politics. On the other hand, however, Graham's definition is deeply significant for understanding one of the ways he sought to oppose the activist politics of Martin Luther King, Jr. We must remember here the obvious point that King frequently called upon churches, white and black, to be generals in his religiously inspired and politically driven campaigns against local, state, and federal governments. To be sure, the civil rights leader used local communities and local politics as stages for his political theater, but the local dramaturgy always had implications for state, federal, and even international politics: King's local politics was always more than local. As revealed in his campaigns, the civil rights leader's definition of the word "politics" never referred simply to "the community life of a town or a city"; it also pointed to social institutions, roles, and practices on all levels of political society.

By contrast, Graham's understanding of politics reflected rural American parochialism—a small-town sense that one's hometown is the center of the political universe. It is true that the evangelist devoted much of his own preaching to national and international problems, but when speaking normatively about the church and politics, he depicted politics as primarily a local practice and claimed that one of the key purposes of the church is not to protest state and federal policies, but "to be an influence for good in the community."[11] Compare this to King's statement in a 1966 interview: "I see the church as the conscience of the community, the conscience of the nation, the conscience of the state, and consequently, the church must be involved in all of the vital issues of the day."[12] While King sought to activate the church in politics at all levels, the parochial evangelist sought to limit the church's purview to the school board, the borough council, and the mayor.

Boys Town and Bloc Voting

On the surface it seems that Graham's politics of localism could have served local civil rights campaigns in communities like Montgomery or Birmingham, but other obstructions made any collaborative work impossible, including the type of politics favored by the evangelist. While the liberal King extolled a politics of social justice, the conservative Graham highly favored political action in terms of local acts of kindness and generosity. Politics was less a matter of enacting legislation that would effect lasting structural change than it was of volunteering ten hours a week at the orphanage on the corner of town.

Unsurprisingly, Graham turned to the example of Jesus when setting forth ideas of political action for local churches. Although he identified Jesus primarily as the Lamb slain for the sins of the world, he also depicted Jesus as the best practitioner of "applied Christianity." Refusing to stay in the safe confines of the temple, Jesus "went out into the streets where the sick, the needy, and the dying were. No musty temple or dusty church could contain him."[13] Graham even granted special attention to Jesus' presence with "the least of these" in Matthew 25—the hungry, the thirsty, the naked, the sick, and the imprisoned. Graham's Jesus was not a holy roller stuck in a white-clapboard church, or even a monk sequestered in desert caves, but a local activist who sought to improve the lives of individuals stuck on the margins. And if his followers are to be with and mirror their Lord, they too will leave their darkened churches and feel the Spirit blowing in the margins of life. "As long as there is enslaved one man who should be free, as long as slums and ghettos exist, as long as any person goes to bed hungry at night, as long as the color of a man's skin is his prison, there must be a divine discontent."[14]

What does "the least of these" passage have to do with the church's role in politics? Matthew 25 is a classic text that social gospelers, liberation theologians, and liberal Christian activists frequently appeal to as biblical justification for their politics of justice. King, for example, used the text to condemn the United States for its failure to formulate and implement policies that would move political society toward the beloved community; he also used the text to criticize churches that failed to take part in the movement.[15] For the civil rights leader, Matthew 25 was a text that called for the church to engage in politics, including direct action against political institutions at all levels and in all branches, in order to establish roles, institutions, and practices that would reflect the love and justice of God as revealed in the one who identified himself with "the least of these."

But Graham never used Matthew 25 in the same way. Rather than citing this text to encourage a politics of justice, he used it to call for the church to become an active participant in a local politics of charity. In *Peace with God*, for example, he cited Matthew 25 as the introductory part of an argument commending church-based charity: "We have but to look about us at the many hospitals, homes for orphans, aged, and helplessly poverty-stricken, which have been organized by churches to recognize how powerfully this teaching has taken hold."[16] As suggested by these words, Graham was far less inclined to march with King than to send money to Boys Town, the Nebraska home for abandoned and abused boys that Newt Gingrich touted when he was Speaker of the House. Gingrich was merely a pale imitation of Graham. The Speaker's political opponents rightly criticized him for trying to localize a national problem and dismissing the Oliver Twistian abuses that orphanages are also known for, but his local politics of charity was exactly what Graham had long understood as the proper form of church engagement in politics: The church should not seek the formulation and implementation of state and federal policies that would correct social injustice, but rather build and sponsor local institutions of charity.

But this is not altogether fair. Although he consistently favored a politics of charity, the early Graham occasionally encouraged church involvement with local electoral politics and public policy. A few years before King united African American churches in pursuit of the desegregation of busses in Montgomery, for instance, the evangelist had written: "United church action can and frequently does become an important instrument in correcting abuses of civil power and in raising community standards."[17] And three years after the beginning of the boycott, he preached that the church should "be the church" by uniting its members on the local level to elect Christians to political office so that local government might be infused with Christian values.[18] Graham was not proposing that the church identify itself with a particular political party; although politically conservative, Graham was no Pat Robertson or Jerry Falwell, at least in the sense of equating the will of God with a particular party. But the evangelist did suggest, in words that sounded a lot like those we would hear from the Christian Right of the 1980s, that the church should act as a voting bloc designed to elect officials who would then implement Christian values in the local community.

Of course, as A. James Reichley has noted, Graham did not enjoy the success that Falwell and Roberston did in terms of energizing conservative Christians in the public square.[19]

Although Graham tended to emphasize charity over justice, then, there is evidence to suggest that he, like King, preached that the church has an obligation to form and transform the institutions, roles, and practices of local politics. One might thus imagine that in those overlapping areas the two leaders could have joined hands on the local level and called for united church action to bring about "the beloved community" in particular communities. But that, of course, did not happen, and the reason for the nonoccurrence is unsurprising: the two leaders focused on widely different policy issues at the local level. Just consider the local issues Graham highlighted in *Peace with God*: "Whether it is a campaign for more honest law enforcement or better garbage disposal, the cause of humanity at large is being served, and constructive service is one of the first duties of the church just as it is for every sincere member of it."[20] One might excuse Graham for excluding the issue of race as a major factor in local politics because he drafted *Peace with God* before the Montgomery bus boycott, but in the 1958 sermon highlighted above, the evangelist yet again ignored race and focused on the issue of crime in the local community. The evidence is quite clear: While King's local politics focused on substantive issues of importance to African Americans, Graham's tended to target issues near and dear to local whites. For the evangelist, the purpose of direct church involvement in local electoral politics was never about establishing justice for disenfranchised, poor blacks; it was about safeguarding the white community from crime, or, even less significant, ensuring that garbage is collected in a timely fashion.

Graham would stop calling for "united political action" several years into the King era, but he would never stop focusing on charity as the best form of political engagement for the church, even though life in the United States following the Depression showed that it was simply wrongheaded to believe that local forms of charity could solve social problems of national and international scope. As we will see in later chapters, Graham came to realize as much, but his recognition of the limits of charity would never transform his vision of proper politics for the church. Perhaps the evangelist could not bring himself to move away from charity because of the examples he found in the Bible. After all, his favorite texts on the subject, including the parable of the Good Samaritan, were not really about structural transformation. The parable, for example, is a story about practicing interpersonal charity in a society that practices discrimination; the Good Samaritan personally helps a wounded individual who is lying alongside the road, ignored by those who are not part of his class and community. Consider Matthew 25, too. Jesus does not call for his followers to appeal to the government in order to eliminate poverty; he simply asks them to feed the hungry, give drink to the thirsty, clothe the naked, and visit those in prison. His plea seems to be little more than a call for interpersonal ministry with the needy.

But Graham did indeed take an extra-biblical step when he suggested that the church should move beyond interpersonal charity and help build and support institutions of charity. There is simply no biblical warrant for the construction of charitable institutions per se. Also interesting here is that the parable of the Good Samaritan does not even serve Graham's desire to restrict the church to practices of local charity. The Good Samaritan is not in his community at the time he practices his good works; in fact, he actually represents a foreigner traveling on the road between Jerusalem and Jericho. The problem with appealing to the parable, then, is that while it serves Graham's desire to elevate a politics of charity over a politics of jus-tice, it counters his emphasis on localism. More pointedly, if the evangelist wanted to remain with what "the Bible says," he would have offered the church no political advice at all, primarily because Jesus offered his moral lessons to his immediate followers—a small movement of disciples—not to established social institutions we now vaguely refer to as "the church." Church support for charitable institutions, let alone united church action in local politics, was not even a small part of the message of the biblical Jesus as he exhorted his followers to practice radical discipleship. Graham's polit-ical advice to the church on local charity and united church action, there-fore, was far less biblical than it was reflective of traditional political conservatism—the same type of politics that sought to stifle the progressive politics of the civil rights movement.

Proclaiming God's Message through Government

As the King years progressed, Graham's statements on church and politics addressed the growing tendency in the ecumenical church to make public pronouncements on all types of social issues. Like King, who often appealed to Isaiah on peace, Amos on social justice, and Hosea on social blasphemy, the evangelist drew from "the prophets of old" when discussing the topic. "Certainly," Graham preached in 1964, "there comes a time when the church must speak out on moral conditions. Certainly the indi-vidual pulpit must touch on social evils as did the prophets of old."[21] To understand Graham's comment here, which was quite common in his ser-mons throughout the King years, it is important to note that there are at least four qualifiers: First, the evangelist never went so far as to suggest that the church's public voice should be "the conscience of the state." In fact, in a 1967 sermon on "the real role of the church," he seemed to counter this very point when he suggested that "there is a sense in which the church is to advise, warn, and challenge society by proclaiming the absolute crite-ria such as the Ten Commandments and the Sermon on the Mount, by which God will judge mankind, *by proclaiming God's purpose through government in a fallen society*, and by preaching the whole counsel of God, which certainly involves man's environment and physical being, as well as his soul."[22] The difference could hardly be more striking: While King implored the church to speak against government, especially on matters of race, economic justice, and peace, the evangelist invited the church to advise *society* that government is the locus of God's purposes in a fallen world. In effect, this means that Graham wanted the church to shift the object of its preaching away from government, and therefore to preserve government from ecclesial critiques—the prophetic critiques that King spent his life imploring the church to make. Graham's focus away from the government also meant that he dismissed the many biblical prophets who publicly ranted and raved against kings who had disobeyed the commands of Yahweh.

Second, the evangelist often qualified his statements about political preaching by drawing attention to the so-called lack of political and economic expertise within the church. "A President of the United States," he wrote in 1965, "told me that he was sick and tired of hearing preachers give advice on international affairs when they did not have the facts straight."[23] Sharing this story, of course, was Graham's way of saying that he too was sick and tired of the same thing. In a 1964 press conference in Columbus, the evangelist passed on a similar complaint from then Secretary of State John Foster Dulles. Apparently, Dulles had called a meeting with the evangelist shortly after he had made a public statement about sending surplus U.S. wheat to starving India. During the meeting, the Secretary had politely lambasted Graham's political and economic naiveté. "Now when I was President of the Federal Council of Churches, I used to make statements like that, but since I've become Secretary of State, it's far more complex than that." The smitten Graham apparently took this statement to heart, telling the gathered press that it was wrong for the church "to give simple answers to complex problems." Take the case of calling for surplus wheat to be sent to India, he said. If we in the United States were to give our surplus to India, we "would upset the entire economy of China or Australia, of Egypt and different parts of the world." That was what Dulles had taught him—that "it's not quite as easy as your statement implies. And he was very kind to give me a lesson in economics."[24]

Graham was not offering a lesson on economics but suggesting in no uncertain words that the church would do well to refrain from making statements about issues beyond its expertise. Which issues did he have in mind? In 1965 he was especially disturbed by ever increasing church resolutions on disarmament, federal aid to education, birth control, and the United Nations. But he did concede that "there are certain issues we know to be wrong—racial injustice, crime, gambling, dishonesty, pornography. On these matters we must thunder forth as the prophets of God."[25] But why crime and not the Vietnam War? Why gambling and not a guaranteed annual income? Why pornography and not the United Nations? At first glance, it seems that Graham distinguished between general statements on moral issues, like race, and specific policy recommendations, like disarmament and birth control, arguing that while it is okay for the church to make statements about general issues, it is not permissible for it to comment on or demand specific action on particular public policies. But that twisted defense quickly collapses: Would not a stance against racism necessarily support policy recommendations aimed to desegregate society? And would not a stance against gambling entail support for public policy that criminalized slot machines? Of course, but Graham never followed the internal logic of his own thought here; nor did he ever define the criteria by which he included or excluded issues for church comment, thereby leaving the unfortunate impression that the substance of his own political views mattered more to him than the so-called lack of expertise within the church. Incidentally, the evangelist also dismissed his own belief that Jesus Christ is "all and in all," for if Christ is "in" the realm of military or educational or reproductive affairs, whatever that might mean, it would seem that the church would want to discover what he is doing there so as to follow him and inform others. By resorting to the traditionally conservative argument about the lack of political expertise in the church, Graham was guilty of his own charge against those who would compartmentalize their faith, boxing off huge areas of concern as if Christ did not matter to them at all.

Third, it was not just the lack of expertise that troubled Graham; it was also the sense that the church, especially mainstream Protestant churches and the ecumenical movement, lacked sufficient authority to pass resolutions on public policy. Like a good independent-minded Baptist, Graham wrote in 1965 that he was "not sure that the leaders of the church have a right to speak without consultation for the whole membership of the church."[26] The evangelist further explained this point, albeit with a bit of a stumble, during a 1968 press conference, shortly after King was assassinated. "I think there is a vast difference," he stated, "between a church, church leaders, people for their constituency without consulting the constituency on certain political issues, than an individual, like myself, and a private citizen."[27] Of course, he never defined what he meant by "consultation," nor did he dare explain exactly how the major churches and church organizations would consult with their members in a timely fashion during urgent political crises. But his main point was unmistakable—the church should refrain from making and publicizing political resolutions passed by only a select group of its members.

Fourth, Graham rarely allowed his statements about the church's preaching on social issues to stand alone; he usually followed them with a "but" or "however" that led his listeners into a discussion about "the main purpose of the church." For example, the evangelist followed the above statement ("Certainly the individual pulpit must touch on social evils as did the prophets of old") with a qualifying conjunction ("But the main concern of the pulpit and the church corporate is . . . .").[28] The qualifying conjunctions became more pronounced as the King years advanced because of the growing number of resolutions passed by denominations and ecumenical councils, and because of the politicization of the church encouraged by the civil rights movement. These political trends in the church alarmed the evangelist mostly because of his neo-evangelical belief that the primary purpose of the church is far from the realm of politics at any level—far from the place where King wanted to steep the church as deeply as possible.[29]

The Primary Mission of the Church

"What is the church's primary mission? Is it redemptive or social—or both?" This is the loaded question that Graham posed in 1965, in reply to his sense that the church was putting its "greatest emphasis on ecclesiastical organizations, resolutions, pronouncements, lobbying, and even the law itself to bring into being and enforce the social changes envisioned by church leaders as a part of the world where the church shall be the dominating influence."[30] If this statement seems like a shot across the bow of the political church King longed for, it was exactly that. Disturbed by the politicization of the church, the evangelist turned his eyes toward Jesus and, with a considerable hermeneutic stretch, claimed to discover the church's real mission in Luke 12: "Someone in the crowd said to him, 'Teacher, tell my brother to divide the family inheritance with me.' But he said to him, 'Friend, who set me to be a judge or arbitrator over you?' " In Graham's thought, Jesus' words provided the indisputable answer to the question of whether the church's primary mission is social or redemptive. "This was a genuine economic problem, one on which the church often speaks today and passes many resolutions on." But Jesus took a different tact. "Did Christ look into the case and then pass a resolution? Did he study this economic question?" The rhetorical questions held the answer, but Graham rolled on: "No! Jesus said he had not been appointed to this office of arbitrator or judge in economic matters. . . . Jesus felt that this was a matter for the authorities to decide."[31]

The church should do the same—let the authorities decide. Graham wanted to preserve the right of the church to offer general statements about moral and spiritual issues, but he insisted that the church refrain from dictating policy to government or the market. As he put this issue in the 1968 press conference in Syndey, "I think the church ought to make a contribution in every area of social and political problems. But I don't think that the church should assert their [sic] authority over the state."[32] The church is not appointed by God to arbitrate or judge in specific policy matters, and therefore it is far beyond its proper jurisdiction when it passes resolutions on such issues as disarmament, federal aid to education, birth control, and the United Nations. This time Graham's point was not about expertise or the will of church members; it was about divinely appointed jurisdiction and authority—a proper division of labor.

Graham grounded his understanding of the proper division of labor partly in his interpretation of Jesus' views on human nature. The short version of the argument is something like this: Jesus taught that the human person is a trinity, an individual made up of mind, body, and spirit.[33] Government, coupled with schools, businesses, and hospitals, properly ministers to the mind and body, and even the church, with its educational and social ministry programs, ministers well to the mind and body, with the result that "we have vast programs to feed and to develop our bodies, but we have little or no program to develop the moral and spiritual side of man." And so the spirit languishes. "But who," Graham asked, "is going to minister to the spirit if the church doesn't?"[34]

The question was rhetorical. "It is the job of the church," Graham stated at a 1967 Tokyo press conference, "to appeal to the spirit, which will have its effect on social and political ideas."[35] Tending to the spirit is the main mission of the church exactly because, as Graham put this in the 1967 San Juan press conference, "the primary emphasis . . . in the scripture is to the spirit of man, the spiritual side of man."[36] The Bible says so. More fundamentally, however, Graham also held that the spirit of the triune human individual was the primary emphasis of the life of Jesus. The inheritance story redux: After Jesus decided that the question of inheritance was a matter for the proper governing authorities, he "turned to the main themes of his ministry and said, 'Take heed and beware of covetousness.'" Rather than becoming enmeshed in the social, economic, and political problems, Jesus devoted his primary mission to healing the sinful heart—the locus of all social problems.[37]

But what happened to the Jesus of Matthew 25 in Graham's overly neat division of labor? Where is the Jesus who separates the goats and the sheep according to who feeds the hungry, gives drink to the thirsty, visits the sick and imprisoned, clothes the naked? Where is the Jesus who is so concerned with the body that he consigns to hell the goats that fail to tend to the bodies of "the least of these"? For this Jesus, the most important ingredient of good living is not an abstract decision to accept him as personal Lord and Savior, but a radical commitment to be with and minister to the marginalized. Obviously, Graham was reflecting conservative politics more than Jesus of Mt. 25 when he scolded the church for moving in the direction that King encouraged.

Two Kingdoms: A Political Ethic of Imbalance

Also underlying Graham's sense that the church should not assert its authority over the state is the traditional evangelical appeal to Luther's political ethics, especially his theology of the two kingdoms.[38] Armed with a strong doctrine of human sin, Luther's political ethics, as set forth in *On Secular Authority*, sharply distinguished between "the kingdom of God" and "the kingdom of the world." The former consists of all true believers in Christ and is governed by the church through its priests and bishops.[39] And the primary mission of the church within the kingdom of God is only spiritual; the church relies on the Word of God alone as it forms Christian character and spreads love and mercy throughout the world. Ever the pessimistic realist, Luther also envisioned the world beyond the church as full of "unchristian" people who are like fierce animals intent on destroying everything and everyone around them, and argued that in response to the pervasive wickedness in "the kingdom of the world," God established the secular government as a necessary dyke against the ravaging effects of sin. Rather than relying on the Word of God, as the church properly does, the secular government wields "the sword" in order to hold the unchristian and wicked in check.[40] The primary mission of secular government is thus physical—government holds sinful bodies in check. A later chapter will deal with the use of the sword, but here the key point to note is Luther's belief that God has ordained the existence and work of both the church and the state, and that "care must be taken to keep these two governments distinct."[41] The worldly government must never extend its authority into spiritual matters, and the spiritual government must never extend its authority into matters of the state.

It is impossible to find a two-kingdom political ethic in King's thought, but Graham seemed to accept it fully. Like Luther, Graham held that the primary mission of the church is spiritual—to form Christian character and spread mercy throughout the world—and sharply criticized the church for extending its authority into matters of the state. As Graham described the problem, "the spirit of man in many churches is completely neglected because the church is involved in education, and the church is so involved in social activism, that it doesn't have time to develop the spirit of man—to get down to the bedrock of what makes a man tick."[42] Thus, in his sermon on "the proper balance of the church," he proclaimed that "the main concern of the pulpit and the church corporate is the ministry of the Word of God." Social reform is not entirely wrong, but for the church to neglect ministry to individual souls is "dead wrong, and we are grieving the Holy Spirit. My call today is to the church to be the church and to get back a proper balance in its dynamic proclamation of the Gospel of Jesus Christ."[43]

Notice the evolution from the 1958 sermon, highlighted above, in which Graham said that for the church to be the church it should involve itself in electoral politics. By 1964, the evangelist was equivocating, saying that for the church to be the church it needs to regain a balance. And by "proper balance" he did not mean that the church should devote 50 percent of its time to social ministry and the other 50 percent to evangelism, but that the church should give its primary attention and most of its resources to Christian evangelism, and just a bit of attention and a few resources to what he called "social engineering." In a sermon titled "A Cause to Fight," Graham even went so far as to imply that the "proper balance" meant copying the content of his own radio preaching. "I've talked on everything from bad housing to highway safety," he stated. "However, the social issues of our day have not been the main theme of my preaching. My main theme has been the same as that of the early apostles—that Christ died for our sins according to the scriptures, that he was buried, and that he arose again according to the scriptures."[44] A study of Graham's radio sermons does indicate exactly this. The alarmist Graham would take a few minutes to review the action-packed, salvation-threatening crises of the world, but he would then calm down and devote most of his time to sketching what individuals needed to do in order to save themselves from the crises surrounding them. The Billy Graham Evangelistic Association (BGEA) did the same. A quick review of BGEA's ministry through the years reveals the obvious—that the bulk of its expenses went to the practices of evangelism and mission, along with the supporting administrative infrastructure, rather than to social engineering.

Graham believed that because many preachers and churches did the opposite, focusing primarily on social problems with only some attention to evangelism, at least two results followed. First, the church faced a crisis of statistics. The alarmist Graham announced this crisis, without providing a shred of evidence to support his claim, at a 1964 press conference in Washington, DC: "You see the Protestant church is losing out, the whole church is losing out, in the sense of statistics. We are becoming a rapidly increasing minority in the world . . . because we have lessened our emphasis on evangelism—winning people to Christ, which has always been the main task of the church."[45] Second, the church was failing in social activism: "The social program of the church is failing today because we are trying to get the world to accept the social ethic of Christianity without the new heart of Christianity. Men's hearts must be changed before we can change society. We've put the cart before the horse. We're making great pronouncements on social issues today, demanding that the world keep the social ethic, the Christian ethic, when they've never been born again of the Spirit of God."[46] All the political preaching, all the political resolutions, all the political activism would ultimately fail unless the targeted individuals of those pronouncements and actions were justified by the blood of Jesus; only the converted could even begin to understand, let alone live out, the social implications of the gospel of Jesus Christ. Again, this is a point echoed, with tongue in cheek, by Luther in *On Secular Authority*. "But before you rule the world in the Christian and Gospel manner, be sure to fill it with true Christians . . . to try to run the whole country or the world by means of the Gospel is like herding together wolves, lions, eagles and sheep in the same pen, letting them mix freely, and saying to them: feed, and be just and peaceable. . . . The sheep would certainly keep the peace . . . but they would not live long."[47]

Like Luther, Graham believed it foolish for the church to try to implement its social ethic in a world unredeemed and ruled by wolves. As Graham put all this in "The Real Role of the Church," "the church today is getting off the main track. . . . We have been trying to solve every ill of society as though society were made up of regenerate and born again, converted men. . . . The changing of men is the primary mission of the church. The only way to change men is to get them converted to Christ."[48] Hence, by 1964, when the ecumenical church was loudly political, Graham's sense of "the proper balance" of the church was really the statement of dramatic imbalance that introduced the chapter: "I think the church needs to get back to preaching nothing but the Bible." Graham's diagnosis and prescription were equally unbalanced in a 1968 article for *Christianity Today*, in which he described churches as "blundering social physicians." "The great need," he wrote, "is for the Church to call in the Great Physician, who alone can properly diagnose the case. He alone has the cure." And so the church should shift its primary focus away from social causes. "If we in the church want a cause to fight, let's fight sin. . . . I would call the Church back today to its main task of proclaiming Christ and him crucified as the only panacea for the problems that face the world."[49]

Graham not only preached the need for the church to get back on "the main track," witnessing to Christ crucified so that God could save repentant sinners; he also practiced his ethic of imbalance by joining forces with *Christianity Today* to hold the World Congress on Evangelism in Berlin in 1966, hoping that a "spiritual explosion" would result in the world. At a news conference announcing the congress, Graham pointed to nothing less than the experience of Pentecost as his model. "In the first century there was Pentecost which came, and the church scattered with this tremendous fire and the filling of the Holy Spirit, and Spirit-filled men turned their world upside down. They changed the whole current of history. We are praying and hoping that this Congress in Berlin will make a contribution to a spiritual explosion in our generation."[50] The spiritual explosion apparently did not happen as Graham had wished, because two years later, after being disturbed by the 1968 Fourth Assembly of the World Council of Churches' efforts "to redefine the good news of the Gospel in terms of restructuring society instead of calling individuals to repentance and faith in Christ," Graham began to organize another world congress on evangelism, this one in Lausanne.[51]

While Graham was calling the church back to its primary mission of preaching Christ crucified, while he was demanding the church "preach nothing but the Bible," while he was criticizing the church for focusing on the body and not the soul, while he was insisting that the church restrict itself to its divinely ordained jurisdiction, while he was lamenting the church's focus on restructuring society, Martin Luther King, Jr. was attempting to make racial reconciliation, economic justice, and peace integral parts of the primary conscience and work of the church—to inject a social conscience, as well as social activism, into the church's primary mission, all for the sake of the beloved community. Fewer things disturbed King more than an ecclesiology that called the church to slow down its social activism, or to shift its attention away from the body and toward the soul, or "to preach nothing but the Bible." This is exactly the type of ecclesiology that King sharply criticized in his *Letter from Birmingham Jail*. In this famous letter, the civil rights leader decried churches that "commit themselves to a completely otherworldly religion which makes a strange, unbiblical distinction between body and soul, between the sacred and the secular." Recalling a time when the church was socially active, even revolutionary in its conviction that Christians were called to obey God rather than humanity, King lamented the apolitical church of his day. "In deep disappointment, I have wept over the laxity of the Church."[52] But he also remained hopeful about and grateful for "the church within the church," those "noble souls" who joined the march toward the beloved community. "They have left their secure congregations and walked the streets of Albany, Georgia, with us. They have gone down the highways of the South on tortuous rides for freedom. Yes, they have gone to jail with us. . . . Their witness has been the spiritual salt that has preserved the true meaning of the gospel in these troubled times."[53] King was not writing about Billy Graham, nor was he commending the evangelist's vision of the good church. In his letter from Birmingham Jail, King left no doubt that the "the inner spiritual church, the church within the church . . . the true ecclesia and hope of the world," was not the apolitical church of Billy Graham.[54]

The Good Citizen: Christians and Politics

Yet, for all of his bluster against the church's involvement with politics, Graham joined King, quite remarkably, in calling individual Christians to a life of political engagement at all levels. This may seem an odd point, and perhaps crudely paradoxical, but it simply reflects the traditional evangelical inclination to draw a sharp distinction between the social obligations of the church and those of individual Christians.[55] Such a distinction, most obvious in a press conference comment already cited ("I think there is a vast difference between a church, church leaders, people for their constituency without consulting the constituency on certain political issues, than an individual, like myself, and a private citizen"), is completely foreign to King's political thought, but the evangelist consistently distinguished between the church and individual Christians, and by doing so he opened the door, ever so slightly, for individual Christians to become the political animals that King wanted them to be.

"I certainly do not think," Graham wrote in 1967, "that Christians should be disinterested in the affairs of our government. Christ said, 'Render unto Caesar the things that are Caesar's and unto God, the things that are God's.' "[56] But did Jesus really mean that Christians should be interested in the affairs of government when he told inquirers that they should render unto Caesar the things that are his? New Testament scholar Walter Pilgrim characterizes the Caesar text, which really addresses the issue of paying taxes, as "notoriously difficult to interpret," and describes four different types of interpretation that scholars have given the text through the years.[57] Unsurprisingly, Graham set forth what Pilgrim refers to as "the traditional interpretation" of the text, which, like Luther's theology of the two kingdoms, suggests that Jesus acknowledged "two legitimate realms" in the world—God's and Caesar's—with each realm having "its rightful place and honor." In addition, the traditionalists emphasize "the loyalty and respect owed to Caesar are not inherently in conflict with the things of God. A divinely intended partnership exists between the earthly political realm and the kingdom of God." Recognizing the partnership, the Christian owes "respect and honor" to both Caesar and God. "Accordingly," writes Pilgrim, "taxes are owed to Caesar, while to God belongs the loyalty of one's heart and life."[58]

The traditionalist Graham interpreted the "render unto Caesar" passage exactly this way. When asked about the text at a 1963 press conference, he replied: "I think Christ was teaching that we have a dual responsibility, and that these responsibilities are not necessarily in conflict—that we have a responsibility to the state as Christians, and we have a responsibility to God, and that under normal conditions this is not a conflict."[59] Graham further argued that the individual Christian is a citizen of two worlds—Caesar's and God's—and that with this dual citizenship the Christian has obligations to become good citizens of both worlds. But what did it mean for Christians to become good citizens of Caesar's world?

"I would urge every Christian," he wrote in 1967, "to vote and to show a keen interest in the politics of his community."[60] Voting, of course, was not biblically prescribed, but that did not deter the American Graham; he simply shifted his ethical sources from the Bible to American history. "The ballot," he argued, "is part of our great American heritage and freedom. *It is our only means of keeping government clean and proper.* I think that it is not only the right, but the duty of every American to use his franchise, prayerfully and thoughtfully."[61] To stress the importance of voting, Graham would regularly use his radio program to offer a sermon titled "Cast Your Vote for Christ." In the 1956 version of the sermon, the evangelist decried the "alarming apathy" of American Christians: "While we rejoice that people are interested in the things of God, we must also remember that we must render unto Caesar the things that are Caesar's, and show a proper interest in government," especially through the practice of voting. "I hope that every citizen of the United States," he preached, "will go to the polls next Tuesday and exercise his or her right to franchise. The Bible plainly teaches that we are to participate in good citizenship."[62] The juxtaposition between "go to the polls" and "The Bible plainly teaches" would most likely have suggested for the biblically challenged that the Bible actually recommends voting as a practice of good citizenship, but obviously, this is not true: the Bible neither directly teaches nor subtly implies that Christians are to be good citizens by going to the polls. Given the lack of polls in both Ancient Israel and early Christian communities, Graham's vision of good citizenship was far more American than biblical.

Beyond voting, good citizenship also meant praying for the governing authorities. The evangelist found biblical justification for the practice of praying for politicians in I Timothy 2:1–2: "First of all, then, I urge that supplications, prayers, intercessions, and thanksgivings be made for everyone, for kings and all who are in high positions, so that we may lead a quiet and peaceable life in all godliness and dignity." But Graham also moved far beyond this biblical admonition, when he called upon Christians to pray so that the will of God would reveal itself through the democratic practice of voting. In his 1960 version of "Cast Your Vote for Christ," for instance, Graham made a special push for Christians to hold prayer meetings over the presidential election that was gripping the nation. "Let's ask Him to speak and to show us His will in this election." This election pitted the Catholic John F. Kennedy against Graham's good friend, the nominally Protestant Richard Nixon, and apparently required more prayers than usual. "I have been in prayer about this election more than any single event that I can remember."[63]

Besides appalling psephologists, Graham's admonition to pray that God would direct the outcome of an American election was certainly extra-biblical, reflective more of his devotion to American politics in general and Republican politics in particular than to his commitment to biblical Christianity. But while his American Republicanism was quite clear, unclear was the way that God might direct a democratic election. Would God send more Democrats to the polls than Republicans, or vice versa? Would God direct the African American community to shift its vote from the Republican Party of Lincoln to the Democratic Party of Kennedy? Graham did not answer these inevitable questions, of course; he simply insisted that Christians can and should use prayer as a political practice to invite God to become a key player in American democracy.

More broadly, the evangelist also called upon Christians throughout the King years to offer their prayers during national crises, like the race riots in the 1960s, and international crises, like the raging battle against communism. But good citizenship in Graham's thought also meant a lot more than just praying. When asked in 1960 about Christianity and citizenship, the evangelist also claimed that Scriptures tell Christians "not only to pray for those in political authority, but to participate in and serve his government."[64] Yet again, however, Graham's response was extra-biblical. There is not one biblical text that suggests that Christians should participate in government, and so it should come as no surprise Graham did not cite which text he might have had in mind. He did vaguely point to the "salt of the earth" text at various points ("You are the salt of the earth"), suggesting along the way that politics would be a lot cleaner if Christians would participate in it. But this text is far too general a teaching about Christian witness to use as a specific mandate for participation in government.[65]

Nevertheless, what did participation in government exactly mean in Graham's thought? Part of the answer emerged in 1967, when he directly encouraged Christians, if they "felt so called, to take an active part in politics and to crusade for clean, honest, and upright handling of community affairs through good government."[66] Unsurprisingly, this advice commended the same localism that Graham had emphasized when speaking about the role of the church in politics, but the interesting twist here is his suggestion to focus on the process of local politics—to make sure that the operations of local government are clean, honest, and upright—rather than on local issues. Obviously, this advice ran completely counter to King's own efforts to encourage Christians to lobby local officials on both procedural and substantive issues, such as the integration of restaurants and businesses. We should note, however, that Graham's own political actions suggest that he was certainly open to lobbying elected officials at all levels, not just on procedural issues, but also on substantive issues of race, economic justice, and war—issues directly related to the beloved community. But just as he had done with the church, Graham raised the flag about the everyday citizen's lack of expertise. For example, when the press asked him to comment on the tactic of pursuing Cambodia during the Vietnam War, he replied: "I wouldn't want to enter into that, because that is a tactical and political problem beyond my own comprehension." One of the things he had learned from his friendships with presidents was that they "have facts at their disposal so far beyond the facts that we ordinary people have that many times those decisions are based on facts when we don't have the facts. And I think it would be rather stupid for me to comment on that tactical and political problem."[67]

Still, the historical evidence reveals that Graham rarely let the lack of expertise stand in the way of an opportunity to lobby his political friends. Rather than acting as a public prophet, a fulminator in the public square, Graham frequently assumed the role of private friend when dealing with politicians. On the one hand, doing so was simply part of the evangelist's personality. As Mark Noll puts it, "Graham seems to like everyone."[68] On the other hand, however, the evangelist was no dummy; he fully realized that private friendship meant access to power. If there is any doubt about the matter, consider Graham's own words in reply to the charge that he was no public prophet: "I have far more influence by being private. If I said things publicly and preached to the president from some pulpit somewhere, I'd never get another opportunity to talk to them privately."[69] In his own mind, the evangelist's preference for private friendship over public prophecy was a "strategy of access" to private offices of the world's most important political players, where he could then share his private opinions on national and international issues.[70] More exactly, of course, it was a sycophantic strategy of access—a shrewd tactic of opening doors by bowing fawningly in the right direction.

For some reason, however, the evangelist felt the need to lie in public about his private lobbying. In 1963, for example, he stated: "I had the privilege of seeing Mr. Eisenhower many times and Mr. Kennedy many times and President Johnson a number of times, and I've had the opportunity of expressing my views to them on various issues at different times, not political issues, not foreign policy issues, but primarily spiritual issues."[71] This was sheer deception. It is doubtless that Graham expressed spiritual views to presidents, but he was also far from silent on specific political and foreign policy views in his private communications. Consider just a few examples. In a 1950 letter to President Truman, the evangelist encouraged a military showdown in Korea: "I also urge you to total mobilization to meet the communist threat. . . . The American people are not concerned with how much it costs the taxpayers if they can be assured of military security."[72] In 1954 Graham sounded a similar theme as he lobbied President Eisenhower: "I have been praying for you a great deal in the past few days as you wrestle with the Indo-China problem. Whatever your ultimate decision, I shall do my best through radio and television to make my contribution in selling the American public. My private opinion is that Indo-China must be held at any cost."[73] The evangelist returned yet again to the same theme, this time eleven years later, in a flowery letter to President Johnson: "The Communists are moving fast toward their goal of world revolution. Perhaps God brought you the kingdom for such an hour as this—to stop them. In doing so, you could be the man that helped save Christian civilization."[74] Even more interestingly, upon hearing news of the death of Supreme Court Chief Justice Warren, Graham quickly penned a letter to Johnson, pleading with him to appoint a conservative to the high position. "If this news proves to be correct, it is my prayer that you will give serious consideration to balancing the Court with a strong conservative as Chief Justice." Graham even recommended his friend, then-Governor John Connaly.[75]

The evangelist prayed with the presidents, to be sure, but he also lobbied them hard, trying to win them over to his politically conservative agenda, all the while telling the press that he merely shared spiritual matters with the presidents. And it was not just presidents that Graham lobbied; he also lobbied local officials, and U.S. senators and representatives, on issues that ranged from the deployment of troops in Little Rock to highway safety in North Carolina to the selection of vice presidential candidates. Nevertheless, while an active lobbyist himself, Graham did not call other Christians to lobby political officials on issues of national and international scope. As a citizen, Graham felt free to lobby politicians on all kinds of social issues and thereby seemed to offer his tacit approval of such lobbying, but he clearly failed to stress, at least in public, that individual Christians should lobby their elected officials beyond the local level.

In addition to local lobbying, participation in government also referred to Christians actually running for political office or offering their support to individuals tossing their hat into the ring. During the presidential race of 1964, Graham echoed Luther once again when he claimed "that Christian men owe it not only to our country but to the kingdom of God to offer themselves as candidates for public office, which should be considered as a sacred trust." The evangelist was not just talking about running for the local school board, either. "One of the deep-rooted troubles of the nation today," he noted, "is that so many leaders who control national affairs either do not know God or they deliberately deny his existence by the way they live."[76] We should not miss the expanding definition of politics at this point. When speaking about the church and politics, Graham largely restricted the meaning of politics to local community life, but in his comments about Christians and politics, the evangelist had in mind party politics, electoral politics beyond local communities, public policies that affect the life of a nation, and even partisan politics. The expanded definition is critical for recognizing that Graham understood the importance of traditional political action for social change. The evangelist never stopped believing that Christian conversion was the best political tool for social change, but he fully conceded that traditional political action was a second-best option for individual Christians. Even partisan politics was an acceptable option for Christians: "I know men who are in government who have high principles, fine motives, and unquestioned integrity. They have dedicated themselves to a life of public service because they sincerely want to help their fellow man."[77]

Graham himself played an active role in lobbying individuals to run for high office. In an August 19, 1955 letter to President Eisenhower, for example, he wrote that he felt "constrained to add my voice to many others from every part of the Nation, urging you to be a candidate for re-election."[78] In an August 4, 1960 letter marked "extremely confidential," this one also to Eisenhower, Graham extolled the president's speech at the Republican convention, adding: "I hope you will stump the country making this type of speech on behalf of Nixon. . . . I believe Nixon has a fighting chance only if you go all out."[79] And in a September 1, 1960 letter to Richard Nixon, the evangelist revealed that "privately I intend to do all in my power to help you get elected."[80] Interestingly, doing all in his power included lobbying Martin Luther King, Jr. Shortly after meeting with King in Rio de Janeiro during the Baptist World Alliance, Graham wrote in an August 23, 1960 letter to Nixon that "Kennedy had just invited [King] to his home for three hours. King was greatly impressed and just about sold. I think I at least neutralized him. I think if you could invite him for a brief conference it might swing him. He would be a powerful influence."[81] Graham felt so free with his good friend Nixon that he offered highly confidential advice with a markedly anti-Catholic tone. For example, in a June 21, 1960 letter that the evangelist had asked Nixon to destroy after reading, the conservative Graham offered the following sensitive advice: "In my opinion, if you make the mistake of having a Catholic running mate, you will divide the Protestant vote and make no inroads whatsoever in the Catholic vote. Therefore, I hope you will discard this idea at all cost." Graham even went so far as to recommend his good friend Walter Judd to be Nixon's running mate.[82]

Given these few examples, it is impossible to understand Graham's ongoing claim that he was politically disengaged as anything less than laughable, hollow, and disingenuous. And yet he made this claim throughout the King years. In 1964, for example, after he had already lobbied Truman, Eisenhower, Kennedy, and Johnson, the evangelist stated that he "must stay completely out of politics. Christ said, 'My kingdom is not of this world, else my disciples would have fought.' "[83] But these words of Christ seemed strangely absent when the evangelist offered an invocation at a Nixon rally just before the 1960 election and when he sat down to write confidential letters about how best to support Nixon's candidacy. Graham did not technically offer public endorsements of particular political candidates, but his public comments about Nixon preceding the 1960 election were a virtual endorsement without calling the candidate by name. "I think this strategy," Graham wrote Nixon, "carries greater strength than if I came all out for you at the present time."[84]

In short, it was massively deceptive for the evangelist to claim, as he often did, that he was politically neutral.[85] The last thing Billy Graham ever wanted throughout the King years was to be removed from or neutral in politics. Even after Harry Truman had banned him from the White House, well before the onslaught of the politicized King years, the evangelist was pounding on the door, asking for admission and pleading with the president to come to the crusades. Not until Jimmy Carter would a president again adopt a no-nonsense approach to the supplicant Graham.

Back to the good citizen. For Graham, the good citizen is an active politico who votes at the polls, prays for politicians, lobbies local leaders, recruits candidates, and even runs for political offices. Nevertheless, the primary mission of the individual is to make disciples of Jesus Christ; political actions are always secondary to that primary vocation. But the secondary mission was still deeply important to Graham. On the one hand, the evangelist urged Christians to fill voluntary agencies that served the cause of charity at the local level—hospitals, orphanages, and homes for the elderly and the poverty-stricken. On the other, he wanted Christians to be soldiers, employees in governmental departments, and politicians in high places. Individual Christians should take their Christian principles and apply them as well as possible in their individual work places, especially in the sacred vocation of government. In Graham's political thought, the more Christians involved in government, the cleaner government could become: Good Christians make for good government.

The Politics of Accommodation: Christians and
Civil Disobedience

Is there any type of work in Caesar's world that a Christian may not do? What about the type of political protests that King led throughout the civil rights movement? Graham enthusiastically encouraged Christians to run for high political office in the United States, but what about grabbing a bull-horn and marching in the streets for something as basic as civil rights? A similar question was put to Graham in a 1964 press conference in Columbus, Ohio, when the press asked him what he thought of Christian preachers leading open demonstrations in the civil rights movement. "Well," Graham stammered, "I think that is entirely up to the individual pastor. We have great freedom of conscience in these matters, and I think the individual himself must make that decision before God and his con-science."[86] This was not exactly the type of ringing endorsement that the evangelist offered to would-be evangelical politicians, but neither was it the unshirted condemnation that other southern evangelicals and fundamental-ists were making of Christian participation in the protest movement. By shifting authority to individual pastors or individual Christians, Graham was simply being true to his individualistic Baptist theology, with its great emphasis on the freedom of individual conscience to decide on matters in which there was no clear-cut answer. Theoretically, this commitment to individual conscience could have provided miles of common ground for Graham and King to cooperate in the civil rights movement, but, again, that did not happen.

Nowhere did Graham ever join King in explicitly calling for Christians to march in the streets, lead demonstrations, participate in sit-ins, ride the busses, go to jail, and offer their bodies to be beaten and scourged and bruised, all for the sake of the beloved community. Compared to King, Graham was the quietist of quietists. Why? Perhaps his understanding of political authority holds helpful clues.

Romans 13:1–7 was the evangelist's favorite text on the subject of polit-ical authority. In this text, the Apostle Paul contends that Christians should subject themselves to the governing authorities because they have been instituted by God, possess authority from God, and properly carry out the divine work of executing wrongdoers. Government is a gift from God, and the governing authority acts as "God's servant" to keep order and establish justice. "Therefore," Paul wrote, "whoever resists authority resists what God has appointed, and those who resist will incur judgment" (13:2).

Martin Luther King, Jr. largely dismissed this text, arguing that it was the result of Paul's mistaken belief that the Second Coming was just around the corner. "Feeling that the time was not long," King wrote, "the Apostle Paul urged men to concentrate on preparing themselves for the new age rather than changing external conditions."[87] Just so, Paul's words no longer apply to contemporary living. "Today we live in a new age, with a differ-ent theological emphasis; consequently, we have both a moral and religious justification for passively resisting evil conditions within the social order."[88] King also downplayed Paul's sense that government is "God's servant" for executing wrongdoers; more often than not, King depicted government as a deeply sinful entity that wrongly punishes individuals striving for freedom and justice. Without apology, he thus swept Romans 13:1–7 into the dustbin of history.

As he did so, King wholly embraced Acts 5:29—"We must obey God rather than any human authority"—when explaining the ultimate justifica-tion for the civil disobedience practiced by the civil rights movement. In Acts 5 the Apostle Peter faces questions at his arrest for having taught in the name of Jesus, and then defies the high priest of Jerusalem, claiming that his allegiance belongs not to the Jewish leaders of his day but to God and God alone. King loved this text and used it repeatedly to explain and justify his civil disobedience, stating that when human authority conflicts with divine authority, Christians must always give their allegiance to God. Thus, when he was criticized for his actions in Montgomery in 1955, he simply stated, "As Christians, we owe our ultimate allegiance to God and His will rather than to man and his folkways."[89]

Compare King's view of political authority to Graham's words in New York City in 1957, shortly following the violence perpetrated by racists rabidly opposed to school integration in Little Rock, Arkansas. "The Bible," Graham preached, "orders us to be in subjection to the powers that be, for the powers that be are ordained of God."[90] Graham would use these words not only to squelch white violence in Little Rock, but also to condemn the civil disobedience practiced by the civil rights movement throughout the King years.

Unlike King, Graham believed that God personally selects individuals to fill political offices. For example, on the Democrat Truman, Graham wrote: "We believe our President to be a man of God. We believe him to be God's choice for this great office."[91] God apparently favored the Republican Eisenhower, too: "In probably the most unique way in American history," Graham wrote, "you have been placed in the office of President, not only by the overwhelming confidence of the American people but also by Divine Providence."[92] Graham said similar things about Presidents Kennedy, Johnson, and Nixon. Yes, the people had expressed their will through the democratic practice of voting, but God had directed the outcome. Because the electoral winners were really God's personal favorites, to oppose them was nothing less than opposing God. "Revolt against duly constituted authority," Graham preached, "is an offense against God."[93] Christians are thus to be subordinate to rulers and their laws.

When discussing civil disobedience in America, Graham held that Christians should obey all laws. King, of course, disagreed. In his letter from Birmingham City Jail, the civil rights leader clarified the meaning and practice of civil disobedience by describing the difference between just and unjust laws. Inspired partly by Thoreau, King held that just laws are in accord with natural and divine law, both of which serve and uplift the human personality, and are willingly assented to and followed by the whole citizenry. Unjust laws, on the other hand, counter natural and divine law, and so distort the human soul and degrade the human personality. In addition, unjust laws are codes that a majority does not follow but instead inflicts upon a minority population with no right to vote or legal means of redress. In King's view, citizens have a moral obligation, and Christians have a faith obligation, to obey just laws and to disobey unjust laws.[94]

Graham, however, flat-out opposed King's theology of law, as well as his ethic of resistance. "Every law," Graham preached in New York City, "may not please every person at all times, but there is an obligation that we as Christians are to obey it."[95] What about laws that establish and maintain systems of segregation? Obey them. What about laws that establish a tax code that does harm to the poor? Obey them. What about laws that draft

poor African American men in disproportionate number for an unjust war?
Obey them. Just because God has granted authority to the powers that be,
Christians have an obligation to respect and honor the work of the governing authorities, including laws that would directly undermine the
beloved community.

To support his law-and-order approach to civil disobedience, Graham
always came back to Paul and the biblical witness. In 1962, six years after
the Little Rock crisis, the evangelist stated: "Despite the tyranny of
Rome . . . I read no speeches in the Bible by Peter, John, or Paul against
the political regimes of their day. They preached Christ and they preached
Christ alone . . . and did it within the context of a tyranny that eventually
imprisoned them and killed them."[96] Graham also cited the political life of
Jesus. In the 1961 sermon titled "Jesus, the Great Revolutionist," for example, he preached that Jesus accomplished a revolution in the world, setting
in motion a church that has lasted longer than all political empires, all the
while refusing to speak against or disobey the governing authorities. "He
didn't even bother to lift his voice against the tyranny of Caesar."[97] Finally,
Graham also appealed to the politics of the early church. "During the three
hundred years when the Roman emperors declared Christianity an illegal
religion," Graham stated in 1964, "Christians were marked as criminals by
civil law simply because they were Christians. Against the tyranny of such
a government . . . Not only did they obey the laws of this tyrannical government, but they pledged their prayers and paid their taxes, as Paul had
told them to."[98] With the force of these ethical sources behind him,
Graham aptly summarized his position at an Atlanta press conference in
1964, stating that as a representative of "the kingdom of heaven," he must
offer his support to "whatever type of government we have. I must pray for
those in authority, and I must preach the Gospel in the midst of it."[99]

One of the questions to arise here is whether Graham's use of sources
was accurate. It seems that while Graham was right in his assessment of at
least part of Paul's politics—Pilgrim characterizes Romans 13 as "an ethic
of subordination."[100]—his appeal to Jesus is questionable. This is no place
to detail the political thought of Jesus, but a critical response to Graham's
own ethic of subordination must at least point out that while Jesus was not
a political revolutionary by any stretch of the imagination, neither did he
present himself subordinate to the state. There are no reports of Jesus
describing the governing authorities as "God's servant"; neither are there
any indications that Jesus ever called his followers to pray for those in
authority, or to honor and respect them as divinely appointed by God. On
the contrary, Luke 13:31–35 suggests that Jesus did not hold an ethic of
accommodation at all. When he learns that Herod wants to kill him, for
example, the Lukan Jesus does not fall prostrate in front of the throne, or
bow his head and pray for the governing authority, or reach into his pocket
and try to pay his taxes ahead of time. Instead, a defiant Jesus says, "Go and
tell that fox," revealing contempt for one who would stand in the way of
his healing ministry. After describing his own governing authority as a

"fox," Jesus then states that he will defy Herod's efforts and continue his divinely appointed mission to bring healing to the people of God. As Pilgrim puts it, "Jesus will not be forced into submission out of fear or respect, even toward his own ruler."[101] There are other texts that suggest a similar stance by Jesus, like the texts in which he cleanses the temple, but Graham ignored them all in his discussion of civil disobedience, thus revealing an arbitrary hermeneutic tainted by evangelical quietism. Once again, Graham was not as biblical as he claimed to be.

If King's notion of political authority ultimately led to a political ethic of resistance, Graham's led to an ethic of subordination. For the evangelist, the proper political stance for Christians is one of willingly suffering on earth, preaching Christ crucified, praying for and honoring those in authority, obeying all the laws of the political authorities, and trusting that one day God will make all things right and good for the people of God. Ultimately, Billy Graham was a quietist, and so just after King's assassination, and just before the Poor People's Campaign, it was no surprise at all when he announced: "I am against all civil disobedience."[102]

An Exception

But Graham's claim that he was against all civil disobedience was not entirely true. Sometimes he offered a predictable exception to his blanket condemnation. In 1964, for instance, he stated: "The only time I would ever do otherwise [than subordinate myself to the governing authorities] would be if my free worship were interfered with. For example, in a Communist state or something like that. Then I might have to disobey the government."[103] It was an exception that Graham had embraced for years, even as far back as 1957, when he preached: "Every law may not please every person at all times, but there is an obligation that we as Christians are to obey it unless it interferes with our right to worship God according to the dictates of our conscience."[104] Behind Graham's exception was his love for the Pilgrims, his Baptist heritage, and more fundamentally, biblical stories about believers who refused to bow down and worship their rulers—including Paul and the apostles in the Book of Acts, as well as martyrs in the Book of Revelation.[105]

Allowing for the exception meant that Graham had to leave behind Paul's unqualified assertion that governing authorities were God's servants and that Christians should subject themselves to the governing authorities. Interestingly, it also meant that there was some common ground between King's and Graham's theologies of political authority. Like King, Graham finally conceded that political authority has its limits, and that when government moved beyond its proper jurisdiction, Christians had an obligation to resist.

In reality, however, there was no common ground between the two preachers as they surveyed the political conditions of the United States.

Unlike Graham, King had an expansive notion of the conditions under which political authority dissipated, and interpreted the Acts passage broadly enough to allow for civil disobedience of any unjust law—not merely a law infringing upon religious freedom. Graham could never bring himself to do the same and, in fact, found all civil disobedience in the United States to be downright sinful. His reasoning was simple: The United States allowed for religious freedom, and so there was no compelling reason to understand U.S. government as anything but God's servant for the good. In the final analysis, then, the two men could never have been full partners in the civil rights movement.

The Primacy of Evangelism

This chapter has identified numerous reasons for the chasm between Graham and King. But there is an additional reason—the overarching vocation of individual Christians. In Graham's thought, the primary vocation of Christians is essentially spiritual, far removed from the realm of worldly politics. "We as Christians," Graham argued, "have two responsibilities: first, to proclaim the Gospel of Jesus Christ as the only answer to man's deepest needs; and second, to apply as best we can the principles of Christianity to the social conditions around us."[106] Graham allowed for the church and individual Christians to be politically engaged, albeit in a limited way, but he consistently maintained that the primary mission of the church and its members is to continue to surrender their lives to Christ, especially by seeking the conversion of their neighbors. The Christian community can best serve political society not by political preaching, voting, praying, lobbying, or even running for and serving in high office, but by making disciples for Jesus Christ—men and women whose hearts will embrace the virtues of love, peace, and justice.

Graham's dogged devotion to Christian evangelism shone forth especially in his comments on the outlandish possibility of running for the U.S. presidency. "I was approached about running for president," he revealed in 1964. "And some quite prominent people and financiers and people like that came to see me over about a period of a year. I never gave them any encouragement." The evangelist reported that he was more inclined to listen to Nixon and Johnson, who advised him to keep on preaching: "They said you're making your greatest contribution to our way of life in that field, and God, you see, called me to preach, and *I consider that a greater calling and a greater office and a greater responsibility than any political office in the world*, and I have no intention at any time of going into politics."[107] The evangelist considered political office a "sacred" office and the state to be "God's servant," but he understood his vocation of evangelist to be the most important of sacred trusts. And that, of course, was because of his unshakable conviction that evangelism addresses the individual heart—the foundation of political society. Without clean hearts in the citizenry, the beloved community can never even begin to form. Ultimately, then, all political action targeted at individuals whose hearts are not redeemed by the blood of Jesus falls far short of the reign of God.

At last, this position leads to a few obvious questions: If politics ultimately fails in an unredeemed society, why should the Christian community devote any of its resources to political action? Because the conversion of political society to Christianity remains an unfulfilled dream, at least for Graham, would that not entail a singular focus on evangelism as the one and only proper political practice for Christians and their church? Did not Graham himself put "the cart before the horse," as he accused the ecumenical church of doing, when he called for the church to engage in local politics, and individual Christians to become politically active at all levels of unredeemed political society? Graham, it seems, suspended or ignored his strategy for social transformation—first, conversion of the heart, and second, political engagement—when he suggested that the church and its members participate in politics *at the same time* they practice evangelism. The mere suggestion that the church and Christians may engage in political action in an unredeemed society is simply illogical in light of the evangelist's belief that the redemption of society is required before Christians can formulate and implement policies reflective of Christian ethics.

However confused, Graham's notion of the primary vocation of the church and its members, in addition to his political ethic of subjection, stands in direct opposition to King's political church, as well as to his hope that Christians would fight the state, even disobey its laws, on the march toward the Promised Land. Even as he stepped out of the pulpit and entered the Oval Office, and even as he encouraged Christians to become politically engaged, the evangelist simply could not join King in calling for the church and its members to leave behind their political laxity and become full and active participants in a movement intent on breaking the law in order to lead political society to a new law, a better law, a law more reflective of the love of God in Jesus. Graham's version of American patriotism, as we will see in the following chapter, only added a few more feet to the wall of division separating him from King.

CHAPTER THREE

"True Christian Loyalty in Our Hearts": A Christian Defense of American Patriotism

"Third, we should earnestly seek, as Americans, a revival of patriotic loyalty." With typical dramatic flair, Graham was preaching yet another *Hour of Decision* sermon, this one titled "Labor, Christ, and the Cross," but the title was not really helpful. The sermon had less to do with labor than it did with the talk of the town in 1953—the infamous McCarthy hearings. Graham was a rabid anticommunist from the earliest days of his ministry, and he simply could not let the hearings pass without commenting on American subversives and the faithful patriots who sought to squelch them. With a hermeneutic stretched to the limits, he began his patriotic reflections with none other than Jesus: "His whole ministry pointed like an arrow to Golgotha and the fulfillment of the divine purpose for his life." Divinely faithful, Jesus was the best example of loyalty for any individual who would serve God and country, no matter the cost. Just so, "his unwavering spirit of loyalty has inspired patriots to willingly die for what they believed to be right."[1]

If only all Americans would be so inspired. "In these days," Graham continued, "when it would seem that the embers of patriotism and loyalty are burning low, all true Americans should experience a revival of true Christian loyalty in our hearts." And all true Americans can indeed experience this if only we ensure that all our words and actions mirror the life of Christ, and then kneel in prayer, asking God for the courage to exercise a new loyalty to our "God-given ideals," the neglect of which is leading our country directly into "moral bankruptcy."[2] The evangelist did not unpack in this sermon what he meant by "God-given ideals," but in 1961, at the high point of the Cuban Missile Crisis, he listed them as "the dignity of the individual, faith in God, an adherence to the authority of the Scripture, and a respect for human life."[3] More needs to be said about these later—they are far from nugatory—but there is one more step to highlight on the evangelist's path toward ideal loyalty. What we really need, he preached, is "a revival of patriotic loyalty. Every day we are shocked by the refusal of men before government investigation committees to answer whether or not they are members of the Communist party." True Christian loyalty was adamantly opposed to such political subversives: "While nobody likes a watchdog, and for that reason many investigative committees are unpopular, I thank God for men who, in the face of public denouncement and ridicule, go loyally on in their work of exposing the pinks, the lavenders, and the reds who have sought refuge beneath the wings of the American eagle, and from that vantage point, try in every subtle, undercover way to bring comfort, aid and help to the greatest enemy we have ever known—Communism."[4]

Enter Robert Bellah's groundbreaking work on civil religion—"a genuine apprehension of universal and transcendent religious reality as seen in or, one could almost say, as revealed through the experience of the American people." In his original article on the subject, Bellah argued that civil religion has been invoked in the United States not only to serve good causes, like defining the identity and purpose of our democratic republic, giving meaning to the practice of sacrifice for the common good, and mobilizing support for attaining national goals of justice and peace, but also to support causes far less worthy. "On the domestic scene," Bellah observed, "an American-Legion type of ideology that fuses God, country, and flag has been used to attack nonconformist and liberal ideas and groups of all kinds."[5] Graham's ideology of "true Christian loyalty" was the perfect example from 1950s America. The American Legion evangelical blatantly cloaked his vicious attack on "the pinks, the lavenders, and the reds" in a civil religion that fused God, America, and Old Glory, giving no thought to the possibility that the practices he identified—loyalty to Christ, devotion to God-given ideals, and a revival of American patriotism—might actually conflict with one another. In the end, Graham was McCarthyite in more ways than one: not only was he as anticommunist as the senator was, he was also no less sketchy in the details of his argument.

Just a year after this sermon, Senator McCarthy would face a devastating question that would expose his politics of deception and mark the beginning of his fall from grace—"Have you no decency, sir? At long last, have you left no sense of decency?" The McCarthy hearings came to a relatively quick halt after that, but Graham's patriotism knew no end. As McCarthy and his ideological janissaries were felled and silenced, "the Great American," as Graham was characterized in a 1967 awards banquet, grew all the bulkier in his patriotic cloak and became all the louder in his clarion call for fervent patriotism.[6] Indeed, Mark Noll is too limited in claiming that "early in his career Graham's evangelical faith was matched by a conventional faith in American."[7] Not just early in his career but throughout the King years, Graham expressed a civil religion that identified America as virtually chosen by God and fused Jesus and American history. Graham's American-Legion religion also confused Christianity with the destiny of America, blended the virtue of Christian sacrifice with offering one's life for America, and assaulted liberal dissidents who stood between Jesus and American patriotism. Perhaps for these reasons Roderick Hart has characterized Graham as the "arch civil religionist."[8]

But civil religion comes in different forms, and there was another great American, Martin Luther King, Jr., who offered the country a competing civil religion. Sickened by the American-Legion type, King invoked the God of the founding fathers not to bless and baptize America, but to judge the nation and its public policies for failing to build the beloved community. If Graham's civil religion usually reflected white American Legionism, King's embodied the experience of African Americans who, though consigned to the back of Memorial Day crowds, nevertheless waved their own red, white, and blue flags. But this is too simply put to be fair, for Graham's civil religion also assumed a transcendent, prophetic role that at times criticized America for the same sins that King had identified. For the most part, however, Graham's public faith focused on the sin of American sins—secularism—when it dared to criticize the country at all.

Virtually Chosen: America as Blessed and Favored

For Graham, patriotism was a Christian virtue—in America. When the evangelist spoke of the virtue of patriotism, he directed his comments not at Russians, Cubans, Chinese, or others living behind the Iron Curtain, but at Americans: Good old-fashioned Christian patriotism was for the land of the free and the home of the brave. Many of the regular flag-saluting themes in Graham's whitewashed patriotism, at least as it took form throughout the King years, appeared in a remarkable sermon he preached on Thanksgiving Day in 1956. The evangelist began this particular message by suggesting that God would bless America as long as citizens continued to remember, honor, and glorify God: "Continued blessing and favor from God is conditioned by our attitude toward him. Unlimited favor awaits us if we will remember his works, his redemption, and his commandments. But if we forget him, as did Israel of old, we put ourselves in the path of judgment, poverty, and adversity."[9] Did this mean that America, like Israel of old, was God's chosen? The short answer is "not exactly," but the full answer depends upon the evangelist's definition of "chosen."

Graham offered a definition of sorts in his first sermon at the 1958 crusade in Charlotte. "We have an idea," he preached, "that we Americans are God's chosen people, that God loves us more than any other people, and that we are God's blessed. I tell you that God doesn't love us any more than he does the Russians . . . the Chinese . . . the Africans. God doesn't love us any more than any other people. There . . . is no partiality with God."[10] A few weeks later, the evangelist once again sounded the same theme, this time warning against the "national pride" of believing that God's love for America is deeper than it is for other nations.[11] Graham dismissed the notion of America as chosen on other levels, too. For instance, in the 1956 sermon "God and Crime," he answered the question of chosenness with "an emphatic 'No!' We do not have any special immunity from the judgments of God."[12] But the evangelist also stated, in the very same sermon, that America was certainly "blessed" and "favored" because of its "right-eousness," its faithful obedience to the God who had created America.[13] Thus, although he argued that America was not chosen, if that means to be loved more than other nations, or to be immune from the judgment of God, Graham certainly believed that America was virtually chosen, nearly chosen, as close to chosen as a country could be.

What was the substance of God's blessings upon America? In the Thanksgiving sermon, Graham listed three things that should cause Americans to humble themselves before God in a spirit of gratitude. First, he invited his audience to "be thankful this week for peace." By "peace" he did not mean "peace of heart," as he had emphasized in other writings and sermons, but "temporary respite for America from hostility and blood-shed." Graham considered it tragic that hostility was occurring across the globe, especially in forsaken Hungary, which could do little against the threatening power of godless Russia, but how grateful he was that America, on Thanksgiving Day 1956, enjoyed a period of peace—which he could not help but interpret as an unmistakable sign of God's favor and blessing. Second, "we should be thankful for freedom . . . not just the freedom to do as we like, but the freedom to do the will of God . . . freedom under law, freedom under moral law, freedom under God." Graham was grateful not for libertinism, or for an irresponsible freedom, but for a strong social order that permitted the flourishing of Christian practices and the proclamation of the Christian gospel. And third, the evangelist invited American Christians to thank God for freedom of opportunity: "In America, the land of free enterprise, business and industry, there are no respectors of persons . . . by freedom of opportunity, we do not merely refer to the mak-ing of money . . . .[but also] opportunity for education, for service, for friendships, and for spiritual enrichment and development. . . . No nation has been so blessed by Almighty God."[14]

Other sermons throughout the King years also provided substance for Graham's theology of divine favor. In "The Cost of Freedom," for exam-ple, he preached that "God blessed us with a material prosperity beyond that of any nation in the history of the world."[15] This line of thought went far beyond his earlier baptism of American capitalism; here his civil religion took the form of a bourgeois gospel of prosperity. Never mind Job, who had lost his possessions in spite of being among God's favorites: For Graham, God was Midas, and the gentle touch of his golden hand had turned America into pure gold. The evangelist suggested in "The Cost of Freedom" that America's military strength was yet another sign of God's blessing and favor. The superior capability of American soldiers, the over-whelming power of American bombs, the unmatchable precision of mili-tary jets—all these were indicators that God had blessed and favored America. Never mind the nonviolent Jesus who had died on the cross. In Graham's civil religion, God was Herculean, and the gentle touch of his muscular hand had given America an unmatched ability to scorch Germany and Japan, Korea and Vietnam, Russia and China.

Finally, Graham's civil religion also set forth American democracy, "the greatest government in all the world," as a sign of divine favor and blessing.[16] Negatively, he identified democracy as the best system for a sinful humanity. "In a government of unredeemed humanity," he argued, "democracy is the only fair and equitable system."[17] But Graham also offered a positive reason for embracing democracy—its courageous enactment of Christian principles. In reply to an individual concerned that Christian preachers "talk as if democracy and Christianity were one and the same," Graham argued that while no government is perfect, democracy, just like Christianity, allows for "the power of choice," embraces "the dignity of the individual," and "believes in the power of the governed to choose those who govern them."[18] Although not the same, Christianity and democracy were largely interdependent, and so Christians should be faithful democrats.

The America that Graham depicted as "blessed" and "favored" was foreign to the black experience in 1956, 1957, or at any other point during the King years. In fact, there were always at least two Americas in this era—Graham's and King's—and rarely did the two ever meet in matters of everyday life, let alone civil religion. Consider just a few of the divergences. While Graham was depicting "peace" as a sign that God had blessed America, King's house was being bombed, his followers were suffering beatings at the hands of police, and his phone rang off the hook with death threats from racist thugs. Should we remember lynching, too? Had King heard Graham's sermon, one suspects the civil rights leader would have mouthed the damning words of the prophet Jeremiah: "They have treated the wound of my people carelessly, saying 'Peace, peace' when there is no peace" (Jer. 8: 11). Or perhaps the civil rights leader would have asked the logical question: If peace is a sign of God's favor, does the absence of peace suffered by the movement mean that God despised and rejected African Americans?

There were other points of divergence. While Graham was celebrating social order as a sign of divine blessing, King and his followers were suffering at the hands of state-sanctioned disorder, of a police force that ignored their safety concerns and collaborated with racist thugs. Further, while the evangelist was extolling "freedom of opportunity" as a sign of God's blessing, King and other activists were vigorously protesting an omnipresent Jim Crow and his enslavement of opportunity. The so-called free enterprise system that Graham adored was the one and the same system that prevented African Americans from accessing a market with livable wages and professional opportunities, and the so-called freedom of education lauded by the evangelist was nowhere available for little black boys and girls studying in poor schools with few books and fewer pencils. King understood all too well that freedom of opportunity was an abstract notion in an African American family living without food on the table, books in the library, and friends in corridors of business and government. Again, there were inevitable questions bubbling up from the black experience: If freedom was a sign of God's favor, did the painful experience of discrimination and seg-regation mean that God did not favor blacks? If freedom of religion was a sign of God's blessing, did the shocking experience of church segregation mean that God did not bless them? If freedom of opportunity was a sign of God's favor, did the lack of opportunity mean that God had turned away?

Finally, while Graham was weaving democracy and Christianity into a seamless web, King was arguing that although pure democracy was reflec-tive of Christianity, real democracy in America was rarely so reflective. As the civil rights leader put it, American democracy was nothing less than "anemic democracy," terribly lacking in the colors of its minority citizens.[19] More damning, however, American democracy had wrongly cleared space and time for "the antithesis of democracy"[20]—segregation—and then allowed "states' rights" to run roughshod over God-given rights, like the right to equal opportunity.[21] Rather than praising American democracy uncritically, the civil rights leader appealed to America's founding documents as sources for critiquing the oppression of blacks in the land of the free. Although an ardent supporter of democracy in its pure form, King was an endlessly critical patriot who sharply condemned the impure democracy that Graham's civil religion had conveniently overlooked.

When Graham's theology of blessing embraced the virtue of patriotism in America, then, it did so at the expense of African Americans for whom dreaming the American dream was a practice hollowed out by whites who sat on clean curbs on the Fourth of July, saluting the American flag carried by white veterans, waving at the white belle lucky enough to be crowned queen, and smiling as if white America was the only America. They were wrong, of course, when they denied blacks from participating in their Fourth of July parades, and so was Billy Graham when he whitewashed the African American experience in his depiction of America as almost chosen. But the whitewashing should not have come as a surprise. When used poorly, as it was by Graham, civil religion always sanitizes the dirty little secrets of a nation that oppresses minorities.

Christian America?

Graham's civil religion identified part of the cause of God's blessing and favor as the faithful history of the United States, beginning with the writ-ing of the Mayflower Compact, when the Pilgrims "acknowledged their debt and gratitude to God and . . . Jesus Christ as their Lord and Master." The Pilgrims, Graham believed, "had come to this country to found a nation in the concept that God is to be God and that this nation was to be under God." And they succeeded, with Jesus Christ as their guide: William Bradford, the governor of the Plymouth Colony, was devoted to Christ, John Winthrop and the other heads of the early colonies were truly "men of God," and the awe-inspiring constitutions they had written acknowledged

"God as Supreme majesty."[22] Moreover, in 1777 the Continental Congress had approved the spending of $300,000 for Bibles for the colonies and "the ethical and moral concepts of Christianity are found all the way through the Declaration of Independence. . . . How many men came to our shores with Bibles in their hands and faith in God and founded this country! That's one of the secrets of the blessing and prosperity of this nation."[23]

Graham revealed another "secret" too. "God has not blessed America simply because a few Pilgrims prayed at Plymouth Rock," he preached in 1956. "We have been favored because periodically, as a nation, we have returned to God in repentance and corrected our manner of life before the hand of judgment fell."[24] That is what America did in the 1730s when European atheism hit the nation shortly after the new colonies had turned to gold rather than God, in the 1780s when liquor manufacturing began in America, and in the early 1800s when the gold rush made everyone "money and pleasure mad." During each of these periods, a revival took hold in America, the country humbled itself in prayer, and God "refreshed" the land aplenty.[25] Graham also gave other examples of faithfulness in American history, as when George Washington prayed for victory at Valley Forge, when Franklin called for prayer as the Constitutional Convention struggled to ratify a document, and when Lee prayed that the will of God be done during the Civil War. On each of these occasions, God heard the humble petitioners and responded with blessing and favor upon the nation: Washington went on to victory, the Constitution was born, and "[t]he shackles of slavery were thrown off."[26]

The real secret of America, then, is not in its material resources or technological expertise or military power or even democratic principles: "It is found in her heritage of spiritual susceptibility and response to God"—an ongoing history of confession, repentance, and acceptance of God's guidance.[27] Make no mistakes in interpretation here: Graham, unlike general practitioners of civil religion, was talking about God in Jesus Christ, and his depiction of early America was primarily of a Christian America. Christian Pilgrims, the Christian William Bradford, the Continental Congress's funding of Christian Bibles, Christian educational institutions (such as Harvard and Yale), Christian morality embedded in the Constitution—all these indicated that early America was Christian America.

Graham's history lessons, while helpful in their own right, were far from comprehensive, as the eminent historian Edwin Gaustad's work has shown. To be sure, Franklin had led the Convention in prayer, but he was a deist who questioned the divinity of Jesus, and who, just five weeks before his death, wrote: "Here is my Creed: I believe in one God, Creator of the Universe. That he governs the World by his Providence. That he ought to be worshipped. That the most acceptable Service we can render to him, is doing good to his other Children."[28] Absent from his deist creed, of course, was any reference to Christ and the need for men and women to confess their sins and believe in Jesus as Lord and Savior. Further, the hyperrationalist Washington might have prayed at Valley Forge, but he preferred to use such rationalist titles as "Higher Cause," "the Supreme Dispenser of all Good," and "Governor of the Universe" when publicly referring to God. And "the howling atheist," Thomas Jefferson, published an Enlightenment-inspired version of the life of Jesus that excluded references to miracles, apocalyptic teachings, and the resurrection, all in favor of the ethical example and teachings of Jesus.[29] The suggestion that early America was Christian America, especially a Christian America that monolithically held the views of the pious evangelicalism of Billy Graham, was crudely dismissive of the overwhelming evidence of deism and rationalist Christianity in the civil religion of our founding fathers.

King would have found Graham's history lessons more than suspect. Indeed, the two preachers had significantly different foci when recounting early America. Whereas Graham focused on the faithful Pilgrims, the civil rights leader looked far beyond the Pilgrims—and to the history of his own people. For example, with lines he would recount many times King stood before his Alpha Phi Omega brothers in Buffalo, in 1956, and gave them a history lesson that white schools rarely if ever taught at the time. "You will remember that it was in the year 1619 that the first Negro slave was brought to the shores of this nation. They were brought here from the soils of Africa and unlike the Pilgrim fathers who landed here at Plymouth a year later, they were brought here against their will."[30] Unlike Graham's we-gather-together civil religion, King's did not express a glorified historical beginning of America. The slaves did not set sail with religious freedom in mind; they sailed the seas in chains, bound for a land that held no promise of peace, no promise of freedom, and no promise of equal opportunity. America was not the land of opportunity; it was the land of slavery and death.

King's lessons in early American history simply reminded Americans that the white stars of Old Glory were surrounded not just by brilliant blue but also by the shades of his people—black, blacker, and blackest. And it was not just the history immediately preceding or following the arrival of the Pilgrims that King sought to remember for the nation, either: "For more than 200 years, Africa was raped and plundered, a native kingdom disorganized, the people and rulers demoralized and throughout slavery the Negroes were treated in a very inhumane form."[31] Just so, the orderliness of Graham's civil religious history turned downright disorderly in King's: Washington might have prayed for victory at Valley Forge, but at the same time American whites were subsidizing the dismantling of African governments. Franklin might have prayed at the Convention, but at the same time American whites were paying for the rape and pillaging of Africans. And the Constitutional Convention might have authorized money for the distribution of Bibles, but at the same time American whites were ensuring that African slaves could not read the Queen's English. If Graham's civil religion gave good reason for whites to wave their flags, King's gave African Americans just cause to see the flag as a symbol of an evil empire that sought to make them subhuman. It is little wonder, then, that the mature King never once claimed that early America was even a little bit Christian.

All this is not to say that King's own brand of civil religion did not appeal to the founding fathers and America's greatest leaders in positive ways. But when he did honor America's heroes, it was never for the same reasons cited by Graham's civil religion. For example, King honored the slave-owning founding fathers, not because they prayed at the nation's beginning, but because they were the authors and signers of the Declaration of Independence and the U.S. Constitution—documents that enshrined the principle that all are created free and equal. King celebrated the work of Thomas Jefferson, not because he was a believer in God, but because he institutionalized a federal government that respected both states' rights and God-given human rights, allowing the latter to trump the former when the two conflicted.[32] Similarly, the civil rights leader frequently cited Lincoln, not because he prayed during the Civil War, but because he courageously acted on his principled conviction that the proper business of the state is to mold reconciliation out of a divided society.[33] While Graham's civil religion piously obsessed on the faith of the founders, King's focused on their political acts of liberation and reconciliation.

Graham was never too interested in speaking about either the cerebral faith of the founding founders or about their keeping of slaves, but he did eventually give pause to the thought of a Christian America, primarily because of his Baptist conviction that the experience of becoming Christian is an individual event. Thus, by 1957, he was qualifying his earlier comments about Christian America. "There is no such thing as a Christian nation," he argued, "nor can there be. Only individuals are capable of becoming Christians."[34] The evangelist continued to hold this position throughout the King years. In a 1967 press conference in Tokyo, for example, he argued: "The United States is not a Christian nation. We are a secular nation." Interestingly, at this point Graham was concerned that the Japanese might dismiss his western brand of Christianity because of American policy in Southeast Asia, and so he conveniently added: "There are many Christians in America . . . but no country can be said to be Christian, and you cannot judge Christianity by the domestic or foreign policy of any government."[35] Later in the press conference, however, he returned to his main point: "There is no such thing as a Christian nation. You couldn't say that unless the vast majority of the people had been born into the Kingdom of God, and I know of no nation like that."[36] Though born in Christ, America would remain a secular nation as long as "the vast majority" of citizens did not commit themselves to Jesus as Lord and Savior.

The shift in characterizing America as secular necessitated a complementary shift in explaining "the secret of America," and Graham began to make this adjustment in 1957, as well. In *The Revival We Need*, for example, he argued that God spares, blesses, and favors America because of "the very nature of God"—love, mercy, and compassion—and because of "the great number of born-again Christians in the world."[37] What was the real secret of America? "If it were not for God's people in this country it would have been in Hell long ago. It's the Lord's people that God is honoring. Don't you despise that godly Christian who lives next door to you. Don't you laugh at that Christian student. . . . I tell you he is one of the reasons that this nation has the blessings and prosperity that it has."[38]

Again, King's civil religion saw all this a bit differently. Rather than depicting born-again Christians as the primary reason for the nation's ongoing prosperity, he identified good Christian whites as a major reason that his people suffered alienation and poverty. It was white Christians who had lynched his people for all those years and then justified slavery with obscure passages from the Bible. It was good Sabbath-keepers who demanded that African Americans surrender their bus seats to whites, who refused to hire African Americans for their downtown businesses, who incited German shepherds to attack black children, and who sent young African American men to fight on the front lines of the war while educated white men stayed in college or enrolled in graduate school or seminary. Not all opponents of racial and economic justice were born-again Christians, of course, but King knew from his own experience that the resistance included so-called Christians who gathered together in the safety of white clapboard churches with steeples striving to get near to the heart of God. Driving by these churches and knowing of the support their members gave to the anti-civil rights movement, King found himself asking one question: "Who is their God?"[39]

Graham's civil religion differed from King's not only in its interpretation of American history, but also in its portrayal of the manifest destiny of America. Unlike King's, Graham's preached in "The Revival We Need" that America was born in Christ and made for Christ, just as one of the greatest American Calvinists had once declared. "Woodrow Wilson once said, 'America was born a Christian nation for the purpose of exemplifying to the nations of the world, the principles of righteousness found in the Word of God.' " For good measure, the evangelist heaped on another quotation from an American president, this one a founding father. "John Adams, our second president, said, 'The destiny of America is to carry the gospel of Jesus Christ to all men everywhere.' "[40] The Great American thus stood between Adams and Wilson, holding their hands high and proclaiming that the divinely ordained destiny of America was to evangelize the world—to share the Gospel of Jesus Christ not only from sea to shining sea but also across the globe, where heathenism and tribalism needed to be wiped out so that natives could be saved for eternal life, so that they, too, could begin to build nations with Christian histories and Christian destinies.

King's civil religion had another destiny in mind. The mission of America was never about transforming heathens or anyone else into Christians; that would have been yet another example of American arrogance and bigotry. For the civil rights leader, the divinely willed destiny of America was to build the beloved community—a time and place where races, classes, religions, and nations would be so reconciled, so consciously interwoven, that no one would study war any more. The mission of America was not to create a master race, a master class, a master religion, or a master nation, but to construct a world house marked by universal, redemptive good will for all the various parts of humanity. Individualism and diversity were not causes for distress, but reasons for affirmation and celebration as necessary parts of a whole community devoted to the common good. In this sense, King's civil religion held the seeds of the destruction of Graham's: the destiny of America was to provide the conditions under which American civil religion, with its national borders, would die a peaceful but quick death. In the beloved community, civil religion, insofar as it was bound by any borders, including religious ones, was ultimately uncivil.

Taking God out of American Life

Nevertheless, for all its flowery words about America's Christian history and destiny, Graham's civil religion also sought to transcend the American experience and judge it on behalf of God in Christ. It is unfair to suggest that the evangelist embraced a wholly uncritical civil religion, a blind love of country, or a religious nationalism out of control. Such superficial criticism ignores the basic point that Graham felt divinely anointed to save America from the flames of hell. Although the evangelist was no doubt a flag-saluting patriot, he was also a critical prophet, or at least when compared to King, a prophet in minor key. Unfortunately, Graham himself would downplay his prophetic identity when responding to sniping critics during the Nixon years. "God," he would state, "has called me to be a New Testament evangelist, not an Old Testament prophet."[41] But Richard Pierard has rightly suggested that such a comment "was unfortunate because he has in fact played the role of prophet."[42] Indeed, Graham assumed the role of prophet in different ways. The pages ahead will show that in the King years alone, a prophetic Graham criticized America for its sanctioning of segregation, its full-bellied satisfaction with economic injustice, and even its godless warmongering. But Graham was far more than a secular or religious prophet who ranted merely about social injustices. As America's evangelist, he was primarily a Christian prophet who devoted his shrillest condemnations to the sin that threatened to send America back to the jungle—the sin of secularism.

In the mid-1950s Graham faulted America mostly for practicing an unhealthy number of the seven deadly sins. "In my opinion," he wrote in a book on the subject, "sex is probably America's greatest sin." Humanism and behaviorism had "taught that man was only an animal, and our young people were urged to give free expression to their passions and feelings," with the result that premarital sex had soared to new heights in America. "No wonder our country has plunged into an unprecedented immoral spree that threatens the very structure of our society!"[43] Sex was making the country impotent.

It will become clear, however, that Graham's identification of America's "great sin" changed in response to the various issues confronting America through the King years. Interestingly, sometimes his view changed even within the same publication. For example, apparently forgetting he had just written that sex was America's great sin, Graham also wrote in *The Seven Deadly Sins*, "The great sin of America is greed and avarice. We are so bent on making money that we do not have time for God and spiritual exercise."[44] The prophet lambasted America for a number of other sins, too, and many of them he would later downplay or ignore as civil rights and Vietnam began to capture the country's attention.

Secularism, however, was the one American sin that wove in and out of Graham's sermons throughout the King years, mainly because he depicted it as the root national sin, the sin that gave birth to premarital sex, crime, gambling, and all other American sins. Graham explained the godless emergence of secularism in a classic 1956 sermon titled "Americanism." During the past ten years, he preached, "we substituted rationalism, mind culture, science worship, the working power of government, Freudianism, Naturalism, Humanism, Behaviorism, Positivism, Materialism, Idealism and all the rest. We thought we had found better gods than the true and the living God."[45] But we had not—and great danger was on the way.

Even American democracy, that seemingly unshakeable form of government that ranked higher than any other form in the world, was on the brink of a collapse. As a good civic republican, Graham often preached that democracy would fall hard if unsupported by "moral sentiment," by which he meant Christian principles and values.[46] "It is the Gospel of Jesus Christ," he preached in 1955, "that made America great. That is the heart and core of American democracy."[47] Christianity was so essential to the success of democracy because it instilled within the citizenry the moral values that had given democracy its first breath and all breaths to follow—the values of human dignity and freedom. And so if Christianity fell by the wayside, giving space and time to godless secularism, democracy itself would collapse, leaving us to fend for ourselves in the amoral jungle. Just look at Africa, Asia, and Latin America. It was "very difficult for democracy to work" in these countries, Graham argued in 1964, because there was neither an "informed electorate" nor the requisite "moral basis."[48] They were stuck in the jungle and could not escape to civilization.

More damage was on the way, too. The rise of secularism meant that the whole American way of life, not just its governmental system, was on the verge of implosion, a collapse not unlike the one experienced by Ancient Israel and the Roman Empire. Unlike early American civil religion, which had frequently appealed to the theme of an American Israel to justify Manifest Destiny policies, Graham's often pointed to the fall of Israel rather than to its expansionism. Consider again the quotation cited at the beginning of the chapter: "But if we forget him, as did Israel of old, we put ourselves in the path of judgment, poverty, and adversity." The signs were ominous for Graham. "I am convinced that our nation is in peril," he preached in 1957. "The handwriting is on the wall. The signs of the time are everywhere. American people cannot long continue in their moral degeneracy. There is a cancer eating at the heart and core of the American way of life."[49] A year later, inspired by Edward Gibbon's *The Decline and Fall of the Roman Empire*, the evangelist also adopted the American Rome theme, proclaiming that just like decadent Rome, America was soon to fall into the wasteland of once-great nations.[50]

The themes of the Great American Fall resurfaced with vengeance in the 1960s, when the Supreme Court made the prophet even more prophetic than he had been in the 1950s. Few things disturbed the orderly civil religion of Billy Graham as much as the possibility that America was turning toward secularism during his years of revivalist preaching, but creeping godlessness seemed undeniable as he surveyed decisions made by the Supreme Court in church–state issues in the 1960s. Initially, the Court set off a four-alarm fire in Graham's sanctuary of civil religion when it ruled, in *Engel v. Vitale* (1962), that it was unconstitutional for the New York Board of Regents to require its public schools to recite a prayer drafted and approved by the Board ("Almighty God, we acknowledge our dependence upon Thee, and we beg Thy blessings upon us, our parents, our teachers, and our country").[51] But the alarm sounded even louder a year later when the Court ruled, in *Abington Township School District v. Schempp*, that the Establishment Clause of the First Amendment did not allow for the practice of devotional Bible reading or the reciting of the Lord's Prayer in public schools. Graham's response to *Schempp* was brief, pointed, and unequivocal: "I am shocked at the Supreme Court's decision. Prayers and Bible reading have been a part of American public school life since the Pilgrims landed at Plymouth Rock. . . . At a time when moral decadence is at every hand . . . we need more religion, not less."[52] Of course, "more religion" had not prevented early America from killing Native Americans and sanctioning the slavery of African families, but Graham ignored this point. Instead, his civil religion simply made the conservative case that prayers and Bible reading were indispensable tools for keeping anarchy at bay; they helped to diminish moral deterioration and thereby contributed to a stable social order.

Graham was not the only one to cry foul. The rulings of the Court provoked protests from evangelicals and fundamentalists all across America, including in the hallowed halls of Congress. Representative Frank Becker of New York, for instance, attempted to counter the Court's efforts by proposing, just one day after the *Engel* decision, a constitutional amendment that would have allowed for praying in public schools and invoking the help of God in governmental institutions and activities. Becker's Amendment quickly lost steam, but it took on new life, with considerable energy in the public square, just after the controversial *Schempp* ruling. Without surprise, the liberal *Christian Century* condemned the amendment, saying that it would "destroy the First Amendment's guarantees of religious liberty and then . . . deny that it has done so."[53] But Graham disagreed. "Yes, I support the Becker Amendment," he announced at a 1964 press conference in Phoenix. "I have read it. It's completely voluntary. It does not give any authority to any state or any government to authorize prayers or to prepare prayers or devotions."[54]

But Graham must not have read the amendment very well, because there was no doubt that it would grant government the requisite authority to use prayers in any of its settings. But specific issues were never the evangelist's forte—he was not a policy wonk. More comfortable on the level of generalities, the evangelist added that the Becker Amendment was necessary because "it's simply recognizing God in our national life, which I think is very important, because if we allow this present trend to continue, it means ultimately we'll take chaplains from our armed forces."[55] Like other evangelicals and religious conservatives, Graham believed that he had detected a slippery slope of secularism deeply embedded within the Court's decision. With the Bible and prayer reading dismissed from public schools, chaplains would have to leave the military and Congress, prayer would be banished from the opening of the Supreme Court itself, and the president would be unable to place his hand on the Bible when he takes the oath of allegiance. By contrast, the Becker Amendment would shore things up, returning America to its spiritual roots and preventing the country from slipping further into anarchic waters.

A week after the Phoenix press conference, the San Diego press asked Graham to speak more directly about the importance of prayer and Bible reading in public schools, and he enthusiastically obliged, once again placing his answer in direct dialogue with the Becker Amendment: "Yes, I think school prayers are very important, because, you see, psychologically it tells the child that we believe in God. That's right. It tells the child that the Bible is an important book." If the school does not introduce the student to the Bible, "he has the idea that it's been disapproved, it's no good, we've rejected it. . . . This is what I think the Becker Amendment could help solve." Graham acknowledged that some of his Christian colleagues disagreed, sensing that it would be dangerous to tamper with the Constitution. "But I see a great danger in the opposite direction of taking the whole idea of God from national life, and therefore I support very strongly the Becker Amendment."[56]

King was one of the Christian colleagues who disagreed with Graham, but not because tampering with the Constitution was a dangerous practice. In 1965, when a *Playboy* interviewer asked about the decision on school prayer, the civil rights leader displayed his religious liberalism in full bloom: "I endorse it. I think it was correct. Contrary to what many have said, it sought to outlaw neither prayer nor belief in God." Unlike Graham, whose civil religion highlighted the Christian heritage of America, King also set forth one of the early public arguments in defense of religious pluralism: "In a pluralistic society such as ours, who is to determine what prayer shall be spoken, and by whom? Legally, constitutionally or otherwise, the state certainly has no such right." The civil rights leader then criticized the likes of Billy Graham and his conservative friends in high places: "I am strongly opposed to the efforts that have been made to nullify the decision. They have been motivated, I think, by little more than the wish to harass the Supreme Court. When I saw brother [Governor George] Wallace going up to Washington to testify against the decision at the congressional hearings, it only strengthened my conviction that the decision was right."[57]

But "taking the idea of God from national life" was simply anathema to Graham's civil religion. Without God, America would no longer be great, its children would no longer be leaders in the free world, and its land would no longer be the Promised Land. "When the Bible goes down," he preached, "anarchy will rule. And this generation must face the appalling fact that it's either the Bible or back to the jungle."[58] Curiously, though, the evangelist did not support the Becker amendment strongly enough to want to testify before a congressional committee. The congressman had hoped that Graham would offer his testimony at committee hearings held from April 22 to June 3, 1964, but the evangelist declined, and merely sent the committee a letter of support. "Because our Nation and our public school system had its origins in direct relationship to the Christian faith and believing Christians," Graham wrote, "it does not follow that now, because there are a few atheists and unbelievers in our schools, that it is time to accommodate them by ceasing to pray and in fact, making it illegal to do so." Predictably, Graham's obsession with order also reared its pragmatic head: "At an age when morals are degenerating at an alarming rate, it would seem that if for no other reason we would recognize the fact that a mistake has been made in removing prayer and Bible reading from the public school system."[59]

Because of such strong language, one might think that Graham's failure to attend the hearings must have been due to a scheduling conflict, or perhaps another minor issue, but the evangelist suggested otherwise in a November 1964 press conference in Atlanta: "My position has been that if it is not clarified . . . we may need such an amendment. But at the moment I would rather wait and see what the Supreme Court says in the future. . . . I would rather wait until further decisions have been made before commenting as to whether we need another amendment. I did not go and testify on this because I was not really sure how to testify."[60] As suggested by this equivocating quotation, Graham's position had begun to reflect the ambiguity within the evangelical community on the issue of school prayers. On the one hand, the community affirmed the Court's commitment to the separation of church and state, but on the other, it characterized the decisions as part of a dangerous trend toward secularization. Graham eventually seemed to adopt the position of *Christianity Today*, which, as Steven Green puts it, "called for restraint among evangelicals and recommended a 'wait and see' approach."[61] Nevertheless, although his earlier protestations were rendered pianissimo, there is no doubt that Graham's evolving restraint was coupled with ongoing regret. "I think it would have been far better," he reflected, "had the Supreme Court never touched these things at all, never handled them . . . if they take another step, then of course some of us are going to be very disturbed at the trend toward secularizing America."[62]

Graham would indeed become "very disturbed" as secularism spread throughout the remainder of the King years, and his threatening mantra would remain the same, as evident in this 1966 sermon: "If we get away from our original moral and spiritual moorings, we are in serious danger of disaster. The only possible explanation of America's phenomenal rise in the past 200 years is God. If we leave and neglect God, we can fall much more quickly than when we rose."[63] Graham's civil religion, then, was not uncritical nationalism, but a prophetic patriotism that anathematized secularism for the sake of social order. As an evangelist faithful to his calling, Graham believed that he was divinely anointed, even when addressing a country he deeply honored and respected, to inform America that it stood under not only the grace of a loving God but also the judgment of an angry God violently opposed to secularization. In Graham's civil religion, the trend toward secularism had set America straightaway on the road to hell— a chaotic jungle that was the exact opposite of America's divinely ordered history and destiny.

Like Graham, Martin Luther King, Jr. believed that America was in the hands of an angry God. Even during his first speech to the throngs of people gathered to protest the bus situation in Montgomery, he suggested in no uncertain terms that America was close to the end of its so-called greatness: "The Almighty God is not the only . . . God just standing up saying through Hosea, 'I love you, Israel.' He's also the God that stands up before nations and said: 'Be still and know that I am God, that if you don't obey me I will break the backbone of your power and slap you out of the orbits of your international and national relationships.' "[64] And with greater intensity as the civil rights years progressed, King depicted God as on the verge of slapping America silly. During the last year of his life, for example, while he was visiting Memphis, he invoked the biblical story of Dives and Lazarus in a harsh condemnation of America. "Dives went to hell," King said, "because he sought to be a conscientious objector in the war against poverty." And as the God of justice consigned Dives to hell, God would do the same to America: "If America does not use her vast resources of wealth to end poverty and make it possible for all of God's children to have the basic necessities of life, she too will go to hell."[65]

Although they agreed that America was on the verge of a meteoric fall from greatness, the civil religions of King and Graham parted paths when identifying the sins that would cause the fall. As a liberal pluralist, King never once characterized secularism as problematic for America's destiny. In fact, he was remarkably supportive of what Graham had identified as the manifestations of secularism—for example, rationalism and faith in government. As a product of Boston University's personalism, a rigorous exercise in theological rationalism, King embraced and practiced rationalism in both theology and politics. And because he was a political activist devoted to a radical redistribution of social resources, he also placed great repose in the ability of government to work for the beloved community; God needed government for the construction and flourishing of the beloved community. For the most part, King identified and emphasized three main sins that set America on the road to hell—segregation, economic injustice, and militarism. Graham saw each of these as problematic on some level, but he never once emphasized them as much as the civil rights leader had. On the contrary, he seemed to lose sight of these sins as he became obsessed on the American trend toward secularization. For Graham, far more problematic than segregated busses or the structuring of welfare or even war in Vietnam was the disturbing trend of an activist, liberal Court to render decisions that would remove God from American life. Godlessness alone would be the downfall of America.

My Country, Right or Wrong

Because Graham's civil religion held a double attitude toward America—it saw America as beautiful in birth and destiny and yet marred by the overwhelming sin of secularism—it embraced a dialectical patriotism. On the one hand, Graham held that patriotism meant becoming a full partner in America's greatness—supporting America's riches by becoming a contributing member to the free enterprise system, buttressing America's strength by paying taxes (or, if required, joining the military), and embracing religious liberty by going to church and worshipping the God who blessed America. In effect, to be patriotic meant to live the American dream of Eisenhower's America—to be an outstanding community member with a good job, a solid house, a warm apple pie in the oven, a little Christian citizen in the womb, and a respectable neighborhood church for the family to attend, preferably a Protestant one with a flag in the chancel.

Clearly, the Christian America that Graham longed for so deeply throughout the King years was not just any Christian America but an evangelical Protestant America. Although known for his ecumenical and even interfaith actions, Graham took significant steps to undermine the political influence of faiths other than his own evangelical Protestantism. For evidence, one might point to the recently discovered Nixon tapes on which Graham is heard to bemoan Jewish leadership in America. Still, other relevant evidence abounds, and primary among this is the evangelist's actions during the Kennedy–Nixon campaign. There is no need here to recount the behind-the-scenes machinations already detailed by William Martin's fascinating account of Graham during the campaign, but suffice it to say that the evangelist, like other Protestant leaders of the day, sought to spread more than a bit of fear about the possibility of undue papal influence within the Oval Office: Graham was no Kennedy fan, and took active measures to undermine his campaign.[66] Equally significant, we should note that the evangelist always supported God-fearing Protestants over Pope-obeying Catholics for political office; if there is any evidence that Graham supported a Catholic for political office, it has yet to be uncovered. For the evangelist, a Roman Catholic America would have been wholly unreflective of America's historical roots in Protestantism and of the country's commitment to freedom of individual conscience. Simply stated, the America that God first ordained through the courageous Pilgrims was not a Roman Catholic America.

Nevertheless, the evangelist consistently maintained that the electoral winner was God's choice, even if it happened to be the Roman Catholic John F. Kennedy, and that American citizens must humbly submit themselves to presidential authority and actions. True patriotism could never mean violating the unwritten law of *lese majeste*—undertaking an action that would undermine the authority of American politicians and their laws (unless they became distinctly un-American and took away the right to religious liberty). On the contrary, American patriotism translated into an abiding obligation and responsibility to pledge allegiance to the flag of the United States of America and to practice an ethic of subordination—paying taxes in full, praying for politicians, lobbying and recruiting politicians devoted to Christian principles and values, and (because the government allowed for religious liberty) obeying the U.S. government under any and all circumstances. This last point is also fundamental for grasping the full meaning of Graham's civil religion. The evangelist understood America to be not just any country with just any government, but to be *the* country of God's blessing and favor, with *the* greatest form of government on earth. The American government was God's servant for the good, God's tool in a demonic world system, and God's beacon to all other governments that wished to reflect Christian principles and values.

Graham's civil religion might not have been a form of uncritical religious nationalism, but it sometimes came close to a crude form of religious statism—a dangerously shallow ideology that understood and positioned the American government as God's will on earth, not to be disobeyed under any conditions.[67] Obviously, this is not to say that Graham never criticized the American government, but it is to say that his civil religion never once found justification for civil disobedience against the American government. Because all American laws reflected the authority of the divine will, they were to be accepted and obeyed, without question, by all citizens, especially Christian citizens. While King, as Michael Eric Dyson rightly notes, "argued that those who practice civil disobedience were superior citizens because they were willing to suffer for their beliefs by submitting to legal punishment for breaking bad laws," Graham contended the opposite—that superior citizens were those who practiced civil obedience to all American laws, including bad ones that cause undue suffering and hardship, like laws that implement discrimination and segregation.[68] Just so, Graham's civil religion—its understanding of American government and the meaning of superior citizenship—came perilously close to blatant idolatry. The idolatrous dimension of his civil religion came to fore especially during the Vietnam years, when war protestors journeyed to Canada, threw blood at the Pentagon, and burned their draft cards. The last chapter will focus on the Vietnam War in some detail, but just a few words here about Graham's views on war dissenters will help clarify the argument that the evangelist presented an American-Legion type of ideology that fused and confused God, country, and flag.

"Christianity breeds patriotism." Such was Graham's conservative reaction to the young men and women, many of them Christian pacifists, protesting the raging war in Vietnam in 1965. Their dissent was a *malum in se*. Sickened by the burning of draft cards, the evangelist warned that the young people's actions bordered on treason and reflected the larger "moral and spiritual decay" in the country. "We should support the government and be faithful to it," he added, "as long as it is faithful to God."[69] Graham's civil-religious rhetoric against dissenters increased appreciably as the Vietnam years marched forward, with a striking culmination in March 1968. When members of the press asked him if he would advise a young man to participate in the war, Graham replied: "Well, I think that when our nation makes a commitment, right or wrong, I have a responsibility to my nation. . . . I think when we are called upon we have to serve."[70] Absent here, of course, was any understanding of the limited power of civil law that King had expressed in his letter from Birmingham Jail, or the notion of civil disobedience that he had clarified for dissenters, or the vision of restricted political authority that he had preached throughout his public ministry. Politically, Graham's patriotism did not dissent.

With his patriotic mantra—"my country, right or wrong"—and with his masculine efforts to put a quietus on dissent, Graham revealed what is perhaps the clearest example of idolatry within his civil religion. As a disciple of Jesus, Graham should have known better: Jesus, after all, was not a patriot who preached the virtues of love of country, especially during wartime, but rather a man who sought to transcend national loyalty in order to express singular devotion to loving God and your neighbor as yourself. In fact, Graham did know better. As he sought greater access to preach in communist countries, for example, he shrewdly presented himself less as an American citizen and more as an ambassador for the reign of God. "I am a representative of the kingdom of God," he announced in 1967 Zagreb, seeking to extricate himself from his anti-communist Americanism.[71] Three years earlier, Graham had even observed that the reason for China's opposition to Christianity was quite simple: Christianity had become "too identified with western democracy."[72] But Graham was terribly inconsistent, and when push came to shove in times of war and dissent, his Americanism always trumped his claim to world citizenship. In the final analysis, Graham was exactly that—far more American than Christian in his view that Christianity breeds patriotism.

One Way Out

When his critics accuse Graham of being an uncritical patriot, it is usually because they have in mind his political ethic of subjection. But, again, Graham's civil religion was not merely about propping up the political powers that be; it was also about counteracting the sins leading America to anarchy. So what to do about America's plunge toward hell? How to save America? In a 1964 sermon titled "Turn Back, America," Graham pointed to King Jehoshaphat as the best example for America to follow as it contemplated turning secularism back to the hell it came from: "When he sought peace and social progress for his people, what was his course of action? Did he try new laws, new social plans, new educational projects, and new financial programs?" We should pause here to read the contextual subtext: Did King Jehoshaphat do what King and his followers were seeking from America—the formation of new laws to eliminate segregation, new social plans to combat poverty in the African American community, new educational projects to give African American boys and girls a "head start," and new financial programs, like the guaranteed annual income, that would provide a safety net for African Americans underemployed and unemployed against their will? "No!" Graham preached. "Spurning all of these, he went back to the Word of God. . . . King Jehoshaphat demanded that his people learn the Word of God, that they study it, that they live by it every day, and that they humble themselves before God." And the results were impressive. "When Judah returned to the teachings of the Bible, one of the great triumphs in military history occurred . . . and for many years thereafter, peace ruled the land."[73] Graham hoped the same for America. He did not call for a radical restructuring of American society, he did not call for Christians to march in the streets against America's greatest sin, and he certainly did not recommend an ethic of subjection to the sins plaguing America. Instead, he called for a good old-fashioned American revival and for American patriots to repent and surrender their lives to Jesus Christ. In short, Graham's patriotism counseled individual citizens not only to adopt a political ethic of subjection, but also to practice a Christian ethic of repentance.

What we must remember here once again is that Graham held an atomistic view of society, and thus he saw American society not as an impersonal collective but as the sum of individual citizens. If America was plunging toward anarchy, then, it was ultimately the fault of individual American citizens. "Many of you," Graham preached in 1958, "will blame the Republicans or the Democrats [for America's pending fall from greatness]. It is not the politicians that should take the blame. It is the American people as individuals. We backslide as individuals before we begin to decay as a nation."[74] The evangelist had blamed individual American citizens a bit more colorfully two years earlier: "The basis of the ills and troubles of our land is that the people are not right with God. No nation ever fell that was right with God. Let me repeat: no nation has ever fallen in the history of the world that was right with God."[75] But thank God that "there is still time to repair the breach. We are still on this side of judgment, though time is quickly passing by." And because there is still time, we need not become like fallen Israel and fallen Rome. "Rome's fate need not be ours if we repent and turn to God."[76]

Individualistic in its essence, Graham's civil religion pinpointed Christian repentance as the most patriotic act an individual can ever undertake. "Thus today," he preached in 1958, "the greatest contribution you can make to your nation is to give your life and heart to Jesus Christ because when you make your decision for Christ, it is America through you making its decision for Christ and trust in God."[77] Graham also presented this individualistic approach at several presidential prayer breakfasts, including the one in 1963: "The greatest contribution that any citizen can make to the nation's strength at this hour is his personal faith in Jesus Christ."[78] After sketching this point yet again at the 1964 presidential prayer breakfast ("if we surrender to Jesus, God will save America"), Graham kicked his civil religion into its highest gear. "Yes," he preached, "there is a way out. It is the way that our fathers took—the early colonists who came to the shores of the New World. It is the way that George Washington took at Valley Forge. It is the way that Benjamin Franklin and others took during the Constitutional Convention. . . . It is the way that Abraham Lincoln took in the darkest moments of the Civil War."[79] This one way out—turning to Jesus—is now available to each and every citizen, and if individual citizens would just take it, they will assure that America will not fall from greatness, at least for now.

The True American Patriot

In Graham's civil religion, then, true American patriots were Christians who surrendered their lives to Jesus and loved America so much that they would follow the teachings of the Bible and lay down their lives for the divinely ordained state and its laws. But for King, the true American patriot was the individual (Christian, Jew, Muslim, agnostic, or atheist) who loved America so much that he or she would lay down his or her life, not for America, right or wrong, but for God's will for America—the beloved community. The differences between the competing visions of true patriotism were so sharp that King was far from a patriot in Graham's civil religion, and vice versa. According to Graham's civil religion, insofar as King advocated civil disobedience, he was little more than an extremist, a revolutionary, an anarchist, and an un-American leader of a lawless movement. And according to King's, insofar as Graham disavowed civil disobedience of unjust laws, he was little more than the typical Southern conservative who sacrificed the beloved community on the high altar of law and order.

With different versions of true patriotism, the civil religions of the two figures also presented competing visions of America the Beautiful. King's final goal was a pluralistic society devoted to integration, economic justice, and peace, but Graham's was a Christian if not a Protestant society whose main purpose was to proclaim the Gospel of Jesus and save individual souls from hell.[80] Although he gave lip service to religious pluralism, Graham really wanted everyone to bow down and confess Jesus as Lord; his pluralism always melted when it came face-to-face with his evangelical fervor to make disciples of Jesus Christ. By contrast, King never dreamed of a Christian America devoted to the teachings of the Bible, especially if those teachings encouraged, as Graham's had, an uncritical devotion to the political authorities. Nor did King ever dream of an America that would make Christians of all citizens; although inspired by Jesus, King's beloved community was far more inclusive, far less provincial, and far less Christian than Graham's beloved America.

Graham's civil religion would safeguard his seat in the White House, and as part of the inner circle of American power, the evangelist would offer counsel to presidents of both major political parties, speak at presidential prayer breakfasts first organized in 1953 by his friend Abraham Vereide, and even lead Sunday services at the White House. These were Billy Graham's ways of acknowledging and serving the political authority that he felt flowed from God—and of doing his part to save America from falling from on high. His opponents were relentless in their criticisms that Graham was little more than a fawning court chaplain, but he remained dedicated to forming friendships with presidents and politicians in high offices, stating that it was only access made possible through friendship and faithful service that allowed him to share his confidential views, sometimes critical, behind closed doors. While the Great American Graham was being ushered into the White House, however, Martin Luther King, Jr. was becoming *persona non grata*. The big house would eventually shut its doors to the black man, and it was his love of the beloved community that finally did him in—a love that made him publicly criticize President Johnson's handling of an unjust war against poor peasants in Vietnam. In the American-Legion civil religion that Johnson had learned from Graham, King's single-minded devotion to a peaceful community, especially during America's struggle on foreign soil, was reason for public banishment.

But there was not always such marked conflict between the missions to save America as undertaken by King and Graham. As the following chapter will show, the two religious leaders sometimes came together on issues of vital importance to the beloved community. In these rare moments, the civil religions of the two preachers enjoyed a rare moment of mutual civility if not a foretaste of the feast of the beloved community itself.

CHAPTER FOUR

"He Belonged to All the Races": The Evolution of Graham's Race Ethics

"Southern-born, I was reared in a community where typically Southern attitudes prevailed. If there were Negroes who chafed in their status as second-class citizens, I was not aware of them."[1] As a child in North Carolina, young Billy Graham was raised by parents supportive of Jim Crow, attended segregated schools and churches, drank at "whites only" water fountains, shopped in stores that refused service to African Americans, and benefited from the everyday labors of African Americans on the Graham farm. It is little wonder that he adopted the racist attitudes of the rural South "without much reflection."[2] Graham's early racism, however, was more than just a matter of not seeing African Americans chafe under second-class citizenship; young Billy also did his own small part to keep Jim Crow alive and kicking in North Carolina in the 1930s and 1940s. Biographer Marshall Frady, for example, reports that Graham adamantly refused to join his white friends for trips to "colored" barbershops, saying: " 'Long as there's a white barbershop in Charlotte, I'll never have my haircut at a nigger barbershop. Never.' "[3].

Young Billy supported Jim Crow in countless other ways, too, even in spite of a deep fondness, if not love, for Reese Brown, the African American foreman on the Graham farm. Brown was "one of Daddy's best personal friends," and because of that he was among the highest paid farmhands in Mecklenburg County at the time. "Everyone respected him," Graham recalled, "and I thought there was nothing Reese did not know or could not do." Graham even played with Brown's children, ate with his family in the tenant house, and felt like he was just "another uncle."[4] His positive experiences with the avuncular Brown would encourage him in later years to emphasize interpersonal friendships as one of the fundamental building blocks for improving race relations in America, but the presence of Brown on the Graham farm, even in a leadership role, did little to erase segregationist feelings from the heart of young Billy.

His life-transforming conversion to Jesus Christ at a segregated revival led by the racist Mordecai Ham did not help much, either. Given all that the adult Graham would state about the explosive social implications of individual conversion, we might expect that his conversion at the age of sixteen would have led him in short time to decry the evils of discrimination and segregation. In fact, Graham would frequently suggest that from the moment of his conversion, he simply could not understand segregation, especially as it took form in the church.[5] Curiously, however, his autobiography does not give any indication that his conversion provoked significant change in his racial attitudes. On the contrary, he claimed that he could not "point to any single event or intellectual crisis that changed my mind on racial equality."[6] The evangelist put the point a bit differently in 1960 when he stated that because of the system of segregation in which he was steeped, "even after my conversion, I felt no guilt in thinking of my dark-skinned brothers in the usual patronizing and paternalistic way."[7] What is so curious about this is that Graham would preach throughout the King years that conversion of the heart was the most effective and faithful method for reaching the goal of racial reconciliation. Perhaps he was wrong.

But he was not exaggerating when he reported that his conversion did not radically change his segregationist beliefs and practices. Just consider his life trajectory in the years subsequent to his conversion: Following high school, Graham enrolled at Bob Jones University, whose namesake embraced and preached the party line of white Southern segregationists. Unhappy at Bob Jones, Graham then transferred to the Florida Bible Institute, where he became a member of the Southern Baptist Convention, a staunch advocate of racial segregation. After graduating from Wheaton College, which prevented African American students from living in white dorms and dating white students, Graham then joined Youth for Christ (YFC) and preached at countless segregated YFC meetings. And during the early years of his crusade ministry, he planned and preached at numerous segregated crusades throughout the South. Young Billy Frank might have been an innocent victim of segregationist turpitude, but as he grew into moral responsibility in the years following his conversion, he certainly did his own part to keep Jim Crow alive. The point is this: If the power of conversion really opened one's heart to loving African American neighbors, as Graham would later claim, the younger Graham must have ignored or dismissed the tugging affections of his converted heart when laying out his educational and career paths. Though converted to Christ, Graham remained unconverted to racial justice.

The Long Road to Racial Conversion

Nevertheless, it does seem that a bit of racial sensitivity began to take root in Graham's moral character, however shallowly, during the 1930s and 1940s. At Wheaton, for example, he began to see African Americans not only as farm laborers but also as students with intellects that could rival and surpass those of whites. "They were the first blacks I had ever gone to school with," he recounted years later.[8] Equally significant, Graham also started to accept African Americans as friends who could teach him about race. "At Wheaton College," he recalled, "I made friends with black students, and I recall vividly one of them coming to my room one day and talking with deep conviction about America's need for racial justice."[9] With a major in anthropology, he also came to admire and virtually memorize *Up from the Apes*, an anthropological study, written by Harvard's Earnest Albert Hooten, which suggested that race was a social construct and that "the great cultural achievements of humanity have been produced, almost invariably, by racially-mixed people."[10]

Graham's contact with the racially progressive views of his colleagues in the new evangelical movement, especially Carl Henry, who held that fundamentalists wrongly ignored the evils of racial hatred, also pricked his developing racial consciousness, as did his cross-cultural experiences with YFC. Eventually the glaring lights of the media pushed Graham along, too. When the national media began to focus its lenses on him in 1949, the young evangelical preacher, now with his own team, found it increasingly difficult to practice his "pattern of silence and segregation," as Jerry Hopkins puts it in his excellent study of Graham and race.[11] Indeed, in the following year, the press began to question the evangelist rather pointedly about the discrepancy between his message of universal love and his practice of conducting segregated crusades throughout the South, and especially in Atlanta, where African American ministers scoffed and turned a cold shoulder when Graham offered to hold a special service for them alone (and this after ignoring the issues of discrimination and racism in his services for the whites).

Graham later recalled 1950 as nothing less than a watershed year in terms of his attention to the issue of segregation. "Not until 1950," he wrote for *Reader's Digest*, "was the religious and moral issue involved in segregation brought sharply to our attention."[12] We may look a bit cynically at Graham's claim that it was not until 1950 that segregation presented itself so "sharply," but it is doubtless that the relentless press questions, coupled with his experience in Atlanta, where he had alienated so many of the people he had wanted to reach for Christ, shook his practice of holding segregated meetings to its very core. In fact, we should take special care here to identify Graham's concern for winning souls as one of the major reasons that he first began to address the issue of segregation publicly. Simply stated, the evangelist had come to realize, especially in Atlanta, that his practice of segregated seating, when publicized through the national media, precluded him from winning as many souls as possible—and this deeply troubled the pragmatic soul winner.

The year 1950 was also significant because it was then that a white president of a black college, whose name Graham never identified, pulled him aside and delivered life-changing advice that the evangelist would always hold near to his heart: "The Negro is emerging, Billy. He is not the same person we knew in our boyhood. His leaders, mostly well-educated and responsible, are soon going to call for an end to discrimination. Human justice is on their side; but more than that, religion is, too. You're taking leadership in the field of evangelism, and this is something you're going to have to face." After this breakthrough conversation of sorts, Graham returned to his team, and together they started "thinking, praying—and searching the Bible."[13] Unfortunately, they also continued to plan for segregated services. However meaningful his conversation with the college president would eventually prove to be, and however much the Atlanta experience had shaken his practice of segregation, Graham continued to hold segregated crusades in 1951 and 1952, even while answering to a media skeptical of his integrity in racial matters. It seems that segregated services just ran too thick through his Southern blood as he dealt with places that demanded segregation.

But the problems would not abate, and neither would Graham's developing racial conscience. The growing problem of little African American participation in his crusades, the ongoing glare of the media, and his deeper commitment to biblical study on themes of race all combined in 1952 to lead the evangelist to begin speaking more publicly about the "sin" of racism and to take a few bold steps against extreme white segregationists. For example, when the Mississippi Governor Hugh L. White, a perfect example of ole boy Southern racism, demanded that he hold entirely separate services for African Americans during his 1952 Jackson Crusade, Graham firmly resisted, inviting whites and African Americans to all of his services (with their segregated seating arrangements). In Jackson, Graham also preached in a moment of newly found courage that "there is no segregation at the altar," thereby earning both the scorn of the governor and the rare approbation of the *Christian Century*.[14] But, disappointingly, at least to African Americans and white integrationists, the evangelist immediately backslid into old patterns, by stating unequivocally that he and his organization would still "follow the existing social customs in whatever part of the country we minister," and that the Bible "has nothing to say about segregation or non-segregation."[15] Graham apparently feared that he would lose the support of his white base.

By 1953, however, even Graham had enough of his own circumlocutions and equivocations, and so he assumed an absolutist stance against segregated seating at the Chattanooga Crusade. During these groundbreaking services, Graham "went into the building as the people were beginning to gather one night and personally tore down the ropes separating the white from the African American sections—ropes that had been mandated according to the custom in those days by the local committee. My actions caused the head usher to resign in anger right on the spot . . . but I did not back down."[16] Whatever the immediate cause might have been, it was a deeply significant move for a man who had grown up supporting Jim Crow—a profoundly prophetic move that demonstrated flexibility and maturation within Graham's character. But, once again, the courageous stance was short-lived. Following Chattanooga, the flip-flopping Graham found himself preaching to a segregated audience, this one at the Dallas Crusade, and then to an integrated audience in Detroit, and then back again to a segregated audience in Asheville, North Carolina. But these flip-flops, which made the evangelist appear more than a bit hypocritical on the race question—racially progressive in the North and racially conservative in the South—were far from unsurprising. Rare, indeed, was the segregationist whose moral character matured without detour, who progressed without reaching back into the past and taking comfort in the customs that had molded his or her early moral character. Billy Graham, for all his stunning progress, was simply not that rare.

With even this cursory glance at Graham's maturation and growth, and his backsliding and equivocations, during the 1940s and early 1950s, it is clear that racial conversion, at least on the issue of desegregation, did not occur during or anytime soon after his conversion to Christ. On this point, a revealing 1957 *Ebony* article quotes Graham as saying: "In 1953, after the Supreme Court desegregation edict was handed down, I decided definitely that segregation was wrong."[17] It is more than fair to assume here that Graham was referring to the 1954 decision in *Brown v. Board of Education of Topeka*, and that either he or *Ebony* mistakenly identified the year of the decision to declare segregation in public schools as unconstitutional. But whatever the case may be, if Graham was telling the truth about his reaction to the *Brown* decision—and we have no reason to doubt that he was—twenty years had passed from the day of his Christian conversion to the moment he finally acknowledged, once and for all, that segregation was wrong.

Why such a long period? Why did it take his converted heart twenty years to see the evil of segregation? It is doubtless that Graham's interpersonal experiences with African Americans, his moderating education at Wheaton, his re-reading of the Bible (which we will explore below), his cross-cultural experiences with YFC, the glare of the media, and his concern for increasing the number of converts all played a key role in opening Graham's eyes to the problems of segregation. But the answer to the question of protracted timing ultimately lies in the evangelist's high if not idolatrous respect for political authority. For Graham, the voice of government, at least one that allows for religious liberty, was virtually the voice of God, full of divine authority and intent. Thus, if secular law or customs backed by the force of law sanctioned the practice of segregation, Graham would honor segregation. To be sure, Governor White of Mississippi was a governing authority, but when he demanded that Graham hold different services, one for whites and another for African Americans, he was not speaking with the force of law, either moral or political. On racial matters, the U.S. Supreme Court was *the* authoritative voice of law in Graham's theological system, and so when the Court struck a significant blow to segregation in *Brown v. Board of Education*, the evangelist understood the ruling to be definitive, an echo of the divine voice from on high.

Why was segregation wrong? Graham's evangelical logic determined it to be wrong not only because of biblical teachings and jolting human experiences but finally because the Supreme Court, a servant of God, ruled that it was wrong. Why did it take Graham twenty years to acknowledge that segregation was wrong? It took so long just because the Supreme Court had not ruled definitively on segregation until 1954. It was as simple as that: Graham's racial conversion depended on a Supreme Court ruling. But with the ruling from on high, the evangelist could finally express supernal confidence that segregation was directly opposed to the will of God.

It is also important here to backtrack and correct the record. If his conversion had made him more racially sensitive than before, as Graham frequently claimed throughout the King years, it did not immediately lead him to believe or act as if he believed that segregation was wrong in the eyes of God. Contrary to many of his sloppy claims, neither did his converted heart lead him to desegregate his crusades once and for all in 1953, 1952, or earlier. Yes, 1953 marked the beginning of his integrated crusades, but it did not at the same time mark the end of his segregated ones; 1954, the year of the Supreme Court ruling and twenty years after his conversion, was the first full year that saw the beginning of uninterrupted desegregated crusades. Thus, Graham was at least misleading when he claimed in a 1960 interview with F. Lee Bailey that "when we first started our work . . . we desegregated our audiences in about 1952."[18] He was imprecise again in 1960, this time in a *Reader's Digest* article, when he stated that "in 1952 we decided we could no longer have segregated audiences."[19] He was unambiguously wrong in his 1964 reply to a member of the press who asked if all of Graham's Southern crusades had been desegregated. "I think we held only two or three that had any segregation at all."[20] And he was as wrong as ever in Dortmund, Germany, in 1970, when he stated that for twenty years he had been holding "the largest demonstrations in the country . . . all totally integrated with both races."[21] And these are just a few examples of Graham's whitewashed history.

The evangelist was not the only one who sought to make his early crusade years a bit more racially palatable than they actually were; the Billy Graham Evangelistic Association helped, too, especially when it reported in *One Body, One Spirit*, an official statement on Graham and race, that the evangelist had "held his first deliberately integrated crusade at Chattanooga, Tennessee, in March, 1953. This was more than a year before the Supreme Court's decision of May 17, 1954."[22] Of course, this was a true statement, in and of itself, but the report omitted a few key details, like the number of segregated crusades the evangelist held after the Chattanooga crusade. Contrary to *One Body, One Spirit*, as well as some of Graham's own shaky recollections, the best evidence clearly suggests that the evangelist was not as trailblazing on racial matters as he and his organization wanted us to believe. Thus, when one now reads Graham's comments on desegregation in *Peace with God* (1953)—"The church should have been the pace-setter. The church should voluntarily be doing what the federal courts are doing by pressure and compulsion"—we should acknowledge either that Graham was preaching to himself or that he was a racial "hypocrite," as Hopkins puts it, merely saying one thing while doing another.[23] Perhaps that sets up a false dilemma, however: maybe the racial hypocrite was really preaching to himself.

An Occasional Prophet

This pointed and blunt clarification of the historical record should in no way detract from the significance of Graham's prophetic efforts to integrate his crusades even before the onset of the King years. What we must recall here is that at the time the evangelist desegregated his Chattanooga Crusade, the South was still ablaze with KKK crosses, still sparkling with new "whites only" signs, still a land of lynching, and still a safe haven for Jim Crow and the rest of his family. When set within this racist context, Graham's first integrated crusades, coupled with his early statements on the sin of racism, were nothing less than powerfully prophetic, sharply judgmental of a social system that had prevented individuals from acting as if they were really of "one body, one spirit."

Graham's prophetic stance was so remarkable because he assumed it in an abattoir filled not only with the viciously racist White Citizens Council but also with well-meaning friends, whose cautious analyses suggested that he would lose his white base in the South were he to integrate his crusades. Clearly, it is the moment when one's friends step into the opposing camp that a true prophet is tested most acutely—and Graham did not fail. By integrating his crusades in Chattanooga against the rabid racists and his racially moderate friends, Graham revealed himself as capable of becoming the type of Hebrew prophet who could see what his people could not see, who could say what his people could not say, and who could do what his people could not do. Like the prophets of old, Graham transcended his sinful culture, looked down on it with love, and judged it in light of the Word of God from on high.

Clearly, Graham's heroic stance against segregated meetings in the South revealed dramatic growth in his moral character—growth that the evangelist himself recognized. "My earlier meetings were segregated," he confessed to *Ebony*. "I was reared in the South and had never thought it through. But I hope that through the years, I have grown in many directions."[24] By the time of the article, Graham had already grown considerably since those days when he refused to have his hair cut at a barbershop owned and operated by African Americans. Compared to many of his colleagues in the South, and to his own denomination, the evangelist proved to be a leader far ahead of his own people.

His pioneering role as a desegregating evangelist in a racist culture came with benefits: it gave him peace of mind, a sense that he was following the will of God, and great personal satisfaction. One of his most personally satisfying moments during the 1950s was the day an African American minister approached him at the integrated Louisville Crusade. "I want you to know," the minister shared, "that one of the greatest experiences I have ever had in my life was standing outside the Coliseum and having my people come up to me and say, 'Pastor, is it true that we can sit anywhere we like?' I raised my hand, made a wide sweep of the auditorium and said, 'Anywhere.' " Although Graham had not seen African Americans chafing at their second-class treatment during his childhood, this time, upon hearing the African American minister say "anywhere," the older Graham could not see for a different reason: "There were tears in my eyes."[25]

Nevertheless, Graham's vision, even after it sharpened its focus on the problems of segregated seating at his crusades, was still far from 20/20 in racial matters. Just a few months before the beginning of the Montgomery bus boycott, for example, he wrote a personal letter to President Eisenhower, stating that the American people "are now united as they have not been in decades."[26] But Graham saw unity in America, as did many other white Americans at the time, only because he was not looking through the lenses of the black experience in 1955, a time when the *Brown* decision faced fierce resistance, when Southern courthouses did all they could to keep African Americans from registering to vote, and when Jim Crow still ruled the South with an iron fist and an occasional rope. If Graham did not see that white bus drivers were bullying African Americans, calling them vulgar names and demanding that they surrender their seats to whites, it was because he had narrowed his vision, closed his ears, and shut out the African American experience of disunity.

As race is a social construct, so is American unity. And this much no one knew better than Martin Luther King, Jr., when he stood next to Mrs. Rosa Parks, feeling in his own converted heart that injustice anywhere, even on a bus in backward Montgomery, was a threat to justice everywhere, and that the injustices suffered by his people for centuries really meant that there were two Americas—one white and the other black. Graham's response to King and the civil rights movement, beginning with Rosa Parks in Montgomery, requires its own multi-volume study, and so the task before us in the remainder of this chapter is not so much to provide a chronological account of all of Graham's views and actions on race during the King years, but to test the grand claim made by the evangelist on a number of occasions—the claim that he "supported" the civil rights movement from its beginning.[27]

Deconstructing Racist Biblicism: The Bible

Does Not Say Blacks Are Cursed

"There are a lot of segregationists who are going to be sadly disillusioned when they get to heaven—if they get there."[28] With the arrival of desegregation on center stage during the early years of the civil rights movement, Billy Graham, now converted to racial reconciliation, did not hesitate to join Martin Luther King, Jr. in delivering sharply worded statements against the evils of segregation. In fact, Graham offered considerable support to the civil rights movement by expressing a prophetic rage against segregation, warning its supporters that one day they would have to stand before the judgment of a wrathful God and answer questions about the ways they have treated their neighbors. Unlike King, however, the evangelical Graham was more than ready and willing to threaten unrepentant segregationists with the everlasting fires of a real hell. In heaven there would be no color line, no Jim Crow, no master–slave relationships, no White Citizens Council, and no Ku Klux Klan—everything that made racists feel comfortable and secure in their little enclaves on earth. So beware, segregationists, Graham would say: There will be a Judgment Day, and on that day a scorching future fire awaits those who would dare to burn crosses in support of segregation. (Interestingly, by setting forth such a fire-and-brimstone position, the evangelist was actually making the argument, albeit unintentionally, that he too had been on the road to hell during all those years he had embraced Jim Crow. And this makes for a fascinating image—an image of Graham converting thousands of sinners at segregated crusades while he himself was on the straight and narrow road to hell—but the evangelist never quite played out this thought, never quite followed the logic of his own prophetic stance.)

Although numerous factors played catalytic roles in his racial conversion, the evangelist emphasized the primary role of the Bible and frequently expounded on his Bible study to convert hell-bound segregationists. Without surprise, then, after his backsliding in Chattanooga, Graham no longer touted the position that the Bible "has nothing to say about segregation or non-segregation." On the contrary, with the onset of the King years, he energetically attacked the segregationist reading of the Bible and mustered numerous Biblical texts which, in his view, revealed God's will that segregation was a vicious evil to be conquered and overcome. The Bible, once silent, had become a fiery manifesto against segregation.

The converted Graham immediately set out to deconstruct the distorted biblicism of the segregationists who twisted the Bible this way and that to back their perverse position. Especially disturbing to him was the segregationist appeal to the biblical story in which Noah curses Canaan because his father Ham (Noah's own son) had witnessed Noah lying naked after a night of drunken revelry. Believing that African Americans were descendents of Canaan, segregationists had long pointed to Noah's words—"Cursed be Canaan; lowest of slaves shall he be to his brothers" (Gen. 9:25)—to explain that Africans were cursed by God to a life of slavery and subjection. In response to this peculiar but common justification of segregation, Graham passionately argued three points. First, he argued that Ham and his brothers Shem and Japheth were all "blood brothers," that all of the earth was peopled through them, and that no discrimination existed among them. Second, he claimed that the curse lacked divine legitimacy because it was Noah, not God, who had cursed Canaan. And his third argument was that the Canaanites "were all white tribes, and that the Negro peoples are descended from Canaan's brothers whom Canaan was to serve."[29]

These were wonderfully creative arguments, considerably more insightful and interpretive than his usual proof-texting, but they would have held persuasive power only for those who believed that the story of the curse of Noah had actually happened, and that there was a possibility if not a probability that the story really did explain the historical reasons behind slavery and segregation. And this gets us to a major and obvious point: When making the case against segregation, Graham targeted his brothers and sisters in the white evangelical and fundamentalist traditions—traditions largely ignored, misunderstood, or simply not well known by liberal whites and African American leaders. Of the several major figures in Protestantism at the time, Graham alone could speak the language of segregationists, Graham alone knew their thought patterns inside and out, and Graham alone realized that he could help transform the attitudes of his people with a bit of compelling internal criticism. The evangelist was the one figure who did not have to lob boulders onto his people from outside their scriptural and theological traditions. Instead, he could offer the criticism of a friendly reviewer—a reading of the Bible that provided a biblicist alternative to biblicist segregationism. In this respect, it is difficult to overestimate the significance of the unique role that Graham played in transforming the religious views of a white people stuck in racist biblicism. Martin Luther King, Jr., who interpreted stories like Noah and Canaan metaphorically, would have found the segregationists' biblical arguments, as well as Graham's counter-biblicism, to be pre-modern nonsense, hardly worthy of intellectual engagement. But Graham met his people where they were, not by dismissing their arguments on foreign terms, but simply by turning them on their head and offering a biblicism that rejected segregation as a violation of the written Gospel of Jesus Christ.

The evangelist offered the same type of upside-down biblicism in response to the segregationist claim that the will of God revealed through the history of Israel was to keep the races pure and separate. "Again and again," Graham countered, "God worked to impress two lessons: (1) that the standards of lasting and constructive fellowship are religious—not racial; (2) that the purpose of the separation He commands is for service— not superiority. In every case that can be cited the standard of separation and segregation is religious rather than racial."[30] On a similar note, Graham also expressed upside down biblicism in response to segregationists who found justification for their position in the Apostle Paul's advice to slaves: "Slaves, obey your earthly masters with fear and trembling, in singleness of heart, as you obey Christ" (Ephesians 6:5). Segregationists held this text near and dear to their hearts, of course, because Paul had said nothing about eliminating the institution of slavery; he did not even characterize slavery as evil in the sight of God. But Graham pulled the rug out from under the segregationists and offered them a new way to think about Paul. "The Bible," he wrote, "certainly approved of master and servant relationships, but not along racial lines. Paul told the young Christians of his day that masters are to be kind to their employees and that servants are to obey their masters faithfully as unto the Lord. . . . Not once did he indicate that a particular race was to be a master and another to be a servant."[31]

Graham's sharp critiques encouraged the segregationists not to accept modern biblical criticism, which they considered anathema, but simply to read the Bible more closely for what it really was—the Word of God, plain and simple—rather than as an object to be distorted by race-colored lenses. This counter biblicism proved to be powerfully effective among the many Southerners who wanted to believe and follow the evangelist's path to salvation. It was a stroke of sheer brilliance—and the quiet thundering of a prophet from on high.

A Swarthy Jesus: What the Bible Really Says

Beyond pointing to obscure biblical texts, Christian segregationists also attempted to justify their practices by insisting that Jesus had never explicitly denounced slavery. It was a negative argument: If Jesus did not say slavery was bad, it must not be bad. But such reasoning was "silly," according to Graham, because Jesus "constantly emphasized neighbor-love, and every violation of it is a sin."[32] With the advent of the King years, Jesus became the theological *fons et origo* of the evangelist's evolving race ethics. While a segregationist, he had apparently read the Bible without ever seeing Jesus as racially progressive, but once on the road to racial conversion, Graham read with new eyes and discovered a desegregating Jesus throughout the Gospel. Once silent, Jesus had become an advocate for desegregation.

Graham's biblical hermeneutic became so racially sensitive that he spotted a racially inclusive Jesus even from the time of his lowly birth in a manger. "Consider how fortunate we are," he wrote in 1965, "that Christ was born in Palestine; for being a Mediterranean Jew his skin was darker than mine, though lighter than an African Negro's."[33] He had offered this same point, though a bit more vaguely, five years earlier: "I don't think that Christ's skin was as light as mine, or perhaps as dark as the West African's. He was born in a part of the world where his skin was probably more of a brown or swarthy color."[34]

Graham was yet again targeting white Christian segregationists. Tapping into their pious desire to love Jesus just as he was in everyday life, Graham informed them that Jesus was not a blond-haired, blue-eyed Aryan—not the male version of Betty Crocker at all—but a brown-skinned Jew. Years later Graham would make a similar point to African Americans. Near the end of the King years, the evangelist felt the need to oppose the frightening emergence of a black theology that boldly identified Jesus as a black man whose primary mission in life was to set the captive free.[35] But just like whites, African Americans could not properly claim Jesus of Nazareth as "one of their own kind." As Graham put this at a 1968 press conference, "Christ probably did not have skin as white as mine or as dark as an African, but he had a more swarthy color. He had an in-between color. He belonged to all the races."[36] If Jesus was not the Great White Hope, neither was he the Great Black Liberator. At last, Jesus was a swarthy Jew who included and yet transcended white and black ethnicities.

Graham also came to believe that Jesus embodied and practiced desegregation during the three years of his public ministry. In 1957, Graham appealed to Matthew 25 to suggest that Jesus had directly identified himself with those segregated to the edges of society—"the least of these." Sounding themes familiar in King's own sermons, Graham spoke like a true prophet: "The horror of discrimination will never be fully realized until we remember the sobering words of our Lord: 'As you did it not to one of the least of these, you did it not to me.'"[37] Placed in context, Graham's depiction of Jesus was remarkable. In effect, it sought to overturn churches that worshipped a white Jesus who safeguarded the white baptismal font, the white altar cloths, the white communion linens, the white Bibles, and the white Easter lilies.

Indeed, Graham's swarthy, marginalized Jesus was also an active multiculturalist. "Jesus broke down the barriers," the evangelist stated in 1957. "He lauded the faith of the Gentiles. He lived for days among the despised Samaritans. He said that many would come from the East and the West and sit down with Abraham and Isaac and Jacob in the kingdom. He said that when he was lifted up he would draw all men unto himself."[38] This was not a passive Jesus who sat by idly in the Jim Crow system of the Middle East; this was a Jesus who stood up for love and justice for his oppressed neighbors.

In these early years, "neighbor love," with its unmistakable ring of old-fashioned Southern hospitality, became one of the evangelist's favorite themes when discussing Jesus and race. Again in 1957, this time during the Little Rock crisis, Graham implored his audience "to reexamine the teachings of our Lord Jesus Christ on the subject of neighbor love," especially in the story of the inquiring lawyer: "The lawyer asks Jesus, 'Who is my neighbor?' Jesus indicated that our neighbors are people of different races. No matter who they may be, we are told to love our neighbors as ourselves."[39] Graham's implied point was clear to all who heard him that night in New York City and beyond: No matter who our neighbors may be, even African Americans in Little Rock, Jesus commands us to love them as we love ourselves.

The evangelist also argued that Jesus taught the same type of love in his parable about the Good Samaritan. In a 1963 sermon titled "Solving Our Race Problems through Love," for example, he preached that "Jews [in Jesus' day] . . . had no dealing with the Samaritans, yet the Samaritan showed who his neighbor was by helping a person of another race who was in need."[40] This illustration built upon an argument the evangelist had made in 1957 in reference to the story of Jesus meeting the Samaritan woman at Jacob's well: "This [story] points up to the racial strife which existed between the Jews and Samaritans in Christ's day, as it exists in America today, even among church people. Though Christ was primarily concerned with the redemption of the individual, he did not hedge on the race question. . . . Jesus put no color bar on the Golden Rule."[41]

Like "neighbor love," the colorful expression "did not hedge" became part of Graham's stump speech on Jesus and race. Less frequently, partly because it was a theological concept favored by liberals like King, the *imago Dei* also made its way into Graham's pronouncements on Jesus and race. "Christ," Graham wrote in 1960, "did not hedge on the race question. He emphasized and enlarged upon the Old Testament revelation that love is due man—every man—as a creature made in the divine image." Enlarging upon the notion of *imago Dei*, Graham's Jesus revealed himself to be "the antithesis of hate . . . he does not divide people by skin color or political allegiance. . . . To Christ, we are either his—or not his."[42]

Like a fresh convert who sees with new eyes, the racially converted Graham saw a desegregating Jesus all over the place—at his birth, in his life example and teachings, and especially in his tragic death. "When Christ died," Graham wrote, "the veil which separated man from God was ripped vertically from top to bottom and the way was open for all men to have access to God. . . . The horizontal separation of man was broken at the same time as the vertical."[43] Again, do not miss the prophetic dimension of all this. When one considers the traditional emphasis of fundamentalists and even evangelicals—that Jesus died for our sins so that we may have life everlasting—Graham's claim that the veil was ripped horizontally at the same time it was torn vertically was stunning in its theological progressiveness. To someone like King, trained in the social gospel and black church theology, such a claim would have been mundane, but for Graham and those in his community, it was downright revolutionary: It turned upside down pious pulpits that clung to the cross only because it was the place of individual salvation.

The cross became the centerpiece of Graham's belief that segregation was unqualifiedly antithetical to the will of God. To be sure, he sometimes appealed to the Hebrew Scriptures and creation theology when explaining the biblical case against segregation. For example, in "God and the Color of a Man's Skin," he took a page from creation theology by arguing that although the Bible does not indicate the origin of different skin colors, "it does say that we are 'made of one blood.' It tells us that God, in the sense of creation, is the heavenly Father of all the races."[44] And as the Creator of us all, God focuses not on the color of one's skin—God is no respecter of persons—but on the heart of the individual. This type of creation ethics also appeared a bit more forcefully in his comments during the Selma era of the civil rights movement: "The Bible teaches that there is a unity of the human race. We're all descendents of Adam and Eve. . . . We're all descendents from a common pair, and . . . man's descent from a single pair constitutes also the grounds of man's obligation of natural brotherhood for every other member of the human race."[45] Further, it was this very obligation that Moses, perhaps the greatest of our faith ancestors, practiced in his own life. "I think it is very evident," Graham stated in a 1962 press conference, "that Moses had an Ethiopian wife whose skin was dark."[46] The shocking news for segregationists everywhere was that the lawgiver of lawgivers—Mr. Law and Order—was married to a black woman.

Beyond progressive creation theology, Graham also cited the so-called barrier-breaking theology of the early church, especially as expressed by Paul in his letter to Philemon, "the greatest passage in all the Bible concerning race relations." In Graham's retelling of the story, Onesimus, a slave who had robbed his master and then fled, was converted to Christ through the powerful witnessing of Paul. "As in all true conversions, immediately the Holy Spirit filled Onesimus's heart with the love of God. He wanted to go back to his master and make amends. This is a sign of every true conversion. Paul sent a letter to the master of Onesimus, whose name was Philemon. He did not command Philemon but appealed to him on the basis of Christian love that he receive Onesimus not as a slave but as a beloved brother. As someone has said, 'The death of slavery was struck here.' "[47] Graham's creative retelling of the story, however, was not as accurate as he might have thought, primarily because it was Paul, not Onesimus, who decided that the runaway slave must return to his master, whatever the consequences might have been. Paul attempted to soften the harsh punishment typically awaiting runaway slaves, but he also decided that he would respect the institution of slavery, and the legal rights of Philemon over his runaway slave, by sending the converted Onesimus back to his master. Needless to say, this has not been a favorite text of the African American community; but Graham sanitized the apparent sanctioning of slavery and declared the text exemplary for Christians in a racially segregated world.

One other item stands out in his appeal to the early church—a peculiar point about God's desire to save pagan Africans. "It was God's purpose," Graham claimed, "to send the Gospel south into Africa, below the Sahara Desert. That is why he brought Phillip from a great evangelistic campaign to deal with the Ethiopian." In Graham's thought, then, the biblical story of Phillip and the Ethiopian reveals that the Christian Gospel is not just for white Europeans or swarthy Middle Easterners; it is also for dark Africans. Further, "the important thing about the Ethiopian is not the color of his skin. The Bible tells us that God is no respecter of persons. The important thing is that he believed."[48]

Although he appealed to creation theology and the witness of the early church, Graham found such appeals to be insufficient and ultimately grounded his anti-segregationist stance in the old rugged cross. Take away the cross, and his case for desegregation, while it does not collapse altogether, certainly loses its vibrant center. Graham believed that although each of us has common parents in Adam and Eve, the fall ruined God and Adam's plan "to build a wonderful world together in which there would be no suffering, no earthquakes, no war, no hate, no pride, no lust, no death."[49] Sins like segregation thus came to rule the world without challenge—until, that is, the cross of Jesus was erected at Calvary. Stretched on the cross, Jesus ignored all artificial barriers and offered love and forgiveness, fellowship, and "a new direction" to all gathered there.[50] The color of their skin did not matter; the only thing that mattered was that they were within the circle of the cross, within the possibility of a new community free of racial barriers. By offering himself as a sacrifice that satisfied God's thirst for justice, Jesus overcame not only the division between God and humanity but also the barriers between human individuals, including the great racial wall between whites and blacks. In the crucified Jesus, then, we can see just how wrong segregation is—and we come into contact with a divine power that makes possible reconciliation between the most sinful individuals of the human race. If desegregation is finally possible in Graham's thought, it is only because Jesus offered himself as a sacrifice to satisfy God and thereby defeat the sins—the artificial divisions—of the world. In this sense, only the cross of Jesus is the nexus of racial reconciliation.

Finally, Graham pointed to the Spirit of Jesus living in the world today. Jesus' words, as recorded in Matthew 25, do not make merely for a nice lesson from the past, for the Spirit of Jesus continues, right here and right now, to be with those on the margins of society. And the stories of Jesus on the cross, as recorded in the Gospels, do not make for mere history; the power of reconciliation made possible at the crucifixion two thousand years ago is still available today, right here and right now, to any and all sinners who "come to the foot of the cross." At the "foot of the cross," Graham preached, the Spirit of Jesus looks down upon us without discrimination and offers each of us "not only a full and free pardon, but a changed life, lived in fellowship with God," and in community with our brothers and sisters throughout the world. Just like the historical Jesus of Nazareth, the Spirit of the living Christ desegregates the segregated, unites the divided, and binds those discriminated against. As Graham put this in *World Aflame*, "Wherever there is discrimination, Christ is at work with His sword cutting out hatred and intolerance."[51]

★ ★ ★

Given Graham's wide-ranging appeal to the main characters of scripture, from Adam and Eve to Moses and from Jesus to Paul and Phillip, it should be no surprise that the evangelist came to believe that "the whole weight of Scripture is for treating all men with neighbor-love, regardless of race or color."[52] What the Bible really says is this: (1) in the shadow of the cross, there is neither slave nor free, but only those who would believe in him and those who would not; and (2) those who come to the cross have a divinely mandated obligation to treat their neighbors as Jesus would—lovingly, without concern for race. Though markedly different from King's liberal heritage, Graham's evangelical Biblicism, coupled with his cruciform theology, thus supported the civil rights leader's insistent claim that segregation was a sinful obstruction to the beloved community and that desegregation was the path society must take if it is to move closer to the Promised Land of milk and honey. In many ways, Graham had become the evangelical King.

The Loss of American Prestige and the

Extinction of the White Race

Graham's case against segregation did not end with his appeal to the Bible and Jesus. The evangelist understood his people well enough to know that they held two things near to their heart—God and country, though not necessarily in that order—and so when trying to loosen their grip on Jim Crow, he described not only what "the Bible says" but also the negative effects of segregation on white America. Graham, in other words, called upon his fellow American patriots to defeat segregation not only because it was unbiblical, but also because it was un-American, especially in the sense that it posed a dangerous threat to the land of the free and the home of the brave. Obviously, this was yet another brilliant move on Graham's part, at once wholly responsive to his people's love of country, deeply reflective of his own version of civil religion, and yet somewhat supportive of King and the civil rights movement.

After noting the importance of Bible study, the evangelist often claimed that international travel was a major catalyst in his racial conversion. Consider his 1957 sermon "Four Great Crises": "I want to tell you this: after traveling all over the world I am convinced that one of the greatest black eyes to American prestige abroad is our racial problem in this country."[53] Oblivious to the problems of racially tainted language, Graham used the "black eye" metaphor more than once or twice, and his main point was always to draw attention to America's loss of prestige in a world beginning to see the harsh discrepancy between democratic ideals and the harsh practices of segregation. Especially because of his travels in North Africa, India, the Far East and Western Europe, Graham felt that "our racial tensions are causing some of the people of the world to turn away from us, to doubt that we have the moral and spiritual qualities to lead the Western world in this desperate hour. Race prejudice is a cancer eating away at the heart and core of American life and, therefore, threatening to eclipse the dawn of peace and justice for all humanity."[54]

The evangelist attributed the loss of prestige partly to the world's press, which he thought tended to exaggerate racial incidents in America. Following the violence used by Bull Connor in the Birmingham campaign of 1963, for example, Graham stated that the events had been "exaggerated out of all proportions by the world's press."[55] It is difficult to imagine the possibility of exaggerating the significance of a police dog attacking an African American girl, or of a white tank rolling through the streets of downtown Birmingham, but Graham believed that the world press did exactly that: It blew such racial incidents completely out of proportion so that America would end up with a "black eye" in world opinion.

Enter Graham's rabid anti-communism. When making his case against segregationists, Graham would frequently preach that banishing Jim Crow was necessary in order to deny the communists "their most powerful weapon in the battle to win the minds of the 70 percent of the world's population that is colored."[56] With the world's press as their unwitting tool, the communists were posing as defenders of minorities and seeking to capture the hearts and minds of colored people, and as they did so, America was losing its one and only chance to make the world safe for democracy and free enterprise. As Graham put this dramatically in 1960, "Many foreign experts who look at us objectively think that these problems [racial discrimination included] may weaken us to the point where Communism will gain the ultimate victory."[57]

This was yet another fitting argument for a man trying to convert the hearts of conservative segregationists. Graham was smart enough to realize that telling stories about little black girls who could not swim in the community pool all summer, little black boys who had to attend school in dangerous buildings without sufficient heat, or black men and women who were unable to earn a livable wage would fail to capture the hearts of his conservative white audience. These were stories for King to share with his followers and the liberal world beyond the South. For Graham, more helpful would be stories about the sacred object of conservative loyalty—America the beautiful. And thus he argued that it was American prestige that segregation damaged, it was American democracy that segregation undermined, and it was American wealth that segregation threatened as communists took control of the world. In Graham's account, it was impossible to be an American patriot and a racial segregationist.

Graham also threatened his people with the possibility that colored people would take control of the white-dominated world. "It must be remembered," he wrote in 1960, "that 70 percent of the world's population is colored. They are growing in power, strength and numbers." As the power of the colored people increased, the power of the whites would shrink, shrivel, and pass into history—unless segregation was ended. "If we do not end our racial discrimination," Graham wrote in 1960, "the gloomy prophecy of Dr. Martin Niemoller of Germany may come true when he said that a hundred years from now *the white race may well be extinct.*"[58] It was a racist argument—perfect for appealing to racist whites. Especially effective was Graham's warning about brewing racial wars.

In Selma, for example, after African Americans were beaten back by white police officers as they began their march to Montgomery, Graham wrote that "America could be in a bloody racial war by summer. Our very existence as a democracy is threatened. For God's sake, let's reason together."[59] Graham was not above appealing to self interests and scaring his own people with extinction. Gone would be summer afternoons with iced tea on front porches, gone would be waitresses roller-skating with hamburgers and milkshakes in hand, gone would be July 4 concerts next to the courthouses where Gramma and Granddaddy received their marriage license. For the sake of white America, the time had came to reason together.

Compliance

We have thus far seen that Graham's anti-segregation crusade in the King years included the desegregation of his crusades and sharply worded public criticism of segregation, both of which offered significant support to King as the civil rights movement gained footing in the South and began to move throughout the rest of the country. On the one hand, Graham's desegregated crusades provided his followers with an actual picture of what they could not see, an image of the unimaginable, so that they could move toward a desegregated society. On the other hand, the crusades offered his followers an actual experiment in reality, a real opportunity to enter into a stadium and realize the unrealizable—a place where whites and African Americans would sit side by side and worship their common God. In this sense, the crusades were nothing less than dramaturgical events that provided hardened whites with a historically unimaginable reality in which desegregation was not only really real, if only for a brief moment in time, but also really real without violence, anarchy, and a noteworthy loss of white power.

Like his desegregated crusades, Graham's spoken and written comments about segregation were constructive in the sense that they encouraged whites to meditate on a desegregating Jesus and to mirror his birth, life, and death by practicing neighbor love toward African Americans. But at the same time, Graham's vocal opposition to segregation was less constructive than was the positive image of his desegregated crusades. As we have seen, the evangelist's words sought not to articulate a grand vision of "the beloved community," but to deconstruct the white myths of segregation and threaten whites with the extinction of America the beautifully white.

Whatever the methods were, Graham's overarching goal was to convince his people that segregation was wrong, and more practically, to prepare them to accept and implement *Brown v. Board of Education of Topeka*, as well as other race-related legislation that would come to affect their everyday lives. In other words, he integrated his crusades, constructed a desegregating Jesus, deconstructed the white myths of segregation, and delivered a sentence of death to segregationists so that he could ensure that his people would find themselves prepared, spiritually and morally, to obey the law of the land. Order remained one of Graham's primary political values throughout the King years, and his emphasis on this value, like his desegregated crusades and public criticism of segregation, sometimes served King and the movement quite well. For example, in a March 27, 1956 letter to President Eisenhower, Graham wrote that he would do "all in my power to urge Southern ministers to call upon the people for moderation, charity, compassion and progress toward compliance with the Supreme Court decision [in *Brown v. Board of Education of Topeka*]."[60]

Like Eisenhower, Graham was deeply concerned that whites would not obey the law of the land but would violently protest the decision to desegregate white schools. So he went to work behind the scenes, meeting with Southern ministers, African American and white, in order to encourage them to push their own flocks into compliance with the Supreme Court decision. His June 4, 1956 report to Eisenhower was optimistic: "As soon as possible after our talk in March, I went quietly to work among denominational leaders in the South. I had several private meetings with outstanding religious leaders of both races, encouraging them to take a stronger stand in calling for desegregation and yet demonstrating charity, and, above all, patience. I met with excellent and overwhelming response."[61] Of course, hell would break loose in Little Rock, in 1957, when Governor Orval Faubus ordered the National Guard to help block African American children from attending formerly all-white public schools, but here again Graham would serve the civil rights movement well by appealing to the importance of law and order. When the Little Rock crisis reached its apex, Eisenhower called Graham to ask for advice regarding the use of federal troops to enforce compliance with *Brown*, and the evangelist's advice was pointed: "I think you've got no alternative. The discrimination must stop."[62]

At the time, Graham was preaching at the New York Crusade, and his sermon during the crisis appealed not only to neighbor-love, as explained above, but also to his unwavering belief that Christians must obey the law of the land. It is thus unfair to claim that Graham was a good ole boy who used the law-and-order argument merely to keep African Americans in their place. His appeal to law and order was far more complicated than that, and far more progressive than we might expect, for just as he had done with racist biblicism, Graham took the traditional appeal to law and order and turned it on its head when arguing against the segregationists who sought to deny implementation of *Brown* at the local level. On the one hand, he argued that because *Brown* had become the law of the land, it was now the obligation of all whites to accept and implement the law—to revolt against *Brown*, after all, would be to revolt against God. On the other hand, when whites did revolt against *Brown*, the evangelist held that the duly constituted authority, in this case, President Eisenhower, faced a divine obligation to stop the anarchists and enforce compliance with the law.

Graham offered a similar type of law-and-order argument when discussing civil rights legislation passed by Congress and signed into law by the president. For example, after President Johnson signed the Civil Rights Act of 1964, a member of the press asked Graham what he thought of the legislation. Graham's stammering reply, typical of his responses following the successful passage of other race-related laws, focused on the duties of being a law-abiding citizen rather than on the merits of the civil rights legislation. "Well," he said, "I think that it is now law, and whatever people think of it, I think we must obey the law. And I have been delighted with reactions so far in the South . . . people don't realize that the South is largely a law-abiding part of the country. And the people don't like the law, but I think the people are going to obey the law, and I think that tremendous progress is being made in the South in this matter of race relations."[63] Did Graham himself like the law? Or was he one of "the people" who did not like being forced by the U.S. government on so-called local racial matters? Absent here was any ringing endorsement of the merits of the legislation, or any sense that the new law was a great step toward justice for African Americans. The conservative Graham simply stated, at least in this press conference, that the civil rights legislation was the law and that "the people," that is, conservative whites like Graham, would most likely obey it. That was about as grudging an endorsement as was possible. Nevertheless, it was positive in the sense that it encouraged whites to throw down the Confederate flag and obey the powers that be.

More generally, Graham also served the civil rights movement by eventually conceding that civil rights legislation was a necessary tool in the process of breaking down the walls of segregation. In the early King years, Graham refrained from offering enthusiastic support for specific race-based laws, but he did generally acknowledge that "we need anti-segregation in this country."[64] The evangelist usually offered this general concession quickly and without explication, but as the years progressed he expounded a bit more on the need for civil rights legislation. In 1965, for example, he wrote that while love was most important for eliminating segregation, "men are frail and unfortunately love and understanding need a little prodding in the way of man-made laws. In America that prodding takes the form of civil rights legislation." Civil rights laws were necessary because sinful segregationists refused to desegregate voluntarily. Graham even moved his race politics from negative concession to positive affirmation in his 1965 article when he praised the Voting Rights Act of 1965, though not by name. The act, he said, "will help do much toward eliminating the artificial barriers which set men apart from one another in a way contrary to the will of God. I believe this legislation will in time provide a strong framework upon which America will build a lastingly multi-racial society."[65] With these relatively glowing words, Graham was not only affirming the civil rights legislation; he was also suggesting that citizens should accept and obey this new law of the land. As he put this explicitly in the same article, "We must first learn to obey the law of the land."[66]

Only shallow criticism, therefore, would suggest that Graham dismissed legislation as a necessary tool in the battle for civil rights. Rather than dismissing legislation altogether, the evangelist conceded its necessity in light of the sinfulness of unbending segregationists and eventually affirmed it as helpful for moving America toward becoming a multi-racial society. This prophetic stance revealed dramatic change in a man who in earlier years had fully embraced Jim Crow (and, by implication, the argument for states' rights that underlay the system of Southern segregation). It also revealed his bold willingness to separate himself from his family and friends—among them, Nelson Bell, his father-in-law—who consistently derided anti-segregation legislation in favor of voluntary desegregation resulting from a converted heart. By first conceding and then embracing civil rights legislation as necessary and helpful, Graham clearly sought to undermine the arguments of the segregationists and the voluntary desegregationists in favor of the position that King and his followers pushed—that desegregation would never happen unless backed by the power of law and order.

Graham's Boycott of Apartheid

Graham supported the goals of the civil rights movement not only by desegregating his crusades, speaking against desegregation, and encouraging compliance with civil rights legislation, but also by taking his crusades to the land of the slaves—Africa. While racists were spewing "Go back to Africa" to African Americans throughout the King years, Graham himself packed his bags for a preaching tour of Africa in 1960. Graham's tour was far from completely successful. He faced strong opposition from Muslims who protested his unsympathetic condemnations of Islam, and preaching the Gospel to native Africans, who lived and breathed animism, juju, and shamanism, proved to be more than challenging for a farm boy from the hills of North Carolina. On this latter point, William Martin's biography includes a delicious story about Graham attempting to share the Good News of Jesus Christ with a half-naked, painted, and inebriated African during a drunken dance in Tanzania. As Martin characterizes the precious moment, "The hapless tribesman, more baffled than angry at the incongruous apparition squatting beside him, kept saying, 'I too drunk. I do not understand.' "[67] Graham gave up.

Nevertheless, however difficult his trip proved to be, and however problematic twentieth-century Christian evangelism now appears, it must have been deeply significant for American citizens at the time to witness Billy Graham showing love, in his own inimitable way, to the people on whose shoulders American slavery was built. And in the context of the civil rights movement in America, it is doubtless that Graham's trip took on an unmistakably prophetic dimension. By traveling to Africa and sharing his faith with Africans, Graham showed Americans, in word and deed, that whites were not the only ones worth saving—that blacks, even the blackest tribal ancestors of African Americans, were special individuals for whom the open gates of heaven were made. By courageously inaugurating integrated services in certain parts of Africa, the evangelist also demonstrated that slavery and discrimination need not have been, and should never have been, the result of white contact with the dark continent: Slavery was not the inevitable result of a curse from Noah or even God, but the sinful choice of a sinful humanity. Graham even emphasized the blackness of the Gospel of Jesus Christ after he came back to America. "All over Africa," he stated, "faces lit up as we told how Christ belongs to all races . . . that he was born near Africa, that he was taken to Africa for refuge, and that an African helped carry his cross."[68]

This was not all. Remarkably, Graham also engineered his own boycott of white racism while touring Africa. Long before students protested apartheid at the South African embassy in Washington, DC in the 1980s, and long before they offered their bodies for jail in sympathy with the imprisoned Nelson Mandela, Billy Graham adamantly refused to preach in the land of apartheid. Upon learning that the government would not allow blacks to attend his crusades, he flatly refused any invitation that came his way from South Africa. Graham's recollection of the event in his autobiography is summed up in merely one sentence: "Churches in another nation, South Africa, strongly urged us to come, but I refused; the meetings could not be integrated, and I felt that a basic moral principle was at stake."[69] This is a humble reflection, but Graham's boycott was of tremendous symbolic significance to segregated blacks everywhere, and the boycott took on even greater significance in his decision to avoid setting foot in South Africa altogether (that is, not just for preaching). Graham made the decision while traveling with Howard Jones, the first African American evangelist on the Graham team. Partly because of criticism about his lily white organization, partly because of a conscious commitment to set an example for segregationists, and partly because of a desire to help save more blacks from the fires of hell, Graham decided to integrate his team in 1957 by adding Howard Jones, a pastor from Ohio, as a staff evangelist. Jones's work was racially significant: he helped to increase the number of blacks attending Graham's crusades, coordinated pre-Crusade meetings between whites and African Americans, preached his own crusades, and frequently acted as a liaison between Graham and the African American community. By Jones's own account, based on years of experience, Graham was racially progressive. And this much was certainly true over the skies of Africa in 1960. Flying with Jones, the evangelist directed his pilot to follow a longer flight schedule rather than stopping for a layover in the land of apartheid, primarily because the longer route would avoid any possible embarrassment to or harassment of Jones on South African soil, as well as any possibility of a report that Graham had sanctioned the policies of South Africa through the back door. To top it off, the evangelist also offered prophetic comments about South African apartheid while on his broader tour of Africa. "I don't see," he said, "how the South African approach can possibly work. Race barriers will ultimately have to end."[70]

Graham's pointed comments about apartheid, as well as his boycott of South Africa, were heavily publicized, and although it was far from the type of boycott that King had led in Montgomery, the evangelist's small boycott showed Americans, in no uncertain terms, the importance of taking uncompromising action in the face of racial discrimination. In fact, although no one has ever drawn a direct connection between Graham and the boycotts of South Africa during the 1980s, it is nevertheless true that his boycott in 1960 helped blaze a trail for the many boycotts to follow in the subsequent years.

Democratic, Faithful, and Effective: A Positive Interpretation of Civil Rights Demonstrations

Given Graham's boycott of South Africa, one might think that he would have been fully supportive of the practices of the civil rights movement— the boycotts, the sit-ins, and the marches, all designed to confront a racist government. Although that was certainly not the case, it is nevertheless wholly inaccurate to characterize Graham, unqualifiedly, as a mere opponent of the strategies and tactics of King and his followers. Consider, for example, just a few of Graham's wide-ranging comments on the movement's practices.

In 1964, a member of the press asked the evangelist if he believed "there is justification for people marching or demonstrating for a moral principle that they believe in, such as civil rights." By this time, of course, the civil rights movement had practiced boycotts, sit-ins, and marches, and so Graham knew exactly what the press member had in mind when asking about demonstrations. "Yes, I do," he replied, "if [the strategy] is nonviolent, and if it doesn't lead to extremism, and if it is peaceful. I think this is the American way. We have strikes for example. We have the right to strike. If it had not been for the right to strike, labor might never have made the progress it has made."[71] Graham, as we will see, went on to qualify this answer even more and also to divert the issue away from justification for the practices, but the important point here is his "yes," his concession, however grudging it might have been, that sometimes there was moral justification for civil rights advocates to march in the streets, hold sit-ins at universities, or boycott certain industries. Significantly, Graham did not provide a moral or spiritual argument for supporting civil rights demonstrations, as King and his colleagues frequently had. Instead, he merely characterized the practices as "the American way," as justifiable expressions of the democratic right to dissent. Ultimately, the nonviolent demonstrations were examples of red-white-and-blue democracy in action. By appealing to "the American way," of course, the evangelist was yet again targeting and tugging at the patriotic affections of his own people, especially when he spoke of the right to strike—a right that few blue-collar Southerners would have characterized as unjustifiable.

Beyond preaching about the American way, Graham also observed on occasion that the demonstrations served a helpful cause. Following

President Johnson's famous 1964 speech on civil rights, for example, the evangelist stated: "Demonstrations have served their purpose in arousing the conscience of the nation."[72] In a 1965 interview, Graham even offered a stamp of approval for the nonviolent demonstrations that had already helped to bring about racial changes in the South. "I think that many of the peaceful demonstrations have aroused the conscience of the nation," he said. "Demonstrations have brought about new, strong, tough laws that were needed many years ago. I think that in the South we are going to see a peaceful solution to the problem."[73] These are the most laudatory words Graham ever spoke, at least during the King years, about civil rights demonstrations. As we will see, while he was commending the demonstrations, he was also calling for their end. But Graham's critics should not move to this latter point until we first recognize his willingness to depict the demonstrations, on the one hand, as virtual alarm clocks on the shoulders of a nation hazily contemplating its immoral practices against a racial minority, and on the other, as tools of political realism, an effective means for pushing and pulling a sinful nation to take legislative action to correct a social problem. Graham might have called too quickly for the end of demonstrations, but as a Christian realist, he well knew that a sinful nation required significant pressure to reconsider and change its immoral practices: Nice conversations simply would not do.

Graham could pay no higher a compliment of the demonstrations than to say that they were democratically sound, morally faithful, and politically effective. These comments, although few and far between in Graham's thought, are not to be taken lightly, as if he was just tipping his hat at the civil rights movement. The evangelist was always aware that millions of his followers looked to him for moral, spiritual, and political guidance, and that his positive words about the demonstrations would enter the consciousness of millions of Americans who were wondering what to make of the demonstrations they encountered on television and in their newspapers. In this sense alone, Graham's positive comments about the civil rights demonstrations clearly offered support to King and the civil rights movement as it struggled to save the soul of America.

Rebuilding after the Bombs

In addition to offering occasional vocal support for the demonstrations, Graham also supported the movement when it took vicious hits, as it did in 1963, when white racists bombed Sixteenth Street Baptist Church in Birmingham, killing four beautiful black girls who had been in Sunday school at the time of the bombing. In response to this horrific event, Graham cooperated with Washington columnist Drew Pearson in waging a heavily publicized campaign to raise funds for rebuilding the bombed church. This was not the first time that Graham and Pearson worked together for the cause of healing racial rifts; they had also joined forces in

1958 when Pearson asked the evangelist to join Americans Against Bombs of Bigotry, a committee charged with raising funds to help rebuild an integrated high school in Clinton, Tennessee that had been bombed by white racists.

Graham was not content merely to raise money for these distressed areas from a safe distance, however, he also made it a point to travel to them with his team and hold integrated rallies in an effort to show that the unifying Spirit of God would ultimately triumph over the divisive forces of evil. Shortly after the Clinton bombing, for example, the evangelist traveled to the town and spoke at an integrated fund-raising rally where he called for "tolerance, forgiveness, cool heads, and warm hearts."[74] And a few months after the Birmingham bombing, Graham journeyed to that troubled city for an integrated Easter crusade attended by 35,000 whites and African Americans who heard him identify "heart trouble" as the ultimate cause of the world's problems.[75] Nor were these the only times the evangelist responded to violence with integrated crusades that emphasized the power of nonviolent love over violent hatred. Following the violence in Selma in 1965, Graham toured Alabama—with stops at Dothan, Tuscaloosa, Auburn, the Tuskegee Institute, and Montgomery—in an attempt to create a new climate in which African Americans and whites could work together to solve their race-based problems. In each of these places, the evangelist held desegregated meetings that showed African Americans and whites what it meant to sit and worship together in a spirit of unity—to experience a foretaste of the heavenly feast to come, where there is no color line, no racial barrier, no segregated seating.

Graham's reactions to the violence in Clinton, Birmingham, and Selma revealed that he was far more than a passive player in the fight for civil rights. When the movement needed significant funds so that it could rise out of the smoldering ashes caused by racist bombs, Graham got off his knees, stepped forward, and helped raise cash. He could have remained in the background, continuing his own hard work of raising money for his evangelistic crusades across the globe, but he speedily rose to the occasion and joined hands with the movement on a few of its most depressing days. And when the movement needed a constructive, energizing, spiritually moving vision of integration that no divisive bombs could overcome, Graham got off his knees and organized integrated rallies in violent communities.

The good deeds continued, too. Graham's experience in civil rights committee work in Birmingham and Clinton, his personal friendship with and deep affection for President Johnson, and his deep ties to the evangelical voting bloc made him a perfect candidate for a national citizens' committee to help implement the Civil Rights Act of 1964. Johnson lobbied Graham to serve as chairperson, but the evangelist declined the leadership role, stating that his "schedule of preaching engagements and crusades is just too heavy to permit my giving adequate time to the leadership of this important committee." Still, the evangelist did not opt out completely, taking a safe route that would not further irritate many of his white acquaintances in the South. "I shall be delighted," he wrote the President, "to serve as a member of the Committee, and I shall do all I can to assist Governor Collins and Mr. Dean in this important work."[76] His willingness to serve on a heavily publicized national committee charged with implementing the Civil Rights Act of 1964 suggested, in no uncertain terms, that he believed in the fundamental importance of implementing federal legislation for moving America toward some of the racial goals favored by King and his followers. This is significant, of course, because of the states' rights position touted by white preachers and politicians throughout the South, even long after the successful passage of civil rights legislation in 1964. As Graham's decision to work with mainstream Protestants decreed a divorce from fundamentalists, his willingness to serve on Johnson's committee effected a break from states' rights advocates in the South, many of them friends and acquaintances. Mugwumpery was turning out to be the evangelist's specialty.

Graham's decision also reflected his slightly skewed view that whites should be the ones to show initiative in improving race relations. This argument was a tad disingenuous, primarily because King and his movement had already taken the initiative to improve racial issues in the South and beyond, but the evangelist offered it anyway ten full years after the beginning of the Montgomery bus boycott. In 1965 Graham stood before an integrated audience and announced that although racial prejudice was not "confined to the whites," he was convinced that "the initiative must come from the majority of whites in this country and that once we set the example, what prejudice exists toward us by the Negro will vanish in due time."[77] Needless to say, this was yet another argument crafted especially for Graham's own people. Although disingenuous, the argument was smart in the sense that it offered the promise of power to whites already disempowered by the civil rights movement. The argument was also creative in the sense that it appealed to white power as the catalyst that could best effect a transfer of power from whites to African Americans. While King called upon African Americans, especially from 1965 to 1968, to create black power—economic, political, and cultural—and thereby undermine white power, Graham appealed to white power and implored his white followers to recognize their powerful status and transfer their power, willingly, to a people who threatened the white way of life. Although targeted toward his own people, Graham's comments on white initiative certainly served the movement, albeit in a backhanded way, by calling for a peaceful transfer of power.

A Great and Tremendous Movement

Finally, Graham backed the civil rights movement during the King years by occasionally offering general praise for Martin Luther King, Jr. and the movement as a whole. He did this especially in 1957, when he invited the civil rights leader to offer the invocation for one of the services at the New York City Crusade. Although his sermon indirectly belittled King's tactics, Graham's introduction that night left no question about his general support for the movement: "A great social revolution is going on in the United States today."[78] More important, however, was the general symbolism of the moment—the African American leader of the civil rights movement occupying center stage with a former Southern segregationist, the nation's foremost Christian evangelist. By inviting King to offer the invocation, Graham appeared to be offering his own benediction upon the young Baptist minister and his budding movement against segregation.

Significantly, Graham never extended another similar invitation to the civil rights leader throughout the remainder of the King years, but the evangelist did try to maintain cordial interpersonal relations with his Baptist brother. In 1960, for example, he hosted a dinner at the Baptist World Alliance meeting in Rio de Janeiro as a tribute to King and his work. "The dinner," Graham recalled, "was in honor of Mike [MLK], and I invited Southern Baptist leaders from the United States to come. I wanted to build a bridge between blacks and whites in our own South, and this seemed like a good opportunity to move toward that goal." Graham's strategy in Brazil, typically evangelical in its focus on interpersonal connections and friendships, apparently made a difference in the eyes of some of Graham's Baptist colleagues. "During our brief stay in Rio," he recounted, "some Mississippi Baptists came up to Grady [Wilson of the BGEA] to welcome him. As they were talking, Mike came by and slapped Grady on the shoulder and greeted him warmly. Our friendly relationship with Mike made the point with my Baptist friends."[79]

Words of praise, at least for the movement, flowed again when Graham was asked to comment on the Nobel Peace Prize awarded to King in 1964. In reply to a press member's question—"Do you see Martin Luther King's award of the Nobel Peace Prize as an encouragement to 'men of the cloth,' both white and black?"—Graham replied: "Yes, I think that Dr. King has well expressed that he feels the prize was given to him as a representative of a movement that many people have been involved in. I thought that his statement at that point was very good because it was quite true. It was the recognition by the Nobel Peace Committee of this tremendous movement in this country."[80] There are other important things to note about Graham's response, but significant here is his acknowledgment that the civil rights movement was a "tremendous movement in this country." However faint his words of praise appeared to some civil rights supporters, Graham could not help but concede that the tremendous movement had forced America to begin correcting a social problem with spiritual roots.

As Branch and Martin have already noted, Graham also provided support for King and the movement by sharing their public relations tactics and organizational expertise with the civil rights leader and his staff.[81] If not envious, King was at least curious about Graham's ability to attract huge crowds and international publicity for his crusades. By comparison to the grand crusades, King's public appearances, often limited to churches and college campuses, were relatively smalltime affairs, and so King's team sought and received counsel from the Graham team on publicizing and organizing King's appearances and the work of the movement. In fact, the King team took the Graham team's advice on everything from planning the Crusade for Citizenship to timing the release of King's letter from Birmingham Jail. At one point early on, King even dreamed of holding integrated crusades with Graham, but the following chapter will suggest that King's dream was more than unrealistic; the evangelist was far too evangelical to hold integrated crusades with the social activist King. Nevertheless, the evangelist's willingness to share his public relations and organizational expertise with the King team revealed good faith and good will from a man who had once refused to visit an African American barber.

A Partial Conclusion

Did Graham support the civil rights movement from the beginning, as he frequently claimed both during and especially after the movement? The answer to the question is far more complex than the partial answer this chapter has only begun to describe. It is also far more nuanced than Dullea's description of the evangelist's race record as "excellent,"[82] or Pierard's unqualified gushing over Graham's comments on race as "not just the utterances of an evangelist but even more of a prophet!"[83] These paeans to the evangelist are far from helpful, but it is possible to argue at least this much so far: As a young Christian evangelist, Graham fully accepted the customs of Jim Crow and held segregated services throughout the South, but by the time of the Montgomery boycott, the evangelist was vocal in his opposition to segregation and consistent in his refusal to practice segregated crusades. Throughout the King years, but especially when the movement was focused on Jim Crow, Graham built a homiletic case against segregation, primarily by deconstructing the biblicism of segregationists and by constructing a biblicism that depicted a desegregating Jesus. Although Graham met with white and African American religious leaders, lobbying them to join forces for an all-out ecclesial fight against segregation, his target audience throughout the King years was primarily white evangelicals and fundamentalists—an audience that fell outside the activist core of the civil rights movement. The evangelist sought to convert individual members of this audience away from segregation by appealing not only to scripture, one of their primary moral sources, but also to their loyalty to America—their virtue of patriotism—claiming that segregation was leading America to a fall from domestic and international greatness. More pointedly, Graham also wielded a white power argument, threatening conservatives with the extinction of the white race and thus with the need to cede power voluntarily if white strength was to continue to flourish.

Beyond his efforts to convert whites away from discrimination and segregation, Graham supported the civil rights movement by conducting his own personal boycott of sorts against South African apartheid, thereby showing the world the importance of refusing cooperation, any cooperation, with the unjust system of segregation. And more directly, upon returning to America, he supported the civil rights movement by demanding law and order from whites contemplating non-compliance with civil rights legislation; by characterizing the movement's peaceful demonstrations as "the American way," democratic, faithful, and effective; by calling for white initiative in supporting the goals of the movement; by helping to rebuild black institutions bombed by white racists; by showing his Baptist friends, primarily in the early King years, that King was a true personal friend; and by publicly referring to the civil rights movement as a "great" and "tremendous" movement that served America well.

Did Graham support the civil rights movement from the beginning? If we consider only the argument made thus far, we could tentatively nod our heads with Mark Silk's argument that Graham was "a bit of a liberal" on race matters.[84] Still, mounds of evidence remain for us to wade through, and thus it would be far too shallow to argue, unqualifiedly, that Graham supported the civil rights movement from the beginning. As the next chapter will show, there is another part of the story to tell—a part that should make us more than wary of Grant Wacker's flowery characterization of the evangelist's "longstanding position on race relations" as "difficult to criticize."[85] Interestingly, Graham subjected himself to criticism quite a bit. In 1965, for example, he replied to a student who had questioned his inaction in civil rights by saying, "It's true I haven't been in jail yet. I underscore the word *yet*. Maybe I haven't done all I could or should do."[86] With this confession as our guide, perhaps it will be far easier to criticize Graham than the sympathetic Wacker would have us believe.

CHAPTER FIVE

"This Is Freedom Out of Control!": Graham's Dissent from the Civil Rights Movement

"Just behind the white church school was a public school for black children." So begins a fascinating story that Graham shared with his radio audience in 1965, at the time of the Selma movement. The playgrounds of the two elementary schools were adjoining, and there was no Jim Crow fence between them, which meant that the white and black students could freely play with one another in a large common area. Little Susan was one of the children who attended the white church school, and her mother had encouraged her along the way to invite a friend for Saturday lunch; all she had to do was to let her mother know ahead of time. One day Susan came home and excitedly reported that she had indeed extended an invitation to a girl she had made friends with on the playground. Pleased but cautious, Susan's mother, already steeped in segregation, wondered aloud if the friend was white or black. And in Graham's classic retelling, "Susan replied, 'I don't know, but I'll look tomorrow.' "[1]

The lesson he drew from this innocent story was virtually impossible for his audience to extract, but it was also pure Graham: "There is a possibility in the cross of Jesus Christ in that he breaks down every barrier. When we have been born again of the Spirit of God, he breaks these barriers down and love fills our heart, not only for God but for each other."[2] However beautiful in its simplicity, Graham's heart-tugging illustration left many questions unanswered: For example, did he believe that there should have been two different schools, one for blacks and another for whites? If not, what should Graham's audience do, if anything, about the problem of racially segregated schools? Should they seek a more equitable distribution of resources among the white and black schools? Should they dare to integrate the public white and black schools? If so, should they seek to integrate right away or wait a few years? And how does the all-white private Christian school fit into the racial mix to begin with? Should churches, in a post-*Brown* age, be in the business of opening all-white or all-black schools? With its unanswered questions, Graham's illustration made for the type of pious treacle that frustrated many African Americans during the civil rights movement. Consider the acidulous critique of Chuck Stone, a columnist for the *Chicago Defender*, in response to Graham's general belief that the cross breaks down all racial barriers:

What the sinner is supposed to glean from this kind of vapid, silly declaration is that if he simply kneels down and prays to Jesus Christ, somehow his troubled racist heart will be changed and he'll love his black brother.

Shucks, Billy Graham himself isn't even able to come out and unqualifiedly denounce racial segregation and those who practice it . . . he's too busy praying.

You don't see Billy Graham walking into the Southern temples of racial segregation and telling the racists to get out because they defile God's house with their denial of love and brotherhood.

You don't see Billy Graham walking any picket lines or even admitting they have a spiritual redemption for the sinner.

You don't see Billy Graham telling white people that Negroes are so unremittingly their brothers that they must live together next door to each other as neighbors and accept Negroes with love as neighbors.

And this is the tragedy of a Billy Graham—not his antiseptic evangelism that would keep us enslaved by simply "kneeling at the cross," waiting for a miracle to transform our souls, but his failure and refusal to invigorate the teachings of the Christ of Nazareth with the spiritual requisites of a jet-age society torn asunder by horse and buggy racial hatred.[3]

Stone's truculent criticism, published in 1964, was not entirely fair—by 1964 Graham had unqualifiedly denounced racial segregation, and although he never told whites that they must integrate their neighborhoods, he did preach that whites must accept African Americans as their neighbors—but the commentary does provide us with excellent evidence to note that in spite of all the positive words and deeds noted in the previous chapter, not all African Americans were enamored with Graham's race politics in the 1960s. In fact, many African Americans, including King and his staff members, were deeply disappointed with the evangelist's lack of progressive leadership since the early days of the civil rights movement. The frustration was multilayered, stemming from Graham's early refusal to travel to the Deep South, his ongoing politics of diversion, his consistent separation of the Gospel from integration, his arguments against "forced integration," and his public decrying of the movement's timing and speed. Ivy-tower scholars like Wacker may now find Graham's race politics "difficult to criticize," but at the time of the movement, street-level activists like King and his followers could have provided a whole laundry list of reasons for faulting Graham's race politics.

Absent

One of the key areas of disappointment in the early King years was Graham's glaring absence from the states in which the civil rights movement had begun to flex its muscles—a point that the civil rights leader addressed directly in his August 31, 1957 letter to the evangelist. The first chapter noted that King took the occasion of the letter to request that Graham conduct interracial crusades throughout the Deep South, perhaps in Mississippi, Tennessee, and Alabama, where the effects of a crusade "would be immeasurably great."[4] And now we need to ask why King would dare to make such a suggestion. Surely, part of the reason was King's frustration with Graham's decision to keep a safe distance from the moral issue of racism as it played out in the Deep South during the volatile years of the beginning of the movement.

Well aware of public criticism of his absence from the Deep South during the early years of the movement, Graham mounted a vainglorious defense in 1970, two years after King's assassination: "The first violence we had in America on the race question was in Clinton, Tennessee. I went there immediately and held an integrated meeting because I was challenged by a columnist in America." Not only that—Graham also claimed to have helped save the local leader of the White Citizens Council, who then promptly resigned from his position. In addition, the evangelist defensively reported that he "went to Little Rock in the middle of their crisis and held a great integrated meeting in their city. . . . I toured the state of Alabama in every major stadium in Alabama with integrated audiences, with police guns before me, behind me, and around me"[5]

Graham, of course, was clearly wrong to suggest that Clinton marked the first occasion of racial violence in America—what about all those years of slave-whipping and lynching?—but there is little else to dispute in this vigorous defense, except for the missing facts. In 1955 and 1956 thousands of African Americans in Montgomery organized a bus boycott that reached national and international audiences, all the while claiming that their movement was spiritual, not merely political, in motivation. This largely Protestant movement held its organizational meetings in African American churches, sang old-time Gospel hymns, regularly prayed and worshipped, and elected ministers as its leaders. Opposing this spiritual movement was the group of "good Christians" who had birthed and fed Jim Crow year after year—white men and white women who went to church on Sundays and who loved to listen to Billy Graham preach yet another fine, moving sermon on the radio. More to the point, many of the oppositional white Christians were members of Graham's own denomination—the Southern Baptist Convention—and recognized the evangelist as one of their Spirit-led leaders.

So where exactly was their Spirit-filled leader—the one whose personal touch with white religious fundamentalists could have helped to resolve racial crises in the South? Where was the unofficial preacher of American

Protestantism—the one who emphasized the spirit over the physical—when his black Protestant brothers and sisters were belting out Protestant hymns in order to regain fuel for their mighty spiritual battle against "the flood of mortal ills," as Luther put it in "A Mighty Fortress"? Far from Alabama and the rest of the Deep South, Graham was in Europe, Canada, India, and the Far East during 1955–1956. Yes, he also traveled to Richmond, Oklahoma City, and Louisville for his crusades during these years—but the Deep South was nowhere to be found on his itinerary.

Graham's absence left a deep vacuum. By the end of 1956, African Americans struggling in the civil rights movement had a clearly identified religious leader of national and international import, but Southern whites, either conservative or moderate, had no similar religious leader to help guide them through the ever-flowing stream in which they, too, had found themselves stuck. This was so troubling, of course, because individuals in crises desperately look for leaders who will step forth, outstretch their hands, and offer the wisdom and charisma needed in times of difficulty. This is exactly what a smart politician will try to do, for example, when a massive natural disaster strikes the country—he or she will travel to the affected area and tell the people that they will have all the resources required to address their situation in a speedy and effective manner. On another level, this is what a good parish minister will do when a crisis affects the parish—he or she will make it a point simply to be with the people and offer them the sheer comfort of presence.

But Graham refused to step forth. It is virtually impossible to unpack with any certainty what his intentions were for staying away from the volatile Deep South during the time in question. Hopkins suggests that Graham told friends that his concern over the race controversies had led him to think it unwise to hold crusades there, but whatever his intentions really were, the message of his actions certainly suggested that he had no interest in being present with his fellow Christians, black or white, as they found themselves drowning in the sea of discrimination and racism.[6] In fact, even in later years, when Graham did venture into Tennessee, Arkansas, and Alabama, it always seemed that he had to be pulled into the racial crisis. He went to Clinton only after Senator Estes Kaufman and Drew Pearson had publicly challenged him, he traveled to Little Rock only after the Little Rock Ministerial Association had pleaded for his presence (and then, after consulting Arkansas Representative Brooks Hays, he waited a full year before making the trip), and he conducted his tour of Alabama only after President Johnson had encouraged him to preach in that state (ten full years after the bus boycott). If nothing else, Graham's reticence, most likely due to a concern over alienating his own white followers, suggested that he was far from an active supporter of the civil rights movement as it burned throughout the South during the King years.

Not only was Graham personally absent from the Deep South during the early King years, he was also directly lobbying President Eisenhower to keep a safe distance from the racial crisis developing there. For example, he encouraged the racially moderate Eisenhower in a March 27, 1956 letter "to stay out of this bitter racial situation that is developing." Graham suggested that the president could take whatever steps he felt were "wise and right" following the election, but that he should allow the Democrats to "bear the brunt of the debate" in the period leading up to the election.[7] The evangelist also reiterated this partisan point, but with a different twist, in a June 4, 1956 letter to the president: "I am somewhat disturbed by rumors that Republican strategy will be to go all out in winning the Negro vote in the North regardless of the South's feelings. Again I would like to caution you about getting involved in this particular problem." For some reason, Graham also informed Eisenhower that he had "the confidence of white and Negro leaders." He was wrong, of course: Martin Luther King, Jr., perhaps the most significant African American leader at the time, had little if any confidence in Eisenhower's willingness to act on racial matters. But Graham plowed ahead anyway. "I would hate," he wrote, "to see [this confidence] jeopardized by even those in the Republican Party with an ax to grind."[8]

At the same time Graham was writing these letters, King and his followers, though depressed by Eisenhower's earlier inaction, were nevertheless hoping against hope for presidential leadership to help solve the boiling crisis; but the President, true to his silent moderation, would remain stubbornly inactive on matters of race throughout his tenure. There is no evidence to suggest that King was aware that Graham had been encouraging Eisenhower to keep his distance from the racial problems developing in the South, or of the evangelist's hope that the Republicans would ignore African Americans in the North in order to win the emerging Republican stronghold in the South. But it is doubtless that such news would not have surprised King and the movement as the civil rights years progressed. After all, just two years after the 1956 presidential election, he found himself especially concerned over Graham's close identification with segregationist politicians—and concerned enough to write a letter about the problem of public perception. In 1958 C. William Black, a Baptist minister in San Antonio, had asked King to write Graham about a scheduled appearance of Texas Governor Price Daniel, a staunch segregationist, at one of Graham's crusades in San Antonio, and the shocked civil rights leader quickly complied, penning a short but pointed letter. Addressing the letter to "Dear Brother Graham," King argued that "if Governor Daniel is identified with you on the eve of the Democratic Primary, July 26, in which Mr. Daniel is seeking reelection it can be well interpreted as your endorsement of racial segregation and discrimination." And such a move would have disastrous results in the civil rights community. "Any implied endorsement by you of segregation," King wrote, "can have damaging effect on the struggle of Negro Americans for human dignity and will greatly reduce the importance of your message to them as a Christian Minister who believes in the fatherhood of God and the brotherhood of man."[9]

This letter marks the first point of fracture between the two leaders. Up to this point, King had been hopeful of publicly working with Graham to address the racial crisis. Taylor Branch has already reported that the two leaders had met privately a number of times following King's presence at the New York Crusade, and that "on King's side, there were even dreams about a Graham-and-King crusade that would convert racially mixed audiences first in the North, then in border states, and finally in the Deep South."[10] This hope was merely a continuation of King's earlier enthusiasm for the potential impact of Graham's crusades on America's racial problems—an enthusiasm that had bubbled over during King's meeting with Graham prior to the 1957 invocation. "Your crusades," King had stated at that point, "do more with white people than I could do. We help each other. Keep on."[11] But the possibility of cooperation for a Graham-and-King crusade eventually broke down over "the emphasis between politics and pure religion." In additional talks King's lieutenants "found Graham increasingly unwilling to talk about the worldly aspects of the race issue."[12] And shortly after the collapse of the talks, the King letter arrived in Graham's mail.

Graham's response to the letter, offered through his associate Grady Wilson, only widened the growing gap between him and King. Suggesting that King's appearance at the 1957 Crusade was on moral par with Daniel's at the San Antonio Crusade, a belligerent Wilson wrote: "Perhaps you should know that we received scores of letters and telegrams concerning your coming to our meeting in New York, and yet Mr. Graham was happy to have you come as a fellow minister in Christ."[13] Predictably, Graham denied King's request, closely identified himself with the segregationist Daniel, and thereby lost the confidence of many African Americans, including King, in the process. Meanwhile, the segregationist Daniel went on to win both the primary and the general election.

A Politics of Diversion

While appearing with Southern segregationists seeking high office, Graham also sought to divert national and international attention away from the South. Throughout the civil rights movement, King attempted to focus the world's attention on Southern towns and cities—Montgomery, Birmingham, and Selma—as part of his overall strategy to eliminate discrimination and segregation from America. It was a big strategy of micro proportion—a regionally based, and therefore more easily manageable, tactic designed to affect a national and global problem. But Graham, a favorite son of white North Carolina, would have none of it and actually took steps to vitiate the movement's microcosmic efforts. During the Selma movement, for example, he released the following statement through his public relations team: "It is wrong for people in other parts of the country to point an accusing self-righteous finger at Alabama. To single out one state as a whipping boy often becomes just a diversion to direct attention from other areas where the problem is just as acute."[14] What is so interesting about this argument is that while he was accusing others of diversionary tactics,

Graham himself was practicing a race politics of diversion—a diversion away from King's efforts to turn Selma into the cynosure of world politics.

This was far from a new tactic. During the Little Rock crisis, one of Graham's main points was that "racial tension is not limited to the Southern part of the United States. . . . Very few parts of the world can point a self-righteous finger at Little Rock."[15] Of course, pointing a finger *away* from the South meant a loss of focus *on* the South—the type of result he sought a year later when he pointed his own finger at the devil. A firm believer in the devil as a personal force of evil, Graham told a primarily white audience in Charlotte that the devil and his demonic hordes were the real ones behind the racial crisis in 1958: "We see the forces of evil stirring up racial tensions all over America. It is not limited to the South . . . and it seems as if the whole world is a pot and the devil has a big stick stirring everybody up. Why, he has even got the church stirred up."[16] Perhaps more than any other, this statement best reveals the countless miles of impassable Southern swamps between King and Graham during the early years of the movement: While King envisioned the civil rights movement, as well as the tensions it brought to the surface, as the work of the Spirit of God in Jesus—a Spirit that frees the slave, gives sight to the blind, and reconciles the irreconcilable—Graham, at least in 1958, saw racial tensions not as a divinely mapped stage that would lead African Americans and whites to the Promised Land, but as the direct work of a demonic spirit that divided people and caused chaos in communities of law and order.

Graham's blaming of the devil, of course, also shifted the responsibility for racial problems away from the very white racists whom the movement sought to implicate. The evangelist continued this diversionary tactic, though in different ways, for years to come. In 1960, for example, he argued that "Jim Crow is a world figure—not just a Southern U.S. vagrant or a creature of South Africa's apartheid policy."[17] Crow's "footprints" were everywhere, in Great Britain, India, Australia, and especially behind the Iron Curtain. Unsurprisingly, the anti-communist Graham was quick to report in 1963 that racial rioting had broken out in Czechoslovakia and that scores of African students were being harassed in the Soviet Union. "Yet," he lamented, "the stories are played down in the press while the slightest racial incident in the American South makes headlines."[18] In 1963, of course, that "slightest racial incident" might have been police dogs ripping into the flesh of African American boys and girls protesting segregation, or the water of high-powered hoses shooting directly at the vital organs of these same children, or perhaps the white tank of the racist Bull Connor bullying its way past and through Birmingham's civil rights protestors. Nevertheless, this was not the worst of Graham's diversionary tactics. The absolute low point came in 1964, just following the Birmingham bombing that killed four little African American girls, when he stated: "A Western newspaperman told me yesterday that there's a growing suspicion that the bombings may be from professionals outside Alabama who want to keep the racial problem at fever pitch in the South."[19]

The problem with Graham's position was not that he was wrong about the extent of racism throughout the United States and the world beyond, but that he was consciously diverting attention away from a region that the civil rights movement, at least in its early years, was trying to spotlight for the nation and the whole world. Graham's diversionary politics ran directly counter to King's tactics and goals for the movement. The civil rights leader wanted the world not to glaze over in light of racism everywhere, but to focus on one Rosa Parks as she refused to surrender her seat on a Montgomery bus. He wanted the world not to lose perspective by seeing racism across the universe, but to concentrate on the sarcastic grin of one Bull Connor as he fired his hoses upon the very people he was supposed to protect. King wanted the world not to experience a sense of helplessness in the face of a universal Jim Crow, but to feel the acute pain of one elderly African American woman trampled by white police thugs in riot gear. By narrowing the problem of segregation and discrimination, by giving concrete shape to it in an everyday life visible from people's backyards, and by personalizing the system of racism in small Southern towns, King believed that he could help people of good will grasp segregation and discrimination as real problems with nearby, achievable solutions. Conversely, he well knew that if he presented race-based problems as abstract, amorphous, and distant, the problems would rarely if ever move people of good will to a sense of outrage, let alone direct action.

But Graham dug his heels in and cried foul—and not just about King's focus on *Southern* racism but also about, more broadly, his targeting of *white* racism. Graham took personal affront to the movement's stereoscopic focus on white racism and sought to counter it by constantly raising the issue of black attitudes and actions against both blacks and whites. Consider Graham's less-than-subtle counterpoint to the civil rights movement in 1957: "The slaves were captured and sold largely by Africans." To be sure, Graham noted "the everlasting shame of the Dutch, the English and the northern Americans," but his first point, especially when addressing the problems of slavery, segregation, and discrimination in America, was usually about black failures, black prejudice, and black hatred. In the same article just cited, he also wrote: "In a southern city this summer I talked with a Negro leader who understood but could not conquer his own feelings. 'I have as much prejudice in my heart against a man because his skin is white as any man had against a Negro because his skin is black,' he told me."[20] Significantly, Graham offered not one similar illustration of white racism—he rarely did—thereby leaving his audience primarily with a personalized and easily remembered sense of black prejudice.

Even the most cursory study of his writings and sermons reveals that Graham strongly emphasized black prejudice over white racism throughout the King years. In the 1957 *Life* article, for example, he argued that "the responsibility for discrimination is not all one-sided. The Negroes, too, must share the responsibility." His backing evidence for "two-sided" discrimination, believe it or not, was the number of African Americans who

attended his desegregated crusades—a number lower than the average
number at his segregated crusades. "I asked many Negroes about it," he
wrote. "They said they felt much more comfortable sitting by themselves."[21] Graham sharpened this one-sided point in 1963 when his radio
audience heard him report that "a New York Negro leader told me some
time ago, 'I hate all whites.' "[22] Even in Harlem, in 1965, the evangelist
observed that racial prejudice "is not confined to the whites. I have dis-
cussed the problems with Negroes and some of them hasten to inform me
that . . . they genuinely feel prejudiced toward the white man."[23] These
few examples, however, pale by comparison to Graham's troubling introduction of race problems in his bestselling *World Aflame*. The evangelist
could have introduced racism by describing the killing of four Birmingham
girls, the bloody beatings of freedom riders, or the African American children whose flesh was ripped in demonstrations for freedom. Instead, he
chose to introduce the topic of racism by highlighting a seventeen-year-old
African American boy who had murdered a white person. "His mother,"
Graham wrote, "said he used to be such a wonderful boy, but that the black
nationalists made him hate the white man."[24]

Graham was not wrong to observe that black prejudice was a real phenomenon, but he was wrong to emphasize black prejudice to the exclusion
of white racism. The evangelist was far from inclined to tell stories about
white prejudice, share any personal conversations he might have had with
white racists, or report that certain white leaders hated all African
Americans. By far, most of his illustrations were not about white racists at
all, but about the black prejudice he had allegedly encountered in meetings
and conversations with African Americans. No doubt, Graham intended
for his illustrations to compensate for the movement's focus on white prejudice and racism, but his counterweight obsession on black prejudice
revealed his own racism as well as a shallow understanding of race politics.
Nowhere, after all, did he attend to the different reasons underlying black
prejudice and white prejudice. He dared not suggest, for example, that
black prejudice resulted primarily from a history of systemic discrimination
carried out by whites, and that white prejudice, with no similar roots, was
of a whole different species, political and psychological, than black prejudice.

Graham's illustrations also left his audience with the distinct impression
that African Americans were the major perpetrators of prejudice in racially
torn America. Given his heavy emphasis on black prejudice, it would have
seemed to the average white person listening to Graham that the fault for
America's race problems lay primarily with the African American leaders
who hated all whites, or with the African Americans who dared to stay
away from the evangelist's crusades, or who told him that they felt as much
prejudice as any white man could. Of course, nothing could have been further from the truth, but truth was not the goal of Graham's race politics—
diversion was. Once again, by pointing his finger away from white
prejudice, Graham sought to divert attention away from a primary target of
the civil rights movement—white racists—and by pointing his finger

directly at black prejudice, he attempted to undermine the protagonists of the civil rights story—African Americans suffocated by systemic white racism.

Race Is Not the Gospel

Graham also diverted attention away from the civil rights movement by claiming time and again that the message of racial justice was not the same message as the Gospel of Jesus Christ, and that Christians and their churches would do well to focus or refocus their efforts on proclaiming the unadulterated Gospel. Consider part of his 1963 sermon on prayer and race: "I am also concerned about some clergymen of both races who have made the race issue their gospel. This is not the Gospel. The Gospel is the good news that Jesus Christ died for our sins, and that he rose from the dead, and that God is willing to forgive us our sins and give us new life and joy and peace. Slavery was practiced extensively in the days of Christ, and the early apostles and the slaves were largely white people. And yet the apostles never made it their gospel, although their teachings eventually meant the end of slavery."[25] But what it meant for Christians to avoid the pitfall of making race their gospel was remarkably unclear in Graham's thought. "This does not mean," he preached, "that the race problem is not to be preached and taught, but it is not to be our Gospel."[26] Presumably, the evangelist meant to say that issues of race should not be the primary message, or the primary motivation, of the Christian church and its members. And, indeed, this was his main message at the 1964 press conference for the World Congress on Evangelism: "I think that some men have made the race question their gospel. That is not the gospel—that is a result of the Gospel. The Gospel is the good news that Christ came into the world that first Christmas to save the people from their sins, and this is to be the major emphasis of the church."[27]

Perhaps more than any other, this statement, made at a high point in the civil rights era, reflected the radically different social contexts in which Graham and King operated as ministers of the Gospel. Unlike King, the evangelist naturally stayed in his *querencia*—safe, white-controlled environments, far removed from attack dogs and high-pressured hoses and bully sticks, deeply sheltered in the plush offices of business leaders and politicians, protected by the soundproof walls of radio and television stations, or surrounded by the lush fairways of exclusive golf resorts. In such comfortable settings during the 1950s and 1960s, it must have seemed relatively easy if not altogether fitting to argue that race was not the Christian Gospel. Conversely, it must have been relatively difficult if not altogether impossible to preach an individualistic notion of salvation and heaven while white thugs hammered away at nearby African American girls and boys, while one entertained daily death threats from white racists, or while one's friends and family members clawed their way to a land where the color of their skin would not be the measure of their character. Given the daily pressures within King's context, it must have seemed downright mind-boggling if not offensive for anyone to suggest that he should not make race his primary emphasis. To refuse race as a primary emphasis, after all, would have alienated him from his own people, destroyed his vocation as a prophet in a sinful land, and vacuumed the air out of everyday life.

Graham's comment also revealed the virtually unbridgeable chasm that had grown between his gospel and King's. For Graham, the Christian Gospel was that Jesus Christ, God incarnate, came to the world so that whoever believes in him may not perish but have everlasting life. But for King, the Christian Gospel was so much more than that—it was the Good News that Jesus Christ, the highest revelation of God, was divinely anointed to set captives free, right here and right now, so that they may be wholly capable, in attitude and actions, of experiencing freedom and realizing the love and justice of God on earth. Given the meaning he attributed to the gospel, it would have made no sense for King to understand racial justice as anything but the Gospel: If liberating African Americans from their white oppressors was not the Gospel, nothing was. In the end, for those in the civil rights movement, Graham's point that race was not the Gospel was little more than a meaningless abstraction made by a white man with little connection to the everyday sufferings of the black people of God.

Against Forced Integration

As if his politics of diversion was not enough, Graham also took great pains to undermine legislative, executive, and judicial efforts to formulate and implement integration.[28] Interestingly, during an interview on ABC's "Issues and Answers" in 1969, the evangelist stated without qualification that he had been "for the civil rights legislation."[29] He had offered a similar statement a year earlier, during a New York City press conference: "I supported all the civil rights legislation."[30] But Graham was once again setting forth revisionist history—a history that betrayed his actual practices during the King years.

In his 1957 article for *Life*, the evangelist made the intriguing argument that although the Bible was clearly against racial discrimination, "there can be voluntary alignments on the basis of social and other preferences, where personal choice alone is involved and where the Christian ethic is not at stake."[31] Curiously, Graham made no effort to expound on this sentence, perhaps the most intriguing one in the entire article, but he did so in a 1960 article for *U.S. News and World Report*: "The Bible also recognizes that each individual has the right to choose his own friendships and social relationships. I am convinced that forced integration will never work. You cannot make two races love each other and accept each other at the point of bayonets."[32] Graham used virtually the same words three years later, in a 1963 sermon on race. "The Bible," he preached, "recognizes that each individual has the right to choose his own friendships and social relationships. I, for one, am convinced that forced integration will never work."[33]

In both cases, Graham was making two different points. The first was about biblical opposition to "forced integration," and the most fascinating point about this argument is that nowhere did he ever cite any biblical texts to support his view. Graham was normally masterful at detailing the texts that backed his opinions, but his absolutist claim that forced integration was biblically wrong was simply devoid of references. Of course, this should come as no surprise to biblical scholars, or even casual readers of the Bible, who know that they would have to look long and hard, and then without success, to discover biblical words on "the right" of an individual to select his or her friends and acquaintances. They simply are not there.

Graham's rights-language might have revealed the influence of his segregationist father-in-law, Nelson Bell. There is some evidence to suggest at least the possibility that Bell's segregationist beliefs had some spillover effect on Graham's public statements. In personal correspondence dated 1956, Bell warned a Mrs. R.H. Peake of Norfolk to be very careful when interpreting the wording of the evangelist's statements on race. Although Graham might encourage churches in the South to lead the way in improving racial relationships, he noted, the evangelist certainly did not call for the same churches to fight for integration. "I do not believe," Bell also added, "that we can legally discriminate against the Negro, nor do I believe that we can feel in any way that they have a different standing before God than those of us of white skin. But, I feel *strongly* that the Church, nor the Government, has any right to force social contacts which are not desired by individuals."[34] Of course, it is quite possible that Bell's thoughts were the result of Graham's influence, or that the two simply fed off each other when speaking of the problems of "forced integration," but whatever the case might have been, Graham and Bell were soul brothers in their opposition to forced integration.

Like Bell's, Graham's first argument was that forced integration was wrong, and his second was that forced integration would not work: "You cannot make two races love each other and accept each other at the point of bayonets. It must come from the heart if it is to be successful. Otherwise, we can build walls of hatred and prejudice that will take generations to overcome."[35] Interestingly, King also argued that integration would not be ultimately successful until the hearts of individuals changed. For the civil rights leader, desegregation was "eliminative and negative"; it eliminated and negated a sinful system that denied blacks equal access to schools, housing, and transportation, among other places. But integration, unlike desegregation, was "creative"—"the positive acceptance of desegregation and the welcomed participation of Negroes into the total range of human activities."[36] In effect, integration was true reconciliation, and for this to exist, all members of society must express an attitude of acceptance—an attitude that accepted each person as a worthy member of society and equal in value to all other persons. In this view, desegregation "will not change attitudes but it will provide the contact and confrontation necessary by which integration is made possible and attainable."[37]

Understanding justice as desegregation and love as integration, and claiming that the former is the means for effecting the latter, King held that government can assure justice but not love, that government can desegregate but not integrate society. The demands of desegregation can be "regulated by the codes of society and the vigorous implementation of law-enforcement agencies," but the demands of integration "concern inner attitudes, genuine person-to-person relations, and expressions of compassion which law books cannot regulate and jails cannot rectify." In King's view, then, government can establish justice, but only "a higher law produces love"—an "inner law, written on the heart."[38] And it is the proper work of religion and education to move political society toward this inner law.

Graham's notion of "forced integration" was not even remotely similar to King's notion of fully developed integration. In fact, the meaning Graham attributed to "forced integration" seemed to equate with King's notion of enforceable desegregation—"the contact and confrontation necessary by which integration is made possible and attainable." Graham did not provide specific examples of "forced integration," especially "at the point of bayonets," but one of the images that must have come to mind for those who read his 1960 column was the image of African American children being escorted by federalized troops to white schools in Little Rock.

Perhaps helpful here would be a look at Graham's underlying views on the implementation of *Brown*. The evangelist never explicitly opposed the implementation of *Brown*, but one had an unmistakable sense that he often couched his own views by publicizing those of the denominational leaders he consulted on matters of race. For example, in 1957, while he did not explicitly state that he opposed the speedy implementation of *Brown*, he did heavily publicize his interpretation of the views of unnamed denominational leaders in the South. "Most of them," he wrote in *Life*, "feel that segregation should be ended now on buses, in railroad and bus stations, hotels and in restaurants." Glaringly absent from this list, however, was the group of foundational institutions in local communities—public schools, industries, and courthouses, to name just a few. Regarding schools alone, Graham added: "However, most of [the leaders] feel that it is far too early to implement school integration in some sections of the deep South. They seem to feel that the day will come when both races will be psychologically and spiritually ready for it, but that the time has not come yet." It is likely that this position was also Graham's at the time, partly because of his claim that the denominational leaders were "not extremists on either side," and partly because of his own self-characterization as a racial moderate.[39]

Graham was not saying that *Brown* was a law to be challenged and overthrown, but he was stating that implementing *Brown* too speedily in certain areas of the Deep South would have been imprudent, as well as negligent of those ill prepared to have their children study and play with children of another race. Activists in the civil rights movement, including King, disagreed, stating that justice delayed would be justice denied. Waiting a year to respect the feelings of those ill prepared for integration would simply deny justice for a child who had waited to hold a new book and write on a new tablet. Unlike Graham, King placed his emphasis not on the uneasy adults, white or black, but on the children for whom justice had already been denied for far too long.

We can and should push this point further, too. If we take Graham's numerous statements about "forced integration" seriously, we can rightfully claim that he was opposed not only to a speedy *implementation* of *Brown*, but also to *any* legislative effort that forced integration upon the white citizenry, including, presumably, *Brown* itself. To be sure, this is a controversial thesis, but it is also an unavoidable one: *Brown* encouraged forced integration, and Graham was adamantly opposed to forced integration. So perhaps we should avoid making the evangelist more racially progressive than he really was. To put the point bluntly, no matter what he said in later years, Graham was no integrationist, at least in the sense that King and others in the civil rights movement were integrationists. Their short-term goal was integration enforced by government and its forcible means, but Graham's short- and long-term goal was voluntary integration, a form of integration that would not interfere with or trample the rights of whites to associate as they please, to choose their own friendships and social relationships. In short, Graham's stance against integration "at the point of bayonets," as well as his elevation of the right to free association as biblically sound, was diametrically opposed, in principle and practice, to King's unqualified calls for the forceful implementation of the laws of desegregation.

Even a Fool Knows

On a related note, mounds of evidence suggest that although Graham conceded the necessity of legislation for effecting racial justice in America, he also emphasized his belief in the insufficiency of legislation at the same time that King and his followers were going to jail in their quest for the formulation and implementation of just race laws. The first chapter has already noted Graham's belief in the insufficiency of legislation for social transformation, but here the task is to expound on this general point in relation to his specific emphasis that legislation is an insufficient response to racial issues.

"Even a fool," Graham wrote in 1965, "can see that we cannot settle the racial problem by legislation alone." Perhaps unwittingly, but quite amusingly, the evangelist followed this rather pointed comment with his favorite story about Hubert Humphrey: "A day after the 1964 Civil Rights Bill was passed, the then Senator Hubert Humphrey came over to the table where I was sitting in Washington and said: 'Billy, legislation alone can't do it. It must ultimately come from the heart.' How right he was!"[40] But this was not a new thought that (the fool) Humphrey had suddenly planted in

Graham's thought. Even at the beginning of the King years, the evangelist had consistently emphasized the insufficiency of legislation as a remedy for solving race-related problems. Shortly after the Little Rock Crisis, for example, he had stressed not the need for legislation to establish racial justice in schools, or to curb the violence of white racists intent on keeping African Americans out of schools, but the inability of legislation to move political and civil society in ultimately helpful ways: "Legislation is often necessary, but it will not change the individual. The law of the land can never be perfectly enforced . . . cannot give people the desire to obey the law. . . . The law lacks the power to make us love. . . . Yes, ladies and gentlemen, you cannot legislate morals."[41]

This was a criticism sickeningly familiar to King and the civil rights movement—the politically conservative charge that the attempt to legislate morality, however well-intended, was wrongheaded, impossible, and ill-fated. The civil rights leader stressed otherwise, of course, especially in the first period of his life. "We must continue," he stated time and again, "to struggle through legislation,"[42] which he understood to be one of the indispensable "tools of justice."[43] To be sure, King conceded that legislation was ultimately insufficient for establishing love, but unlike Graham, he also stressed that legislation can control "the external effects of one's internal feelings."[44] It can prevent whites from lynching African Americans, or consigning African Americans to inferior schools and jobs, and just because it can coerce and control the behavioral effects of feelings, legislation is necessary for effecting racial justice in political and civil society.

The politically conservative Graham, however, saw the emphasis on legislation as yet another example of the modern tendency to enlist "big government" for virtually every social crusade. "We have become so accustomed to thinking that big government can solve everything," he preached in 1963, "that we are frustrated when we realize that there are some things that big government cannot do."[45] Like what? For Graham, big government could not even begin properly to address the real cause of racial injustice—the problem of sin in the human heart. When asked in 1964 how he would solve the problem of de facto segregation, the evangelist answered: "I don't think there is any ultimate solution to it at all outside a moral and spiritual awakening on the part of both races in which there is love and understanding in the heart. There are certain things you cannot legislate."[46]

Graham reiterated this point especially following the passage of the Civil Rights Act of 1964. After Johnson delivered his famous civil rights speech at the passage of the Act, Graham released a statement that highlighted the insufficiency of the Act, even while praising "the greatest speech on civil rights of any president since Lincoln." Yes, the nation was making a "heroic attempt" to offer political, economic, and social equality to African Americans. "However, a thousand civil rights laws will not ease the racial tension in America unless we have a spiritual renewal that will change our hearts and give us a new love for each other."[47]

Further, when racial tension did not ease following the implementation of the Act, Graham reiterated his point all the more: "We were given to understand by some people that the Civil Rights Act of 1964 would solve the race issue in the United States. What has happened since indicates that we need something more, something deeper than legislation." Something deeper than legislation was required, because the race problem in the United States was essentially spiritual and psychological. "There is a psychological barrier that I believe could be overcome by a spiritual *renaissance* that would plant in our hearts love for each other and the recognition that we are of one blood under heaven."[48] Remarkably consistent, Graham again stressed the ultimate failure of all legislation after the successful passage of the Voting Rights Act of 1965. The Act would be helpful in its own way, he conceded, "but I am not so naïve as to believe that the solution to the racial problem lies in the mere passage of man-made laws."[49] Ultimately, only the supernatural love of God in the heart of individuals, available at the foot of the cross of Jesus during a Billy Graham revival, could solve the race problem. It was a good old-fashioned spiritual revival, not a legislative remedy, that America desperately needed.

It is impossible to overstate the difference between King and Graham on this point. While the evangelist conceded the necessity for legislation in a sinfully racist world, his emphasis was always and everywhere on what America *ultimately* needed—hearts transformed by the love of God in Jesus. And with this ultimate need in mind, Graham deliberately refused to call upon his followers to seek legislation that would eliminate segregation and establish racial justice for African Americans. In addition, Graham himself was far from inclined to make public statements calling for the successful passage of civil rights legislation. Although the press frequently asked him to comment on specific pieces of civil rights legislation before Congress throughout the King years, his usual answer was little more than a "no comment."

For example, in 1964, when the press asked if he would give his thoughts "on the current legislation pending Congress on civil rights" (that is, on the legislation that would eventually result in the Civil Rights Act of 1964), Graham's taciturn answer was simply "No, not on this particular bill."[50] Seven days later, he would offer a slightly revised answer to a similar question: "Well, I haven't made a statement about it yet because I'm for all the objectives of the civil rights bill, but whether this particular bill, I didn't want to get involved in all the controversy on a particular bill, because they obviously are going to change it."[51] This was the type of answer that Graham would frequently offer when asked about specific pieces of civil rights legislation. One might suspect that he was simply being faithful to his own belief that Christians would do well to steer clear of comments on specific policies, but in the first press conference just cited, Graham was more than willing to offer specific comments on the Becker Amendment, the highly controversial bill that sought to reinstate prayer in public schools. So specificity was less likely an issue than, Graham's firm conviction in the wrongness of forced integration, which is what the civil rights legislation sought, or perhaps his fear of losing his fundraising Southern base.

Whatever the case might have been, Graham continued to refuse to offer specific comments on civil rights laws throughout the King years. Just before King's assassination, for example, the press asked him to comment on open-housing legislation passed by the Senate. "I don't have any comment about that at this time," Graham replied.[52] It was this pattern in Graham's reaction to civil rights legislation—a pattern of deflection, delay, and deafening silence—that is important to keep in mind when reading the evangelist's own interpretation of his response to civil rights laws. As noted above, Graham often claimed without qualification that he supported all the civil rights legislation, but it was usually only after civil rights bills had become law that Graham would offer his "support." For example, after having refused to support the civil rights legislation that resulted in the Civil Rights Act of 1964, Graham offered his grudging support primarily after the Act had become law—and then he limited his support only to *obeying* the Act. "Well," he stammered, "I think that it is now law, and whatever people think of it, I think that we must obey the law."[53] In short, Graham tended to arrive at the legislative party a few hours late, after the table was set and the roast beef sliced. Only then would he dare pick up the fork and proclaim that he would eat whatever was on the table—whether he liked it or not.

Too Far Too Fast

Graham was short of words, even tongue-tied, when asked to comment on specific civil rights legislation, but he was certainly loquacious when demanding delays to the movement's push for racial justice. Indeed, the evangelist's implicit call for a delay in implementing *Brown*, as mentioned above, was just a small part of an overall strategy of delay in matters of race politics. Early in the King years, in 1956, Congressman Frank Boykin of Alabama had rightly recognized the mark of gradualism in Graham's race ethics and had even implored Eisenhower to use him as a resource for encouraging moderation in the Southern race crisis. "I believe our own Billy Graham," Boykin wrote, "could do more on this than any other human in this nation; I mean to quiet it down and to go easy and in a Godlike way, instead of trying to cram it down the throats of people all in one day, which some of our enemies are trying to do. I thought maybe if you and Billy talked, you could talk about this real, real good."[54]

Boykin was not mistaken in his homespun analysis of Graham's gradualism, or of the president's potential interest in his suggestion. Eisenhower promptly took Boykin's advice and consulted with Graham, who confirmed in a subsequent letter that patience was indeed the hallmark characteristic of his race politics. Further, he informed the president that he was encouraging patience, above all other attitudes and actions, from both sides in the crisis. "I believe that the Lord is helping us," Graham added, "and if the Supreme Court will go slowly and the extremists on both sides will quiet down, we can have a peaceful social readjustment over the next ten-year period."[55] Apparently, Billy Graham was not the only gradualist moderate—the good Lord was, too.

Graham's call for a go-slow approach to racial issues increased in frequency and volume as the King years progressed. Making his gradualist approach public, the evangelist took the occasion of his 1957 *Life* article to admonish African Americans to go slowly in their efforts to achieve justice in an unjust world. "For the Negro today," he wrote, "the Bible has many words of comfort and also a word of warning: 'If when you do right and suffer for it you take it patiently, you have God's approval . . . because Christ also suffered for you, leaving you an example, that you should follow in his steps.' " Graham also boldly appealed to African American history. "You have been known," he observed, "for your patience and faith as a people."[56] The evangelist's paternalistic point was unmistakable: As the slaves had so wondrously exhibited patience in a world that had beaten, enslaved, and then beaten them some more, African Americans should do no less in 1957.

Graham continued to encourage a gradualist approach in his 1960 article for *Reader's Digest*, where he tried to add a bit of depth to his rationale: "Some integrationists, both Negro and white, are trying to go too far too fast. I am convinced that you cannot force integration any more than you can force segregation. I realize that, among the impatient, 'gradualism' connotes appeasement. But the fact is that as a rule men's attitudes are changed gradually." Rather than pushing too hard too fast, the integrationists "should not try to drive people but lead them." Graham offered what he considered to be the perfect illustration of his point—a story about a young minister who was more than eager to work on transforming the racial attitudes and practices of his Southern parishioners. "After his first five sermons, all on race prejudice, he brought in a Northern Negro to instruct his people further. His congregation got up in arms, and an element from town gathered about the church with clubs and pitchforks. His bishop told me: 'While he was right, his method was wrong. Instead of leading his people in love, he was driving them—and nobody likes to be driven.' "[57]

But Graham was driving in his own way—by consistently putting the brakes on the civil rights movement as it sped ahead through the 1960s. In December 1963, just a few weeks after the assassination of John F. Kennedy, the evangelist took the occasion of a Miami press conference to demand yet again that the movement slow down. "Well," he replied to a press question, "I think that you cannot turn the Queen Mary on a dime in Mid-Atlantic. You can't have a social revolution in one summer . . . social change takes time." He also remarked that "responsible Negro leaders" recognized the necessity for going slow when turning the Queen Mary. "It's going to hurt the whole cause to push too fast," he added, "and yet some pressure must be kept up."[58]

Graham's sympathetic interpreters might draw attention to that last point—"some pressure must be kept up"—but the evangelist's statement in Miami was little more than a poorly veiled critique of Martin Luther King, Jr. Graham simply resented and despised King's politics of urgency, especially in 1963. The year is important to note because it was then that the civil rights leader wrote his famous letter from Birmingham City Jail—a widely publicized letter in which King depicted himself not as a "responsible Negro," but as an impatient leader who demanded racial justice right now. If there was anything that distressed King while incarcerated in Birmingham, it was the group of refined clergy who claimed to be sympathetic to civil rights while remaining insistent that he slow down his approach and tone down the urgency of his demand. In response to this gradualism, King wrote an eloquent defense worth quoting at length here:

> For years now I have heard the word "Wait!". . . . This "Wait" has almost always meant "Never". . . . I guess it is easy for those who have never felt the stinging darts of segregation to say, "Wait." But when you see vicious mobs lynch your mothers and fathers at will and drown your sisters and brothers at whim; when you have seen hate-filled policemen curse, kick, brutalize and even kill your black brothers and sisters with impunity; when you see the vast majority of your twenty million Negro brothers smothering in an airtight cage of poverty in the midst of an affluent society; when you suddenly find your tongue twisted and your speech stammering as you seek to explain to your six-year-old daughter why she can't go to the public amusement park that has just been advertised on television, and see tears welling up in her little eyes when she is told that Funtown is closed to colored children and see the depressing clouds of inferiority begin to form in her little mental sky, and see her begin to distort her little personality by unconsciously developing a bitterness toward white people; when you have to concoct an answer for a five-year-old son asking in agonizing pathos: "Daddy, why do white people treat colored people so mean?"; when you take a cross-country drive and find it necessary to sleep night after night in the uncomfortable corners of your automobile because no motel will accept you; when your first name becomes "nigger" and your middle name becomes "boy" (however old you are) and your last name becomes "John," and when your wife and mother are never given the respected title "Mrs."; when you are harried by day and haunted by night by the fact that you are a Negro, living constantly at tiptoe stance never quite knowing what to expect next and plagued with inner fears and outer resentments; when you are forever fighting a degenerating sense of "nobodiness"; then you will understand why we find it difficult to wait. . . . I hope, sirs, you can understand our legitimate and unavoidable impatience.[59]

This lengthy passage is so worth quoting exactly because it highlights the radical differences between the civil rights leader and Graham. King, of course, did not address his letter to Billy Graham, but Jonathan Bass rightly reminds us that although the letter was addressed to eight white clergy in Birmingham, addressees could have easily included all who had objected to King's campaign, including one Billy Graham.[60] It is not just the 1963 comments in Miami that prove as much. During the beginning of the Birmingham campaign itself, shortly after Bull Connor had released his hounds on nonviolent protestors, Graham publicly called for civil rights leaders to "put the brakes on a little bit" and seek "a period of quietness in which moderation prevailed."[61]

Like the obstructionist clergy of Birmingham, Graham did not "understand," as King put it. Sheltered in the Lincoln room at the White House, sequestered among white politicians with African Americans fetching cigars and cleaning bathrooms, and isolated on a gorgeous mountaintop home with a family that had no material needs, the evangelist did not even begin to sense the urgency that King felt. On the contrary, just like the eight white clergy in Birmingham, the evangelist was a card-carrying racial moderate deeply opposed to the tactics and timing of King's strategy, favoring small and quiet steps over a long period of time, rather than loud marches designed to effect immediate structural change. If historians rightly depict the Birmingham clergy as well-meaning but pathetic conservatives far behind the liberating spirit of the times, they should do the same with Graham.

Beyond 1963 Graham continued to express a politics of slow, steady change, with the emphasis on slow. Following Johnson's famous civil rights address at the time of the passage of the Civil Rights Act of 1964, the evangelist argued "that racial demonstrations should cease until the nation has had time to digest these new laws. Demonstrations have served their purpose in arousing the conscience of the nation. Future racial differences should be settled in the courts and at the ballot box."[62] King, of course, turned a deaf ear and sped forward to Selma.

Once Graham caught up with King's plans in Selma, he once again urged the civil rights activists to delay their push forward: "The Selma crisis will not be solved until the emotions of both sides have cooled off." Ignoring the activists' desire to push ahead with what would become their most famous march, Graham suggested three specific things to facilitate a discussion "in a spirit of Christian love, understanding and brotherhood." First, he urged President Johnson to call King and Governor Wallace to the White House for a discussion that would take "long enough for both sides to express their views." Second, he requested that Selma's clergy, African American and white, hold a joint prayer meeting. And, third, he implored both races in Selma to meet together for "a great evangelistic meeting" that would "get the eyes of the people off their problems and on the Lord. It is hard to hate each other when we are praying, singing and worshipping together." Graham also added that he would be "most willing to come and help in such an effort if the clergy invited me."[63] And thus his major response to Selma—stop the marches, cool down, and pray and worship together—simply ignored King's words from Birmingham: "We must come to see with the distinguished jurist of yesterday that 'justice too long delayed is justice denied.' "[64]

Graham best summarized his own gradualist approach in 1965: "I believe that only through a moderate approach can the ends sought by the Negro minority be realized. The serious situation this country now faces was not born overnight. It will take time to right the wrongs and heal the wounds of segregation."[65] No doubt, this was the most consistent position in Graham's race politics throughout the King years. While the civil rights leader kept shouting "*Now!*" Graham kept throwing up his hands and yelling "*Wait!*" Just so, Graham broke a promise he had made to King in 1960, when the two were spending a few days together in Puerto Rico, on their way to a meeting of Baptists in Brazil. According to Graham's own recollections, it was during this time that King had invited Graham to call him "Mike," the name that only a few friends used when speaking to the civil rights leader. Graham happily obliged, and the two spoke frankly about their relationship. "We had a wonderful two days of fellowship and discussion there," Graham remembered. "I told him, 'I certainly am not going to ever condemn you for your street demonstrations. So let me do my work in the stadiums, Mike, and you do yours in the streets. I don't expect you to condemn me for my stadium demonstrations.' " King agreed. "And he told me, 'Billy, I realize that what I'm doing will never work until the heart is changed. That's why your work is so important.' "[66] Unsurprisingly, Graham frequently cited King's compliment of his work, but the evangelist never noted that he had broken his own promise to the civil rights leader. Although there is no record that King ever publicly criticized Graham's revivialism, there is overwhelming evidence that the evangelist publicly condemned both King and his street demonstrations. King's politics of urgency found a hard-nosed opponent in Graham's politics of gradualism.

Prayer as the Solution to the Race Problem

Graham's pious response to King's sense of urgency in Selma—let us turn our eyes toward Jesus—was yet another example of the evangelist's ongoing politics of diversion. Calling Americans to get on their knees and pray was standard in Graham's corpus of reactions to the civil rights movement. King had heard the evangelist's call to prayer shortly after the beginning of the Montgomery bus boycott and then throughout the remainder of the King years. Graham's clarion call, however, was shrillest in a sermon he preached in 1963—"Prayer, the Solution to the Race Problem"—a slight revision of a 1955 sermon.

As African Americans were walking miles to work in 1956 Montgomery, and then as they were offering their own bodies for beatings and jailing in 1963 Birmingham, Graham announced to his radio audience that "prayer is the most important thing we can do in the time of crisis." Prayer, not self-sacrifice in bus boycotts or marches, even for Christian principles, is the most important practice a Christian can undertake. "Jesus showed us," Graham preached, "that prayer is more important than evangelism or mission work. Prayer is more important than social work. We can accomplish more through prayer than we can by appointing committees or devising new organizations or planning new strategy."[67] For Graham, a whispered word to God, even from one individual, was far more important than the Montgomery Improvement Association, formed by African Americans to combat segregation on buses, or the Southern Christian Leadership Conference, designed to help save America from its own racism, or the nonviolent strategy of King and his followers.

Graham also argued that even when completely surrounded by racial injustice and laws that condone discrimination and segregation, Christians should realize that the best thing they could ever do is to bow their heads, submissively and humbly, in a moment of prayer. "We see injustices being done on both sides," he preached. "We may see laws passed which we consider to be unjust. The attitude of the Christian is to be one of prayer and love." Placed in its social context, Graham's advice meant at least the following: When the bus driver curses at you for being black, pray. When the courthouse turns down your application to become a voting citizen, pray. When the police give free reign to white racists who would harm your children, pray. When you cannot find a job that would pay enough to feed your family, pray. "Otherwise," Graham preached, "the hatreds, the resentments, and the prejudices of the world will infect us." Further, if we do turn to God in prayer, we should expect that miracles will indeed happen. "I am convinced," he added, "that if Christians all over America would fall on their knees in prayer, we would see a great change in the approach to the racial problems . . . at this hour." Characteristically, however, Graham was not specific in his call to prayer. He did not suggest that Christians should pray for a change of mind among racists, or for the safety of African Americans as they sought to secure justice for themselves, or for the conversion of the white church from its apathy in matters of race. He did suggest praying for "a peace that would be morally right in every sense of the word," but he did not even begin to unpack his thoughts on the substantive content of such a peace.[68]

King did not heed Graham's call. Contrary to the evangelist, King found prayers like Graham's to be vacuous, unhelpful, even harmful, and so the civil rights leader offered his own prescriptions. Around the time Graham delivered his first sermon on prayer and the race problem, King encouraged people to pray not just in general but for those who were fighting the good fight. "We ask people everywhere," he wrote, "to pray that God will guide us, pray that justice will be done and that righteousness will stand."[69] King was praying not for peace but for justice and righteousness—for the rights to be wronged in the battle against discrimination and segregation. He also invited his followers to pray not just for the civil rights movement but also for the racists who would obstruct the movement in the most violent of ways. "We must pray," he stated, "for a change in attitude in all those who violate human dignity and who rob men, women, and little children of human decency."[70]

Perhaps most importantly, however, King stood firmly against Graham's evangelical belief that prayer is more important than social action, and that prayer is a proper tool for directing one's focus away from everyday problems and toward personal salvation. Although he prayed regularly, King characterized prayer as a wholly insufficient resource on the march toward the beloved community. As he put it in a sermon published in *Strength to Love*, "God, who gave us minds for thinking and bodies for working, would defeat his own purpose if he permitted us to obtain through prayer what may come through hard work and intelligence. Prayer is a marvelous supplement of our feeble efforts, but it is a dangerous substitute."[71] King criticized President Johnson's proposal for a Day of Prayer in response to the 1965 inner-city riots exactly on this point. "As a minister," he stated, "I take prayer too seriously to use it as an excuse for avoiding work and responsibility."[72] In effect, this was also a critique of Graham, who had actually called upon the president to proclaim the Day of Prayer.

For King, then, Graham was tragically wrong when he merely bowed his head at crusades, trying to show his fellow Christians that prayer was the solution to the race crisis. The racial crisis demanded immediate action from public personalities, not another well-crafted prayer from a Christian hiding in the closet.

Extremists Out of Control

Beyond calling for polite prayers, Graham's reaction to the civil rights movement also turned downright hostile from 1964 through 1968, with one of the most marked turns, at least in his public statements, happening shortly after civil rights demonstrations at the 1964 World Fair in New York City. When asked to comment on demonstrations shortly after the fair, Graham replied that he supported them if they were nonviolent and did not "lead to extremism." But he also observed that he was especially concerned with the tendency for demonstrations to become violent as they progressed through the years: "I think that we have seen that tendency develop in this country in the civil rights among certain extremist groups." Calling this "a dangerous trend," he added: "I think responsible civil rights leaders are beginning to realize this, and are beginning to call a halt to it. For example, what happened at the world's fair, where a group of people tried to interrupt the President of the United States. They did not stand up during the signing of the national anthem. This is irresponsible demonstration, and this is the type that does a great deal of harm [to the civil rights movement]."[73] Graham did not call for an end to the demonstrations at this point, but for a type of demonstration that was safe, orderly, and respectful of political authority—in effect, a patriotic bow to whites in power.

A year later, however, in a patriotic sermon titled "To Keep Our Flags Waving," Graham spouted a hotter rhetoric against all types of civil rights demonstrations, not just the violent ones. "The United States," he announced, "is rapidly becoming a nation of picketers, demonstrators, squatters, and sitters. What a spectacle we have become to the world!" And to Billy Graham. "Where is this going to end?" he asked. "This is freedom out of control!"[74] This was not the type of raw rhetoric that Graham would have delivered just anywhere (in Harlem, for example), but this time he was speaking to his radio audience—his friends, his followers, his family members, the ones who would become the core fervent supporters of the white Christian backlash to the civil rights movement of the mid- to late 1960s.

Graham's own backlash to the civil rights demonstrations increased in volume and intensity from 1965 to 1968, especially when violence erupted in the inner cities. This is not to say that his key leadership in the backlash movement began in 1965; Graham had long been fomenting discontent among whites by depicting African Americans as extremists out of control, always on the edge of executing a violent revolution against innocent whites, and always demanding way too much from white America. The lowest point of this early effort occurred in 1958, shortly after a mentally unstable African American stabbed King at a public event. "Thank God," Graham responded, "that Martin Luther King . . . was not stabbed by a white person. If he had been, we might have seen a racial war in New York with blood flowing down the street."[75]

It was exactly this type of backlash effort, wholly insensitive to the plight of African Americans, that Graham engineered with considerable intensity as the inner-city riots erupted. In 1967, after riots in Detroit and Milwaukee, the evangelist gave an unqualified tongue-lashing to all civil rights demonstrations. In a sermon titled "America Is in Trouble," the conservative patriot told his radio audience that "Supreme Court Justice Hugo Black said, 'It's high time to challenge the assumption . . . that groups that think they've been mistreated have a constitutional right to use the public streets, building, and property to protest whatever, wherever, whenever they want, without regard to whom it may disturb.' Justice Black went on to say, 'The crowd moved by noble ideals today can become the mob ruled by hate, passion, greed, and violence tomorrow.' Indeed! The crowd of yesterday has already become the mob of today."[76] It is this type of *unqualified* response to the riots of the 1960s that made Graham an unofficial but loud and visible leader of the white Christian backlash to the civil rights movement. Leaving behind the words of a racial moderate, Graham unabashedly used the riots as the perfect excuse to scorch all civil rights demonstrations, not merely the violent ones. As a primary leader of the

Christian white backlash, Graham seemed intent on turning America back to the white orderliness of the Eisenhower era.

Strikingly, Graham's white backlash was evident even in the days following the assassination of King. One would think that the assassination would have tempered his condemnation of demonstrations but at a press conference just one month later, Graham took center stage, announcing that all civil disobedience was wrong, primarily because it "will lead to violence and violence will lead to anarchy and all of us will lose everything as far as the country is concerned."[77] This type of backlash, with its appeal to the emotions of order-loving Americans, was yet another example of the fear mongering that Graham often relied on to capture his audiences and move them to nervous concern about the safety of their future. Throughout the King years, Graham had depicted communism as a godless force intent on taking over the whole world and threatening our freedom to go to Sunday school, pray to Jesus, and wave the American flag; and from the mid- to late 1960s, he added civil rights "extremists" to his list of bad people who, like the communists, would run roughshod over our American rights, make a mockery of our American flag, and rob our American homes.

Graham held a fluid notion of the identity of the civil rights extremists. On the one hand, he clearly implied, as he did in his 1956 correspondence with Eisenhower, that King himself was an extremist; in fact, for Graham, anyone who was not a racial moderate, like Eisenhower, was a racial extremist. This implication also turned explicit at certain times throughout the King years. During the Birmingham crisis in 1963, for example, Graham blamed the city's racial problems on "extremist groups" that refused to exercise love and patience and understanding. Given this definition of extremism, it was more than clear that King's absolute refusal to go slowly in the civil rights battle in Birmingham qualified him to be the extremist of extremists. Further, when preaching in Alabama in 1965, Graham characterized "extremists in the civil rights organization" as those who would not give the Southern state "time to digest the new civil rights laws."[78] As it turned out, of course, King was one of those extremists who decided to continue protests in Alabama long before the state would even pick the laws off the legislative plate.

But Graham had other particular civil rights activists in mind, too— subversive, elusive, shadowy communists. Influenced by J. Edgar Hoover, the infamous director of the FBI during the King years, Graham was convinced beyond a shadow of a doubt that communists had penetrated the civil rights movement and were using the movement—and King—to advance the communist agenda of world revolution. In 1964, at the time of his campaign for the presidency, Senator Barry Goldwater, also influenced by Hoover, stated that King himself was a communist and implied that he had plans to take over white America and hand it on a platter to the Soviet communists. Anti-communism, of course, still ran at a feverish pitch in the mid-1960s, and Graham saw fit to add plenty of fuel to Goldwater's fire.

"New York City officials," he proclaimed, "say the communists are taking advantage of America's race problem." Citing an unnamed "communist official in Geneva, Switzerland," the McCarthy-like Graham reported that the reds were carefully planning to "use the race issue to divide and ultimately destroy the United States."[79] The evangelist never publicly labeled King as a communist, but the historical record certainly suggests that he wholeheartedly joined Goldwater's efforts to discredit the civil rights movement by characterizing it as a puppet of godless communism.

The word "extremists" came to mean other things in Graham's thought, too. As racial tensions became more violent during the King years, it became clear, at least to Graham and other white moderates, that there were African Americans far more extreme than even King, and that these radical extremists were far more dangerous to the American way of life than King ever was. The youthful movement started by these so-called radical African Americans—Black—Power became Graham's new bugbear.

The years 1966 to 1968 witnessed a strong surge of opposition to King from within the ranks of civil rights activists, and nowhere was the dissent more visible than in the Student Nonviolent Coordinating Committee (SNCC), whose mantle of leadership had passed from the nonviolent John Lewis to the loudly militant Stokely Carmichael, the young activist who had popularized the phrase "black power" during the 1966 march to support James Meredith's admission to the University of Mississippi. During Carmichael's tenure, SNCC and all other Black Power advocates began to promote the philosophy of black nationalism, the development of black-controlled institutions, and the acceptance of violence as a means for establishing justice for African Americans.[80] Faced with this new black militancy, Graham did not stop implying that King was a racial extremist, but he did largely shift his negative focus to Black Power advocates, who wore their militancy on their sleeve and everywhere else so that others, especially "the white man," like one Billy Graham, could see it without squinting.

In typical fashion, King had a double reaction to the Black Power movement. On the one hand, he stood against its embrace of a separate black state, permanently separate black institutions, and the use of forcible means to establish justice. On the other hand, however, he deeply appreciated the movement's "cry of disappointment" in response to oppressive white structures. In this sense, he saw Black Power as the "response to a feeling that a real solution [to black disempowerment] is hopelessly distant because of the inconsistencies, resistance, and faintheartedness of those in power."[81] The civil rights leader also admired the movement's psychological call for "somebodyness" to take root within each African American self—an unabashed sense of pride in being black.[82] Perhaps more significantly, however, Black Power inspired King to speak more about the need for power made possible by social, political, and economic resources controlled by African Americans alone. Troubled especially by integration without power, King even made advances toward the black separatist position near the end of his career, declaring "we don't want to be integrated *out* of power; we want to be integrated *into* power," and suggesting that "temporary segregation" might be required for African Americans to achieve the power required for realizing justice.[83] Finally, prompted by the radical dimension of Black Power, King also began to emphasize the language and social hermeneutic of revolution, stating that America must experience a revolution of values—a dramatic turn away from the racial discrimination, economic exploitation, and militarism deeply embedded within American institutions and interpersonal relations.[84]

But unlike King, who believed that the positive dimensions of Black Power aided and abetted the civil rights movement, Billy Graham did little more than to characterize Black Power advocates as extremists gone wild, as dangerous radicals with terrifying designs to overthrow white America. Predictably, Graham was appalled by Black Power's call for segregation in certain social, political, and economic forms—a position he stated most clearly on ABC's "Issues and Answers" a year after King's death. "The difficulty I think that many people are facing today," Graham argued, "is that many of the blacks are beginning to talk about apartheid or separatism. . . . It seems to me that if we're going to live in peace and harmony in this country, we're going to have to live with each other and treat each other as equals."[85] Absent from this statement, of course, was any recognition that Black Power advocates were calling for separation exactly because integration *with* power was not happening, or that the white power structure was adamantly refusing to treat blacks as equals. With few nuances in his thought, Graham merely insisted that Black Power was blatantly racist, as negative a movement as the white power movement. "People like the extremists to the right and to the left which are advocating either white power or black power and preaching racism," he argued in 1967, "are trying to destroy the relationship that I think is building up. . . . I think that we are on the threshold of solving this problem if the spoilers don't come in and destroy the relationship."[86]

Equally predictable, Graham sounded alarms about Black Power's call for revolution, suggesting countless times that the Black Power advocates were political subversives whose only intention was to teach violence, defy authority, foster racial discord, and promote national anarchy. From the mid-1960s through the end of the King years, Graham argued that the inner city riots spreading at rapid pace through America provided direct evidence of the subversive teachings and practices of Black Power. In 1968, for example, he criticized the Kerner Commission Report for failing to "put enough of the blame on those that are going around the country inciting riots." Given the context, it would have been clear to all informed observers of American society and culture that Graham was indicting primarily Black Power advocates for the riots. "We've got people going about today with a great deal of hate, both black and white, who are preaching race hatred and urging people to get guns, urging people to get ready for war. I think that these people are going to have to be stopped or we could have some real trouble in the next 24 months."[87] Although he made it a point to note that whites were preaching hatred and encouraging violence, Graham never once targeted them as pointedly in his public comments as he did Black Power advocates.

For Graham, then, Black Power spoiled the civil rights cause by espousing violence and a black racism contrary to the spirit of the movement, let alone the love of God. Fascinatingly, the evangelist tried to grant legitimacy to his vitriolic stance against Black Power by citing King himself. In a 1967 press conference in San Juan, for example, Graham argued that "now there are certain extremists in the civil rights movement that are hurting the cause of civil rights in the United States, so that now, in the university level . . . you can't get the enthusiasm anymore, because they want to be identified with these more extreme elements . . . that are far, far more extreme and to the left of Dr. King. And I think Dr. King himself feels that."[88] Graham was partly right in the sense that King recognized that the Black Power's embrace of any means possible, as well as its strident nationalism, could add to the rising backlash, but the evangelist failed to mention King's positive interpretation of Black Power. More significantly, however, if Graham was looking for someone to blame for the lessening of enthusiasm for civil rights demonstrations—no doubt, a real phenomenon in 1967—he had to look no further than the mirror. As we have just seen, Graham had publicly identified the civil rights movement with extremists and communists long before Carmichael ever assumed power in SNCC, and so it was more than a tad ironic that the evangelist accused Black Power advocates as the major if not the only cause of the backlash to the civil rights movement. Pointing his finger at Black Power advocates as "the spoilers" was perhaps the height of hypocrisy of Graham's racial politics during the King years. On a practical level, of course, it was yet another strategy for conquering the wider civil rights movement.

Another Kind of March: The Quiet Revolution

Graham was dismayed and distressed by the emergence of Black Power not only because of the violence and the so-called racism of black nationalism, but also because of its potential negative effects on what he saw as remarkable progress in civil rights during the King years. He stated as much in his most substantive response to Black Power, a 1967 speech titled "The Quiet Revolution." "We have made the greatest progress in civil rights in the last fifteen years of any country in the history of the world," he preached. African American family income was on the rise, unemployment was down among married African Americans under the age of twenty, and African American presence in white-collar occupations was increasing. Moreover, the U.S. Senate and the Supreme Court both held an African American member, and more than half of all African American students were completing their high school education. "Yet," Graham wondered, "why is it that with all the progress made in civil rights there is racial rioting and bloodshed in our streets—and the threat of more to come?"[89]

King could not disagree more with the evangelist's major premise. For all of his victories, from the desegregation of buses to the elimination of literacy tests for voting, the civil rights leader believed in the year of his death that the battle for America's soul, and for the guarantee of the right to life, liberty, and the pursuit of happiness for all African Americans, had only begun. King conceded that the civil rights movement had resulted in important achievements, but in 1968 he emphasized that such achievements were far too limited: "We made some strides toward the ending of racism, but we did not stride into freedom."[90] Freedom for African Americans, indeed for all Americans, would remain an elusive goal until the three interrelated obstructions of the beloved community—racial discrimination, economic exploitation, and militarism—were defeated at long last.

But Graham, in typical fashion, downplayed the limited nature of the effects of the civil rights movement and focused instead on what he saw as America's tremendous progress in civil rights especially when compared to other countries. With his emphasis on progress, he seemed to suggest that African Americans would do well to stop the pushing, reflect on the massive gains, and give thanks for America's willingness to grant civil rights denied to minorities in other countries. It was as if he was saying, "Look at how far America has come. Blacks should be grateful for our progress, rather than demanding more and more and more."

For Graham, the civil rights push for greater freedom in the mid- to late 1960s, especially from Black Power advocates, was not only arrogant and ungrateful, but also anarchistic, a bitter foretaste of the future downfall of America. "All the elements of anarchy, insurrection, and revolution are now building up in the United States," he threatened. "What we have read about in Algeria, Cuba, Angola, the Congo, and even Vietnam, is beginning here. National violence often starts with a legitimate grievance, a discontent, or a frustration. Radical leaders soon rise to mobilize the discontented. Eventually terrorism and guerilla warfare begin."[91] Importantly, this became Graham's interpretation of the evolution of the civil rights campaign in America: In the beginning there was a legitimate grievance against segregation, as exemplified in the Montgomery boycott, but then extremists, like communists and Black Power advocates, infiltrated the civil rights movement, assumed leadership positions, and appealed to the sighing masses, who eventually responded to the teaching of "any means possible" by taking up arms and inciting riots that threatened another revolutionary war, this one unfavorable to white America. Once good, the movement had become bad.

But Graham also believed that the Black Power movement would ultimately fail, and that its evolution would implode primarily because of "a false assumption on the part of some of the Black Power advocates," —the belief "that all Negro problems are caused by the white man." Graham found Black Power's finger pointing at the white man to be far too limiting, because "the Negro is also a man and shares with the Caucasian and the Oriental the disease of sin." Contrary to the teachings of Black Power, the crime and violence sweeping inner cities was not caused by poverty and discrimination engineered by the white man, and racial injustice was not caused only by the white man. "It is a result of the natural rebelliousness against God and his fellowmen on the part of all races since Adam and Eve rebelled against God in the Garden of Eden."[92] So rather than preaching a violent and blatantly racist revolution against whites, Black Power advocates would do well to join forces with the white man and become part of a stronger, more effective, and certainly more faithful movement—the "quiet revolution" sweeping across America. Even nonviolent activists, Graham argued, could do no better than to leave behind their dramatic demonstrations and take a leading part in this noiseless revolution, with its potential to save America's soul.

Unsurprisingly, by "revolution," Graham meant "renewal of a personal faith that will get at the root of our problems by changing the men who cause our problems"—a renewal made possible only by coming to the foot of the cross and making Jesus Christ one's personal Lord and Savior. "Christ," Graham preached, "is the greatest revolutionist of all time." He was not the type of revolutionist one saw in Stokely Carmichael, Rap Brown, or even Martin Luther King, Jr.; nor was Christ's revolution even remotely similar to the types of revolution embraced by the Black Power advocates and the civil rights movement. Straining to sound hip and radical, Graham stated:

> The word "revolution" means "a complete or drastic change," and Christ's dialectic was revolutionary. He talked about change, not only in government, not only in culture, but primarily in the human heart. Most revolutions are accomplished by violence and by dramatic events, but not so with the spiritual revolution that Christ brings. Like the quiet power of spring when new life surges through nature— giving the trees color, the flowers new beauty, and the whole world a new freshness and a new hope—Christ comes quietly, touching our lives with a new radiance, a new meaning, a new purpose, a new glow, and bringing with it a new satisfaction.[93]

Graham's revolution was nothing other than the old, old story he had been preaching for years—the story of God loving the world so much that he gave his only begotten son so that whoever believes in him shall not perish but have everlasting life.

There were significant divergences between this old-time Gospel revolution and the revolutions proposed by Black Power advocates and King. For example, while King's and Carmichael's revolutions focused primarily on changing the social institutions, roles, and practices of the white power structure in America, Graham's revolution began and ended with the individual heart. King's revolution used dramatic means, like dramaturgical marches held at symbolic locations and on symbolic occasions, and

Carmichael's embraced forcible means, but Graham's, with its reliance on the invitational prayer at a crusade service, was quiet, noiseless, and unthreatening to white power holders. King's and Carmichael's revolutions demanded radical change now, but Graham's was patient, longsuffering through the winter, and yet always expectant for the buds to appear and burst forth in their own time and without any external force. King's and Carmichael's revolutions were not content with relying on means that would indirectly transform the social institutions, roles, and practices of white America over a long period of time, but Graham's was content merely to move from one heart to another, and to wait for however long it might take to melt the winter of the soul.

The most fascinating response to Graham's revolution ever to come from the African American community was James Cone's influential *Black Theology & Black Power*. "When Billy Graham can speak of a revolution," Cone wrote in 1969, "we clearly require a tighter definition of the term. Revolution is not merely a 'change of heart,' but a radical black encounter with the structure of white racism, with the full intention of destroying its menacing power." Cone also clarified his meaning of the definition a bit more vernacularly. "I mean confronting white racists and saying: 'If it's a fight you want, I am prepared to oblige you.' This is what the black revolution means."[94] But that, of course, is not what Billy Graham meant.

In addition, unlike Cone and others, Graham was convinced that the quiet revolution, although a matter of the individual heart, "could reverse many of the disturbing trends in society," including the trend toward greater racial division, and he claimed to have seen the noiseless spiritual revolution all over America, especially at his Southern crusades.[95] Speaking of his 1965 crusade in Alabama, for example, Graham extolled what he called "another kind of march." Not to be confused with civil rights marches, Graham's was "the march of hundreds of men and women of both races out of the stands at Cramton Bowl every night to receive Jesus Christ as Lord and Savior." This "other kind of march" was not loud or abrasive or aggressive; it was a quiet march whose image burned brightly in one's memory. "As long as I live," Graham preached, "I shall never forget the marching feet of the hundreds of people as they came forward night after night in the stillness and quietness and hush to receive Jesus Christ as their Lord and Savior." It would have been clear to all who heard Graham that he was comparing his march to the civil rights marches, but for good measure, he made the comparison a bit more explicit. "I saw [both races] walking quietly, orderly, with no barriers making demands, with no loud speakers blaring slogans."[96]

Graham gave lip service to supporting the civil rights marches throughout the King years, but the march he really supported with all his heart and mind and soul was not the type organized by King and other civil rights leaders— the loud, demanding, slogan-wielding, government-focused, and (occasionally) disorderly marches. "In my opinion," Graham stated, "this [crusade] march in Montgomery is far more significant, more constructive, and more revolutionary than the other marches we've read about in our newspapers and watched on our television screens." And this was so because, unlike other marches, Graham's apparently effected "a spiritual unity . . . centered in the person of Jesus Christ," the one and only solution to sin-sick hearts. Governments, laws, and courts may try their best, but only "Christ can change the world by changing the hearts of men."[97]

An Interpersonal Politics of Kindness

But what about *after* one accepts Jesus Christ as Lord and Savior? Was Graham ever inclined to suggest that other converted Christians should join the marches, demonstrations, sit-ins, boycotts, and other practices of the civil rights movement? Again, the answer is an unambiguous "no." Graham had plenty of advice for Christians seeking to respond positively to the racial crisis of the 1950s and 1960s, but virtually all of it centered on creating a "local climate of goodwill." More particularly, Graham suggested seven "practical possibilities" that a converted individual could undertake in order to help create a local climate of goodwill: remember that "love is patient and kind"; demonstrate courtesy, patience, humility, and unselfishness; teach love for the other races at home; accept responsibility for one's brothers and sisters in Christ; "take a stand in your church for neighbor-love"; be honest about the human tendency to think one has done enough; and "act soberly and thoughtfully, but . . . on principle. Never condone a wrong for the sake of expediency."[98]

If Graham supported the marches, or any of the other practices of the civil rights movement, his support was altogether absent in this 1957 advice—advice that would remain consistent throughout the King years. What Graham primarily recommended beyond Christian conversion was not structural engagement with white institutions but personal and interpersonal practices—ensuring that one's heart is morally pure and then saying "hello" to one's neighbor, practicing courtesy in local institutions, and politely nudging one's church to be nice to African Americans. Most revealing of his interpersonal approach was his favorite illustration for improving race relations:

> And remember this simple, eloquent example: shortly after the close of the Civil War, a Negro entered a fashionable church in Richmond, Va. one Sunday morning while communion was being served. He walked down the aisle and knelt at the altar. A rustle of shock and anger swept through the congregation. Sensing the situation, a distinguished layman immediately stood up, stepped forward to the altar and knelt beside his colored brother. Captured by his spirit, the congregation followed this magnanimous example.
> The layman who set the example was Robert E. Lee.[99]

Graham's favorite race-related example throughout the King years was not the courageous Mose Wright, whose life was threatened because he decided to testify against two white men accused of killing his nephew Emmett Till; or Rosa Parks, who refused to surrender her bus seat to a white person, knowing full well that she would be charged with a crime; or Martin Luther King, Jr., whose house was bombed when he fought for "forced integration"; or James Reeb, a white minister murdered for taking part in the civil rights movement; or James Meredith, a young black student shot while marching to gain entrance into the University of Mississippi; or Fannie Lou Hamer, who was ridiculed beyond ridicule for insisting that African American voters should have been represented in Mississippi's Democratic Party; or the thousands of unnamed African Americans beaten and jailed in their pursuit to transform the structure of white racism in America. For Graham, the prime example for bettering race relations was a white Confederate general who, having already ordered the slaughter of individuals fighting for the abolition of slavery, one day allegedly decided it civil and perhaps Christian to kneel next to an African American hoping to partake of the simple elements of bread and wine.

Graham did not say anything more about the "magnanimous example" of Robert E. Lee. He did not go on to suggest that Lee sought to change the segregationist practices of his church and denomination, nearby churches and schools, or courtrooms and pressrooms. None of this, after all, was ultimately significant. What ultimately mattered was not the changing of social structures in Richmond, but the simple interpersonal act of one individual Christian for another. And thus, for Graham, interpersonal acts of Christian kindness were the firmest foundations for solving the nation's race problem.

A More Developed Conclusion

Did Graham support the civil rights movement from its beginning? The prior chapter argued that by the time the civil rights movement had begun, Graham was vocal in his opposition to segregation and consistent in his refusal to practice segregated crusades, and that as the King years progressed, he supported the movement by calling upon whites to comply with race-based legislation, characterizing peaceful marches as "the American way," helping to rebuild black institutions bombed by whites, referring to King as a personal friend, and characterizing the movement in general as a "great" and "tremendous" movement. But this chapter has offered additional information that requires qualifying the earlier depiction of Graham as a supporter of the civil rights movement. Indeed, the substantive evidence in this chapter suggests that Graham was not telling the whole truth when he characterized himself, unqualifiedly, as a supporter of the civil rights movement from its very beginning.

If Graham was a supporter of the civil rights from the beginning, his support was nowhere to be found in the Deep South at the start of the King years. Perhaps fearing the loss of his white constituency, Graham stayed away from the Deep South in the early years, failing not only African Americans but also his fellow white Baptists, members of his own denomination, who desperately needed strong leadership for the crises before them. During these same years, Graham also lobbied Eisenhower to steer clear of the racial crisis stirring in the South, and encouraged Southern ministers, white and black, to adopt a go-slow approach in the emerging campaign for civil rights. Graham preached against segregation and refused to hold segregated crusades, but he also did his best to remove himself and others from the crucible of the civil rights movement in the early years, thereby suggesting that his primary concern was not the integration of buses or schools, but the possibility that his ministry and Republican politics would go up in flames.

Aware of Graham's obstructionist tactics, King vocalized his opposition in a 1958 letter, but the evangelist continued to act in ways that countered the tactics and goals of the movement. More particularly, Graham sought to undermine the movement by diverting attention away from the Southern communities that King had targeted; by emphasizing black prejudice over white racism; and by proclaiming numerous times that because race was not the Christian Gospel, Christians and the church would do well, no matter what situation they found themselves in, to deemphasize racial issues in favor of the good news that Jesus Christ died for the sins of the world. Graham also sought to undermine the movement by arguing that "forced integration"—the type of legislative policies that King and the movement sought—was biblically unsound as well as ineffective in people's everyday lives, and by arguing numerous times that "you cannot turn the Queen Mary on a dime in Mid-Atlantic." Like the addresses of King's letter from Birmingham City Jail, Graham deeply opposed the timing of King's strategy—his ceaseless pushing for immediate legislative, judicial, and executive action—and called instead for the movement and the nation to bow in a moment of prayer for peace. Perhaps most seriously, from 1964 through 1968, Graham became one of the most outspoken leaders of the white Christian backlash to the civil rights movement, taking the occasion of the urban riots, as well as the emergence of the Black Power movement, to call for an end to all demonstrations. As a leader of the white Christian backlash, Graham sounded alarms about the threats made by Black Power advocates, giving all of his attention to fear mongering and none of it to the movement's ongoing attempts to correct structural racism and discrimination. Finally, true to his evangelical roots, Graham attempted to undermine the movement by continuing to shift his followers' attention away from structural issues, emphasizing instead his ongoing conviction that what ultimately mattered was the transformation of the individual heart and the local, interpersonal acts of kindness that flowed from a heart imbued with the Spirit of Jesus Christ.

No, Graham did not support the civil rights movement from the beginning. Although deeply opposed to segregation and steadfastly committed to law and order in communities struggling with the new civil rights legislation, he could never bring himself to declare his support for "forced integration"; nor could he ever embrace the tactics and timing that King adopted in the quest for integration. Just so, although Graham was an anti-segregationist, he was far from an integrationist, at least in the sense that King was. And as an anti-integrationist, he continually sought to undermine both the goals of the civil rights movement, especially forced integration, and the civil disobedience designed to effect integration. It was only as the civil rights movement pushed for integration that Graham's full position on the movement became clear, but when he laid out his campaign against both "forced integration" and the movement's hard push for immediate governmental action, his message was simply unmistakable: a big government that pushed for racial integration was as unchristian as Jim Crow himself.

★   ★   ★

This is only one part of the complicated story of the relationship between Graham and King's beloved community. And here we would do well to remember that, for King, the beloved community is marked not only by racial reconciliation but also by economic justice and peace. As we will see in the following chapters, Graham occasionally supported King on matters related to economic justice and peace. He smoothed the way for King's poverty politics at certain points, and he supported the practice of nonviolence among African Americans. But in the end Graham depicted economic justice and peace as laughable goals for a fallen world.

CHAPTER SIX

"The Tramp, Tramp, Tramp of the Little Man": Graham's Conversion to the War on Poverty

Billy Graham was a child of the Depression. "Growing up in those years," he recalled in his autobiography, "taught us the value of nickels and dimes." Apparently with good reason: During the Depression, his father lost the family savings of $4,000 in the Farmers' and Merchants' Bank of Charlotte, and the family dairy farm faced ruin when the price for a quart of milk plummeted to five cents. Far from indigent, however, the Graham family had an established dairy farm, replete with cows, barns, land for gardening and farming, and even laborers. "We all simply believed in hard work," Graham wrote. And as hardworking laborers, the family recovered in a matter of months from the loss of personal funds. Through it all Graham's father kept faith in the system of free enterprise, and perhaps more importantly, he had passed on this faith to young Billy long before the onslaught of the Depression. "My father early on," Graham reflected, "illustrated for me the merits of free enterprise. Once in a while when a calf was born on the farm, he turned it over to my friend Albert McMakin and me to raise. When it got to the veal stage, we marketed ourselves and split the proceeds."[1]

Workers, Be Content!

By the arrival of the King years, Graham had already developed a reputation for being an advocate of the merits of free enterprise—a reputation sealed in part because of his occasionally subtle but always unmistakable preference for capital over labor. The evangelist's preference for owners and management in labor relations should come as no surprise if we remember that Billy and his family, unlike the African American laborers on the Graham farm, owned and managed the means of dairy production. Indeed, the Grahams recovered so quickly from the stock market crash not only because they were hard workers, as Graham thought, but also because they were part of the ownership class that had enough capital and laborers to avoid the bread lines and continue their self-employed status.

To be fair, Graham was, as McLoughlin put it, sometimes "circumspect in his treatment of the problems of capital and labor," primarily because he sought to appeal to the working masses.[2] To this end he frequently offered apparently neutral statements on capital and labor, as he did in this 1952 sermon: "The church should be impartial toward the labor union as it is to other economic groups. We must not place halos on the heads of one group, and horns on the heads of another. We must treat all with equal fairness and try to be neither pro-labor nor pro-capital."[3] But there is no doubt that the thin veneer of neutrality frequently cracked, especially because Graham found labor unions to be obstructionists of free enterprise. McLoughlin rightly noted significant problems with the evangelist's "description of the Garden of Eden as that happy place where there are 'no union dues, no labor leaders, no snakes, no disease,' " and in ongoing claims that strikes could paralyze the nation and damage the abilities of the U.S. military.[4] Even in the 1952 sermon just cited, Graham argued that "organized labor unions are one of the greatest mission fields in America today," while at the same time failing to identify the class of owners and managers as another of the greatest mission fields.[5]

Graham had a vague sense that organized labor had carried out important work in its early years. When asked in 1958 if unions were justified, he responded: "I know that the history of labor certainly justifies the union method when labor is exploited. The working man in America has risen to a place of respectability as a result of refusing to be taken advantage of." But the evangelist also insisted that labor of old was not the same as labor of 1958. "Recently," he observed, "the trend has been more in favor of the union than of industry. Unions are seeking to take advantage of industry and exploit them, just as they were once exploited."[6] In Graham's mind, by 1958 the exploited had become the exploiters, which meant that the leaders of industry had become victims of greedy labor leaders.

With a preferential option for capital, Graham continued his crusade against unions in the following year, taking the occasion of Labor Day to tell workers that they should be grateful rather than greedy for their extraordinary material blessings. "No workers in any land," he preached in 1959, "enjoy higher wages, a better standard of living, and better working conditions than America's laboring people. Even those in relatively low income brackets live like kings compared to other laborers throughout the world." Rather than asking for more from leaders in industry, the American worker should "be grateful to God that he is free to select the kind of work he is able to do. He should be grateful that he lives in a land where collective bargaining and a fair deal for the working man is encouraged . . . that he lives under the stars and stripes where the government bends every effort to obtain the dignity he justly deserves as an honest workman."[7] This admonition was simply a variation on a theme that Graham had been preaching for years. In his 1956 Thanksgiving sermon, for example, he had implored Americans to be thankful "for opportunity. . . . In America, the land of free enterprise, business and industry, there are no respecters of persons. . . . But in America there is opportunity for education, for service, for friendships, and for spiritual enrichment and development."[8]

Graham did not completely absolve capital from responsibility in his 1959 sermon, but instead called on both labor and capital to practice justice. "Justice in God's accounting," he claimed, "means a fair deal for both capital and labor. An employer who exploits his employees for the purpose of unfair profit stands condemned before the court of God's justice. But, on the other hand, workers who demand higher wages from industries which can't afford them stand condemned as greedy and unfair." Once again, however, his apparent neutrality broke down when he demanded that American workers should be grateful for their wages, whatever they may be, while also failing to demand that owners should be content with whatever befalls them. Predictably, the evangelist pointed to Jesus to back this advice: "Jesus said to the soldiers of his day, 'Be content with your wages.' "[9]

But Graham was wrong. Nowhere do the Gospels ever report Jesus as having said that; it is rather in the Gospel of Luke where we read that John the Baptist ordered soldiers not to extort money by threat or lies, but to be satisfied with their wages (3:14). Still, this minor point makes little difference in the long run, because in the years to come the biblicist Graham would point to other verses to back his gospel of content. Among his favorites was Philippians 4: 11 ("I have learned to be content with whatever I have"[10]), which he loosely interpreted to mean that the Apostle Paul "was not dependent upon circumstances for happiness. He did not cherish a grievance against life when he was short of money, or deprived of comfort or exposed to unfair criticism. He thought more of what he could give than what he could get."[11] Of course, there were other texts that Graham could have cited—for example, the famous story of Moses' efforts to set his people free from slavery in the oppressive land of Egypt. As one of the most important figures in the Hebrew scripture, Moses provided a brilliant counterpoint to Paul's tired conservatism; no biblical character was more discontent with economic stations in the history of Israel than Moses was. But Graham ignored all this. Reflecting his own social location as an owner, the evangelist hid Moses in the bushes and highlighted the Philippians passage as the economic gospel of success.

Far from academic, Graham's suggestion that American workers adopt Paul's attitude of content was his consistent reply to everyday economic situations. Consider one example. In 1960, when a common laborer asked the evangelist how to be content in light of not having had a raise for four straight years, Graham's reply seemed oblivious to the strains of shrinking income and growing household budgets: "There are two ways of being rich—have a lot, or want very little." And lest the worker doubt the implied advice, Graham once again returned to the source of sources.

"Jesus," he wrote, "was the most satisfied man that ever lived, and He had less than most of us. 'The foxes have holes, and the birds their nests, but the Son of Man has no place to lay His head.' He had learned the secret of adjusting His wants to His needs."[12] Ultimately, then, Graham did indeed ground his gospel of content in Jesus, not merely in the writings of the Apostle Paul. But the Jesus of Graham's economics was not the one he cited at other points in his ministry—the one who was divinely anointed to feed the hungry—for Graham well knew that this Jesus had long empowered poor workers to band together for collective action against owners and management. Rather, the Jesus of Graham's economics was the man who had no livable wage and not even a home to call his own, and yet lived better than anyone else. Given the significance Graham attributed to the practice of imitating Christ, would his Christology not mean that homeless people should be content with their homelessness? Or, more radically, that the people of God should become homeless? As the owner of a beautiful home atop a gorgeous mountain in North Carolina, the evangelist did not pursue these exact questions.

His bottom line, however, was this: "We don't need to learn how to get more, but how to get along with what we've got, and get on with the business of really living."[13] Usually directed at everyday workers, this advice was consistent throughout the remainder of the King years, although it assumed different forms at different points. In 1967 Graham buttressed his gospel of content with the theological claim that one's economic station is part of God's plan for one's life. Consider his response to a laundry woman who described her work as "very hard and uninteresting" and wondered how to respond to job complaints she had heard from her colleagues. Rather than inviting the woman to contemplate collective action for better economic rewards, Graham replied: "For the believer in Christ . . . there is little cause for complaint. We are told that we are to do our assigned tasks 'as servants of Christ, doing the will of God from the heart' (Ephesians 6: 6–7). . . . Your life is planned, and your complaint is against His plan."[14] Her status as a laundry worker in a dead-end job with little economic benefit and no personally satisfying rewards was not the result of a capitalist system out of control; it was the beautiful outworking of God's special plan for her individual life. Was it also God's plan for certain laundry owners to become wealthy by paying lousy wages for unfulfilling work? Given Graham's grand vision of providence, one would think so, but the evangelist wisely left such questions unanswered.

Graham's reply to the tired laundry woman was deeply pious: accept Jesus and celebrate your job as God's plan for your life. Beyond offering this pious advice, Graham also counseled Christian workers to work hard in whatever they do and thereby demonstrate the strength of Christian love. In reply to a factory worker who wondered if "doing just one thing all day long on an assembly line" constituted a life "worth living," Graham advised him to give his life to Jesus. "The next thing," he stated, "is to do the best you can in the task assigned to you. Be a faithful and efficient worker, even if it is screwing a nut on one bolt after another. Others are working all around you. Let them see how a Christian should live."[15] And how should a Christian worker live in the everyday drudgery of Industrial America? "If you will welcome Jesus Christ into your heart and take Him along with you through each day," Graham counseled, "life will become a joy, not a drudge."[16]

According to Graham's gospel of content, then, everyday workers should understand their workplace as part of the divine plan, be content with their work, and encourage others to be similarly content. After all, to fight against one's divinely ordained economic station, attitudinally or otherwise, is nothing less than to rebel against God's economy and to fail in one's mission to witness before others.

Complementary to his gospel of content was a Calvinist respect for frugality. In short, Graham told discontented workers to scale down their economic consumption. By exercising frugality, workers could become less needy, more independent from the demands of the material world and, of course, more content with their lowly economic stations. The Bible, Graham wrote, "does encourage frugality and thrift. Even Jesus said to His disciples after He fed the multitude, 'Gather up the fragments that remain that nothing be lost.' Although our Lord had the power to create, He himself lived frugally and without luxury."[17]

Graham knew exactly what he was espousing—a "new Puritanism," as he later put it, an ethics of austerity in which individuals would gather around a table with little food, in a shelter with little heat, and among a people plainly dressed, all the while giving thanks to the Lord for the simple gifts before them.[18] It was an economics perfectly reflective of an American Thanksgiving during the hard years. Never mind that this was not Graham's own personal practice, in fact, it was light years away from the personal lifestyle of the man who ate in lavish restaurants, rested at a stunningly beautiful mountain retreat, and, though not foppish, basked in sartorial splendor. It was Graham's advice for others, especially those who did not have the luxury to be like him—everyday workers struggling for economic security, hoping for a better economic life for their children, and worrying about their identification with the unions that the evangelist condemned.

It should be clear by now that Graham's gospel of content served the ownership classes quite well. Happy workers who understood their jobs as God's plan and who lived frugal lives would find little reason to join unions and battle for better wages, sustainable pensions, or increased health care for the family. If nothing else, the evangelist's puritanical economics was vigorously anti-union and proudly slavish to owners. All this is not to say that Graham did not encourage the ownership class to mirror God's love and grace; he did exactly this countless times throughout the early King years.

But even here he revealed his bias for owners. For example, in the 1959 sermon noted above, his one and only example of love and grace in the workforce was a company where the *employees* lent the owner ten percent of their salaries for sales and upgrades (and this long before workers regularly contemplated bailing owners out of dire economic situations). Graham's economic thought, then, implored workers not only to be content with their wages and practice frugality, but also to be discontent with the earnings of their employers in difficult situations and to lend some of their meager wages back to employers struggling to maintain businesses or industries. Apparently, the gospel of content did not always apply to the struggling members of the ownership class.

As suggested by the personal company he kept through his years of public ministry—oil barons and CEOs of the most prestigious companies—the evangelist was never one to stand with labor over capital during the King years. His preferential option for capital was evident in two other areas. First, his bias was immediately clear in his vitriolic depiction of unions as entities opposed to Christianity and in favor of the secularization of America—a description the evangelist proffered especially in the beginning of the King years. With no evidence to back his claims, Graham proclaimed in 1952, for example, that "certain labor leaders would like to outlaw religion, disregard God, the church and the Bible." This was a claim he repeated countless times throughout the 1950s. Counseling the "laboring man and his family" to remember that "the father of all trade unions is Lord Shaftsbury, and Lord Shaftsbury was converted under the preaching of John Wesley," Graham argued that rather than modeling the "haughty, proud, rich and self-satisfied" labor leaders of today, workers would do well to humble themselves before God and accept Jesus as their personal Lord and Savior.[19]

Second, as the 1950s progressed, Graham's bias became evident in the eagerness with which he publicized the criminal elements of unions. Indeed, one of the few times he appeared to be a fan of Robert Kennedy was in 1958, when he poured lavish praise on Kennedy's efforts to expose the ties between labor (more specifically, one Jimmy Hoffa) and organized crime. While effusive about Kennedy's work, Graham was also highly critical of the church over the same issue. "Could it be," he asked, "that the church has failed and thus gangsters have taken over in some parts of the labor movement?"[20] Unsurprisingly, the evangelist emphasized "gangsters" rather than "some" in this riveting sermon and thus left his radio audience with the distinct impression that unions were little more than morally bankrupt organizations whose criminal leaders should be indicted and imprisoned by the federal government. Graham did little to qualify that characterization a year later, when he stated that "ruthless men have wormed their way into many of our laboring organizations and have used their positions of power for personal selfish gain."[21] If there was ever a den of greedy thieves in lust with iniquity, Graham suggested, it was in the unions.

The King of Discontent

Graham's anti-union messages stood in sharp contrast to King's positive message that organized labor was an indispensable ally for reaching the beloved community. Unlike Graham, King had a deep and early appreciation for organized labor, partly because some of his key advisers were union organizers. This was a key point of difference: Whereas Graham kept company with leaders of business and industry, King's closest associates always included union leaders. For example, E.D. Nixon, the man who first invited King to assume a leading role in the civil rights fight in Montgomery, was head of A. Phillip Randolph's Brotherhood of Sleeping Car Porters. Randolph himself, who also acted as a King adviser, was "the nation's pre-eminent black labor leader."[22] As a union leader, he had organized marches on Washington by African American labor leaders and worked hard to become part of the executive council of the AFL-CIO. In addition, A.J. Muste, who played a catalytic role in King's commitment to nonviolence, was a general secretary of the Amalgamated Textile Workers of America, directed Brockwood Labor College, and helped develop the practice of sit-in strikes.

Influenced by labor leaders, as well as by the poverty of his own community, King approached organized labor from a different social location than Graham did. As part of the class of white owners, Graham argued that by 1958 workers were exploiting industry owners and managers, but King, with ties to a people who were virtually nonexistent among owners and managers, argued that African American workers continued to suffer at the hands of owners and managers who either underpaid African Americans or slammed the doors in their faces as they searched for livable wages. The exploiters had not yet become the exploited.

On a related note, as a white owner, Graham saw American workers as blessed with a material security known nowhere else in the world, but King, in the trenches of Southern poverty, saw African American laborers as wrecked by an economic insecurity that strangled their educational and cultural growth.[23] Simply put, Graham and King had different visions of America's economic landscape. Whereas Graham envisioned America as the land of a free enterprise system that favors no individuals over others, King never once thought that American enterprise was free; in fact, he saw it as largely restricted to whites with access to jobs and capital. Further, it was just not true, according to King, that in America "there are no respecters of persons," as Graham put it: America of the 1950s and 1960s respected white men with land and money (men like Billy Graham) over all other types of people, especially poor African Americans. Nor was it true that America was the land of free opportunity for education; poor African Americans were always consigned to a second-class education, compared to whites of all classes.

In addition, while Graham told laborers to be satisfied with their wages—to be content with their economic station in life and practice frugality—King did no such thing. King's vision of the beloved community, after all, was wholly based on the theological premise that God was calling individuals and societies to another place—to the Promised Land, a land of milk and honey, a land that differed, attitudinally and materially, from the desert, where starvation and dehydration ruled the day. And this points to a fundamental difference in the ways in which Graham and King understood freedom. If true economic freedom, for Graham, was ultimately spiritual, grounded in one's commitment to Jesus Christ and thereby liberated from material concerns, for King true economic freedom was largely substantive—having access to a good education, a livable wage, adequate housing, and affordable health care.[24] Even as a high school student, King had sharply argued against an economics of content. "We cannot come to full prosperity," he stated at an oratorical contest in 1944, "with one group so ill-delayed that it cannot buy goods."[25] And he continued to preach this economics of discontent throughout his public ministry. "I never intend," he stated in 1956, "to adjust myself to the tragic inequalities of an economic system which takes necessities from the masses and gives luxuries to the classes."[26] Indeed, the theme of "maladjustment," rather than contentment, became prominent in King's economics as the years progressed, with the civil rights activist claiming, partly in response to the pop psychology of his day, that he would much rather be maladjusted than adjusted to such things as oppression and economic injustice.

Finally, as a law-and-order white, Graham stereoscopically focused on labor corruption, but King once again offered a different view. "The current attacks on organized labor because of the misdeeds of a few malefactors," he stressed, "should not blind us to labor's essential role in the present crisis."[27] Therefore, while Graham was sharply criticizing organized labor, especially in the early King years, the civil rights leader was seeking to establish deeper connections between labor and the emerging civil rights movement, believing labor to be indispensable for raising the living standard of African American workers. "Labor unions," King wrote, "can play a tremendous role in making economic justice a reality for the Negro." If there was anything in labor that earned King's wrath, it was not its secularity or immorality or even ties to organized crime; it was an issue that Graham totally ignored in his evaluation of labor—racism. King noted that although national leaders of the AFL-CIO proclaimed their intention to help eliminate racism from labor and the wider society, many local union halls still barred African Americans from membership. The AFL-CIO had also virtually abandoned its drive to organize Southern laborers because of the fierce resistance of white labor oligarchies. Although disturbed by labor's racism, King nevertheless realized that labor had great potential for becoming a key ally on the march toward the Promised Land, and so he cranked up the pressure, calling the AFL-CIO to use more resources to fulfill its pledge and to pull African Americans more deeply into labor's vision of and efforts for economic justice. As the civil rights leader put it, "The organized labor movement . . . must concentrate its powerful forces on bringing economic emancipation to white and Negro by organizing them together in social equality."[28]

King continued to make overtures to labor in the early 1960s and relied especially on A. Philip Randolph, a vice-president of the AFL-CIO, for access and influence to national labor leaders. In 1961, for example, King addressed the Fourth Constitutional Convention of the AFL-CIO at the invitation of then-president George Meany, taking the occasion to sketch the "unity of purpose" that existed between labor and the civil rights movement. "Our needs," he stated, "are identical with labor's needs: decent wages, fair working conditions, livable housing, old-age security, health and welfare measures, conditions in which families can grow, have education for their children and respect in the community."[29] But King also admonished labor for its racism and invited it to participate more fully in the civil rights movement. "Labor," King criticized, "has not adequately used its great power, its vision and resources to advance Negro rights."[30]

This double attitude toward labor—courting and critical—was present in King's thought throughout the remainder of his life. One only need read his last book—*Where Do We Go from Here?*—to see that although his disappointment with labor's racism grew through the years, he never stopped courting labor as an ally for economic justice for African Americans. In the final analysis, King knew all too well that the well-fed and ruddy-faced laborers Billy Graham described so glowingly in his Labor Day sermons were not the same workers King saw in his travels—the underpaid domestic help of Montgomery, the indentured farmers in the Deep South, the unemployed workers in Chicago, the oppressed sanitation workers of Memphis—and that a powerful political lobby was what the African American community desperately needed if it were to move from poverty toward the economic justice of the beloved community. For King, organized labor was exactly that political lobby, and just so, a primary and indispensable tool for entering the Promised Land—for redistributing resources from the wealthy to the poor.

Can Christians Be Rich?

Importantly, while preaching his gospel of content to everyday workers, Graham also gave comfort to the rich by steadfastly refusing to tell them that they should live like Jesus—frugally and without luxury. "There's nothing wrong with having money," Graham preached in 1960, just as he did throughout the King years. "Nowhere in the Bible is a person condemned for being rich."[31] Apparently, Graham felt that the wealthy were to be content with their economic station in life, too. Possessions were not for fretting over at all—if one had a lot of them.

But this is to put the point far too simply, for throughout the King years Graham also listed three reasons that would call one's wealth into question. First, he held that there was something terribly wrong with being wealthy if one acquired riches by sinful means—through oppression of the poor, for example, or perhaps through lying and deceit. In *The Seven Deadly Sins*, he wrote: "It is not a sin to be rich. If you have gotten your riches honestly, God considers you a steward of that which He has given you."[32] Conversely, if you have gotten your riches dishonestly, God considers you a poor and sinful steward of the gifts of God.

With this use of the language of stewardship, Graham was making reference, albeit obliquely, to Jesus' parable of the talents—a parable he had unpacked a bit more fully in earlier works. In *Peace with God*, for example, he had argued that earthly riches are not a sin because "the Bible makes it clear that God expects us to do the best we can with the talents, the abilities, the situations with which life endows us."[33] The parable of the talents, according to Graham, clearly suggested that the servant who did nothing with his money, a poor steward if ever there was one, justly deserved the wrath of God, and conversely, that those who took their talents and multiplied them as much as possible, while using appropriate means, justly earned God's favor.

It is no surprise here that Graham fully embraced the Protestant work ethic that was a marked characteristic of his Calvinist upbringing. Ever faithful to theologians of the heart, however, the evangelist was more inclined to cite the strangely warmed Wesley than to appeal to the cold intellectual Calvin, as he did in a 1960 collection. "John Wesley," Graham wrote, "had a three-fold philosophy about money. He said, 'Make all you can; keep all you can; and give all you can.' "[34] This was an overly simplistic characterization of Wesley's economic ethics, as Theodore Weber's brilliant book on Wesley has shown, but it certainly served Graham's overall argument that the Protestant work ethic was worth adoption by Christians who claimed Calvin and Wesley as their theological ancestors.[35]

We should note, however, that Graham's work ethic appeared to conflict with his gospel of content. In other words, there seemed to be a marked though partly hidden conflict between encouraging individuals to be content with their wages, living frugally along the way, and imploring them to earn as much as possible. But, of course, he had different target audiences in mind when he spoke these conflicting words of economic advice. To be more specific, he held one ethic for workers dissatisfied with their economic station—work hard, be content with your wages, and live frugally—and another for upwardly mobile individuals and people of means—work hard, earn all you can, save all you can, give all you can, and thereby show God that you are a faithful steward of the many talents God has given you.

The evangelist's use of the parable of the talents as a foundational piece for his economics led him not only to allow for and encourage wealth among Christians, but also to insist that there is no virtue in being poor. "Too many Christians," he wrote, "have . . . taken a most sinful and damaging spiritual pride in being poverty-stricken."[36] Perhaps more than any others, these words reveal that Graham was certainly no Lukan theologian. Nowhere did he ever claim, as the Lukan Jesus did, that blessed are the poor. Instead,

Graham preferred the far less difficult saying of the Matthean Jesus: "Blessed are the poor in spirit" (5:3). And here emerges another reason that Graham believed could call an individual's wealth into question—the allegiance of one's heart and mind and soul.

"What God condemns," Graham preached in 1960, "is the love of money—the madness that makes men worship it."[37] What the evangelist had in mind, of course, was the famous verse of I Timothy 6:10: "For the love of money is a root of all kinds of evil." But did Graham also have in mind Jesus' words to the rich young ruler seeking advice for entering eternal life? "Go," Jesus said. "Sell your possessions and give the money to the poor" (Mt. 19: 21). The Matthean Jesus did not say, "Hold onto your money, but just make sure your heart is right." Or, "It is truly possible for you to love God and be rich—just make sure that you do not love your money more than you love God." Recognizing the peril of wealth for practicing proper devotion to God, Jesus instructed the rich young ruler to sell everything and give the proceeds to the poor. And, according to the Gospel of Matthew, when the rich man failed to do so, Jesus turned to his disciples and said: "Truly I tell you . . . it is easier for a camel to go through the eye of a needle than for someone who is rich to enter the kingdom of God" (19: 23–24).

Graham knew the text well, but he clearly opted not to use it as an inducement to get his many rich friends to sell their possessions. Instead, what he did was what rich Christians have been doing for centuries—he spiritualized the text, arguing that what was really problematic was not the rich young ruler's wealth, but his imperfect heart, his sinful affection for his wealth over God. Hence, in Graham's interpretation, what Jesus *really* meant was not that rich people would find it difficult to enter heaven, but that any one who gives his or her heartfelt allegiance to Mammon, rich or poor, would find no rest in God.[38]

So how to test an individual's allegiance to God or Mammon? Answering this question brings us to the final reason that, according to Graham, could call an individual's wealth into question. It is a reason that extends all the way back to the beginning of the King years, when Graham wrote: "Earn your money as much as you can, according to God's laws, *and spend it to carry out His commands*."[39] The evangelist reiterated this point throughout the King years and perhaps most definitively in 1960, when he answered the question of whether wealthy individuals could still be Christian. "It is not how much money we have," he wrote, "but what use we make of that which is entrusted to us, that is the test."[40] Unsurprisingly, the evangelist never gave much thought to specifying what he meant by spending money in ways that reflected the commands of God. Clearly, he did not mean selling one's possessions and giving the proceeds to the poor. But what faithful spending did mean, other than tithing one's income to the church or building "a better world," simply lacked substantive definition in Graham's economic thought. Laissez-faire at heart, the evangelist let the rich go and decide for themselves.

This was not an uncommon occurrence in Graham's economic thought. In *Peace with God*, for example, he had set forth a remarkably progressive understanding of Christian stewardship, but then left it undeveloped, virtually without any substance at all. "Actually," Graham wrote, "we can possess nothing. It is God who owns everything, and we are but stewards. . . . Everything that we see about us that we count as our possessions only comprises a loan from God." Ownership became even weightier in light of Graham's evangelical belief in heaven. "When we clutch an object or a person," he wrote, "we are forgetting that no matter what we can get, we can't take it with us when we go to make our final accounting before the seat of judgment."[41] Fascinatingly, Graham presented a potentially radical economic ethic here—an ethic that could have called for letting go of one's possessions, sharing the goods that one does not "own," or even sharing all things in common, as at least some early Christians had. But again, Graham never specified what it meant, materially, to live as if our possessions are not our own, to let go of the possessions we formerly clutched, and to prepare our lives for the final judgment. In effect, he let the rich be rich.

Is it possible, then, for Christians to be rich? Of course. "Some of the most dedicated Christians I know," Graham observed in 1960, "are people of means, but their financial interests are subordinate to Christ and his kingdom." It is just as possible for rich people to be Christian as it is for poor people to be unchristian. "I know it is possible," Graham wrote, "for I have met wealthy people who are sincere followers of Jesus, and I have met poor people whose every waking thought centered about money."[42] If the rich earn their wealth with moral means, pledge their hearts to God, and use their wealth to carry out God's commands, they should be content, assured that their place in life everlasting is secure. And the poor should be content, too, trusting that their economic station is reflective of the will of God, living frugally, and remembering that the Son of Man had no place to lay his head.

The Tramp, Tramp, Tramp of the Little Man: Against

Colonialism and Communism

Graham also held that America, as a nation, should be content with its economic status. In 1958, while America was still enjoying the so-called Age of Affluence, the evangelist argued that his fellow citizens were guilty of covetousness "as a nation, as a people, and as individuals," with the result being that America was the most materialist of nations.[43] Fashioning its own golden calf, America had placed its repose in material things rather than in God, thereby ignoring Jesus' conviction that our lives do not consist in the abundance of the things we possess.

With its repose in material things, "our whole economy is geared to getting more. The capitalist wants more profit. The laboring man wants more wages for less hours. And all of us are engaged in a mad race—trampling over each other, cheating each other, lying, stealing, anyway we can get it—to get another dollar."[44] Once we were solid Puritans, content with hard work and simple gifts, but by the Age of Affluence we had become libertine gluttons, lusting for more and more and more, whatever the goods might have been, and equating our happiness with the quality if not the quantity of our possessions. In the process we had also become blind to our own selfish economic desires. "We cannot possibly believe," Graham preached in 1958, "that a person can be happy without a refrigerator or a television set. We cannot possibly believe that there are moral and spiritual principles more important to millions than even a plate of food."[45] Seeing "shocking evidence of selfishness and greed on every hand,"[46] Graham identified this insatiable appetite for more goods, more cash, more property, as "the greatest stumbling block to the kingdom of heaven in America today."[47]

King, of course, had a different take on the Age of Affluence. Especially troubling about this "historic period of prosperity," he argued, was that in "'the affluent society,' the Negro has remained the poor, the underprivileged, and the lowest class."[48] Rather than seeing covetousness, avarice, and greed as the hallmark characteristics of African Americans in the 1950s, King simply claimed that his people were hungry for basic economic justice—a good job, a livable wage, and decent education for their children. But Graham admitted no exceptions in his claim that Americans were guilty of covetousness, avarice, greed, materialism, and gluttony. "You say," he preached in 1958, "'But, Billy, I'm not a rich person.' You have shoes, don't you? You have a suit of clothes; you have a dress. Then you are rich by the world's standards. You had something to eat, didn't you?"[49]

In the early King years, Graham virtually ignored the poverty that characterized his own home region, the rural South, where it would take only a quick car ride to see children, white and black, without shoes, without breakfast, and without coats. The evangelist also dismissed the everyday stresses of working individuals whose shoes were tight and worn, whose suit was patched, whose breakfast was mush, all because they were trying, futilely, to make ends meet in the so-called Age of Affluence. To top off his quick dismissal of American poverty, Graham often followed the above rhetorical questions by comparing Americans to Indians, adding more than a little guilt and shame along the way. "In India tonight," he often preached, "over a hundred million people will go to bed hungry tonight—if they have a bed to go to. And when they drive the trucks down the streets of Calcutta tomorrow morning, they will pick up people that died of starvation . . . .The poorest person in this audience tonight is rich by the world's standards."[50] The implication was clear: Americans who would not die of starvation by the morning were not really poor at all; they were "rich," and probably selfish and greedy, too.

The greedy practice of bowing down before the golden calf, according to Graham, resulted in severe damage to the precious American system of free enterprise.[51] There is little doubt that Graham was an economic conservative during the early part of the King years, and his conservative thought, dedicated to preserving the system of free enterprise, was evident not only in his puritanical ethic for everyday workers, but also in his critique of American economic policy. There were three related areas in particular that he was especially concerned about—the federal deficit, inflation, and the tax burden.

In 1958, a year when economic conservatives were still opposed to overspending, Graham lamented a rising deficit, claiming that the "average American is now so used to deficit spending that he cannot possibly realize that we are on the broad road that leads to the destruction of our national economy." For good measure Graham cited anonymous "economic leaders" to give his point additional substance: "Many of our leading economists have warned that that it is only a question of time before our deficit financing will be at the end of its rope. In 1958 alone we went into the red by nearly twelve billions of dollars."[52] One can only imagine what Graham would say about today's federal deficit.

Graham returned to the conservative theme of rising deficits throughout the King years. In 1967, for example, he delivered perhaps his most stunning indictment of deficits. "We have begun to live far beyond our means," he cried. "Millions now think that society owes them a living." This, of course, was a slap to the sense of economic entitlements that Barry Goldwater was also decrying at the time. "Politicians," Graham continued, "are forced to vote billions of our grandchildren's money to feed our selfish wants and desires. Thus we now have a fantastic national debt. No nation in history has ever owed so much." Graham was so concerned about the rising deficit partly because it offended his puritanical sensibility of not using credit to pay for things, and partly because he believed that it led to the destabilization of the American dollar—and to inflation. "The pressure is beginning to build up on the dollar," he announced in 1967. "The British pound may be devalued again next year, and many economists question whether the dollar can withstand the strain."[53] Graham had sounded this mantra years earlier. In 1960, for example, he had argued that America's greed and selfishness would result in a deficit that would drive the American dollar to "lose its stability and the confidence of the world. This is already beginning to happen as millions of dollars worth of gold flow out of this country every month." And a collapsing dollar, Graham warned, would only lead to "inflation that threatens the very structure of this country."[54]

Although contemporary U.S. economic policy suggests that he need not have done so, Graham also drew a connection between a rising deficit and a higher tax burden on the American consumer. A growing deficit, he argued in 1958, "means higher and higher taxes." If for no other reason, the treason implicit in a higher tax rate should deeply offend American patriots. "[Higher taxes] was one of the basic reasons that our forefathers left the old country," Graham preached. "They wanted to escape the high taxes of Europe." But there were other reasons to be concerned about high tax rates, too, and about inflation and a bloating federal deficit. Graham saw all of these economic problems as the clearest of indicators of the potential demise of America itself. Just look at Rome before its fall from greatness, he preached. Before it collapsed, Rome had high taxes that it used "for free bread and circuses for the populace."[55] And just as Rome collapsed, so too would America—unless it reversed its liberal tax-and-spend policies.

Perhaps more interestingly, Graham also interpreted high taxes, a rising deficit, and inflation as part of a left-wing conspiracy to undermine America's economic greatness. "Few people realize that this is one of the objectives of Communism—to get us to spend more and more on our- selves until we are financially bankrupt."[56] At last, then, America's liberal economists, with their willingness to allow for deficits so that the country could invest in jobs, were little more than communist dupes, unwitting tools of an evil ideology plotting the downfall of America and its vast riches and resources.

If there was anything that the capitalist Graham was opposed to in eco- nomic matters, it was the system of communism as he saw it during the 1950s and 1960s. Although he favored using rhetorical, McCarthyite lan- guage when speaking about communism, Graham did set forth a relatively full description of communism in a 1963 sermon titled, appropriately enough, "Why Communism Is Gaining"—a sermon that addressed the all-important question of whether communism was a Christian practice. Graham's first task was to explain the difference between early Christian communalism and the communism practiced in Soviet Russia or Red China. Here Graham had in mind Acts 4:32 ("now the whole group of those who believed were of one heart and soul, and no one claimed private ownership of any possessions, but everything they owned was in common"). With this controversial passage before him, the evangelist had to concede that some early Christian sects were communal. "But these attempts," he argued, "are sharply different from modern communism. . . . They were all voluntary groups, and they were governed democratically. The leaders were selected by the people, and the laws governing the people were determined by free voting."[57]

Graham did not provide any biblical argument to make his case, and with good reason, because his argument about democracy in early com- munist sects was pure fantasy; democracy was simply absent in the political and economic thought of early Christians. Indeed, Graham himself seemed to have eventually recognized as much, because he dropped the democracy argument in 1967, when responding to a reader of "My Answer," who pressed him on the differences between the radical economics of early Christians and the practices of contemporary communism. In response, Graham returned to his earlier argument, but this time with an entirely different twist: "There is a great difference here. The 'having all things common' of the early Christians was based entirely on love. There were no force or coercion. There were no police to enforce the will of the authorities. In fact there were no authorities; it was entirely a matter of the heart."[58]

Graham's first word, then, was that communism, as practiced by Soviet Russia and China, was not the same as the communal living of early Christian sects. Unfortunately, the evangelist did not attend to any similarities that might have existed between early Christian communalism and twentieth-century communism; doing so, of course, would have been anathema to his conservative economics. Instead, he went on to define communism as an economic system that favors "the replacement of private property and land and capital by common ownership and the replacement of private management by collective administration."[59] Two years earlier, after reading *Life*'s series on communism, Graham had stated essentially the same thing, although in that skeletal description he had actually cited Karl Marx. According to Graham's reading of *Life*, Marx taught that the achievement of a communist society "would take wholesale abolitions of private property, money, buying and selling, distinctions between town and country, and even divisions of labor itself."[60]

Graham's shallow description of Marxist economics, attributable in part to relying on *Life* as a primary analytical source, is not worth addressing here; more interesting is the substance of his opposition to communism. To understand Graham's deep opposition requires remembering the primary characteristic he identified in his distinction between Christian communalism and twentieth-century communism—freedom. Graham, that is, opposed the economics of communism in large part because he believed it undermined the God-given freedom possessed by the individual. The abolition of private property, common ownership, and collective administration—all these were wrong because they undermined an individual's God-given right to choose his or her own labor, to keep the economic rewards of his or her work, and to purchase property for creating a safe haven of Christian love and warmth for one's family.

If we want to see the damage caused by communism, Graham preached in 1959, just take a look at Red China. "Individual freedom is gone and the normal family life existence of centuries . . . is being destroyed. An entire nation is being driven to live in communals where love and home are only memories. It is true that great material progress is evident, but at what a price! Christ said, 'Man shall not live by bread alone,' but Red China is trying it."[61] With its denial of individual freedom, China's economy led to the rise of secularism, the breakdown of the family, the collapse of love—and also the lobotomy of human personality. "In Red China," the evangelist preached, "we see a frantic effort to make a conditioned, brain-washed man to be used as grist for the State."[62] Interestingly, Graham's concluding response to China was a sound byte from the political theology of the Catholic philosopher Jacques Maritain (though Graham, of course, did not cite him): "Man was made not for the state, but for fellowship with God."[63]

Graham opposed the economics of communism also because of what he believed to be its materialistic dimension—its stereoscopic focus on bread alone. In faithful opposition, the evangelist reminded his audience that the human being does not live by bread alone and that any promise of human fulfillment that grounds itself in the quality and quantity of bread for the human body is bound to fail miserably. Just look at welfare states, he argued in 1965. "Some time ago I was visiting in a welfare state where one of the church leaders said to me: 'We in the church have fought for better living conditions and a higher standard of living. In this country we now have security from the cradle to the grave; but we are faced with psychological problems . . . which are just as great and devastating.' "[64] Similarly, communism was utterly devoid of concern for the human heart.

There is yet another reason Graham provided for opposing the economics of communism, especially as he saw it practiced in the Soviet Union—the nature of the ministry of Jesus. When speaking about what he took to be the evil practices of communism, Graham invoked Jesus, and not just any Jesus, but a Lord and Savior who had expressed no preferential option for the poor, who had steadfastly refused to set class against class, and who had clearly chosen not to stand merely with the proletariat. "Although He refused to put class against class," Graham wrote in 1965, "we read that the common people heard Him gladly. Yet he was as concerned for the bourgeois as He was for the proletariat. He had as much time for the rich young ruler as He had for the blind beggar, and He was as concerned for Nicodemus as He was for the poor lame at Siloam's pool."[65] Jesus was no communist, Graham preached, and so his followers should not be, either.

It is not true, however, that Graham merely condemned the economic practices of communist countries. One of the evangelist's most fascinating and positive evaluations of communism is found in his 1956 book on the seven deadly sins, especially in the chapter on gluttony, where he astutely observed that "communism, with its multiplied millions of adherents, promises to help the helpless." For Graham, this promise was important for at least two reasons, one of them biblical and the other pragmatic. On the one hand, the promise was a faithful response to the demands of scripture, and here Graham drew from Amos 6:4: ("Woe unto them . . . that lie upon beds of ivory").[66] If the evangelist admired communism for any reason, it was its adamant refusal to allow its citizens to lie on beds of ivory. Graham openly lamented that while America was lounging beside a swimming pool constructed with the rewards of capitalism, selfishly sipping a lemon-flavored tea every now and then, communist countries were actively undertaking a godly mission to work hard and help the poor out of their misery.

Indeed, Graham preached that one of America's greatest faults in the early part of the King years was its selfish refusal to share its material wealth more fully with the world's poor. "Three-fifths of the world," he reported in 1956, "live in squalor, misery and hunger. Too long have the privileged few exploited and ignored the underprivileged millions of the world."[67] In his New Year's Day sermon of that same year, Graham had made the point much more colorfully, more pointedly, and perhaps more progressively than he ever had before and ever would again:

> I wonder if one of the reasons for our current foreign problem is that
> we've failed to share our supplies with the world's needy. Too often
> we have hobnobbed with the advocates of the colonial philosophy
> and have forgotten the little man. This is where Russia is making great
> gains while we continue to lose face in the areas of the world where
> extreme need exists. *We must reject outmoded colonialism.* We must
> begin to champion the little man. We must have Christian compas-
> sion for the starving, suffering, shackled people of the world and inter-
> pret our words into actions of love and kindness. We must not only
> give of our surplus goods, but we must share our know-how and our
> equipment with those who are starving. All over the world we can
> hear the tramp, tramp, tramp of the little man—the men that have
> not. They're trampling by the millions, and they are soon going to run
> over us unless we are willing to share the surpluses that God has
> endowed us with.[68]

At first glance this remarkable extract, a foretaste of the emergence of post-
colonial Christian theology, seems to be a fine example of progressive
Christian economics—an argument that governments have a responsibility
to take care of the poor. But that is too shallow an interpretation, for in
1956 Graham was calling not for a welfare state that would alleviate the
demands of poverty in the United States, but rather a dramatic revision
within American foreign policy—a shift away from a you-have-we-take
system, what he called "outmoded colonialism," and toward a program of
foreign aid that would provide capital, material resources, and the required
technological knowledge for moving a developing country out of poverty.

Why did Graham suggest a considerable increase in foreign aid for developing countries but not for the elimination of poverty at home? There are
two answers here. The first, addressed in above sections, is that in the early
King years Graham did not have a sense that America's poor were truly
poor. In 1956 the evangelist saw extreme need not among the American
poor but in developing countries such as India. The second reason, which
gets to the heart of his politics, is his sense that if America did not provide
aid for the world's poor, communism would fill the gap and take over
developing countries, which would then join forces with Soviet Russia or
Red China in a bid for world domination: The little man could become
way too big a threat. To be sure, Graham believed that Christian compassion demanded caring for the world's poor, but the threat of communist
domination appeared to be the major reason for his urgent sense that
America must begin to redistribute wealth to developing countries.

Although a few blips would appear on the screen, Graham's alarmist
condemnation of America's foreign aid program became shriller as the
King years progressed, at least until the mid- to late 1960s. In 1962, for
example, he preached a sermon in which he claimed that "the world of

angry, hungry men are looking to us for answers, and we're not giving them answers. . . . They have asked for bread, and we've given them a stone." Africa, South America, and Southeast Asia were all experiencing revolutions, Graham reported, "and we snore complacently while one nation after the other is nibbled away by the purveyors of the Big Lie."[69]

Why was communism the big lie? Graham held many reasons for using this phrase, some of which have already been noted, but in economic matters he believed that communism's biggest lie was its promise of delivering a utopia. The evangelist held that eschatology, the doctrine of the end times, was the one and only key to unlocking the secret and essence of communism. "It took me a long time," he stated in 1964, "to realize that I couldn't debate or argue with a true communist until I understood eschatology . . . because the communist says he's going to change the world. He's going to make a new world."[70] But the promise of delivering a world that would revolutionize capitalism and bring about economic justice for the proletariat is a big lie, primarily because economic justice will arrive only with the Second Coming of Jesus, when "we are going to have two chickens in every pot, and two cars in every garage, and two television sets in every home." Jesus will come again, and when he does, he alone will establish "a tremendously affluent world."[71] The communists will not and cannot do it, the socialists will not and cannot do it, and even the capitalists will not and cannot do it. When economic justice comes to the world—and it will—it will come only through the miraculous work of God at the Second Coming.

King disagreed yet again. Like Graham, King had serious misgivings about communism—its "ethical relativism," its "metaphysical materialism," and its totalitarian forms.[72] Holding that communism's political totalitarianism subjected the individual to the state, King also echoed the political philosophy of Maritain: "Man is not made for the state; the state is made for man."[73] But following in the footsteps of one of his college professors, Samuel Williams, King enthusiastically praised communism as a "protest against unfair treatment of the poor," and thus as a serious challenge to any follower of Jesus, who, after all, was anointed to preach the Good News to the poor.[74] Ultimately, underlying the wide difference between King's and Graham's evaluative analysis of communism was nothing less than Christology: Graham's Jesus embraced the bourgeois and the proletariat equally, but King's expressed a clear preferential option for the poor.

In addition, King, like the communists, set forth his own utopia—the beloved community—and insisted time and again that this community could emerge in human history. In this sense, King sharply opposed Graham's sense that economic justice was possible only at the time of the Second Coming. Compared to King's here-and-now economics, Graham's economic theology appeared to be little more than a vague promise of a pie in the sky, the type of promise that white bourgeois Christians had long offered the hungry masses. In short, King was far too optimistic about the economic possibilities within human history, and far too angry at the delaying tactics of bourgeois Christians, ever to accept Graham's quick dismissal of communism's utopia. Plus, as a liberal theologian, King simply did not believe the evangelical claim that Jesus would really come again to set things straight in the course of human history.

King's economics ethics, however, did converge with Graham's, albeit slightly, on the issue of international aid. Like the evangelist, King lambasted American foreign policy as largely a colonialist practice. "We in the west," he wrote, "must bear in mind that the poor countries are poor primarily because we have exploited them through political and economic colonialism."[75] King eventually recommended a Marshall Plan of sorts to eliminate poverty throughout the world, and especially in Asia, Africa, and South America. But unlike Graham, King was not even slightly inclined to suggest that the threat of world domination by communist states should be the driving force behind a significant increase in international aid. For the civil rights leader, the best reason for developing a new Marshall Plan is the religious conviction that all of humanity is created in the image of God and that each person is of infinite value. "If we accept this as a profound moral fact," King argued, "we cannot be content to see men hungry, to see men victimized with ill-health, when we have the means to help them."[76]

Perhaps more important, however, was King's comprehensive understanding of colonialism. Unlike Graham, King set forth a notion of *domestic* colonialism, and claimed that the American government practiced this colonialism by constructing slums, isolating them from mainstream economic society, and then refusing to eradicate them. Colonialism was not just something that America engineered abroad; it was an economic practice that the U.S. government encouraged and supported within its own borders. King expressed this notion of domestic colonialism most pointedly in 1966, when he became a resident of Lawndale, a slum in Mayor Daly's Chicago, in order to draw attention to the plight of Northern slum dwellers. "It was a vicious cycle," King wrote about Lawndale. Without education, slum dwellers could not find a decent job, and so they had to turn to welfare. But once on welfare, the state prohibited them from owning property, including cars that would give them access to mainstream economic life. Trapped in the ghettos, the slum dwellers were then forced to buy overpriced goods in stores that practiced price gouging on virtually all of their goods. In effect, slum residents became powerless individuals in a colony whose important decisions about daily living were always dictated from outside the slum. "Many of its inhabitants," King added, "even had their daily lives dominated by the welfare worker and the policeman. The profits of landlord and merchant were removed and seldom if ever reinvested."[77] In his fight against domestic colonialism, King gave little thought to the federal deficit, inflation, and a weakening dollar. The main challenge was not to drive down the deficit, but to spend the money required to eliminate poverty.

On Ghettos and Riots

While Graham largely ignored the demands of domestic poverty in the early part of the King years, all this began to change in the mid-1960s, when urban riots broke out in Los Angeles and other American cities. It is not easy to find references to ghetto life in Graham's sermons and writings before Watts erupted in 1965, but once the riots were unleashed, ghetto life became one of his favorite topics for social commentary.

In 1964, one year before Watts erupted, a member of the media asked Graham about the cause of America's "moral and spiritual decay," and his response, typical of his conservative politics, warned against the dangers of relying too heavily on the federal government. "I think," he stated, "that in our affluence . . . we are looking to big government instead of to God. We think we can pass a law in Congress or that we can vote an extra billion dollars and solve any problem in the world. We are beginning to find out that dollars cannot buy everything. And I think that, of course, the basic problem is the human heart."[78] But Graham himself turned to big government in his own way when the riots of Watts took center stage in 1965.

From his safe haven in Montreat, North Carolina, Graham announced that Watts was "only the beginning—a dress rehearsal for revolution," and that Congress should immediately drop all other pressing concerns and "devise new laws to curb the type of violence" erupting in Watts and other places. New "tough laws" were desperately needed because of a primary cause of the riots—"sinister forces . . . trying to set race against race and class against class with the ruthless objective of overthrowing the government." Interestingly, Graham did not merely say that the riots were caused by individuals with sin-sick hearts. To be sure, he felt that the riots suggested the need for "a great spiritual awakening in America,"[79] but his major emphasis in Montreat was that Congress should pass new legislation that would bring control to an anarchistic situation caused by "sinister forces." In effect, he was ignoring his own advice and calling upon big government to become bigger—not to plow investments into poor areas but to add to its mounds of legislation and give enforcement officers more work to accomplish. Graham, it turns out, was not as opposed to big government as he wanted his followers to believe; he was simply opposed to the type of big government favored by liberal economists and social activists like King.

Graham's response from Montreat also implored King to join together with other civil rights leaders and declare a moratorium on all civil rights demonstrations, at least "until the people of the North and West have had an opportunity to digest the new civil rights acts."[80] At times a hardnosed pragmatic opportunist, then, the evangelist took the occasion of the Watts riots to strike out against the civil rights movement, daring to link nonviolent marches with violent riots.

King had a different perspective on Watts. Hearing his fellow clergy members condemn the violence and its perpetrators, the civil rights leader claimed that the clergy should be "as vigorous in condemning Negro conditions causing the riots" as they were in criticizing the violence.[81] King himself described the riots as "absolutely wrong, socially detestable and self-defeating," but he took care to add that equally deplorable was "the continuation of ghetto life that millions of Negroes have to live in. They are in hopeless despair and they feel they have no stake in society. This is the basis of the problem." More particularly, he identified hopeless despair caused by poor economic conditions as the primary cause of the Watts riots. "I hope they will not spread," King stated. "But due to joblessness and housing conditions, every northern community is a potential powder keg." Because he identified the primary cause of the riots as economic, he also suggested that the solution to the riots was primarily economic. "We must get rid of the ghetto," he argued, "and bring Negroes into the economic mainstream of American life."[82] King conceded that the use of police force was required to restrain the rioters in the short term, but he emphasized that the long-term solution to the problem lay in "better housing and economic conditions and opportunities for Negroes."[83]

After his initial comments from Montreat, Graham traveled to Los Angeles and, fitted with a bullet-proof vest, surveyed the riot area by helicopter. Following this well-protected tour, the evangelist shifted his thinking on the riots just a bit, this time conceding that poverty and lack of education were parts of the volatile mix of Watts—something he had not done earlier, or at least with any marked emphasis. However, he again noted his belief that sinister forces were behind the riots, and that the underlying cause of the riots was the spiritual revolt of humanity against God. And he once again publicly linked the riots and the civil rights movement. "I believe the riots have hurt the civil rights cause," he stated.[84] It was as if Graham was forcing the fulfillment of his own dire prediction.

As the riots spread to other cities, Graham continued to call for Congress to pass legislation that would quell the sinister forces that he believed were running rampant in the inner cities. In 1966, after returning from a crusade in London, he even called upon President Johnson and the FBI to "identify these groups who are teaching and advocating violence, training in guerilla tactics and defying authority."[85] The situation, Graham believed, had become too desperate not to inform the American people of the identity of the extremist race agitators.

At first glance, Graham's 1966 statements seem to be merely more of the conservative rhetoric he had spouted during the Watts riots, but there is a significant point of evolution to note. Exasperated by the continuing violence in urban America, Graham took a new step, even a dramatic one, suggesting that President Johnson and Congress "take some of the money we are giving away abroad and get rid of these ghettoes that have no place in affluent America. It has always seemed incredible to me that so much poverty should exist side by side with so much wealth in places like

Manhattan."[86] It is important not to miss this remarkable development: For the first time, Graham was publicly calling for moving funds earmarked for foreign aid, which he had earlier favored as an indispensable tool for fighting communism, to social welfare programs that would eliminate ghetto life in the United States.

Interestingly, just a year earlier, he had stated that tearing down skid rows paled in comparison, at least in terms of its social effects, to saving individual souls.[87] Graham did not let go of that conservative point in 1966, but his emerging thought clearly reflected a newfound discovery in and a correlative emphasis on the benefits of eliminating ghettos. Why? Actually, Graham's development should not come as a great surprise, primarily because it follows from his concern for law and order, as well as from his hatred of communism. Because he believed that the ghettos were breeding grounds for "sinister forces," that some of these forces were communists, and that the threat they posed was increasingly dangerous to the soul of America, Graham came to believe that eliminating ghettos was simply another way of fighting anarchy and communism. More pointedly, it seems that he made the shift in his thinking because he was becoming increasingly fearful that communist-inspired African Americans were plotting a violent overthrow of the U.S. government. Indeed, his concern for the security of white America in the face of an increasingly hostile African American population seems to have been the primary catalyst that fueled his suggestion for shifting monies from foreign aid to domestic programs designed to eliminate ghettoes.

Whatever the cause might have been, however, Graham's call for eliminating ghettos continued as the King years progressed. At the presidential prayer breakfast in 1966, for example, he took a small part of the occasion to suggest that tough love—a love that destroys all that is against love—required attacking ghetto life. "If we love the poor and underprivileged," he stated, "we will want to destroy the slums and ghettos that have no place in American life."[88] Graham found the theme of this sentence important enough to repeat, almost with the exact same words, for his radio audience in that same year: "If we love the poor and underprivileged," he preached, "we will want to destroy the slums and ghettos that have no place in an affluent America."[89] America, according to the Gospel of Billy Graham, was about wealth and prosperity, not about poverty and ghettos, and just being true to the health and welfare of the American character required eliminating this cancerous body known as ghettos.

All this is not to say that Graham did not occasionally slip back into patterns of emphasizing tough legislation, as well as individual salvation, at the expense of his idea of eliminating ghettos. For example, in 1967, during yet another high point of urban rioting, he preached a relatively shallow sermon against linking riots and poverty too closely: "We have been told over and over again by some of our leaders in Washington," he observed, "that poverty is the cause of crime. This just is not true." To understand that this is not true, just remember the Depression, when people were truly poor.

"We are not as poor today," he argued, "as in the thirties; yet there was no rioting, no looting, nor killing of police officers then." For Graham, the comparative evidence suggested that poverty was not the driving force behind crime. "The problem of rioting and crime is far deeper than just poverty. No amount of money is going to change the present situation. We need new, tough laws against the subversive elements that are seeking the overthrow of the American government."[90]

Similarly, during the 1967 riots in Detroit and Milwaukee, Graham thundered forth with these same black-and-white themes in another sermon, this one titled "America Is in Trouble," in which he belittled "naïve psychologists and sociologists who still say that the root cause [of the riots] is poverty or the lack of job." After belittling these professionals, Graham then praised the conservative Joseph Jackson, the president of the National Baptist Convention and, more interestingly, a strident opponent of King's liberal-structural methods for transforming American society. "One of the great Negro leaders of America," Graham announced, "is Dr. Joseph Jackson . . . [who] recently said, 'No sociologist has yet told us what corrupts the human spirit more—poverty or wealth. I am convinced,' he said, 'that men have the power to withstand and defy an evil environment. It's not poverty that makes a person what he is,' says Dr. Jackson. 'It's the person himself and the spirit upon which he feeds.' " Pulling out all the stops, Graham then cited the favorite president of the African American community: "As a boy, Abraham Lincoln lived in terrible poverty, far worse than any known in America today. Yet from this environment he grew to be known as Honest Abe, and his name is immortal wherever men love freedom."[91]

In sermons like this one—and there are many others just like it—the earlier nuances disappeared. Rather than speaking of poverty as a significant factor in the rioting, Graham seemed to dismiss it as utterly insignificant, returning to the themes he felt most comfortable preaching—that humanity's "basic problem is spiritual, not social," and that humanity "needs a complete change from within."[92]

A Conscientious Objector in the War on Poverty?

Clearly, Graham's economic ethics experienced a back-and-forth dynamic in 1966 and 1967. On the one hand, he called for the elimination of slums, and on the other, he dismissed poverty as an unimportant factor for removing despair and violence from ghetto life. But this fascinating back-and-forth movement appeared to break down altogether at a Kiwanis luncheon in April 1967, when Graham sharply criticized President Johnson's Great Society initiatives, including the elimination of poverty. This was not the first time he attacked the Great Society—he had been doing so since 1965—but it was certainly his most colorful criticism to date.

The evangelist told the Kiwanis members that the 1966 congressional elections, held two years after President Johnson's own election, suggested "a growing uneasiness about big government intruding into every area of our lives. People are beginning to sense a melting away of their personal liberty. They are becoming alarmed at the possibilities of federal power and a decay of local government and the wasting away of personal freedom."[93] Swinging away from the Democrats, the voters had expressed their concern that government was becoming too big, too oppressive, and too anti-liberty. Of course, any well-informed Kiwanis member would have understood that the uneasiness of "the people" was actually Billy Graham's, too, and that his expressed concern about big government was a less-than-subtle attack on President Johnson's efforts to transform America into the Great Society. For a variety of reasons, not all of them related, Graham was especially concerned about the Johnson Administration's War on Poverty.

First, Graham believed that that the "big government" required to execute the War would simply chip away at individual liberty, especially through taxation, giving the federal government greater power to control the economics of local communities and individual households. Second, he sensed that the War would provide economic rewards for idleness—a practice that ran directly counter to one of the foundational sources for Graham's economics, namely, II Thessalonians 3: 10 ("Anyone unwilling to work should not eat").[94] Just like the author of this biblical letter, Graham firmly opposed giving free bread to the undeserving poor—individuals who could work but simply chose not to do so. Third, the evangelist was offended by the War's anti-Christian materialism, that is, its dogged obsession with the bodily dimension of human existence. "Little mention of the moral and spiritual side of man," he told the Kiwanis members, "is made in discussions of 'the Great Society.' "[95] In an earlier argument, he had also attacked the Great Society's blatant appeal to self-interest, countering that all Americans would do much better if they were to follow Jesus, who became poor for our sake and taught that humanity does not live by bread alone, and his apostles, who "held worldly goods in contempt and cherished the abiding values of the Spirit."[96]

Fourth, Graham was appalled by the view of human nature implicit in the War—a view that understood humanity as actually capable of eliminating poverty. The evangelist had offered this point most clearly in 1966: "President Johnson's goal of the Great Society is certainly an admirable one. . . . But history does not offer much hope. Human nature has always stood in the way. All previous efforts have failed; and there is no valid reason to believe that this effort will succeed, in spite of good intentions."[97] Like communism, Johnson's Great Society was terribly mistaken in believing that humanity, in and of itself, was good enough, capable enough, and strong enough to bring about the elimination of poverty. Humanity was simply too sinful, too stupid, and too selfish to build and maintain the Great Society.

And fifth, on a related note, Graham was disturbed by the War's implicit eschatological failure to recognize that poverty will indeed be eliminated in human history, but only at the time of the Second Coming, never by human hands alone. If the War on Poverty was to succeed, it would need more than President Johnson and the American people; it would need the power of Jesus Christ descending in the clouds.

Unsurprisingly, Graham's conservative scoffing at the War on Poverty was antithetical to King's own efforts to support the War. In January 1964, when he and other black leaders met with President Johnson at the White House, King was delighted to learn that the War consisted of many of the ideas contained in his own proposal for a government-backed compensatory package that would finally lift African Americans out of the poverty created by years of slavery and discrimination.[98] And King pushed hard, in his own way, for the success of the War after his meeting with Johnson. For example, at the 1964 meeting of the Platform Committee of the Republican National Convention, he lobbied for "a broad-based and gigantic Bill of Rights for the Disadvantaged." Inspired by the GI Bill of Rights of 1944, King claimed that just as the government compensated World War II veterans for the time they had spent away from their families and jobs, the government should also compensate African Americans for years of slavery and discrimination.[99] He pushed the same policy proposal at the Democratic National Convention, where he announced that the government should provide a guaranteed annual income that would lift all poor people out of their poverty. More specifically, he also called upon the government to eliminate ghettos and slums, and to provide the poor with free quality education and training, free health care, affordable housing, and full employment—all of the necessary ingredients for moving the poor toward the beloved community.[100]

Theologically, King suggested that the Bill of Rights for the Disadvantaged was one sure way to establish, on earth, the equality that all of us have in the mind of God. "If we are all really God's children," he argued, "then all of us are entitled to the same opportunities, pleasures, and responsibilities."[101] Politically, he claimed that the proposed bill would finally begin to make human rights a reality within the United States. "If we are to talk of human rights in the US," he stated, "we must face the necessity for a program of aid to the disadvantaged which raises the poor white and Negro from poverty and failure."[102] In King's thought, then, Graham's opposition to the War on Poverty was theologically heretical and politically undemocratic—yet another wrongheaded obstruction on the march toward the beloved community.

President Johnson was well aware of Graham's dismissal of the War, and the great persuader was unwilling to let his favorite preacher stray too far from the warm fold of the Oval Office. In fact, Johnson had asked Graham in early 1967, shortly after the Kiwanis Club speech, to serve on the War on Poverty Advisory Council, rightly suspecting that the evangelist's presence would grant the War considerable legitimacy in the minds and hearts of the millions who believed in the old-fashioned Protestant work ethic. But Graham politely declined the invite. "Please forgive me," he penned Johnson, "for turning down your request to serve on the War on Poverty

Advisory Council. I will be out of the country—Latin America, Canada, Europe and Asia—the greater part of this year."[103] Graham, of course, failed to mention that he could not quite stomach the liberal, unbiblical economics of the War.

But like so many others, the evangelist simply could not resist the persuasive powers of Johnson for long, and just one month after he appeared before the Kiwanis members, slapping the Great Society silly, Graham found himself smiling for cameras in a propaganda film extolling the virtues of the Community Action Program of the Office of Economic Opportunity (OEO), which was run by no one other than Sargent Shriver, the liberal relative of John F. Kennedy. Amazingly, Billy Graham, the onetime pacifist in the War on Poverty, had become a "convert," as he put it, and a zealous one at that, to Johnson's plan for fighting poverty with the powers and resources of the federal government.[104] If Graham was once blind to the benefits of the War on Poverty, he now saw them with remarkable clarity for the first time in his life.

Conversion to the War on Poverty

There were two primary forces, according to Graham's own account, that drove him to conversion to the War on Poverty and then participation in the OEO film—Bible study and careful analysis of OEO programs. The evangelist described both of these reasons in Shriver's *Beyond These Hills: A Rural Action Community Film with Billy Graham*. In the two overlapping versions at the Billy Graham Center and Archives, the film shows a smiling Graham and Shriver visiting the hill country of North Carolina— meeting the state's first Head Start graduates, attending a class in which adults were learning to read, and actually helping to turn on a water system that the hill country did not have before the OEO program came on the scene. "I think that it's wonderful," Graham announced at one point in the film, "that we can work together and plan together and build together and have the help that we are getting today."[105]

It was so wonderful, on the one hand, because the OEO program, in Graham's thought, was a faithful response to biblical admonitions to care for the poor. But what about Graham's earlier belief that poverty would never be eliminated until the Second Coming? Graham did not address this specific point in the OEO film, of course, but he did respond to a question, posed by Shriver, about the biblical point that the poor will always be with us. "Well," Graham observed, "Christ said that, and I think that his prophecy has proven correctly. Here it is the middle of the twentieth century, and we probably, if you take the whole world, have more [poor] people today . . . than ever before in the history of the world." Graham did not surrender his belief that poverty would not be eliminated until the Second Coming, but what he clearly did in this film was to shift his emphasis from the descriptive to the normative. "But [Jesus] wasn't giving us a command," Graham explained. "All of his commands were in the opposite direction. If you turn to the 25th chapter of Matthew, you'll find that Christ is saying that we're to go out and to help. . . . We're to feed those that are hungry. We're to give clothes to those that are naked."[106]

But Graham knew this text before the War ever began, and so the question becomes, Why did he not understand it to be supportive of the War before his conversion to Johnson's liberal economics? This question is impossible to answer with certainty, exactly because it goes to the internal motivations of Graham's so-called conversion, but it does seem that Graham acted out of deeply felt obligation to serve his president. With Johnson's prodding, Graham once again opened the Bible for wisdom, and this time he found nothing less than a biblical war on poverty. "In fact," he announced in the film, "I went through the Bible and chose, oh, I would say, about a hundred scriptures that indicate that we do have a moral and spiritual responsibility to help those that are really in need."[107]

This was a major point that Graham would return to in June 1967, one month after making the film, when he traveled to Capitol Hill and personally lobbied for the War on Poverty. Not once did Graham ever lobby for civil rights legislation during the King years, but in 1967 he decided that he would personally lobby, and not *sotto voce*, for his friend President Johnson's pet project to eliminate poverty. "This is the first time I have come to Washington to speak for or against a government program," Graham stated before a gathering of congressional and business leaders, adding that a recent study of biblical texts on poverty had encouraged him to make the jump into the realm of lobbying for the War.[108] Opening his Bible before the leaders, Graham read Deuteronomy 15: 11: "Since there will never cease to be some in need on the earth, I command you, 'Open your hand to the poor and needy neighbor in your land.' " But this was not all, Graham stressed: "There are 175 more passages in the Bible that teach the same thing, making anti-poverty efforts a major teaching of the Bible."[109]

What happened to Graham's earlier concern about handouts—about giving food and drink to the idle? The evangelist addressed this issue too in the OEO film, telling Shriver, "I think people have the wrong ideas . . . about the poverty program . . . the idea that it's sort of a handout, that you're going around giving money to people, and as soon as the money is spent, it's not going to do any good. And, of course, the Bible teaches that this is wrong, that we should give motivation, that we should give people an opportunity. And this is . . . really what the poverty program is doing, and I was really quite surprised and delighted that you're not going around handing out money."[110] What Graham claimed to discover in his trip to the hills of North Carolina was that the Community Action Program was not handing out free goodies to the undeserving but providing tools for the genuinely poor so that they could help lift themselves out of poverty—tools like Head Start, adult education, and something as simple as pipes for running water. "What I've seen today," a smiling Graham stated, "indicates that what you're doing is training people, and you're giving people an opportunity to do for themselves, and this, to me, is a very important point."[111] On the other hand, then, the OEO program was so wonderful because it avoided the liberal economics of handouts in favor of the more conservative economics of training and education.

There are other points of evolution to note here, too. It was not just Bible study and the nature of the OEO program that led to Graham's shift in thinking about the War on Poverty; also underlying his shift was a significant transformation in his evaluation of the economic practices of "big government." Interestingly, the rhetorically gifted Shriver asked Graham in the OEO film if the federal government should even be involved in the War on Poverty. "Didn't the poor used to take care of themselves?" Shriver wondered.[112] Parting ways with his earlier statements, Graham's response actually made the case for "big government," while not using that value-laden phrase. "It's true," he allowed, "that your father and mine did hard work, but our world has changed a great deal since your father's day and my father's day. . . . Now today individual groups in our tremendous population can't do as much proportionately as they could a few years ago. It takes the action of government, and that's one reason why I have supported the idea of the poverty program."[113]

This was not the first time that Graham made this type of argument, either. For example, when a member of the press had asked him in 1963 to comment on the trend of government handling economic problems for the poor, Graham had replied: "Well, I feel that the government has a responsibility to its people in social welfare, yes, and the church couldn't possibly do it all alone."[114] But Graham downplayed this point when he publicized his critique of the Great Society, and he did not return to it again until his conversion. But once he returned to it, he emphasized it time and again, as he did when lobbying on Capitol Hill. There was a time, he told the congressional and business leaders, when individuals and small groups could pull themselves up by their bootstraps and emerge from their situations of poverty. "But this is impossible now," Graham stressed, "and only by government action can we win the poverty war."[115]

What happened to the role of the church in Graham's new economic thought? The evangelist's words in the OEO film provide some clues for understanding the interplay between church and state in his new economics. "Now the Bible teaches," he stated, "that if a man is naturally lazy and idle and he gets drunk and spends his money on drink and so forth . . . he doesn't deserve our help, except to try to get him remotivated, reconverted, reborn and changed so that he'll work for himself. But if a man or a woman is poor and can't help it . . . then, first of all, the church has a responsibility, and until more recently, the church has done nearly all of it, at least in our Western culture."[116] In short, the church's role was to convert the idle poor, to assist the unintentionally poor as best as it could, and then to allow the state to continue what the church cannot do. And this is exactly the state's responsibility—to continue the church's practice of alleviating the demands of poverty when the church can no longer do so. Such was the case in 1967, according to Graham. The economic climate had taken such a turn for the worse that by 1967 churches and voluntary associations could no longer adequately address poverty, which meant that the state had to fill the gap. And thus Graham's economics expressed, albeit unwittingly, the Catholic doctrine of subsidiarity—the claim that the state should do only what individuals, families, communities, and voluntary agencies cannot accomplish with their own resources, time, and energy. Without using the language of subsidiarity, Graham explained its principles to Shriver, adding that the church no longer had "the resources that can be put at your disposal by government, and this is why I stand back and say, 'Hallelujah! Get going!' "[117]

Another important point of evolution to note is Graham's new understanding of true poverty. While Graham had earlier claimed the American poor were not really, truly, genuinely poor, he dropped this point altogether in the OEO film and, in fact, appeared to adopt a new stance on poverty. This time Graham emphasized that "we have thousands of people in this country in genuine need," and that those who could not see such genuine need "have blinders on."[118] Indeed, this genuine need—this true American poverty—was so great that only the powerful resources of the federal government could begin to address the problem adequately.

Still another mark of evolution is a surprising shift away from his earlier gospel of content. Whereas the earlier Graham had encouraged the poor to be content with their low-paying jobs and their low economic station in life, thus mirroring the Son of Man, who was satisfied though he had no place to lay his head, the converted Graham emphasized a different point in the 1967 film. "I think that it's possible to be comparatively poor and spiritually happy," he stated, "but I believe that Christ teaches that we can have both. And he taught us that while we are to go out and proclaim the Gospel, on the one hand, we're also to go and give a cup of cold water in his name, on the other."[119] This new gospel of relative discontent, although not grounded carefully in the Bible, correlated well to Graham's pragmatic vision of a strong America. As revealed in the OEO film, Graham's conversion expressed a pragmatic edge that was only occasionally, and then vaguely, present in his earlier economic work. "Just from self-preservation and the building of our own society for our own good," Graham stressed this time, "I would still want to help the poor, because I don't think that we can build a great America and have one side of the street riding Cadillacs and the other without water, without food, without education."[120]

This was a remarkable statement for a man who had earlier embraced free enterprise, a gospel of content, and small government. Unbelievably, the economically conservative Graham had become an outspoken advocate of Head Start, adult education, infrastructural improvements, all designed to help move poor individuals and families into the mainstream of American economic life and make America the great country it once was. He was not leaving behind his concern for individual initiative; that conservative principle would remain with him throughout the King years.

But he was fully embracing an economics that provided tools for the working poor so that they could help lift themselves out of systemic poverty.

To top it off, Graham, never one to hide his good works, happily reported on his full conversion to President Johnson in a letter dated June 30, 1967. "I talked to Sargent Shriver last night," the evangelist penned, "and he is releasing a film that he and I have made—in full support of the Poverty Program. I hope that this film can be used to arouse the interest of people everywhere in your magnificent attempt to help the poor, needy, and oppressed, especially in our major cities."[121] At last, the converted Graham shouted from the mountaintop that the federal government must set the captive free.

The Ghetto Tax

In the year following Graham's active lobbying for the War on Poverty, the National Advisory Commission on Civil Disorders, charged with investigating causes of and potential solutions to the riots, issued the Kerner Report. Perhaps most famous for warning that America was "moving towards two societies, one black, one white—separate and unequal," the report argued that white society was a primary cause of ghetto life: "White society is deeply implicated in the ghetto. White institutions created it, white institutions maintain it, and white society condones it." The report also suggested that the riots reflected the pent-up frustration of African Americans with their environment—an environment marked by unemployment, underemployment, poverty, poor education, and inadequate housing, among other things. And in light of these problems, the report recommended that the federal government take decisive action to improve the economic lifestyles of blacks in the inner cities, even by providing a "national system of income supplementation," the guaranteed annual income that King had supported.[122]

The media wasted little time in asking Graham about his reaction to the report, and he wasted little time in publicizing his negative response. "Well," he said, "I have two major problems with the report. . . . One, I don't think that it put enough of the blame on those going around the country inciting riots." This reply was a conservative return to the "sinister forces" that Graham had invoked at Watts, when he called for tough legislation, laws with teeth, rather than for social and economic programs, as the most effective method for combating riots. "I think these people are going to have to be stopped," Graham stated, "or we could have some real trouble in the next 24 months."[123]

Graham's second problem with the report reiterated his long-expressed theological view of humanity. "I don't think that the commission recognized that man is a trinity," he argued. The human individual has a mind that needs education, "and we need to spend tremendous amounts of money in education, especially in the ghettoes." The individual also has a body that needs medicine, food, and a standard of living. "But man is also a spirit, and he needs moral and spiritual instruction which gives motivation to our lives."[124] And thus Graham returned, once again, to the one constant theme of his thought—the human heart. "I don't think that the problem is altogether poverty, and I don't think that the problem is altogether education. The problem is the human heart." The evangelist even cited economic statistics to back his focus on the heart rather than on the body. "It came out," he reported, "that the average income of those rioting in Detroit . . . was $117 a week. . . . This indicates to me that poverty was not the real problem. There was something else, and it comes down to human nature and the rebelliousness of human nature. I think only Christ and God can meet that need and change man."[125]

It seems that Graham's two points of dissension from the report would have constituted relatively hardcore arguments against enacting the report's recommendations, but this did not prove to be the case. To be sure, there was a change of emphasis in his thought: During his lobbying for the War on Poverty, Graham focused less on the heart and more on the body, and in his reaction to the Kerner Report he focused less on the body and more on the heart. But this shifting of focus did not mean that he was dropping his concern for the body—a point he made quite clear when a member of the media asked him if he would "stand behind" his "backing of the poverty program last year." Fascinatingly, Graham replied: "Yes. My only change would be I think we need more money. I think that this riot commission's report indicates that we've got to do something and do it fast."[126]

The evangelist went even further two months after his comments on the Kerner Commission when he announced his support for the goals of the Poor People's Campaign, first organized by King shortly before his assassination in Memphis. Asked after the assassination if he supported the march, Graham first warned that such marches can turn ugly and violent, leading society to disorder and anarchy; the evangelist never once developed a healthy appetite for King's methods. While he quickly condemned the methods of civil disobedience—an early slap to King's legacy—Graham also claimed to back the intent of the march. "I went through the Bible," he stated, "and picked out every passage that I could possibly find on the poor. There are hundreds of passages which I didn't realize were there. There is no doubt that we have a tremendous responsibility to the poor as Christians, as a society."[127]

Although the march was designed to draw attention to both rural and urban poverty, Graham honed in on the problem of poverty in the ghettos and set forth breathtaking ideas for eliminating ghetto life—breathtaking, that is, for someone who had initially opposed the War on Poverty. "I don't think in an affluent society like America there is any room for ghettos," he argued. "In fact, I am in favor of splitting our income tax returns so that you have a domestic tax and you have a defense tax. But we also need a ghetto tax. If we can spend 25 billion dollars or 30 billion dollars a year in Vietnam, then we certainly ought to be able . . . [to] get rid of the ghettos."[128] This argument was progressive beyond progressive for an evangelical molded from political and economic conservatism, especially because conservative critics of the War on Poverty were arguing that a guns-and-butter economy was breaking the backs of everyday citizens—killing them with more taxes than they could possibly afford. But Graham, once blind to the genuine poverty of Americans, stood against this conservative groundswell and argued that if America could spend its money fighting for justice abroad, it should certainly do no less on the home front, and that if a ghetto tax was required for economic justice at home, then a ghetto tax should be on the front burner of the legislative agenda.

The evangelist had another idea in mind, too. "I have wondered," he announced, "if the time hasn't come to think in terms of recalling the Peace Corps volunteers [and] sending them to the ghettos of America and do something in this country and set an example to the world." It was Graham's sense that America's troubles—the assassination of King, urban violence, and ongoing racial and economic injustices—were giving America a huge credibility problem, so much so that "what we say abroad doesn't mean as much as it did five years ago."[129] By the end of the King years, then, Graham had deemphasized his earlier plan to combat communism by pumping foreign aid into developing countries, and sounded a clarion call for the return of the Peace Corps troops, the raising of a ghetto tax, and the pumping of millions of dollars into areas of poverty for the purpose of education and training.

Had Billy Graham become an advocate for the welfare state? At least in its early years, before the rising costs of the Vietnam War, President Johnson's War on Poverty, with social welfare programs designed to help individuals from cradle to death, was intent on building upon the foundations of the welfare state that President Roosevelt had begun to construct during the Depression. The Kerner Commission, with its call for a guaranteed annual income, sought to add to the welfare state that Johnson had envisioned, and King's Poor People's Campaign, with its demand for a massive public works program, the construction of integrated housing, and the provision of free education and health care, among other things, clearly favored a massive welfare state over a minimalist state that would support merely a free enterprise system. Thus, insofar as Graham lobbied for the War on Poverty, endorsed the Kerner Commission's call for more funds to address the bifurcation of white and black America, and spoke favorably of the goals of the Poor People's Campaign, he certainly supported the construction of a massive welfare state—if not explicitly, then at least by implication of his words and, on occasion, his uncharacteristic deeds, like political lobbying.

Near the end of the King years, the major difference between Graham's economics and King's was not the standard difference between conservativism and liberalism, because the two preachers had come together in so many ways, including in their full support for the War on Poverty, as well as in their prophetic sense that if America was resolved in spending millions for a war in Vietnam, the least it could do on the home front was to allot the money required to combat poverty. Rather, the main difference between the two figures lay in the implications that each drew from their respective and overlapping economic theologies. Unlike Graham, King frankly concluded that the best economic system for the twentieth century was the democratic socialism found in Sweden. It was more favorable than any other system, King believed, because it successfully addressed the pressing economic need for a "more equitable distribution of wealth."[130] On the one hand, the civil rights leader held that capitalism was an insufficient system because it failed to address the problems of poverty systemically, and that communism was insufficient because it ran roughshod over human rights in its systematic attempts to combat poverty. On the other hand, he found capitalism to be eminently helpful in the sense that it acknowledged and sought to safeguard individual liberties, and communism to be equally helpful because it demanded a systemic approach to poverty. King thus sought to bring together the strengths of the two systems, claiming that "The kingdom of God is found in a synthesis that combines the truths of these two opposites."[131] That synthesis, he believed, could be found in Sweden's democratic socialism. Unlike political totalitarianism, Sweden's social democracy ensured the preservation of individual liberties, and its socialism, unlike unfettered capitalism, embraced the collective means required to eliminate poverty, like the nationalization of some private industries and the establishment of state welfare agencies.

Graham never took this same step. Although his support for the War on Poverty, a significant increase in expenditures for eliminating the bifurcation of black and white societies, and the goals of the Poor People's Campaign implied a commitment to a welfare state of sorts, he never went so far as King in identifying democratic socialism as the best system for combating poverty. Taking that next step, as King had, must have appeared simply unfathomable for the man who continued to love free enterprise as a gift from the Almighty.

A Closing Backlash

If Graham was more economically liberal at the end of the King years than he was at the beginning, he certainly was not showing his stripes with any sense of pride or regularity after King's assassination. Yes, he had announced his support for the goals of the Poor People's Campaign before the movement pitched its tents in Washington, DC, but once the campaign was well underway, Graham struck a different tone, a qualified reversion to his earlier stance on genuine material need. "This march," he preached one month after King's assassination, "must make millions of people throughout the world smile, because the average income of the marchers is far above that of most people in Asia, Africa, Latin America, and even millions in Europe." Graham did not dare to call the marchers "rich," as he had called the American poor in prior years, but he certainly suggested that the poor marchers were, when compared to the rest of the world's poor, relatively well-off. "There is no doubt," he continued, "that terrible poverty exists, not only in the ghettos of America, but also in many other areas of the country as well. Yet, in comparison to many other parts of the world, even the people in the ghetto have clothes to wear, food to eat, and various social services to call upon."[132]

Further, nowhere in this sermon did Graham suggest that he supported the goals of the Poor People's Campaign. He acknowledged that "the Bible teaches that Christians have a great responsibility to the poor in their society," but he quickly glided past this point in order to get to his real emphasis—the human soul. "Many times," he preached, "we get our values confused . . . Jesus . . . indicated that the spirit of a man is far more valuable than a man's body." The implication here was that the Poor People's Campaign had its values confused—that it should focus first on the soul and only then on the body. In a sense, this argument was Graham's own backlash to his earlier emphasis on lobbying for the War on Poverty. This backlash, targeted directly at the campaign and indirectly at his own earlier actions, exploded with rhetorical flourish in Graham's sermon. "Perhaps," he stated enthusiastically, "we Christians need a march on Washington to dramatize the nation's moral and spiritual condition and man's lost condition before God, and his need of personal salvation. It seems that the only way to get attention today is to have a march, a demonstration, or a riot."[133]

Following King's assassination, then, and shortly after his own endorsement of the goals of the Poor People's Campaign, Graham gave voice to a white backlash that would quickly surrender in the War on Poverty, dismiss the recommendations of the Kerner Commission, and allow the Poor People's Campaign to drown in the summer rains. If Graham had come together with King for awhile—and he had done exactly that—he eventually separated himself once again from King's hopes for economic justice. Once the Poor People's Campaign staked its ground in Washington, the evangelist characterized the demonstrators as materially blessed in comparison to the rest of the world, criticized the campaign's methods as a shallow way of attracting attention, belittled the campaign's focus on material needs, and diverted attention away from the campaign's goals by calling upon Christians to form their own march on Washington to dramatize spiritual poverty.[134]

What accounted for the flip-flop? It is impossible to answer this question with certainty, mainly because it requires reaching into the unknowable regions of Graham's motives, but one thing is clear: by May 1968 Graham was no longer desperately trying to please President Lyndon Baines Johnson. He had moved onto Nixon by that point—and Nixon was no Johnson. Playing on and fueling the fears of the white backlash, Nixon failed to enact the Kerner Commission Report, shifted emphasis away from the War on Poverty, and ignored the ongoing demands of those who had been involved in the Poor People's Campaign. Johnson was not absolved of guilt, of course; his shift of attention to Vietnam had first doomed the War on Poverty. But if Johnson had dug the hole for the War on Poverty, Nixon happily shoveled the dirt back in—and Graham did nothing of significance to stop it.

At last, if Graham had once been converted to the War on Poverty, he became a backslider shortly after King's assassination, and recommitment to anything but the old-time Gospel of survival—no one lives by bread alone—seemed unlikely. So, too, did any possibility that King's dream for economic justice would become real. With the death of the civil rights leader, as well as the encouragement of Graham and others who led the white backlash, the dream of the Promised Land quickly died in what would turn out to be one of America's greatest nightmares—the presidency of Richard M. Nixon.

CHAPTER SEVEN

"I'm Not a Pacifist": On Militarists, Pacifists, and Vietnam

"Strongly urge showdown with communism now. More Christians in South Korea per capita than any part of the world. We cannot let them down."[1] It was 1950 when Billy Graham began offering specific advice to U.S. presidents, whether they wanted it or not, and his first words of telegrammed counsel that year were clear—prepare for war. Lest Truman miss the point, Graham followed up several weeks later with a full letter to the president. "I also urge you to total mobilization to meet the communist threat," he wrote. "The Bible many times urges us to be prepared for war, and Jesus Himself predicted that there would be wars and rumors of wars until the end of time, and warned about those who talked peace when there is no peace."[2] Despite his active lobbying, America did not come close to mobilizing all its forces for a clear-cut victory in the Korean War, and the hawkish Graham did not hide his discontent. In 1953, when the warring parties signed a truce to halt the war, he took the occasion of his weekly radio program to register his dissatisfaction. "It was the first war in American history," he complained, "that we have not won."[3] Throughout the past three years of fighting, "we have shown our moral weakness. We have shown that when pressed we could betray our friends and compromise with the enemy."[4]

If there was anything that disturbed Graham about American foreign policy, it was the slightest hint that the United States was giving ground to the godless communists. "There can be no bargaining," he preached. "There can be no parleying or compromise with evil. Let us put again into our foreign policy moral justice, no matter what it costs."[5] This is the same type of advice that Graham would offer a year later, when Dwight D. Eisenhower confronted the problem of Indo-China. "My private opinion," Graham wrote, "is that Indo-China must be held *at any cost*." Still, ever solicitous of political power, even at the expense of principle, the court chaplain also added: "Whatever your ultimate decision, I shall do my best through radio and television to make my contribution in selling the American public."[6]

Although sketchy, these early pieces of correspondence, penned before 1955, contain several ingredients of the war and peace ethic that Graham would adopt throughout most of the King years—an uncompromising determination to fight communism at any cost, a realistic and apocalyptic interpretation of human history, and a Christology that depicted the love of God in Jesus as a moral basis for using violence. On each of these three points, the evangelist diverged sharply from liberal and Christian pacifists, including Martin Luther King, Jr., whose principled commitment to non-violence set forth the possibility of peace on earth, not merely in heaven.

An Early Manichean

Graham's defense of the justifiability of war grew with remarkable intensity during Hungary's bid for independence—a bid mercilessly crushed by Russian tanks on the streets of Budapest. The evangelist's vitriolic reaction to the invasion was the first indication during the King years that he was less in the mold of a realistic just-war thinker and more like a zealous warrior, a holy crusader with a bayonet in the shape of a fiery cross. Unlike just-war theorists, with their disciplined refusal to label the enemy as demonic, Graham exercised little discretion when characterizing the invading Russians. Calling the invasion "a diabolical action," as well as "a throwback to the Middle Ages for its savagery, torture, pillage and rape," and a move that "would make even Hitler and Mussolini blush," Graham sounded forth like a Manichean prophet, a political zealot with crystal-clear visions of good and evil.[7] "For thirty-five years," he added, "the Communists have taught there is no God. They have taught that morals are relative and not absolute. They have laughed and sneered at the Ten Commandments and the Sermon on the Mount." The "aggression and murder" in Hungary was thus "the natural outgrowth of a godless ideology."[8]

This would not be the last time Graham would use the raw, unqualified language of a crusader to describe communism or the Soviet Union. Four years later, when Khrushchev pounded his shoe on the desk at the United Nations and declared that we live on earth not by the grace of God but by the strength of the Soviets, Graham once again expressed the indiscriminate words of a holy warrior. "If ever there was a spirit of antichrist and blasphemy," he cried, "it is here." The evangelist was not bold enough to preach that Khrushchev was indeed the Anti-Christ, Satan's tool at the end of the ages, but he did suggest that "the person and power of Satan" was deeply present in the Soviet premier.[9] Even if he did not recognize it himself, the Soviet leader was a key locus of "invisible demon activity and warfare." Satan, in the form of Khrushchev and his godless communism, was lining up his demonic legions against the forces of Christ, in the form of American democracy and free enterprise, as part of a concerted attempt to dominate the world. As Graham put this, "there is no explanation for what is happening throughout the world today, except that it is by the supernatural activity of a powerful and omnipotent Satan."[10]

The crusading evangelist also sharply critiqued both the UN and America for failing to resist the Soviet Union as it rolled into Hungary. He was especially livid because he rightly recognized that, prior to the invasion of Hungary, America had hinted that it would come to the aid of any who would dare to rebel against the Soviet Union in a bid for independence. America might have been saintly when compared to Russia, but in Hungary's "hour of peril and crisis, no help came. The United Nations proved almost ineffective. The West was too weak and fearful to help the valiant people who were throwing themselves at Russian tanks and dying by the tens of thousands for freedom."[11] Hence the title of Graham's sermon—*Needed! Strong Men*. America did not need the type of effeminate and fearful leadership revealed in Western responses to Hungary; America needed masculine politicians, Christian politicians, men ready to grab their guns, sound the war cry, and charge against the rolling tanks.

Eisenhower was not a strong man. Graham had been an early and vigorous supporter of Eisenhower's bid for the Oval Office, and an earnest defender of the president's efforts to bring unity and prosperity to the nation. But the anti-communist evangelist could not even begin to stomach the president's decision to let demonic forces trample, maim, and kill the godly forces of freedom and justice. Graham thus concluded that although Eisenhower had once been a great military leader, he finally proved weak and ineffective in response to the demonic strength of Khrushchev.

Interestingly, the politician most admired by Graham at the time was Secretary of State John Foster Dulles. While Graham conceded that the secretary had made mistakes during his leadership of the State Department, he emphasized that Dulles wholly redeemed himself at the time of his death, when he finally began "to realize that this conflict [between communism and democracy] was indeed a spiritual one. He was against any appeasement. He felt that not another inch of spiritual or material territory could be surrendered to the forces of evil."[12] Dulles, in other words, had become a "strong man," a holy warrior who rightly recognized that appeasement in the face of Khrushchev was naïve and sinful, and that America had a moral and political obligation to mobilize all its forces for a crusade against godless communism. Of course, Graham did not need Dulles to see the "strong man" needed in America at the peak of the Cold War; all he had to do was look in the mirror and see the epitome of masculine American Christianity.

The Cause of War Is Spiritual

Shortly after the invasion of Hungary, Graham preached a sermon titled "The Cause of War Is Spiritual," in which he made the general case that war is about material *and* spiritual territory, just as Dulles had recognized.

Rather than citing Dulles, however, the evangelist this time appealed to the strong man of strong men. "Jesus," he preached, "knowing human nature better than any man who ever lived in history, said . . . 'There will be wars and rumors of wars.' " Unlike idealists and optimists, Jesus understood that the ultimate cause of war is embedded in a constant within human nature and history—sin-sick hearts. "The real cause of war," Graham explained, "is far more deep-seated than the desire to defend or expand."[13] The evangelist did not deny that desires for self-protection and expansion of territory, resources, or prestige were factors in a nation's decision to resort to war, but he stressed that these desires were manifestations of something deeper.

"The real cause of war," he continued, "is spiritual." Underlying this major thesis was Graham's favorite verse in matters of war and peace. "The Bible," he stated, "says in James 4, 'From whence comes wars and fighting among you? Come they not from your own lust?' " Ultimately, wars do not come from conflicting social forces, demographic shifts, a lack of material resources, or shifting national borders. On the contrary, "wars stem from spiritual maladjustment. World war is a mass manifestation of the strivings and the conflict which rage in the human heart." The origin of war is thus not social attitudes, practices, or events, but the individual heart. "Nothing takes place in the world collectively," Graham claimed, "that does not take place first in men individually. If the world is wrong, man was wrong first. We see here the real cause of war. It is an outward expression of man's internal conflict."[14]

The nature of this internal conflict is spiritual because the conflict is in the self's "struggle to resist the will of God. It is a battle between the self we are and the person we could be by the grace of God. Project this civil war inside the average individual man to a worldwide scale and you have a world war. The internal battle which is raging in the heart of man away from God is a world war in embryo."[15] Although he did not say so in this sermon, Graham also held that the cause of war extends back to Adam and Eve, the ancestral parents of us all, Russians and Americans. Because of the original sin in the Garden of Eden, hate, greed, prejudice, and the consequences of these sins, war, entered history. If only Adam and Eve had been content with their lives, "there would have been no hate, no greed, no prejudice. There would have been no wars."[16]

Graham often cited General MacArthur to add political weight to his unmistakably evangelical point about the origin of wars. In "The Cause of War," for example, he claimed that his argument about the human heart "is what General MacArthur meant when he told the world that our problems are basically theological ones. He meant that wars were symptoms of a disease called sin, and until the individual problem of sin is met, the problem of war will remain unsolved." The evangelist also further specified what he meant by "sin" in relation to war, suggesting, on the one hand, that the cause of war is "wrong thinking" within the human individual. "Wars come to the world," he claimed, "because man's idea of God and man becomes distorted. When we cease to think of man as a being of spiritual purpose, created a little lower than the angels and in the image of God, we become perverted in our thinking." Secularism, with its drive to eliminate God from the human heart, and communism, with its view of the human individual as a tool of a godless state, were two "wrong-thinking forces in the world," and thus more than likely to lead humanity to the brink of world war. On the other hand, "wars come from hatred within"—a hatred that rebels against God and creation.[17] When there is hatred in one's heart, one consciously decides to "revert to the animal, to the law of tooth and fang, to the law of the jungle. This is exactly what has happened in Hungary."[18] The Russians had reverted to the law of the jungle, and when they flashed their tooth and fang, America and the rest of the West ran and hid, allowing the lion to slaughter the lambs.

What about Satan? If Satan is a demonic being who uses individuals as pawns in the raging conflict between evil and good, is not he, rather than the individual, a primary cause of world wars? Although Graham did not address this question in "The Cause of War," he did raise it, albeit indirectly, in a 1961 article for *Decision*. "This earth," he wrote, "has become the setting of the conflict, and the very center of the conflict is the human heart."[19] But the heart, for Graham, is also the locus of free will, and so if Satan causes wars in the world, it is only because individuals have deliberately chosen, just as Adam and Eve had, to rebel against God and allow Satan to enter and rule their hearts—their passions, desires, and affections. Whether or not we study war anymore, then, is ultimately an individual decision, a free choice to embrace the power of reconciliation made possible only by Christ crucified.

At times this free will argument broke down, as it did in 1962, when Graham argued that "Satan is behind the scenes of the present era, calling the moves that are taking place within this world system, which is largely under his control."[20] Indeed, Graham always had significant problems articulating the power of Satan in relation to the free will of the individual, but at the very least he was consistent in his attempts to place the ultimate power of Satan within the hearts of individuals. The evangelist was also consistent throughout the King years in describing the individual heart as the seed of all conflict—familial, regional, national, and international. This central point was present at the beginning of the King years when Graham wrote in 1955 that "millions have died on the battlefields of the war because the human heart is deceitful and desperately wicked."[21] And it was just as present near the end of the King era, when he claimed that "the real cause of war is man's rebellion against God. He refuses to acknowledge the Prince of Peace, and all he can do is to move from crisis to crisis and war to war."[22]

Graham's legacy in matters of war and peace, then, is not only a Manichean distinction between good and evil but also an indisputably individualistic interpretation of the cause of war. For the evangelist, war between states, or conflict internal to a state, does not emerge from social-structural forces that transcend and are largely separate from the individual; war is a manifestation of a sick heart, a heart in rebellion against God, a heart full of hate, jealousy, greed, and lust. The individualist was Manichean, and the Manichean was individualistic: just so, for Graham, war was always the manifestation of a sin-sick heart in a world marked by clear choices of good and evil.

The Spiritual Counterrevolution: How to

Fight a Spiritual War

The Manichean Graham carried his individualistic point to its logical conclusion, at least within his evangelical system of thought, by arguing that if the real cause of war is a deceitful and wicked heart controlled by Satan, what the world really needs is a bunch of spiritually cleansed hearts. Once again, Graham claimed to be following the teachings of Jesus on war and peace. "He knew," Graham preached just after the invasion of Hungary, "that it was impossible to create better human relations until men had been born again of the Spirit of God. Human nature needs redirecting, changing and transforming."[23]

Graham's prescribed path for political peace was predictable. "There is only one way that man can be transformed and changed," he stated. "There is only one way to make human nature love instead of hate and that is through the regeneration that comes as the Spirit of God transforms the heart that comes to the cross asking for forgiveness and cleansing."[24] When we come to the cross and surrender our lives, Christ gives us the power to control our thinking and feeling in ways that are faithful to him and the rest of humanity. On the one hand, he gives us the power to control and eliminate the lust, hatred, jealousy, and greed that fill our unredeemed hearts, and on the other, he offers us the capacity to love our enemies. As the heart melts within the fold of the cross, so does the cause of war. Thus, the ultimate foundation of all peacemaking in Graham's thought is intensely personal. "You, today," Graham preached, "do you want to make a contribution to world peace? Then receive Christ as your Savior. Give your life to him, surrender to him as Lord and Master, and in doing so you will be making the greatest contribution to world peace that you have ever made."[25] World peace does not begin when diplomats sit down together and share their thoughts and feelings at the UN; the beginning of global security is the moment when an individual surrenders his or her life to the Prince of Peace.

But Graham's thoughts on war and peace were far more complicated than his simple words about conversion might suggest. To be sure, he characterized an individual's personal decision for Christ as the most important practice for world peace, but he also claimed in the early years that beyond conversion an individual has a divinely ordained responsibility to join a spiritual counterrevolution. If world peace could ever be glimpsed and tasted on earth, it would only be because of a worldwide revolution waged by faithful Christians. But what did it mean to join this battle?

Negatively, it meant refusing the politics of militarism. After Khrushchev's infamous shoe-pounding incident at the UN, Graham warned his followers against trusting politicians who "say that the answer to our problems is to spend more money and build bigger military machines." This is one of the most significant, and forgotten, points for understanding the evangelist's theology of war: Graham was deeply opposed to a militaristic posture that reposed its trust in American might and identified increased military expenditures and power as the salvation of America. "I warn you," he preached time and again, "that this is a deception. The world battle is being fought on a spiritual level. Our desperate need is for a spiritual counterrevolution that will throw back the forces of evil."[26] Militarists, even American militarists, were deeply wrong exactly because, like the demonic communists, they were materialists, foolishly blind to the spirits swirling throughout human history.

Positively, joining the counterrevolution meant having right vision— seeing the world as the battleground between the forces of Satan (communism) and those of Christ (democracy and free enterprise). Opposed to secular political theory, Graham's apocalyptic politics called upon Christians to see their Lord and Savior as present within human history, leading a rectilinear march, much as General MacArthur had done, against the invisible principalities and powers of the demonic world system. "I am convinced," Graham preached, "that on the spiritual battlefield of the present day, Christ has taken up His position and is summoning His followers to stand with him." Importantly, the evangelist did not depict Jesus as an Anabaptist counseling his followers not to resist evil; Graham's Jesus was an embattled Christ, a spiritual MacArthur who stood tall on the mountain for all who have eyes to see, and who sounded the clarion call for all who have ears to hear. As Graham put it, "The people for whom God is waiting are men and women who have caught the vision of the battlefield with all its possibilities and perils, who are awake to the devices of the enemy, and who have set themselves in union with the living Christ to attack every position he occupies and give deliverance from the oppression of Satan."[27]

Joining the counterrevolution also meant using the right weapons when following Christ into battle. Yes, onward, Christian soldiers, but the righteous crusaders would do well not to charge until they held the most effective weapons for battling Satan. What were these? Unlike the politics of militarism, with its emphasis on material weapons to the exclusion of spiritual ones, Graham's was an apocalyptic politics that deemed material weapons wholly insufficient for conquering the invisible forces of Satan. What Graham had in mind was a "swordless battle," and here he turned to the biblical story of King Jehoshaphat's victory over his opponents just after he had assumed the throne. "There seemed no possibility of victory," the evangelist preached. "Desperately he called upon the Lord and proclaimed a fast throughout all of Judea and in the wilderness of Tekoa. A swordless victory was won."[28] According to Graham, what was possible for King Jehoshaphat and his subjects so many years ago—a swordless victory—would be possible for Christ and his subjects in the raging battle with godless forces.

Graham's prescribed path to a swordless victory, however, was not entirely the same as Jehoshaphat's. Apparently, fasting was far too catholic a practice for Graham to recommend for his evangelical audience, and so he turned to practices more familiar to pious Protestants. As Christ summons his followers, he preached, "it is in prayer and obedience that we respond. Through prayer and obedience we fight the battle." Moreover, when we pray with the authority of the Son of God, believing with all our heart and mind and soul that God can rescue the perishing, "we can see situations on the earth controlled; forces in the unseen realms moved; changes effected; powers of evil dislodged and routed; and the purposes of God pressed forward to final triumph."[29] God will answer the fervent prayers of Christian soldiers.

Beyond calling for right vision and right weapons, then, Graham also demanded that final triumph be the goal of all counterrevolutionary Christians. Just like General MacArthur, the evangelist would accept nothing less than unconditional surrender in the battle against godlessness. Final triumph was so important, of course, because anything less would amount to compromise with the devil, and on this point, the evangelist once again revealed his holy warrior mentality, perhaps to the surprise of his own children. After demanding total victory over demonic communism, he boldly announced: "I would rather my children be dead than live under this gigantic anti-Christian system. There are those that say we should appease them, that they will be understanding and reasonable if we give them more." But remember what happened when the appeasers gave Hitler more and more—"he was not satisfied until he had plunged the whole world into war." And just like Hitler, the communists would do the same, if we would stupidly appease their demonic hunger for world domination. Rather than shaking hands with the devil, "we must conduct a spiritual, ideological and psychological counteroffensive that will throw back the forces of evil."[30] In his optimistic moments, Graham even assured his followers that if Christians across America would simply drop to their knees, wield the sword of prayer, and let the blood of Christ flow, communism would falter in its tracks. "I am convinced," he preached, "that hell's legions can be stopped and turned back. I am convinced that the invading heathen darkness can be hurled back."[31]

Graham's advocacy for a spiritual counterrevolution was constant, albeit in muted form, throughout the King years. To be sure, there were several shifts in his thought about the plan and targets of attack. For example, as he began to venture behind the Iron Curtain for visits and preaching engagements, he toned down his public rhetoric about the need for a counterrevolution against communism, rightly acknowledging that such rhetoric would not endear him to government officials. Indeed, at some points—for example, when he decried the close identification of Christianity with any particular government and depicted himself as an ambassador of God's kingdom—Graham would even appear to be opposed to his own version of American Manicheanism. Nevertheless, it is important not to make too much of the apparent effects of this shift, primarily because, as we will see below, in the latter King years the evangelist advocated military action against Vietnamese communists in the strongest of holy-war language—even as he courted other communist countries and presented himself as a transcendent internationalist.

Although his Manichean condemnation of all things communist tended to break down a bit, there was one thing that never diminished in Graham's thought about the spiritual battle against godlessness—his affirmation of individual conversion as the fundamental practice of local, national, and global peacemaking. At the end of the King years, Graham was still preaching that internal lust was the driving force behind all wars and that the solution to war was Christian redemption of the human heart. In 1967, for example, he observed that "the achievement of peace is as complicated as the human spirit, and too much time is spent trying to change society instead of trying to change the men who make society what it is. This is why Christ said: 'Ye must be born again.'" [32] Ultimately, then, Graham was an evangelical conversionist in matters of war and peace; he sought to create pockets of peace on earth by saving souls for Jesus Christ.

However, all this is not to say that he excluded other methods for winning and keeping the peace throughout the King years. We have already seen in the previous chapter, as well as in this one, that the evangelist was a vigorous proponent of using foreign aid to combat communism, of executing the war with North Korea, and of considering the possibility of military action to rout Russia from Hungary. It would thus be absurd to claim that he was wholly opposed to social-structural, and violent, methods of peacemaking. In fact, it would even be mistaken to suggest that he emphasized conversion and prayer over the use of violent means for creating peace on earth. Unlike the clear emphasis in his thought about the civil rights movement—that conversion was *the* answer to the race problem—Graham's emphasis in matters of war and peace was consistently and simultaneously two-fold: He stressed the need for using both Christian conversion and violent means to establish peace and keep order. And this gets us to yet another key dimension of Graham's thought. Although Graham claimed to trust that God alone would fight the communists, if only Christians would pray unceasingly and passionately, he certainly was not willing to rely solely on the prayers or evangelistic efforts of the Christian community. Graham's deep aversion to communism quickly ruled out the possibility of an absolutist commitment to nonviolence. Apparently, God needed real foot soldiers.

Is Peace Possible? The Political Realism of

Jeremiah and Jesus

Although he consistently held that the most important weapons for combating evil were Christian conversion and intercessory prayer, then, Graham's ethics of war and peace really favored fighting two battles at once—swordless and sword-ridden. But on what grounds did he move beyond the spiritual? If the cause of war was spiritual, how did the evangelist justify his embrace of material weapons? Answering these questions with some exactness requires a survey of Graham's commitment to political realism and apocalyptic fatalism, especially in relation to war and peace.

Graham was a political and theological realist. Consider, for instance, his response to the 1960 Paris peace summit. In May 1960, shortly after the U2 spy incident, the Soviet Union joined the United States and other world superpowers at a peace summit in Paris, a city not especially known for firm resistance to evildoers. In light of the U2 fiasco, an embarrassed President Eisenhower took the occasion to lament the necessity for all types of espionage. But Khrushchev, riding high on public shock, loudly demanded that the United States halt all forms of spying against his government. On the offensive, the Soviet premier added that he and his people "firmly believe in the necessity of peaceful co-existence, for to lose faith in peaceful co-existence would mean dooming humanity to war. It would mean accepting that war *is* inevitable."[33]

But what Khrushchev condemned, at least verbally, Graham embraced—a sense that humanity was doomed to witness and even participate in wars and rumors of wars. At the time of the Paris conference, the evangelist explained his political realism in an *Hour of Decision* sermon that he framed with the provocative question of the moment—Is peace possible? The final answer, he argued, lay with two major biblical figures: Jeremiah and Jesus.

For Graham, the prophet Jeremiah was the epitome of political sagacity. What made Jeremiah so wise was his realistic acknowledgment that the world has never been, is not, and never will be a place that safeguards humanity from suffering and death. Throughout the King years, Graham consistently proclaimed that Jeremiah's dismissal of those who say " 'peace, peace,' when there is no peace" (8:11) was simply an accurate reflection of human experience in a fallen world. "History," he argued, "gives little comfort to those who believe that peace is just around the corner. In the entire history of the world since Abraham, we've enjoyed only three hundred years of peace." A more optimistic interpreter of history here might have claimed that the three hundred years of peace suggest the possibility of five hundred, six hundred, or even a millennia of world peace, but the realist Graham drew a different implication—the impossibility of world peace. Look at today, too, he continued: "What grounds do we have for thinking peace is possible when riots are everywhere, governments are falling, millions are living without freedom, and the major powers are now engaged in a frantic arms race?"[34] Conflicts and wars were omnipresent, and so if global citizens thought for one second that a lasting world peace could emerge from the Paris summit, they were stupendously naïve, totally blind to the truth of Jeremiah and the evidence of world history.

Graham also christianized his particular version of political realism by citing Jesus' words in Matthew 24: 6 ("And you will hear of wars and rumors of wars"). More than any other, this text constituted the foundation of Graham's war theology during the King years; there was no other text that he cited more often or with greater enthusiasm. The evangelist loved this text especially because he believed it burst the liberal's bubble of idealism in relation to world peace. "Christ," Graham proclaimed, "indicated there can be no universal peace in the kind of world in which we live. . . . Peace is not within the power of sinful man to achieve." On the one hand, this point was obviously christological. The good Lord was no starry-eyed dreamer lazing about in the middle of the pasture, but rather a realist, a hardnosed advocate for seeing the world for what it really was—a place of wars and rumors of wars. On the other hand, his point was anthropological. The sad truth known to all realists, Graham implied, was that the summit's players—sinners in a sinful world—ultimately lacked the power required to transform war and conflict into an enduring peace. The power to create peace on any level was not within humanity in general, a group of individuals, or any one individual. "As long as there are those who rebel against [Christ] and break his law," he continued, ". . . as long as men hate, have prejudice, greed, and lust, there is going to be the terrifying possibility of war."[35] And just because there will always be at least one sinner filled with hatred, jealousy, greed, and lust within human history, the world will never experience a just and enduring peace. Thus, those who imagined that the Paris summit could actually achieve peace had a false notion of both Jesus and humanity.

Graham's theological and political realism was another constant throughout the remainder of the King years. Two years after the Paris summit, for example, he stated at a press conference that "as long as you have one man in the world who hates another . . . you have the possibility of war. As long as you have men in the world greedy for power, there is potential conflict."[36] This is a point he restated time and again, as he did in 1965, at Grove Park Inn in North Carolina: "As long as lust or greed, or hate, or jealousy is in the heart of a single individual, there is the possibility of war and destruction."[37] Even at the end of the King years, the evangelist was preaching the same political realism. In December 1967, for example, when faced with a growing number of pacifists and peace activists, some of whom picketed his speaking engagements, Graham drew directly from Jeremiah's realism to belittle the peace movement: "We talk of peace, we march for peace, and we attend scores of peace conferences across the world. *Still there is no peace.* . . . So long as there is greed, lust, and hate in the world, there will be fighting and war."[38] And exactly two months before the dreamer Martin Luther King, Jr., was assassinated, the evangelist offered yet another stunning indictment of political idealism. "Some dreamers," he claimed, "can see in the future international cooperation, a worldwide willingness to see eye to eye with one's neighbors, mutual understanding among all peoples, and a world government that will really work. This, of course, from a biblical point of view, is all nonsense."[39]

Apocalypse Soon

Graham was no dreamer. Nor was he a realist in the substantive mold of Hans Morgenthau or Reinhold Niebuhr, or the type of run-of-the-mill realist found within everyday conservative politics. On the contrary, Graham was an apocalyptic thinker whose evangelical eschatology distinguished him from virtually all mainstream political realists of his day. And as an apocalypticist, he held not only that there would always be wars and rumors of wars, but also that wars would increase in number and intensity, culminating in the Great Conflagration known as Armageddon. "The Bible," Graham wrote in 1965, "indicates that toward the end, wars will become more widespread, more devastating, and more frequent."[40] More specifically, the evangelist preached that Jesus himself, unlike contemporary appeasers, "indicated that wars would increase in intensity until the great war of the nations, which is called the Battle of Armageddon."[41]

In the early part of the King years, Graham offered a number of details about his understanding of the battle of Armageddon, including the typical point that the prophet Ezekiel held the key for unlocking the future battle. Eschewing mainstream commentaries, as usual, Graham argued that Ezekiel had predicted that in the last days Israel "would be a thorn in the side of her neighbors and would be prosecuted by many nations," and that "the last great battle will take place when the armies of the north, which many believe to be Russia, will move into the Middle East."[42] This was standard fare for eschatologically obsessed, communism-fearing, and Middle East-gesticulating evangelicals and fundamentalists at the time. Most if not all fervently believed that the Great Russian Bear would emerge from hibernation, plow toward the Middle East, and begin to maul the faithful remnant.

But Graham let go of these specifics as the King years progressed, especially as he began to make overtures to countries behind the Iron Curtain, fertile land for his crusades. So by 1965 he was steering his followers less toward Ezekiel and more toward the general words of Revelation: " 'And He gathered them together into a place called in the Hebrew tongue Armageddon' (Rev. 16:16). This will be the final war, the last convulsive effort of fallen man against the law of God."[43] Whatever the specifics may be, Armageddon would be the fiercest war in human history, a war greater in damage and destruction than any known, and most importantly, a war in which God would enact divine judgment against the infidels. The Great

Conflagration would be a crusade of the highest order—and a vengeful God would not spare the rod.

This last theological point is critical for fully understanding Graham's theology of war and peace. For Graham, the essence of God was not unconditional love, especially the type of nonviolent love that King and other Christian pacifists identified in the crucified Jesus. "God," Graham wrote in the early King years, "is a God of love and mercy, yes; but God is also a righteous judge." Unlike some theologians of his day, the evangelist did not oppose love to justice, but saw the two as complementary; love needs justice, and justice needs love. Martin Luther King, Jr. held the same, but while he believed that the essence of God was nonviolent, Graham envisioned the justice of God as including violent wrath. In fact, forcible vengeance was the hallmark characteristic of divine justice in the evangelist's theological system. Remarkably, Graham even saw a metaphor for God in Dwight D. Eisenhower during his World War II days. "It has been my privilege," the evangelist wrote, "to be with President Eisenhower a number of times. . . . I know him to be a very gentle man, a very kind man, a very understanding man. And yet I read in the annals of history of the Second World War that he ordered the execution of men who had been court-martialed and sentenced. He did not want to do it. He loved the men; he liked the men. But in that instance he was a judge . . . true to the laws of the nation."[44] Graham's claim that Eisenhower liked and loved the condemned individuals was certainly far-fetched, but his general appeal to Eisenhower when describing God made considerable sense in the realm of evangelical theology. In this perspective, individuals can experience God's expansive love by receiving Jesus Christ, the one who overcame death, as Lord and Savior. But if they refuse Christ, they will earn the wrath of God, a sentence of virtual execution, a life in hell. Unlike Eisenhower, however, a just God does not merely kill people, allowing their ashes to return to ashes, their dust to dust—a just God consigns people to eternal torture.

Whence love within this vengeful God? "Judgment is consistent with love," Graham wrote in *World Aflame*. "His justice balances His love and makes His acts of both love and justice meaningful. . . . His punishment of the evildoer and His separation of the righteous is a manifestation of God's great love."[45] But the final authority for receiving and enjoying divine love always rests within the individual's heart. "From the cross God has said to the entire world, 'I love you.' However, when that love is deliberately rejected, the only alternative is judgment."[46]

Graham's evangelical hermeneutic resulted in a God who embraced and eliminated, blessed and blasted, saved and slaughtered. But had he followed Jesus' sayings a bit more closely here, the evangelist could have depicted a radically different type of divine moral character. Even a quick read of the New Testament, after all, will show that judgment is not the only biblical alternative in situations in which love is rejected. Recall, for example, the biblical parable of the Good Shepherd (John 10: 11–18). What makes the shepherd so good is that he doggedly pursues both the sheep that have left his care and those that do not know his name at all. The Good Shepherd does not judge the lost sheep, leaving them to their own mistaken devices, and most likely to the slaughter that awaits them. Instead, he chooses love over judgment, steadfastly refusing to let any of the lost sheep stray too far from the fold. Unlike General Eisenhower, in other words, the Good Shepherd signs no death warrants.

But the patriotic Graham loved the General, and with a hermeneutic that always preferred judgment over unconditional love, he left the Good Shepherd behind and found Eisenhower and the killing fields of World War II to be epiphanous, revelatory of the very character of God. Moreover, the evangelist also held that his Eisenhower-like God was teetering on the brink of violent intervention in human history. "I think," Graham stated in 1967, "we are seeing today movements in the world that indicate that Armageddon may be within this century."[47] More sophisticated than most of his fundamentalist colleagues, the evangelist usually tried to stay away from exact predictions about the end times, but sometimes they just came pouring out of his exuberant spirituality, as they did in this sermon.

As an unabashed dispensationalist, Graham frequently identified signs of the end of the times. In the mid-1950s, for example, he argued that history had already witnessed the fulfillment of prophecies predicted in the Bible, including the reformulation of Israel as a nation-state, a rapid increase in knowledge and travel, the emergence of Russia as a military superpower, and an alarming growth of immorality.[48] "These are apocalyptic trends," Graham wrote, "marked by the war, famine, pestilence and death that we know so well are riding around the world at this very moment."[49] This "very moment" extended to 1965, too, when the evangelist added that he saw signs of the end in his generation's "psychological breakdown," in a "moral binge such as was not known even in the days of Rome," in the proliferation of false teachings, in the increase in lawlessness, and in the rise of material affluence.[50]

Graham's dispensationalism even went so far as to suggest that the world's peace conferences were signs of the end of human history. Drawing from Psalm 2, in which the world's rulers "take counsel together," he depicted peace conferences as "the desperate effort on the part of the world's leaders to establish peace." The effort was so desperate because "God is left out of their planning. The Prince of Peace is never consulted about peace."[51] On a closely related note, the evangelist also identified the move toward "world government" as a sign of the end times. "The Bible," he preached, "plainly says in Revelation 17 that there will come a day when there will be a world government ruled over by one man."[52] More specifically, the apocalypticist had in mind the emergence of the favorite subject of evangelical fear-mongering—the Anti-Christ.

Graham was always suspicious of international peace missions, but his suspicions increased markedly when he detected a desire for centralization of power among global policy makers. Ever the reader of world trends, the evangelist was convinced in 1967 that he had identified a worldwide movement to centralize all governmental power and authority in the hands of one individual—"one superman, a giant, charismatic personality, with unique powers of leadership"—thereby proving the biblical prophecy that "there is going to come a world government headed by the Anti-Christ."[53] Graham's evidence, which would have amused liberal idealists, consisted of international peace conferences that addressed the possibility of a world government. How tragically stupid the idealists were, Graham implied; their hopes were nothing other than signs of the imminent rise of the Anti-Christ.

Graham's fundamentalist peers had long considered the Pope—pick one—as a potentially stellar candidate for the position of Anti-Christ, but the evangelist was far too ecumenical to offer the same suggestion.[54] In fact, his commentary on the Anti-Christ was impersonal and relatively general. The Anti-Christ, he conjectured, will be a world governor of sorts, with all political and economic power centralized only in him. As the locus of all earthly authority, he will rule the world with cleverness, establish remarkable prosperity and peace, and thereby develop a loyal following. In the short term, his treachery will hide the demonic truth that "his one dream, his one desire, one ambition will be to destroy even the thought of God on the face of the earth." But in the long term God will expose all of these deceptions,[55] and at the end of the demonic reign there will be "the greatest war of history—the battle of Armageddon," when God will use violence to overthrow the Anti-Christ and his foolhardy followers.[56]

Thus, we finally come to Graham's full answer to the question of whether peace is possible in human history as we know it—no. On the one hand, peace is impossible because Jesus, just like Jeremiah, declared that there would always be wars and rumors of wars—and the good Lord was never wrong, especially about the sinfulness of human nature. On the other hand, peace is impossible because God is on the brink of executing violent wrath at the time of Armageddon. To be sure, Graham conceded that we may see glimpses of peace (for example, in peace conferences and even through the politics of the Anti-Christ), but his main point was always that any form of human peace is not true peace, a complete peace, a peace that would endure. Liberal peacemakers may have some success, then, but human history is rolling toward a nuclear blizzard, a violent divine intervention that peace conferences and centralized political power could never prevent. For the realist, apocalyptic Graham, peace within history as we know it can never be the result of human actions alone.

A Violent Christ

This gets us to yet another major point in Graham's theology of war and peace. As an anthropological pessimist, Graham held that sinful humanity lacks the requisite power and resources for creating a just and sustainable peace. Nothing human—governments, markets, and churches—can ever fulfill the will of God, including peace on earth. Correlatively, as a divine purist, the evangelist preached that only God has the wisdom and power required to lead a wayward humanity into the ways of true peace. More specifically, though, he claimed that only divine intervention through Jesus Christ at the end of the ages can eliminate the scourge of war from the face of the earth.[57] And this is exactly what God in Jesus Christ will do.

Graham's commentary on Apocalypse Soon depicted not only the Great Conflagration but also (to use Kant's famous phrase) Perpetual Peace. At the time of the defeat of the Anti-Christ, Graham preached, Jesus Christ will ascend to the throne of worldly power and begin a thousand-year reign. As he put this in 1960, "There is a glorious day coming when the Prince of Peace shall return and sit on the throne to rule the world with a rod of iron."[58] The Second Coming of Christ will be glorious, of course, because wars and rumors of wars will disappear, just as prophesied in Psalm 72, Isaiah 2, and Isaiah 9; the lion will lie down with the lamb, swords will be beaten into plowshares, and no one will study war anymore.[59]

On the one hand, Graham's apocalyptic peace referred to a political peace that inhered in institutions, but on the other, it also meant peace that ruled in individual hearts. Just so, this comprehensive peace, both social and individual, will not be easy for even Jesus Christ to maintain.[60] "The Bible," Graham stated, "teaches that when the Lord Jesus Christ comes back to earth as king of kings and Lord of lords, he will have to rule with a rod of iron . . . rebellious nations will exhibit the same rebellious spirit when Christ himself comes to act as the peacemaker and the president of the United Nations." In effect, Christ will be the perfect embodiment of political realism; he "will not tolerate illogical ideas of voluntary coopera-tion. He will come as the exponent of true righteousness and will rule with force to preserve that righteousness—the only language which our rebel-lious world understands in its present sinful situation."[61]

The significance of this last point is impossible to overstate. The apoca-lyptic Graham envisioned the Returned Christ not as a nonviolent, liberal democrat but as a right-wing authoritarian who will rule with an iron rod. Christ will not rely on gentle prodding, moral suasion, direct lobbying, vote garnering, or other democratic means to accomplish his will during the thousand-year reign. As the perfect political realist, he will concede the ultimate futility of appeals to the hearts and minds of the citizenry, and so he will use any means necessary, including force, to create the perpetual peace that God wills for the divine creation. In other words, violent means in the hands of a righteous Christ will establish the peace of God on earth. And here, at last, is the foundation of hope in Graham's war and peace ethics. As he put it, "I believe [that Christ] is coming literally and bodily to set up his reign, and that is the hope for peace."[62]

Against Pacifism

If only Christ can create true peace, should the people of God give up any and all attempts to establish peace on earth? Graham claimed that before

Christ comes again, Christians have an obligation to pray and work for peace, just as the Bible taught; but this was never his emphasis. Rather than specifying ways in which Christians could become peacemakers beyond conversion and evangelism—for example, through marches, boycotts, direct lobbying, or the Peace Corps—Graham always highlighted the impossibility of peace constructed through human efforts.

Here enters his assessment of the UN, an institution he belittled and condemned more than a few times in his life. In 1962, as the UN was addressing substantive issues of disarmament, Graham wrote: "I support the United Nations and I certainly support the disarmament conference." But his major point was that both would fail miserably. Yes, they "may establish an era of peace, maybe 25, 50, or 100 years of peace. But the ultimate end is going to be failure."[63] Graham could have focused on the importance of creating peace on even a short-term basis, but as an apocalyptic realist, he always shifted emphasis to the cloud of doom that hovered over human peacemaking efforts, especially those undertaken by the UN.

He unpacked his disenchantment with the UN further in 1965, when he wrote that the institution "was conceived and created by statesmen who knew little of the significance of the Biblical concept of history and the nature of man. When the perspective is wrong, the whole viewpoint will be wrong." The whole viewpoint was wrong because the UN ignored "the basic problem" of human conflicts and wars—sin in the individual heart. "You cannot build a superstructure," he wrote, "on a cracked foundation."[64] International diplomacy carried out by the UN was thus a record of "broken dreams, broken promises, and broken treatises," and its plan to save the world was little more than a delusion of grandeur.[65] Moreover, the UN, not at all unlike demonic communist nations, was a godless entity that refused to invoke God in its founding charter.

Nevertheless, Graham continued to insist that he "supported the United Nations because it offered some hope at least of solving some problems and postponing some major hostilities." He even described it as "man's best attempt in generations."[66] But all this was a bit baffling. After all, if the whole perspective and viewpoint of the UN was wrong, and if the UN was a godless institution, Graham's statement of support would suggest, given his own thought, that he was compromising with the devil. At best, the evangelist's words of "support" were incoherent if not altogether suspect. Less suspect, however, was his description of the UN's peacemaking work as a "delaying action," a "temporary stopgap."[67] But here we must ask why Graham would have supported a delaying action, especially if it delayed Armageddon and, beyond that, the glorious end of human history. Indeed, why would he have supported any human action that delayed the reconciliation of God with humanity? Unfortunately, the apocalyptic Graham never responded to these questions.

The truth is that Billy Graham was not a peacemaker in conventional ways. He was more inclined to embrace General MacArthur than Martin Luther King, Jr., or even Gandhi. He was more inclined to board an aircraft carrier and encourage the troops than he was to stand before a crowd of anti-war activists and support their efforts. And he was more inclined to bless a war than he was to describe it as antithetical to the ways of Jesus of Nazareth. In fact, Graham was opposed to pacifism, especially of the Christian sort, and subjected it to countless criticisms throughout the King years.

We should recall here that one of the tasks before us is to understand the grounds on which the evangelist embraced material weapons—violent means—for fighting godlessness in general and communism in particular. Thus far we have tended to the negative side of his argument. His realism and apocalypticism provided theological reasons for dismissing dreams of a world without conflict and war; until Christ comes again, guns will fire, bombs will explode, and soldiers will die. But this was only a descriptive point; it merely described the impossibility of a world without violence. There was also a constructive, and normative, part of his theological argu-ments for embracing violent means in the war against godlessness, and unpacking these positive reasons requires an exploration of his antipathy toward pacifism.

In 1960, when a Quaker asked him to comment on the pacifist belief that Christianity forbids violence in any form, Graham argued that "the Bible seems to teach defense of the innocent as non-conflictive with Christian principle." He could have cited St. Augustine, the early church father, who saw defense of the innocent as a just cause for resorting to war, but early church fathers were rarely primary sources for Graham's ethics. The scrip-ture he had in mind was Psalm 82:3–4: "Give justice to the weak and the orphan; maintain the right of the lowly and the destitute. Rescue the weak and the needy; deliver them from the hand of the wicked." But his appeal to Psalm 82 was shaky, primarily because the Psalm nowhere suggests that the use of violence is morally permissible; Graham simply assumed that vio-lence might be necessary to liberate the poor and needy from the hand of the wicked. To be fair, though, the evangelist also had in mind the Hebrew stories in which God sent Israel into holy crusades against its oppressors. "While God, in the Old Testament, said, 'Thou shalt not kill' (do not mur-der), yet He sent Israel out to battle." And from these stories Graham drew the conclusion that "there seems to be a difference in 'killing' for personal gain, and taking the lives of those who molest the innocent"; the former is prohibited, and the latter seems morally permissible.[68]

Interestingly, his 1960 reply to the Quaker was markedly tentative ("the Bible *seems* to teach" defense of the innocent, and "there *seems* to be a dif-ference" between just killing and unjust killing). The evangelist even went so far as to suggest that in the final analysis, the question of whether one is a pacifist "is a question each of us must answer for himself—considering his own conscience and background."[69] However, Graham's characteristically Baptist appeal to individual conscience disappeared when he started to experience pacifist dissent during the early stages of the military conflict in Vietnam. Indeed, most of his direct comments on pacifism during the King years arose in the volatile context of the Vietnam War.

In 1965, already confronted with anti-war activists, Graham tried to steer a middle course of sorts between militarism and pacifism. "Our modern hopes for peace," he wrote, "cannot rest on the practice of creating more war." Military power, political alliances, and military structures may assure victory in a specific war, but they cannot assure the peace. But neither can pacifism. "Pacifism will fail, for the pacifist acts as if all men are regenerate and can be appealed to through persuasion and goodwill. The pacifist also refuses to recognize the rule of power in the preservation of justice, alongside the rule of love."[70] This was little more than a popularized restatement of Reinhold Niebuhr's political realism. Graham was never as careful in his analysis of "immoral society" as Niebuhr was, but it is unmistakable that the evangelist, like Niebuhr and Luther, had a deeply realistic sense that society is far too immoral for reason and persuasion to be effective tools in winning and maintaining peace: one simply cannot trust sinners to listen, let alone respond, to the Prince of Peace.

Graham explained his own version of realism further in 1967, warning that "we must be careful not to impose Christian ethics and principles on people who have never yielded to the Gospel message." Biblical teachings on peace may be fine for small groups of individuals and even local Christian communities, but it is wrong to impose these teachings on wider society, for "society itself can never be renovated and renewed until every individual comes under the influence of the Gospel of Christ." And that will never happen within human history. As it stands, and as it will always stand before the Second Coming, immoral society is the locus of recalcitrant sin and chaos. So to prevent the world from imploding, the best we can do is to hold the sin and chaos in check, and if this means we must use force, even physical force, so be it: It is better to use force against the wicked than it is for the wicked to rule the world.

With his Niebuhrian realism in tow, Graham thus argued that "as long as there are gangsters in a community there is need for a police force. Unfortunately, there are also international gangsters."[71] Interestingly, the evangelist did not call for a worldwide police force; he was far too anti-UN, and far too concerned about the dangers of world government and the Anti-Christ, to propose a centralized police force. Nor did he call for each individual nation to develop its own military so that there would be a balance of power; he was far too American-centric for such an egalitarian notion. Instead, he simply suggested that as long as there are international gangsters, America should be the strongest it can be.

Graham's preference for American military might was especially visible in his numerous trips to the Pentagon, where he would often baptize the American military as the virtual will of God. For instance, in 1965, during his fifth trip to the Pentagon, he told 5,000 members of the top brass that as long as human nature remained unchanged, their work in the military was necessary for good order.[72] He did not tell them to leave their positions and begin trying to win sin-sick souls for Christ; he just encouraged them to be faithful to their war-making occupation—and, yes, to give their lives to Jesus.

Graham's argument against pacifism sharpened as pacifists continued to question him. In 1966, when a pacifist reported that he or she had concluded that war is never justifiable, Graham replied: "Aggressive war is never justifiable, but there are hints in the Bible that justify a nation in protecting itself against attack. Jesus himself said, 'When a strong man keepeth (guardeth) his palace, his goods are in peace.' True, he said, 'Put up thy sword. . . . for all they that take the sword shall perish with the sword.' [But] since the drawer of the sword would be the aggressor, he is condemning aggression." Graham could have appealed to the biblical Jesus who instructed his followers not to resist evil, but such a Jesus simply did not fit the evangelist's conservative politics. Reflecting his 1960 statement on pacifism, Graham's 1966 reply also allowed for the defense of not only one's house but also of "the innocent and helpless when they are attacked—motivated by compassion and not hate."[73]

As the protests against Vietnam grew louder, so did Graham's assault on pacifism, even of the Christian sort, and he delivered his most strident attack on pacifism during the 1966 presidential breakfast, with one beleaguered Lyndon Baines Johnson in attendance. This speech is perhaps the most significant for understanding not only Graham's reasons for opposing pacifism but also for grasping the theological rationale behind his early support for the Vietnam War and, more generally, his embrace of violent means in the earthly battle against godlessness. Graham began his speech by referring to two sayings of Jesus—"I came to bring fire to the earth" (Luke 12:49) and "Do not think that I have come to bring peace to the earth; I have not come to bring peace, but a sword" (Matthew 10:34). Both of these verses prove just how wrong are those who would try "to reduce Christ to the level of a genial and innocuous appeaser." Jesus was not a meek, mild, mousey appeaser, but a "fire-setter and sword-wielder."[74]

The optimists of Jesus' day, according to Graham, did not understand these difficult sayings: They did not realize the depth and consequences of sin, they did not understand that a holy God is full of wrath and judgment, and they did not understand that angels did not mean political peace when they spoke of peace on earth. "It seemed to them that everything could easily be put right by better understanding between peoples, by better education, and by social solutions."[75] Only dense attendees at the presidential prayer breakfast would have failed to understand that Graham was drawing parallels here between the optimists of Jesus' day (who these individuals were, incidentally, the evangelist never identified, most likely because they are nowhere in the Bible) and the pacifists who were protesting the Johnson Administration's decision to escalate the U.S. military commitment in Vietnam.

"Jesus had to correct their optimism," Graham continued, "and warn them that His coming did not mean a quick Utopia. He had to make clear that His coming, far from meaning peace, meant war. . . . His message was a society that would set society ablaze with division and strife."[76] Did this mean that Jesus was not the Prince of Peace extolled by Christian pacifists?

Yes. "We've been taught so long that Jesus was the Prince of Peace, and indeed he was. We've been taught that he was the very incarnation of the everlasting love, and indeed he was." But the problem is that these lessons, especially when taught by optimistic Christians, did not properly define "love" and "peace," with the result that we have terribly misunderstood the "divine definition" of peace and love.[77]

"There is a sense," Graham continued, "in which true love is a fire." It is not "complacent and passive," but a fire that purifies everything that is evil. "It is the man who loves his country most who will fight to preserve its freedom. It is the man who loves his neighbor most who will fight against all that hurts, deprives and oppresses his neighbor." Consider Jesus Christ. "Think how Christ, with righteous indignation, drove the money-changers out of the Temple, how he often rebuked the Pharisees for plundering widows' houses, and how he rebuked those who wanted to stone a poor, helpless, adulterous woman."[78] Graham was grasping here when he used the notion of purifying love to connect the violence of a patriotic soldier with Jesus' overturning of the tables in the Temple; after all, one action killed, and the other did not. But the tenuous connection Graham drew between military violence and the nonviolence of Jesus did not stop him from continuing his patriotic description of true love. "Those who have a love of freedom," he added, "will do everything in their power to keep the freedom that they have. Patrick Henry was burning with love of freedom when he said: 'Give me liberty or give me death.' "[79]

Lest anyone miss the connection to Vietnam, Graham made it explicit: "Those who hate tyranny and love freedom will take sides when little nations suffer terror and aggression from those who seek to take their freedom from them." Contrary to the peaceniks, love can never be equated with peace. "To preserve some things, love must destroy others. It is never neutral!" Offering even more evidence, Graham pointed to Abraham Lincoln. Lincoln had a "deep love" for all individuals, "whatever their color," but "his love did not create peace and unity. . . . It created strife and division. It took a war. It took a bloodbath because he hated tyranny, oppression and prejudice."[80] True love, as shown by Jesus, can never stand by idly when evil is perpetrated around us, especially upon the oppressed; and sometimes true love, as shown by Lincoln, Henry, and even Churchill, must use physical force when confronting moral evil. Graham also directly connected these two points when concluding his speech: "Thus we have found that, as Jesus taught, love of God or love of neighbor or love of country does not necessarily bring peace."[81] The pacifists were wrong, all wrong, for true love sometimes results in bloodbaths and wars.

At last, then, we have come to Graham's positive argument for embracing violent means in the holy crusade against godlessness. For Graham, the love of Christ demanded the use of violence in a sinful world. Just as the righteousness of God had required Israel to take up arms against its enemies, the love of Christ commands us to use violence when defending ourselves and our neighbors against godlessness. This is not to say that Graham's positive case for using violence was altogether humanitarian, firmly grounded in the virtue of love for humanity in general; as we will see below, the evangelist restricted the use of violent means to soldiers employed by democratic forces. But it is to say that Graham grounded his embrace of violent means in the positive virtue of Christian love. In this sense, he simply followed the example set by the tradition of Christian just-war theory, with its theological grounding not in vengeance but in neighbor-love.

Graham's critique of pacifists, especially Christian pacifists, was thus multifaceted and comprehensive. He criticized them for having an optimistic view of human nature, misreading human capabilities in human history, failing to understand the spiritual cause of war, relying on faulty methods for achieving peace, appeasing evil, misunderstanding the Prince of Peace, and working with faulty definitions of "love" and "peace." With this case against pacifism, Graham moved away from his earlier sense that the decision of whether to become a pacifist was a matter of individual conscience, and by 1966 he was hell-bent on depicting the pacifist as on the wrong side of the cosmic war between godly democrats and godless communism. Rather than supporting the will of God, pacifists were actually undermining divine love and peace. This was the tragedy of liberal peacemakers: They thought they were making peace possible, but they were actually making peace impossible.

Vietnam as a Holy War

Graham's fiery speech at the 1966 presidential prayer breakfast was far from a challenge for the Johnson Administration to rethink its policies against Vietnam, or to reconsider the level of deployment, or even to push harder for peace negotiations. Rather, it was a virtual baptism of the Vietnam War. Graham was the high priest, and he poured as much holy water as he could hold over the bowed head of Johnson and all his war policies. And as priests warn parents that raising babies in the world is not an easy task, Graham also warned the baptized Johnson that it would not be easy for him when taking sides with little nations suffering at the hands of tyranny. "But Jesus warned [that] when you take sides," Graham preached, "you will be opposed by those who do not understand the deep problem of human nature and a true definition of love." Look at Lincoln. "He was damned and criticized more than any president in American history."[82] Or at Churchill, who was "mercilessly criticized when he warned about the growing power and ambitions of Hitler."[83] In the same way, standing up today for little nations oppressed by evil will result in opposition. The evangelist's message to Johnson was clear: You will be opposed by the naïve, but take heart—like Lincoln and Churchill, you are a righteous crusader, and your cause is holy.

Unbelievably, just one year later, at a press conference in San Juan, Graham denied it all. "I have never," he stated, "taken sides as to the moral issue [of the war], as to whether America should be there or should not be there. I felt that this is a decision that the president, the cabinet, the Congress, who are elected by the people—this is their responsibility, not mine. I do not take sides politically."[84] The statement might have been believable to his uncritical supporters, but it was more than a bit deceptive; after all, his words at the 1966 presidential prayer breakfast alone reveal that he had sided with the president and his war policies against the peace protestors and their policies of appeasement. Nor was this the first time the evangelist had taken sides on the question of military involvement in Southeast Asia.

Graham's support for U.S. military action in Southeast Asia had actually preceded his early embrace of Johnson's war policies. In 1961, for example, the evangelist had sharply criticized Kennedy for allowing Laos to fall out of the Western sphere of influence. "Mr. Kennedy promised we would never surrender Laos," Graham preached, "but the premier of Canada said that it should be now counted as a Communist nation. Thus, the world situation continues to deteriorate."[85] The critique was especially harsh because Graham had begun the sermon by extolling the virtues of General MacArthur, the great victor over evil. "Probably no leader in the Western world, outside of Winston Churchill, could possibly match him in strength, courage and sheer brilliance." Other observers of international politics, like the members of the Nobel Peace Committee, might have mentioned King, but the pacifist leader appeared nowhere on the evangelist's screen of admired leaders. "Millions of people around the world," he continued, "are hoping and praying that another Churchill or MacArthur will appear on the horizon to lead the West in this hour of its greatest peril."[86] Graham, of course, was one of those "millions of people" who found Kennedy weak on communism in general and Southeast Asia in particular, and who longed for the unbending strength of a MacArthur and a Churchill.

The evangelist's critique of Kennedy grew even shriller after Laos had elected a communist to be prime minister. With Laos falling to communism, and with an increased presence of "guerilla forces in South Vietnam," America was lacking "bold, courageous" leadership. "President Kennedy," Graham preached, "once wrote a thesis concerning British apathy prior to the days of Hitler, entitled *While England Slept*. Could it be possible that President Kennedy is now presiding over a nation that is sleeping" while the communists plan for world domination?[87] To be sure, Graham was thrilled when Kennedy stood his ground against the Soviets during the Cuban missile crisis, and he was far from opposed to the president's decision to commit troops to Southeast Asia.[88] But the evangelist had a sense that all this was terribly insufficient, and shortly following Kennedy's assassination, he stepped up his critique of America's lack of resolve in the war against communism. "We have the most powerful military force the world has ever known," Graham preached in 1964, "but we are afraid to use it. The will to fight for freedom and justice is gone. The ease, the luxury, the immorality of the country have affected us like a narcotic; they have destroyed our will to fight for what we believe."[89]

Shortly before this, Graham had sketched out his full argument against · communism in a sermon bemoaning its advances in "the world revolution." His argument is partly embedded in a remarkable definition of communism that is worth quoting here, if for no other reason than to be clear that the evangelist's feelings of antipathy were far more comprehensive than caricatures of his anti-communism might suggest:

> Biologically, the modern communist is an animal without a soul who has arrived by naturalistic evolution. . . . Politically, a communist is one who believes that the state is supreme . . . and that the individual exists only for the welfare of the state. Thus, they destroy the dignity and value of each person. . . . Socially, a communist does not believe in marriage as an institution of God, but merely as a convenient bio-logical arrangement to produce heirs for the communist state. Internationally, a communist is a revolutionary who is behind much of the unrest in the world. . . . Ethically, a communist does not believe in universal standards of right and wrong, and does not accept the Ten Commandments. . . . Theologically, a communist is an atheist, a destroyer of churches, and a denier of all the fruits of Christianity.[90]

Still understanding communism to be the work of the devil, Graham was thus tickled red, white, and blue when Johnson deepened America's mili-tary commitments against the godless communists in Vietnam. Contrary to his 1967 claim about his support for the war, the evangelist did little to hide his early enthusiasm for Johnson's war policies. In a 1965 interview with the journalist Max Goldberg, for example, he offered a direct statement on the morality of the war. "I think," he said, "that the United States has a moral obligation to defend freedom in Southeast Asia." Perhaps Graham had forgotten this statement by the time he was enjoying the warm sun of San Juan in 1967, but the evidence is clear: he had long taken sides on the question of U.S. military engagement in Vietnam, and he had directly commented on the morality of the war. "Of course," he added in the Goldberg interview, "war is a terrible thing—but it becomes necessary sometimes. I'm not a pacifist. I don't believe the Bible teaches pacifism." Beyond pointing to the Bible, the evangelist also identified more practical issues at hand, mustering a few big names along the way: "Mr. Truman, Mr. Eisenhower, then Mr. Kennedy and now Mr. Johnson have all decided that we must defend Southeast Asia . . . if we do not defend the freedom of the people of Viet Nam, other nations, with whom we have treaties, will never believe our word again."[91]

At the same time he was offering public support for Johnson's war policies, he was also sending private encouragement to the president, depicting him as a righteous crusader in the holy war of holy wars. "You are getting some unjust criticism," he penned, "but remember that the most criticized men in America were those whose names shine brightest in history. . . . Also, remember they crucified Jesus within three years after he began his public ministry." By Graham's account, Johnson was just like Jesus: Although righteous in cause, the president was surrounded by sinful critics. "It is what God thinks about our actions," the evangelist continued. "The Communists are moving fast toward their goal of world revolution. *Perhaps God brought you to the kingdom for such an hour as this—to stop them. In doing so, you could be the man that helped save Christian civilization.*"[92] No doubt, this is the best evidence that Graham wholly supported Johnson during the early years of the Vietnam War. It is also the best evidence for suggesting that the evangelist envisioned the Vietnam War as a holy crusade against godlessness, and Johnson as the one divinely chosen to save Christian civilization from the death and destruction wrought by godless communism.[93] Unsurprisingly, Graham denied the charge and told a lie to beat it. "I categorically deny," he stated, "that I have ever by statement or even implication endorsed the Vietnam War as a holy enterprise. . . . I have been extremely careful not to be drawn into the moral implications or the tactical military problems of the Vietnam War."[94]

Graham's early public support came through loud and clear in his radio sermons, too. In a 1965 sermon titled "The Final World War," he announced with considerable pleasure that most Americans supported the president's policy of "no further retreat in the face of naked communist aggression in the form of guerilla warfare in Southeast Asia." At last, Graham preached, godless communism was beginning to taste the wrath of God, just as depicted in Jeremiah 24. Curiously, this was the flip side to an argument that the evangelist had made in the same year—that communism might have been God's judgment upon the affluent and secularizing West.[95] With the increased presence of U.S. troops in Vietnam, Graham discarded this argument and began to interpret U.S. military action as nothing less than God's judgment on the communists.

Another 1965 sermon criticized dissent and depicted the war as a matter of preserving freedom and opposing tyranny. In "The Real Cause of War," Graham defended the war against liberal university professors and students calling for a compromise in Vietnam. The appeasing professors and students, Graham preached, were just like the weak Western allies who had "lost the peace" at Potsdam and "virtually handed a third of the world over to communism." Like the so-called allies, the professors and students were willing to "surrender millions of freedom-loving people of Asia to the communists." Johnson was not the guilty party, after all; the liberal professors and students were the ones with blood on their hands. "President Johnson has called for unconditional negotiation," Graham added, "but the communists have flatly refused. What is the president supposed to do?"[96] The evangelist's answer, of course, was to stay the course and defeat the communists; strong men like MacArthur and Churchill, Jesus and Johnson, did not appease.

But it was not only the liberal professors and students who earned Graham's wrath. In 1965 a group of clergy attracted national attention, and also Graham's righteous indignation, when they placed full-page advertisements in the *New York Times* calling for Johnson to end the war in Vietnam. Graham's major response to these advertisements was to preach a sermon titled "When Silence Is Yellow," which left little doubt as to his opposition to the clergy and their cause. "We have our peace movements," he preached. "But if by peace we mean appeasing tyranny, compromising with gangsters and being silent because we haven't the moral fortitude to speak out against injustice, then this is not real peace. It is a false peace. It is a farce and it is a hoax." The clergy were yellow-bellied weak men, appeasers lured by the sirens of seductive communists, and deceptive in their politics. "These ads," Graham ranted, "failed to take note of the fact that President Johnson has offered peace time after time in speech after speech; and he has never heard a word from Peking or Hanoi."[97] That Johnson's "offer of peace" was really a call for unconditional surrender only made Graham happier in his assessment of the president. The radical clergy, he added, were not only deceptive but also anti-freedom and ultimately anti-American. "History," he argued, "shows that when a people cease to care enough to fight for their freedom, their society is on its way to oblivion."[98] If the clergy had their way, America would fall from grace and descend into oblivion, just as Rome had done. But good Christians must not let this happen; they must stand up against the liberals and offer an alternative voice and vote in the public debate about the Vietnam War. As Graham put this, "A few people who know what they believe, and are not afraid to express it, can change the world."[99] But if they remain afraid, "evil will take over this country."[100]

Unsurprisingly, then, Graham sought to turn the public debate about Vietnam into its own holy war: The liberal peaceniks were evil, the war's supporters were good, and Christ was calling his followers to battle against the godless dissent at home. Urging his listeners to rise up against the liberals, Graham put it this way: "Do it now—for Christ and for what you know is right. God bless you."[101] The evangelist led the way, and when the press asked about his missing signature on the advertisement, he sniffed: "I was not asked to [sign]—and if I had been asked, I would not have signed such a position."[102]

Taking his own stand against evil, the holy crusader also traveled to Vietnam during Christmas 1965, at the urging of President Johnson, and baptized the war effort in the clearest of terms. Graham told the assembled soldiers that he was deeply proud of "what you are doing to help keep Asian communism from engulfing all of Southeast Asia." He could have told the soldiers that the Prince of Peace remained nonviolent in the face of state-sanctioned violence, that he implored his followers to turn the other cheek, that he demanded his closest friends not to resist evil. But Graham once again allowed his hatred of communism to trump the nonviolent life of Jesus and his American pride to trample the Christian virtue of peace. He was proud, he said, not only because the soldiers were saving parts of Southeast Asia from communism, but also because "of the contribution you are making to help keep your own country free."[103] In Graham's conservative logic, the destiny of American freedom was tied to the Vietnam conflict; as Vietnam would go, so would the United States.

The evangelist returned to Vietnam the following Christmas and continued to declare his support for the war effort, although in more muted terms than he had in 1965. "I don't see any possibility for world peace apart from the intervention of God," he announced, "and the greatest thing we can do here in Vietnam is not only to stand by these people at this time, but it's to live in front of them." And the best way to live "in front of them" is by giving one's life to Jesus, because the most fundamental peace in the world is "peace with God," the condition of being right with God. Tapping into the individual soldier's heartfelt fear of death, Graham explained his point further: "To know that if I'm killed, if I die, I'm ready to meet God. . . . Nothing can bring a greater peace to man in the midst of trouble and difficulty in war than to know all that—that all the past is forgiven, not because you deserve it . . . but because Christ paid for it on the cross." The real peace that mattered was not the peace between the democrats and the communists, but the peace of an individual heart right with God.

This was convenient and comforting news for the soldiers, partly because it did not require them to lay down their weapons; they could shoot, bomb, or stab the communists and still be at peace with God in Christ. "Some of the greatest Christians that ever lived," Graham added, "were soldiers." They were soldiers who carried weapons, to be sure, but they also shone forth with peace in their hearts. And so the American soldiers in Vietnam would do well not only to give their lives to Jesus, but also to "let [the Vietnamese] see that there's something different about us, and let them see the peace that's in our hearts and in our lives and the discipline that's in our lives."[104] Of course, being different—the mark of a Christian—did not mean adopting nonviolence. For Graham, it was possible for one to kill with a Christian smile.

Returning to the United States, however, the evangelist began 1967 with a noticeably ambiguous impression of the Vietnam War. In his New Year's message, he conceded that before going to Vietnam, he "was just as confused and frustrated about the objectives of this war as the average American." Although the trip failed to clarify the war's objectives for him—Graham reported no evolution in his thought—his emerging ambiguous feelings did not eliminate or significantly lessen his support for the war. In fact, he reported that he was "impressed with the fact that most American military men feel that the mission in Vietnam is a peace mission. They hold the view that American presence in Southeast Asia is holding back the tyranny of Red China that seeks to dominate not only all of Southeast Asia but the entire world."[105] This was yet another strong statement in defense of the war, and so perhaps Graham's confusion and frustration were primarily about the administration's lack of resolve to win the war at all costs.

Indeed, Graham was still writing Johnson private letters of support in early 1967. "If a man," he wrote, "trusts in God and does what is morally right, *at any cost*—God will be his defense!" Once again, the evangelist connected Johnson's war politics with yet another war story from the Bible: "When Joshua had been appointed leader of the armies of Israel, and he was about to cross the Jordan River to do battle with the enemy, God said, 'Fear not, neither be thou dismayed' (Joshua 8:1)."[106] Like Joshua, Johnson should put his fear away, cross the river, and attack the enemy of God. Holy crusades did not just happen way back in Ancient Israel; they also happened in the jungles of Vietnam.

Against King

The year 1967 also saw Graham step up his verbal attacks on peace activists, including Martin Luther King, Jr. By 1967 the civil rights leader had already called for negotiations to end U.S. military action in Vietnam, but his early public statements on the war, to the consternation of militants like Stokely Carmichael, were relatively low-key and generally inoffensive to Johnson, whom King considered an occasional ally because of his hard push for both civil rights legislation, especially around the time of the Selma March, and the War on Poverty. But King eventually considered his virtual silence a betrayal of his divine mission to be a peacemaker; and in 1967, with the War on Poverty and the civil rights agenda near the bottom of Johnson's daily agendas, King chose Riverside Church in New York City to offer his first major public statement against the Vietnam War. Before reviewing the substance of his dissent, however, we would do well to survey the evolution of King's thoughts on violence and war, especially in relation to Graham's thought.

King was not always a pacifist. While a student at Crozer Theological Seminary in the early 1950s, he had written a paper titled "War and Pacifism," in which he claimed that he could not "accept an absolute pacifist position," partly because such a position would result in sheer anarchy. Finding the pacifists naïve, he wrote: "Since man is so often sinful there must be some coercion to keep one man from injuring his fellows. This is just as true between nations as it is between individuals." Though not a holy warrior, King believed that "some coercion" could properly come in the form of both police action within a society and warring actions between states—a position he justified by pointing not only to the insufficiency of the pacifist's anthropology but also, more positively, to the Christian obligation to love one's neighbor. "If one nation oppresses another," he wrote, "a Christian nation must, in order to express love of neighbor, help protect the oppressed."[107] Fascinatingly, these words, directly traceable to the writings of the Christian just-war theorist Paul Ramsey, suggest that the young King was far closer to the war ethic of Billy Graham than to the pacifism of Quakers, Mennonites, and the Church of the Brethren, at least in terms of justifying the morality of war.

By the time the Montgomery years arrived, King was still holding onto his claim that physical coercion was morally justifiable under certain circumstances. In fact, he believed the death threats against his life constituted a just cause for the potential use of force, and with this in mind he actually applied for a gun permit, which the local authorities promptly denied. King also refused to discourage friends and followers from using their own weapons for defending his family, with the result that many of the early Montgomery activists were not pacifists at all; their position on matters of violence and nonviolence was actually far closer to Billy Graham's than to Jesus' or Gandhi's. But all this would change in good time.

This is no place to trace King's pilgrimage to nonviolence; suffice it to note that the Quaker Bayard Ruston and others involved in peace churches eventually encouraged the civil rights leader to make nonviolence a way of life. In his own mind, though, King came to justify nonviolence on both practical and theological grounds. Practically, he came to believe that violence is self-defeating in the sense that it simply begets more violence. More specifically, he opposed violence as a practice of the civil rights movement for two practical reasons. First, he was realistic enough to observe that in light of the power and weapons controlled by both white supremacists and the U.S. government, it would be suicidal for African Americans to take up arms; only a slaughter would await them. Second, he held that violence was wrong because of his sense that the everyday means of the movement must always cohere with the end goal. In other words, the peaceable beloved community demanded peaceful means; otherwise, the community would be little more than the tragic end of a bloody and violent trail.

Theologically, the civil rights leader came to ground his nonviolence in the life and death of Jesus. King was one of those individuals who, according to Graham, tragically misunderstood the love of Jesus. With the encouragement of Rustin and others, King began to stress that love, as revealed in the cross of Jesus, entails a willingness to suffer for the end of reconciliation. Cruciform love is not about destroying evil with violence, but about facing "evil with an infinite capacity to take it without flinching."[108] When Jesus was hanging on the cross, King wrote, he could have called upon God to "let loose the mighty thunderbolts of righteous wrath and destroy" his persecutors. But Jesus did not strike his enemies—he loved them; he did not call upon his followers to take up arms—he told them to put their swords down; and he did not call upon God to kill his crucifiers—he asked God to forgive them. King's Jesus, unlike Graham's, refused violence, suffered nonviolently, and subjected himself to "inexpressible agony" and "excruciating pain."[109]

The whole world should do no less, King argued. On the one hand, King's evolving understanding of cruciform love led him to insist that the direct action of all civil rights activists should always and everywhere reflect self-sacrifice, ready forgiveness, and a desire for reconciliation with one's enemies. On the other hand, though, he maintained that Jesus' example of nonviolence was a moral imperative for all individuals and institutions, including secular, worldly governments. But there is an important qualification that deserves immediate attention here. Like Graham, King encouraged the U.S. government to enforce compliance with just laws, even through the use of violent means; for example, he frequently called upon state and federal governments to use their armed forces to protect civil rights activists. "Though a pacifist," he wrote in 1963, "I am not an anarchist." By this he meant that he favored "the intelligent use of police power" in situations where law and order broke down within society, especially in a community of white thugs pointing weapons in the faces of civil rights activists.[110] The significance of this, of course, is that King did not seek to make the state accountable to the nonviolent mandates of cruciform love when it carried out responsibilities associated with keeping domestic order. His unstated rationale, of course, was obvious: It simply would have been disastrous for him and his followers to refuse state force when marching among violent defenders of a racist system.

King thus joined the long line of Christian pacifists who had called for the use of police power on the domestic front while condemning the practice of war in the global community. It was a blatant inconsistency: He demanded that the state practice nonviolent love in the global community, but he allowed the state to set aside the mandates of nonviolent love when addressing domestic tension. Unsurprisingly, however, King simply let the inconsistency stand without additional comment; unlike Graham, he could not bring himself to justify violence in terms of Christian love.

With the inconsistency noted, the important point to highlight here is that King left behind his earlier acceptance of war and began to condemn it on both practical and theological grounds. Practically, he came to believe "that the potential destructiveness of modern weapons of war totally rules out the possibility of war ever serving again as a negative good."[111] King held, perhaps unjustifiably, that war would inevitably lead to nuclear war, and that because the very existence of humanity was at stake, war could no longer be helpful to humanity, with its God-given right to life, in any way. In effect, war had become obsolete, and not just because it could no longer serve a good; it had become obsolete also because science and technology had taken away the causes for war. "In this day of man's highest technical achievement," he wrote in 1968, "there is no excuse for the kind of blind craving for power and resources that provoked the wars of previous generations. There is no need to fight for food and land."[112] This remarkable, and naïve, statement is quite helpful for our purposes because it hints at King's understanding of the causes of war. As we will see in his assessment of the Vietnam War, King's thought sharply diverged from Graham's evangelical belief that the root cause of war is a sin-sick heart. For the civil rights leader, the root cause of war is not an unchristian heart, but the interrelated sins of racial injustice, poverty, and disenfranchisement.

Theologically, King came to oppose war largely because he believed it made a mockery of the life and teachings of Jesus. Fascinatingly, as

Graham's argument in favor of war was primarily christological, so was King's unqualified condemnation of war. Simply stated, the civil rights leader maintained that war was wholly antithetical to the cruciform love revealed in the life and death of Jesus; it opposed and undermined Jesus' admonitions to put down the sword, turn the other check, and love your enemies, as well as his undeniable embrace of nonviolence on the cross. King summarized his christological grounds for opposing war in yet another way, too, when he spoke to European Baptists in 1964. "This is the world for which Christ died," he stated.[113] His basic point here, profound in its simplicity, provided a sharp internal critique for a group not known for its love of pacifism: if they really believed that Christ died for the world, King argued, they would stop justifying anything that abuses, maims, or kills the world and its inhabitants.

A few years later, King also would back his christological arguments against war with a progressive theology of creation. "Every man," he would write, "is somebody because he is a child of God. And so when we say 'Thou shalt not kill,' we're really saying that human life is too sacred to be taken on the battlefields of the world . . . man is a child of God, made in His image, and therefore must be respected as such. Until men see this everywhere, until nations see this everywhere, we will be fighting wars."[114] Interestingly, Graham held the same belief in the *imago Dei*, but the evangelist, unlike King, ignored this theological point when making the case for war. And with good reason; after all, it would seem wholly impossible to make allowances for killing "the image of God."

On a related note, Graham and King differed not only on the justifiability of war but also on the possibility of world peace. Although King readily conceded that world war could easily erupt, primarily because of a group of racists and insecure egotists obsessed with their own designs for power, he consistently emphasized that the world stood on the cusp of global peace. In his Nobel Peace Prize acceptance speech, for example, he announced his refusal to "to accept the cynical notion that nation after nation must spiral down a militaristic stairway into the hell of thermonuclear destruction."[115] Unlike Graham, an advocate of just such a cynical notion, King never believed that humanity was too sinful to rise out of the ashes of violence and war; with the help of God, humanity could always make a way out of no way and choose peace in the ruins of violence.

Nor did King embrace Graham's belief that the world was hurling toward the Final Apocalypse. The apocalypse, for King, was not a historical inevitability at all, but simply a metaphorical depiction of divine wrath; and it would happen neither sooner nor later within human history. In short, King found the apocalyptic thought of fundamentalists and evangelicals, as well as their realistic assessment of humanity, to be too fatalistic, too resigned to war, and too dismissive of the human capacity to be peacemakers. He also found their thoughts on the Second Coming to be too pie-in-the-sky. Opposed to the traditional interpretation of the Second Coming—he held that Jesus comes again every time an individual acts for peace and justice—King refused to put all hopes for peace on Jesus at the end of time. Ultimately, the hope for peace lay not in the Second Coming somewhere out there, but in people dedicated right here and right now to the nonviolence that Jesus had exemplified in his own life.

One would think that King would have become more pessimistic about world peace through the years, but this did not seem to be the case. After his acceptance of the Nobel Peace Prize, for example, he claimed that the prize had given him "deeper personal faith that man will indeed soon rise to the occasion and give new direction to" the rage of humanity against humanity.[116] His deepening faith also resulted in general suggestions for world peace, all of which revealed a marked divergence from Graham's belittling of peace efforts. One suggestion, for example, called for renewed commitment to diplomacy centered in the UN, "the best instrument we have at this time to bring about the dream of peace." Unlike Graham, King depicted the UN not as a godless body whose work would ultimately fail, but as a vital institution whose mission of dialogue was essential to peace on earth. As he put this, "the greatest channel to peace . . . is through dialogue—nations sitting down at the peace table talking together about problems that must continue to rise."[117] But King also was realistic enough to believe that dialogue would not always be enough, and so he also pushed for nuclear test ban treaties and a world police force organized through the UN. Perhaps more significantly, while Graham found talk of world government to be heretical and a sign of the emergence of the Anti-Christ, King embraced world government as a key mechanism for creating global peace. World government was not an indicator of the end of the world, but the institutional path for achieving global security and peace. After all, a world government, or at least a strengthened UN in the short term, would possess the requisite power to redistribute land and resources, empower the racially marginalized, and enfranchise the disenfranchised—in other words, to take away the root causes of conflict and violence.

King's constructive suggestions pointed to his abiding belief that although states are sinfully flawed and limited, they are also deeply capable of responding to collective ventures designed to establish world peace. Unlike Graham, King truly believed that states could move away from obsessive concern with their own power, the constant search for more territory and material, and a false confidence in their own political communities as the perfect societies. Indeed, exactly because he was confident in the redemption of the state, King offered constructive suggestions for establishing peace here on earth, rather than pushing the possibility of peace into the hands of an angry God who would return only at the end of human history.

Back to King at Riverside. Partly because his faith opposed war in general, King took the Johnson Administration to task for executing the Vietnam War; but there were other reasons, too. The war was an enemy of the American poor, he preached. On the one hand, it was diverting money from the War on Poverty, and on the other, it "was sending their sons and brothers and their husbands to fight and to die in extraordinarily high proportions relative to the rest of the population."[118] Further, because he saw the issues of classism and racisim inextricably linked, King also labeled the war as racist and bemoaned the disproportionate deaths of not only the poor but also the many poor blacks. In addition, the war was also an enemy of the Vietnamese poor. After Vietnam had declared its independence in 1945, King argued, the United States had failed to recognize it as a sovereign state, choosing instead to support both France's efforts to recolonize the state and then a series of dictators who had opposed land reform that would benefit peasants. In short, the war was nothing other than a U.S. commitment to wealthy landlords who would deny economic justice and political power to hungry, disenfranchised peasants.

King had chosen to make his views known, he said, because doing so was simply part of his vocation as a Christian minister: "To me the relationship of this ministry to the making of peace is so obvious that I sometimes marvel at those who ask me why I am speaking against the war."[119] Of course, his controversial public stance against the war drew sharp opposition from both within the civil rights movement—James Farmer, Roy Wilkins, Whitney Young, and Ralph Bunche were among those who initially questioned King's public stance—and from outside the movement.[120] And one of his most vocal critics from outside the movement was one Billy Graham. Shortly after the Riverside speech, the evangelist appeared before the press and claimed that King was "making a mistake" by "tying the civil-rights movement with the anti-Vietnam demonstrations," and that his opposition was "going to hurt the civil rights movement and give comfort to Hanoi that the United States is divided."[121] Graham added that King's anti-war stance was "an affront to the thousands of loyal Negro troops who are in Vietnam."[122] The evangelist said nothing about the substance of King's faith—his vision of Jesus, his Christian vocation, his commitment to the poor and disenfranchised. Instead, Graham's response to King's prophetic sermon was purely political—suggesting, yet again, that he was sometimes willing to allow his Americanism to trump his own public expressions of faith.

The critics, especially Billy Graham, did not deter King from continuing his dissent from the war and buttressing his position along the way. Throughout the remainder of his life, the civil rights leader characterized the war as classist, racist, anti-Jesus, and anti-love. In 1967, for example, he told his staff that America had an obligation not to kill its enemies but to love them, just as Jesus had taught; love and killing were fundamentally opposed, never to be put together, especially in Vietnam. The civil rights leader also contended that the war was direct evidence of American arrogance and that "God did not appoint America to be policeman of the whole world. And America must recognize that she has not the capacity nor the power nor has she earned the moral right to be an American power, an Asian power, an Atlantic power and a South American power."[123] Beyond his staff, King told his followers in 1968 that "God didn't call America to engage in a senseless, unjust war, as the war in Vietnam," and that if America did not change its policies, God might "rise up and break the backbone" of American power.[124] And just one week before he died, he characterized the war as "one of the most unjust wars that has ever been fought in the history of the world."[125] It took the world to the brink of nuclear annihilation, propped up corrupt dictators, distributed wealth to the military-industrial complex, and opposed the self-determination of the majority of the Vietnamese, among other things.

"I Would Have Handled It Differently"

Graham had little tolerance for King or any other peace activist. Three months after King's Riverside speech, the evangelist proudly penned Johnson a letter about the peace activists picketing his appearance in London. "Wherever I speak," he wrote, "the anti-Vietnam demonstrators are there. As a matter of fact, they've been picketing my hotel." Apparently, he had steered clear of the demonstrators, but he noted that his associates had engaged the protestors in conversation. "We are convinced," he added, "that most of them are completely Marxists and some outright Communists."[126] Like other conservatives of the Vietnam era, Graham found it hard to believe that an American patriot, or even a British patriot, could do anything but support the effort in Vietnam.

This particular letter is most remarkable, however, because it includes indirect advice, if not indirect criticism, that the holy crusader himself most certainly supported. Graham reported to the president that he had recently been "a guest of honor at an extremely high level and important dinner" attended by socialists and members of the Labor Party. "During a discussion of Vietnam," he reported, "I asked them what they thought should be done. I was amazed when a left-winger spoke up and said: 'Win the war as quickly as possible.' Most of them seemed to agree that America cannot pull out but neither can she win at this present method." In effect, this was the evangelist's way of offering what he considered to be wise counsel to the wartime president; otherwise, Graham would not have passed it on. "You can take that for what it is worth," he added. "I was rather surprised at their reaction."[127]

By the end of the year, however, Graham could no longer contain himself, and his criticism turned uncharacteristically public. When the press asked him about the war in December, his answer was both a partial defense and a partial criticism of the president. Calling it a "strange war," as well as "one of the longest and one of the costliest wars in American history," the evangelist suggested that America did not really understand "the determination and dedication and the methods and techniques of communism. And if this is their plan—to get America involved in a great land war in Asia and it's certainly proving costly to the U.S. economy and it's dividing the American people—then I think they are going to do everything possible to keep us there."[128] Not even two million Marines "could actually win the type of war we are involved in without some help beyond that which I see at the moment, because the jungles are so terrific and the use of Cambodia and these other places as places of sanctuary makes it a very difficult war."[129] Struck by Graham's forthright answer, the media continued to press him, this time inquiring about U.S. incursions into Cambodia; but Graham declined to answer, citing a lack of knowledge about tactical matters. Switching tactics, however, the unrelenting reporters then asked him to evaluate Johnson's "handling of the Vietnam War," and with a bit of a stumble, the evangelist offered a sharply pointed criticism. "Well," he said, "there again I would be entering politics, and I, as you know, am a friend of Mr. Johnson, and if I had done it myself, I would have handled it differently. But, I'm not the President."[130]

In effect, Graham had come closer to King's position than he had ever been before, not in the sense of becoming a pacifist, of course, but in the sense of becoming a public critic of Johnson's war policies. As we have seen, Graham had assumed the role of a Hebrew prophet before, but never before had he acted prophetically, at least in a public setting, against the president's war policies. So what accounted for the evolution? Unfortunately, the catalyst behind his apparent ascension to the role of public prophet remains within the heart of Billy Graham, but we would be wholly remiss not to note two possible factors: the emerging groundswell of dissent even within politically conservative circles, and the re-resurrection of one Richard M. Nixon as a possible alternative to Johnson.

How would Graham have handled the war differently? The above letter suggested that he would have undertaken an all-out win sooner rather than later (apparently, the evangelist believed in the Powell Doctrine even before it came into existence), but the December 1967 press conference offered something different. "Well," he stated, "I'm not sure I would have gotten involved to start with, and I don't think we should blame President Johnson for this war. When President Kennedy was assassinated, he had 16,000 troops already in Vietnam and was on record that we could not afford to lose Vietnam . . . that we couldn't afford to lose Laos, and I think that President Johnson inherited a situation that had already been escalated."[131] But Graham's answer, like others he would provide in the years to come, was pure revisionism. In fact, the evangelist had criticized Kennedy for being weak on communism and losing Laos, and he had also strongly encouraged Johnson to recognize his divine anointing to save America from communism, especially as it took form in Vietnam. To say that he would not have gotten involved with Vietnam from the start was to deny all the holy-war counsel he had offered every American president from Truman to Johnson: Do not negotiate with evil, but fight communism at all costs. But Graham, it turns out, had begun his own politics of deception.

Even as he was questioning the war, however, the evangelist continued to denounce the peace activists. In this same press conference just noted, for example, he stated: "I think the form of protest and the technique of protest is wrong when they are trying to overrun recruiting centers, when they burn their draft cards and all the rest." These types of protest "are extending the war. They are actually helping the enemy because when they see this type of protest and this type of violence that is going along with it, the enemy says, 'If I hold out long enough, I am going to win this war.' " Graham even reported his hope that his own son, who was approaching draft age, would not burn his draft card. "I hope that he will gladly go and be willing to give his life for his country."[132] In spite of his misgivings about the war, the evangelist was far too patriotic, too American, too loyal not to offer his own son, Franklin, to the killing fields of Vietnam.

Although Graham criticized the anti-war protestors at this news conference, he also added that he "would not do away with the right of dissent."[133] Now that he had become critical of the president, the evangelist wanted to maintain a distinction between dissent and protest. Although he did not explain the difference in any detail, by "dissent" he meant participation in free, open, and unthreatening debates, and he understood "protest" to be virtually everything that the militant war protestors practiced—holding sit-ins, burning draft cards, and harassing the president. "I would hope," Graham stated, "that [the war] would be debated not only in the United Nations but in the United States Congress and Senate. I hope that this coming year in the election campaign it will be fully debated."[134] This was a significant move for Graham. Rather than his typical act of calling for blind obedience to presidential authority, the evangelist was calling for open debate about the president's war policies.

Predictably, as he joined the circle of Johnson's conservative critics, Graham seemed to lose his easy access to the White House. No longer did the president regularly invite Graham to come to the family quarters or to take a swim in the pool, as he had done so many times before. The distance between the two once-close men was strikingly evident a few weeks before King's 1968 assassination, during a press conference in Black Mountain, North Carolina, when Graham reported that he and the president had not spoken "in recent months."[135] The distance, however, proved healthy for Graham's ability and willingness to offer some of his most pointed criticisms of the president's war policies—criticisms that would have been unthinkable for him to publicize in 1965. At the Black Mountain press conference, for example, he confessed that he agreed with the dissent expressed by U.S. Senator Karl Mundt, a Republican from South Dakota, an ardent advocate of the war in its early stages but by 1968 a vocal critic of the president's execution and public management of the war. "Senator Mundt," Graham explained, "has been a supporter of the commitment there, but he said that he was having grave doubts because of . . . the credibility gap—because of what we are told, on the one hand, and what is actually happening, on the other."[136] This was perhaps the most serious charge that the pious evangelist would ever levy against Johnson and his administration—the charge of lying about military success in Vietnam.

Never mind that Graham himself had lied about his early support of the war; this time the pious preacher was disturbed by the president's own credibility problem.

Graham's "grave doubts" about U.S. military involvement in the war were not simply grounded in the president's deceptiveness, however. "Secondly," he added, "[this] is the first time . . . that a nation has fought a war that they did not intend to win or in which the objectives were not clear cut before the American people." If we take his earlier comments seriously, the so-called problem with objectives was less serious than the tactical problems of the war's execution; after all, Graham fully supported Johnson's so-called divinely sanctioned efforts to safeguard Western civilization from godless communism. Here was the real problem: "The fact that some of the major targets are left untouched and our men have to suffer the consequences—all of this would lead me to believe that the President and his administration are going to have to soon make a decision, either to admit that we have failed in this commitment or that they must win this commitment."[137] The major problem, once again, was that the president was not undertaking a full-scale assault against the godless communists. Just like Eisenhower and Kennedy, Johnson had become a "weak man."

The press, of course, followed up: "What decision do you think we should make?"[138] Would Graham dare to follow King and call for halting military action? Would he counter all his previous words about the evils of compromising with the evils of communism? Would he become part of the appeasers, the weak men he despised so deeply? Or would he hold onto the flag of the crusader and shout "Onward, Christian soldiers"? Would he invoke the name of Christ and counsel fighting communism in Vietnam at all costs? Would he return to the uncompromising call for "total mobilization" that he had telegrammed to Truman years earlier? What decision would he counsel?

"I don't know," Graham replied. "I really don't."[139]

Love Your Enemies: Three Manifestations of

Graham's Nonviolence

By the end of the King years, Graham's early support of the Vietnam War had begun to evaporate, and on the general point of dissension, his position on the war had grown closer to King's. But the convergence of their dissents was always tenuous, primarily because the two men held different substantive reasons for their opposition. Unlike King's, Graham's objection to the war was never grounded in an understanding of Jesus as a pacifist, a practical sense that violence begets violence, a Christian devotion to improving the economic lives of Vietnamese peasants, a negative sense of American arrogance, or a vision of peace on earth. Contrary to King, the evangelist was disturbed by the lack of clear objectives and the apparent

half-heartedness and public deception with which the Administration conducted the war. At times it seemed that Graham would have preferred the
use of overwhelming force to overrun the communist belligerents, but at
other times (for example, when he stated that even two million Marines
would not be able to win the war), it seemed that he was truly unsure about
his own war counsel. Theoretically, however, the points of convergence
on the Vietnam War could have been much more substantive than they
were, and more generally, the level of convergence between their ethics of
war and peace could have been much deeper than it was. To explain this
curious if not controversial thesis, however, requires backtracking chrono-
logically and exploring three major situations in which the evangelist,
believe it or not, actually embraced nonviolence.

Africa

Graham's theology of war and peace during the early years of the decolonization of Africa is notable especially for its embrace of Christian nonviolence. Like other American commentators at the time, the evangelist was
concerned about the potential for a huge bloodbath as increasing numbers
of Africans joined the decolonization movement. The potential for blood-
letting in Korea or Hungary had not given Graham much pause, but the
thought of Africans killing white Europeans concerned him so much
that he began to preach nonviolence. "Don't follow the revolution of those
who agitate violence," he counseled Africans in 1961, referring to the
communists and Muslims who were making their own bids for control in
parts of Africa. "Follow the flag of Jesus Christ, who advocates love."[140]

On the one hand, Graham pointed Africans to the historical Jesus, even
citing the saying beloved by generations of Christian pacifists: "You have
heard that it was said, 'An eye for an eye and a tooth for a tooth.' But I say
to you, 'Do not resist an evildoer' " (Mt. 5:43–44). On the other hand, the
evangelist invoked the spirit of the living Christ. "Christ the revolutionist is
at work in the world," he preached. "He seeks to shed no blood; his own
was spilled on Calvary's cross."[141] Graham's point was christocentrically
clear: Africans who would embrace violence would both rebuff the teachings of Jesus and refuse to follow the gentle spirit of the nonviolent Christ in
the world today. Any blood on their hands would be sin, plain and simple.

Graham's counsel to decolonizing Africans pushed further, too. Not
only did he tell them to refuse the option presented by the bloody sword;
he also demanded that they refrain from lifting their voice at all against the
tyranny of colonization. Leaving behind his theological roots in Augustine,
Luther, and Calvin, the evangelist seemed to find a new source within the
nonresistant Christology of the radical Reformation. Indeed, sounding
remarkably like an Anabaptist, the evangelist argued that Jesus was both
nonviolent *and* nonresistant to tyranny. "He didn't even bother to lift his
voice against the tyranny of Caesar," Graham preached. Again, his advice
was unmistakable: Rather than lifting their voices against the colonizing

powers, or imitating Marx and Lenin, Africans would do better to follow the one who was "far more revolutionary than Marx or Lenin."[142]

It is important to note here that Graham never once characterized the colonizing powers as evil, demonic, or possessed by Satan. In other words, he ascribed a different moral status to the colonizing powers than he did to the communists during the early to mid-King years. The communists were evil incarnate and thus a force to be eliminated, even with violent means, but the colonizers were merely sinful individuals in need of and certainly capable of the redemption made possible by Christ on the cross. Communists were for killing, but colonizers were for saving. Africans should therefore eschew violent revolution and instead begin "a gigantic counter spiritual revolution on the continent of Africa that will center all future developments around the Gospel of Jesus Christ."[143] The task before the Africans, then, was not to eliminate the colonists, but to use intercessory prayer and evangelism in a swordless battle to save them for life eternal and create a Christian continent.

The Civil Rights Movement

There were other occasions when Graham preached nonviolence during the King years. In 1965, for example, he wrote: "I have always tried to preach nonviolence in the solution to the race problem."[144] Although this claim requires minor qualification—Graham favored the use of police force to quell violence carried out by both whites and African Americans—his message to both races did consistently call for nonviolence.

When articulating his nonviolence during the early King years, Graham set forth four major arguments. First, he appealed to Jesus' admonition to love one's neighbor, just as he would do for the decolonizing Africans. At the time of the Little Rock crisis, for example, he argued that racial tension in America would take many years to solve, and that "in the meantime, it is the duty of every Christian to pray and reexamine the teachings of our Lord Jesus Christ on the subject of neighbor-love. . . . Jesus indicated that our neighbors are people of different races. No matter who they may be, we are told to love our neighbors as ourselves." Further, the evangelist argued that Christians were not free to apply this command in certain situations rather than others; the command to love one's neighbor was a moral absolute, and its substance consisted of nonviolence toward one's neighbor. "Now no matter how strongly a Christian may feel on certain interpretations of the law," Graham preached, "he has no scriptural grounds to resort to violence and mob rule . . . certainly a true child of God will not be found giving vent to hatred and malice."[145]

Fascinatingly, Graham also took the occasion of the Little Rock crisis to set violence in contradistinction to democratic freedom. "Violence against any individual," he claimed, "is a violation of the very freedoms that formed the structure of our nation and government."[146] Which freedoms did Graham have in mind? Although he did not unpack his thought in any detail, the Little Rock context suggests that Graham meant the freedom to dissent from unjust laws and customs. Whatever the case may be, however, Graham's second, albeit largely undeveloped, argument was that good citizens in a liberal democracy should always embrace nonviolence in domestic matters.

Third, the evangelist extended this political argument by claiming that "we have a special obligation to the oppressed people of the earth. God told his people to remember that one time you were strangers, and God said, 'Always love the stranger, no matter who he may be.' "[147] Ultimately, faithful living was not just a matter of refraining from violence against one's neighbor as a principle of liberal democracy; it was also about loving the stranger, the one in a foreign land, as African Americans were to whites, and vice versa, in the land of the Deep South and, in many cases, throughout America.

Fourth, Graham argued against violence as a means to solve the race problem because such violence would be a blasphemous revolt against duly constituted authority. Taking matters into one's hands, rather than turning one's discontent over to the political authorities, was bad enough, but taking weapons into one's hands in order to maim or kill one's domestic enemies was simply anathema to Graham's law-and-order ethics. The flip side of this was his belief that the primary role of government is to provide "law and order" for the citizenry. Just as citizens have an obligation not to take matters into their own hands, especially if those hands hold weapons, government has an abiding obligation to take up the sword and protect its citizenry against harm. Graham made this point most forcefully following the Detroit riots in 1967. In response to the blasphemous anarchy of riot-ers gone wild, he encouraged the federal government to wield the sword, through legislation and law enforcement, even violent methods, so that individual citizens would be protected at long last. "The very purpose of government," he emphasized, "is to provide a setting in which citizens may live productive lives free of the fear that others are able to injure them, kill them, or steal from them."[148] For Graham, whose theology of the state on this point was close to Luther's, this meant that the primary purpose of American government was to wield the sword against rioters in order to create a safe space in which individual citizens may live out the freedoms established by American democracy—to safeguard the American way of life. When government does not fulfill its primary mission of wielding the sword, it is simply natural, given the sinfulness of humanity, that individual citizens would take up their own sword, seek their own justice, and kill their opponents, with the end result being the emergence of anarchy—the antithesis of God's divine order for individuals and communities.

Radical Christians

Graham reserved his sharpest condemnation of violence, however, when addressing his own colleagues within the church. In 1967, for example, he lambasted Christians who, at the Church and Society Conference in Detroit, called for violence to change the structure of American society. First, Graham sounded the alarms. "Today within the church," he stated, "there are hundreds of men that are seeking to overthrow the redemptive message of Christ, but even more, to overthrow the United States government . . . working for violence in the overthrow of social structures in the United States." Second, he depicted the wayward Christians as evil and demonic, "the mouthpiece of Satan himself." They were so demonic because they "rejected God's method of redemption, which is the cross of Jesus Christ."[149] In Graham's thought, the very last thing the church should ever do is advocate a violent revolution within the United States. "How different from the attitude of Christ, who, when he was reviled, reviled not again," and how different from the Apostle Paul, who counseled Christians not to avenge themselves, not to repay evil with evil, but to live peaceably with all.[150] Graham had offered a similar argument two years before the Detroit conference, in his bestselling *World Aflame*. At that point he had concluded that the early church embodied and expressed a "distinctive mission to the world that was neither national, ideological, nor political. It was to bear witness to Jesus Christ. This witness was not to employ any kind of state power or to receive any measure of state support. It was not to take the sword and employ force."[151] Graham acknowledged that "God chose blood as the means of redemption," but he emphasized that spilling blood for means of redemption is an act that belongs only to God. "Only God can properly diagnose man's sin; only God can provide the remedy."[152] Thus, when the church advocates the spilling of blood as a means of redeeming society, it wrongly adopts a measure that belongs to God alone. The church also leaves behind, or at least diminishes to a secondary status, its primary mission, as demonstrated by the early church—"to preach the transforming Gospel of the grace of God and to use such means of social relief as would minister to the present needs of man."[153]

A Question of Allegiance

Given these three different examples, it is conceivable that there were possibilities for a deeper convergence between the ethics of war and peace set forth by Graham and King, as well as between their particular dissents from the president's execution of the Vietnam War. After all, in the examples just cited, the evangelist depicted Jesus Christ as essentially nonviolent and called upon Christians to follow the "flag of Christ" by acting nonviolently, spreading "neighbor love," and showing special concern for strangers in a foreign land—the very substance of King's response to both war in general and the Vietnam War in particular.

So why was there not deeper convergence between the two Protestant leaders? One possible answer is that Graham, unlike King, held one ethic for Christians and quite another for the state, allowing the latter to adopt forcible means in light of a so-called divine responsibility to wield the sword (Romans 13). But this would be a wrong explanation, primarily because of one reason: When making the case for military action in Vietnam, the evangelist invoked Christian love as the major reason that should drive the nation to war. Just so, his theology of war and peace did not maintain that the love ethic of Jesus holds only for individuals in general or Christians in particular; the love ethic was for a government contemplating the killing of Vietnamese peasants in order to prevent the spread of communism. Refusing the classic two-kingdoms approach of traditional Lutherans, then, Graham thus directly contradicted his earlier argument—crafted especially for Africans, civil rights activists, and other revolutionary Christians—that the love of Jesus was essentially nonviolent and nonresistant. For America on the brink of killing communists, Christian love demanded the use of violent means.

If Graham was ever a peacemaker, it was only when nonviolence served his conservative agenda of keeping revolutionary Africans in check, halting the progress of the civil rights movement, and opposing the peaceniks of the Vietnam era. Conversely, Graham refused the nonviolence of Jesus when violence served his conservative politics of opposing communism at all costs. In fact, he always allowed his aversion to communism to trump his embrace of Jesus as nonviolent and nonresistant. With the evils of communism before him, the evangelist could not help but transform the nonviolent Jesus into a military general commanding his followers to take up arms and slaughter the godless enemy. At last, a deeper convergence between Graham and King did not happen exactly because the evangelist's allegiance to America the beautiful was far greater than his allegiance to a nonviolent Jesus.

Billy Graham was not a Christian peacemaker in the tradition of Jesus, the early church, and such American pacifists as the Quakers, the Mennonites, and the Brethren. Although he occasionally sounded the themes of traditional Christian pacifism, Graham was first and foremost a politically conservative Christian devoted not only to saving souls but also to killing godless communists with overwhelming force so that the American way of life could be preserved. Ultimately, Billy Graham was an American holy warrior.[154]

Conclusion: "We Are Now in the Violent Society"—A Question of Legacy

"The brutal assassination of Dr. Martin Luther King has stunned the world!"[1] So began Billy Graham's *Hour of Decision* sermon on April 7, 1968, three days after the death of the civil rights leader. It was also Palm Sunday, the day in the church year when liturgically minded Christians remember Jesus' triumphant entry into Jerusalem. Jesus had entered Jerusalem at the time of Passover, a dramaturgical season that brought together large gatherings of dispossessed Jews for public religious observances. The sizable crowds, thick with discontent, made Roman authorities more than wary of the possibility of political insurrection; and, in fact, Jesus was arrested and crucified shortly after his arrival in Jerusalem partly because the violent Roman government had envisioned him and his followers as a threat to their status and role as occupiers. Of course, Christians have long de-radicalized and de-politicized the story of Jesus and his final days, even to the point of marketing Palm Sunday merely as a family event for waving palm branches and prompting small children to pet the hired donkey.

Graham desicated the story, too. Although Palm Sunday 1968 presented him with a fitting occasion for honoring King's prophetic life and poignant death, the evangelist refused. No doubt, the civil rights leader had struggled with a character flaw that Graham would have been familiar with. But it is also doubtless that just as Jesus had defiantly entered the epicenter of oppression in order to set his people free, so had King marched into the very heart of American power, declaring that government and civil society must liberate his own people from racial discrimination, economic injustice, and political disenfranchisement—and for a peaceful life in the beloved community. In this sense, King, like Jesus, was a significant threat to the powers that be—the gatekeepers of a broken community marked by organized racism, poverty, and violence. But any connection, however loose, between the revolutionary politics of the assassinated King and those of the crucified Jesus was totally lost on Graham. By Palm Sunday of 1968 the evangelist saw the slain civil rights leader as neither a Messianic figure nor a Christian martyr, but as an activist with a faulty understanding of the true essence of the Gospel.

More significantly, Graham even dared to use his Palm Sunday radio program to offer substantive counterpoints, albeit indirectly, to the slain leader's goals and tactics. For example, while King had consistently emphasized the need for social-structural remedies to racial discrimination, Graham's message proclaimed that "no amount of legislation or money can do half the good that a smile or an act of love can do." While the civil rights leader had never stopped dreaming of peace on earth, and had praised even the small dream realized through the Great Society, Graham's sermon depicted King's assassination as final confirmation of the folly of lofty dreams. "Instead of the Great Society," he announced, ". . . we are now in the Violent Society, where the law of jungle is beginning to assert itself." And while King had condemned the Vietnam War, the evangelist praised Australia as a partner in the fight against communism. "I feel in my heart," he confessed, "that I would like to be in America at this hour. But in the providence of God, he sent us to Australia, and we will continue our commitments here, preaching the Gospel of Jesus Christ in this great country . . . our allies in Southeast Asia."[2] In short, Graham's Palm Sunday sermon was yet another statement of opposition to King's beloved community and his goals for pushing America to the Promised Land.

Unsurprisingly, then, Graham did not return to America for the memorial service. Doing so would have meant not only having to commemorate a man whose work he had not embraced for years, but also losing the opportunity to save thousands of individual souls for Jesus Christ, Graham's consistent priority throughout the King years. But had he left the golf courses and stadiums of Australia and come back for the service, he could have bowed his head next to his friend Richard Nixon at Ebenezer Baptist Church and listened to King's eerie reflections on his own funeral, delivered just a month earlier, as they played over the sanctuary speaker:

I'd like somebody to mention that day that Martin Luther King, Jr., tried to give his life serving others. (*Yes*)

I'd like for somebody to say that day that Martin Luther King, Jr., tried to love somebody.

I want you to say that day that I tried to be right on the war question. (*Amen*)

I want you to be able to say that day that I did try to feed the hungry. (*Yes*)

And I want you to be able to say that day that I did try in my life to clothe those who were naked. (*Yes*)

I want you to say on that day that I did try in my life to visit those who were in prison. (*Lord*)

I want you to say that I tried to love and serve humanity. (*Yes*)

Yes, if you want to say that I was a drum major, say that I was a drum major for justice. (*Amen*) Say that I was a drum major for peace. (*Yes*) I was a drum major for righteousness. And all of the other shallow things will not matter. (*Yes*) I won't have any money to leave behind. I won't have the fine and luxurious things of life to leave behind. But I just want to leave a committed life behind. (*Amen*) And that's all I want to say.[3]

And this is exactly what we can say when depicting the life and legacy of Martin Luther King, Jr. forty years after his death. We can say that he did try, relentlessly, to reconcile the divided, give bread to the hungry, and bless the peacemakers. And we can say that he died just as he lived—with a burning commitment to serve his neighbors and, most of all, to save the soul of America. Unfortunately, however, we can also say that King and all his well-intentioned followers failed to create the beloved community for which he had longed and fought so deeply. Racial discrimination, though no longer formally sanctioned by federal, state, and local governments, continues to be a harsh reality for people of color, especially in the inner cities. Economic justice, in spite of the globalization of our market through such measures as North American Free Trade Agreement (NAFTA), is far from a reality for millions who fall below the poverty line. And local and global peace continues to elude us as we hunt so-called demonic terrorists lurking somewhere in dark caves in Pakistan and Afghanistan. King failed to save us.

Nevertheless, his unfulfilled dream has powerfully served to inspire millions of people, in America and elsewhere, to conceive of an alternative reality to the broken community of our lives. Drew Hansen has even argued, in his book on the "I Have a Dream" speech, that King's dream "has helped to change our conception of America so completely that it is no longer possible to argue that America should be anything less than the redeemed nation King envisioned on August 28, 1963."[4] Perhaps it would have been more modest for Hansen to claim that the dream normally emerges as one ideal among others in public discussions about the future of America, but his depiction of King's legacy is not far off the mark: Because of the slain civil rights leader, countless Americans believe they know who we should be and how we should act. To be sure, some Americans continue to find King's dream vacuous and vapid, but it would be foolish to deny that it has also inspired millions to imagine a constructive option for our lives—an agapeic community—and to stand up here and now against forces of racism, economic injustice, and violence. A key part of King's legacy, in other words, is a community of dreamers and activists who refuse to resign themselves to economic or political fatalism, or even its kissing cousin, a religious cynicism that places final hope for the betterment of humanity in the life beyond.

At last, this brings us to the inevitable question of Billy Graham's legacy: What will we say of the evangelist and his ministry, particularly during the King era, forty years after his death? However much it may hurt our liberal sensitivities, we will certainly be able to say that he was right in his realistic assessment of King's dream as largely fanciful. From the perspective of our broken communities at the beginning of this new century, King's beloved community seems like a fantasy of epic proportion. And so, for those of us who take his thought seriously, Graham's adamant refusal to join others in extolling King's dream unqualifiedly has left us more realistic and reasonable than we would have been had we listened only to the dreamer of dreamers.

At the same time, however, we will have to acknowledge that there is good reason that the legacy of Billy Graham will never include a national holiday celebrating his contribution to America. Although the evangelist excelled at criticizing the dream—in fact, only Malcolm X provided an equally powerful critique—he also failed to inspire us to be right on integration, right on poverty, and right on violence, and to struggle day in and day out for peace and justice on earth. Graham was deeply courageous when preaching against segregation in the Deep South, and he effectively moved his fundamentalist and evangelical sisters and brothers to open their doors, if not their hearts, to the African Americans they had once consigned to a second-class citizenship. The evangelist was also surprisingly prophetic in his (short-lived) advocacy for the War on Poverty, and he rightly implored his religious brothers and sisters to take a cup of water to the thirsty in their midst. But if this book has demonstrated anything, it is that the Billy Graham of the King years was no drum major for integration, especially what he termed "forced integration"; that before and after his flirting with the War on Poverty, he was rarely a drum major for economic justice; and that apart from calling Africans, civil rights advocates, and Christian dissidents of the Vietnam War era to embrace nonviolence, he was far from a drum major for peace. In terms of advocacy for the beloved community, Graham's record was nothing if not ignominious.[5]

If we remember correctly, we will understand Billy Graham to be the major Protestant obstructionist to the beloved community that Martin Luther King, Jr. dreamed of for America. In the final analysis, Graham was a political, economic, and evangelical conservative who believed that only the Second Coming of Christ can ensure that black children will hold hands with white children, that two chickens will appear in every pot, and that war will no longer plague us. And here is the full reason that there will never be a national holiday marking the birth of Billy Graham: Coupled with his cynical reaction to King's dream, Graham's own dream for a redeemed America, with its promise that social life would reach fulfillment only when Christ comes again, gave Americans little reason to fight for a better life, for liberty and justice for all, right here and right now.[6] In effect, Graham left us mostly in despair over present social inequities and injustices.

The despair continues. As King's dream of the beloved community has failed to come to fruition, so has Graham's promise of the Second Coming: Christ has not descended from the clouds to help us love people of color, feed the hungry, and turn our swords into plowshares. If we accept

Graham's evangelical theology, the tragic reality is that a procrastinating Christ remains at the right hand of the Creator, holding off, for yet another long day and for reasons unknown, to bring salvation and wholeness to a fallen creation. And this, too, is what we can and should remember when we gather forty years from now and reflect on the evangelist's legacy during the King years: Graham's dissent from the beloved community was ultimately deluded in its promise that Jesus Christ would soon return to right the social wrongs. Christ did not save America in the twentieth century, and if the last two millennia are fair indicators, it does not seem that he will save America anytime soon, either. On the contrary, the signs of the time suggest that we will continue to act both like lost sheep in the pastures of race and poverty politics and like a feared Leviathan in the amorphous sea of global politics.

Still, Graham was admirably relentless in preparing America and the world for life eternal. Although he was no drum major for peace and justice, Billy Graham was the world's best trumpeter for personal salvation, for his Lord and Savior, and for the Second Coming.[7] To be sure, the Second Coming never came, but no one sounded the clarion call of evangelical Christianity more mellifluously and effectively than Graham did. Towering above all others, the genteel trumpeter was spirited, authentic, and undeniably charismatic as he played across the world, beckoning his audiences to kneel at the foot of the cross, confess their sins, and proclaim Jesus as Lord.[8] And if nothing else, this revivalist invitation points to Graham's self-created legacy before, during, and after the King years—generations upon generations of individuals who believe that the evangelist gently guided them to receive Jesus Christ as their personal Lord and Savior so that they would be ready for the Second Coming and life eternal.

Unfortunately, however, the trumpeter's tunes did far more than innocently encourage lost souls to march to glory; they also sought, directly and intentionally, to drown out the drum major's cry for the beloved community. But Graham, it turns out, was just not that good a trumpeter: King's cry could not be silenced. Even in death, his hope against hope echoes through our collective soul, encouraging us to refuse religious fatalism, develop our moral imagination, and act constructively for all the good that currently eludes us. Finally, then, this is also part of Graham's legacy from the King years—his ultimate failure to use the sonorous tunes of evangelical Christianity to silence King and the beloved community.

Thank God for that. If Graham was right to suggest that the Violent Society had successfully beaten the Great Society into submission—and it seems he was—perhaps this latter part of his legacy constitutes his best (albeit negative) contribution to the soul of America. Exactly because Graham and other advocates of resignation failed to squelch moral dreamers and actors—the women and men of all colors who work tirelessly here and now to transform our practices, roles, and institutions into bastions of life, liberty, and happiness—we are not yet dead. We have survived the

Violent Society, not only just as we are, but also as everything we still hope to become.

★   ★   ★

Because he is so admired, it is likely that Graham's ardent defenders, including a few perfervid disciples, will come out in full force upon reading this book. Perhaps they will argue that the real Billy Graham played the most important role in the integration of the South; that he was actually the precursor of new groups of evangelicals who focus on social sins and their social-structural remediation; or that he was a tireless advocate of peace, especially in terms of his emerging critique of the Vietnam War. At the very least, the debate to come about Graham's history and legacy will certainly be intellectually engaging and emotionally frustrating; an attitude or act that one critic will emphasize will be the same attitude and act that another critic will deemphasize. All I ask is that the defenders engage and critique my work on its own limited terms—Graham's social thought and action during the King years—recognizing that the evangelist's personal papers are not yet fully available for public research. If the defenders are fastidious about the existing record, I believe that they will concede exactly what I have concluded: Rather than supporting King's tactical strategies and goals, Graham frequently redlined himself far outside the inclusive, just, and peaceful community that the civil rights leader died trying to achieve.

Appendix: Behind the Billy Pulpit

"Today, I am writing the Easter message, so you'll know when you hear it. Billy has been terribly busy, and on the run every minute, so I don't see him much, but he has been so wonderful to work with, and so appreciative of all I have been doing."[1] These words, part of a 1954 letter that Robert O. Ferm wrote to his family from the famous Harringay Crusade in London, suggest that Billy Graham preached sermons ghostwritten by members of his staff.

Shortly before Ferm wrote this revealing letter, he had petitioned for a leave from his position as Dean of Students at Houghton College for the purpose of conducting research for Graham at Harringay. Houghton granted the initial leave and then extended it after the evangelist had wired a personal request to the college's president. Graham's rationale for his request is especially clear in a telegram he sent to Robert's spouse, Lois Ferm, shortly after wiring the president: "I have been greatly aided by his research and other services. In these days of unprecedented revival I have great need of his service."[2] The service rendered by Ferm and deemed indispensable by Graham included the ghostwriting of outlines and manuscripts for sermons that the evangelist then preached, without ever publicly acknowledging Ferm's contribution, at the Harringay Crusade, on the *Hour of Decision* radio programs, and on BBC radio.

Ferm was not the first ghostwriter for Graham. In 1951 the evangelist had approached Lee Fisher, a wayward evangelist then working at a ranch for troubled boys in Florida, with a request to join the Graham team as a writer and researcher. In an interview conducted by Robert Ferm for the Billy Graham Evangelistic Association (BGEA) Oral History Project and recently made public by the Billy Graham Archives at Wheaton College, Fisher reported that Graham had solicited his sermon-writing services by stating, "Lee, I don't have anybody to help me in the writing or the research. I've never had anybody. Would you be interested in helping me in that capacity?"[3] Longing for a return to fulltime evangelistic ministry, Fisher expressed enthusiasm at the possibility of becoming part of a world-wide evangelistic movement, and Graham invited him to begin writing and researching immediately.

Another year would pass before Fisher would formally join the Billy Graham team, but he submitted sermon material to the itinerant evangelist every week after their informal interview. "I was very pleased," Fisher recalled, "to tune in the *Hour of Decision* and see that he was using it."[4] In 1952 Fisher then joined the BGEA as "research assistant," and for the next twenty-three years he labored with a typewriter in a study far from the pulpit at center stage, where Graham would use Fisher's words to exhort millions of people to confess their sins before God, receive the forgiveness made possible by the blood of Jesus, accept Christ as their personal Lord and Savior, and begin to live the Christian life. Restricting himself to behind-the-scenes ministry was not always easy for Fisher, and so he was delighted when BGEA eventually added "staff evangelist" to his formal title. But the Graham team rarely used Fisher as a preacher, and in remembering the promotion he suggested that the change of title actually served to "cover up for the very personal and intimate work I was doing for Billy."[5]

Rather than admitting that others authored manuscripts he regularly preached, Graham reported in his autobiography that although he had turned to key staff members for background research and editorial work on his speeches, articles, and books, he had never relied on his staff for the preparation of evangelistic sermons. "It has always been helpful to talk over with others an article or special speech while I was drafting it. At the same time, I have always adapted and digested material until it was part of me. And I have never been able to have others help me do my evangelistic sermons."[6] This claim, however, is misleading, and the best available evidence for countering it is the small collection of letters that Robert Ferm wrote to Lois, who would later become an employee of the Association, and their family from London in 1954. Because this issue is so sensitive and will surely generate a chorus of Graham defenders, this excursus will document the Ferm correspondence.

One of the earliest letters in the series, dated March 18, 1954, reveals that within the first week of his arrival in London, Ferm was already writing the entire script, including Graham's sermon, for the *Hour of Decision* radio program. After relaying this exciting news home, the researcher was careful to inform his family that "his unusual service in [God's] name" was "top secret," not to be talked about outside the family.[7] The discrete researcher soon discovered that his confidential work was increasing appreciably, so much so that by March 23, shortly after arriving in London, he was sending Graham one manuscript a day—a full sermon outline. "Right now," he penned home, "I am giving B.G. one mss. a day, and that takes time. I am going to attempt two tomorrow, and if so, Friday I hope to visit Stratford on Avon."[8]

Ferm found his new work consuming and lonely but also rewarding and talismanic. "Last night," he wrote home on March 27, "it was another thrill to hear preached a message I labored over here alone."[9] A day later he added: "Billy has been using my messages right along, so although I seldom visit with him, I am sure he must be satisfied. It is a thrill to listen, after I have spent hours in thought and research and prayer, and then see hundreds come to Christ. I know my limitations in preaching, but perhaps this is God's way of making up to me what I lack in other ways."[10] Ferm would suggest time and again that although he was hidden behind the scenes, far from the public eye, his ghostwriting of Graham's sermons was nothing less than the will of God. "You all know what my part in the work is," he wrote his family, "and it is the kind of work that receives no glory and has to be done alone. But God has honored it and I will praise Him for it. Just pray . . . that I will receive special help from His Word as I am serving Him this way."[11]

On April 9 the devout researcher reconfirmed what he had mentioned to his family earlier—that his daily contribution to the will of God now included both the completion of an outline for a crusade sermon and work on manuscripts for Graham's *Hour of Decision* sermons. "After breakfast, I finished one more outline. I feel I must bring at least one a day, beside the H.O.D. messages."[12] Remarkably, Graham had begun by this point to depend on Ferm for the substantive content of the evening messages at Harringay—a dependence that the researcher detailed in a letter post-marked April 9: "When I brought the mss. to [Graham's] room this after-noon, I talked a moment with Ruth, and she said he depended on my daily outline and notes for the evening message, so thank God for this service I can render."[13] Ferm found this news so significant that he repeated it just a few days later in yet another letter home: "[Graham] has been using my messages nightly, and depends on one to be brought to him each day."[14] Equally remarkable, the days for which Graham expected Ferm's sermons included two of the most significant in the church year—Palm Sunday and Easter Sunday—as noted in Ferm's April 10 request of his family: "Be sure to listen to the Palm Sunday H.O.D., for known reasons, and also Easter. Continue to pray for me, that I can do the work, and keep some degree of health to do all B.G. needs done."[15] The researcher also noted in this letter that Graham had asked him to begin writing two books, one on the law of God and one on reconciliation.

Coupled with the intense pressure of writing sermons that thousands would hear at the crusade services and on the *Hour of Decision* was Ferm's acute homesickness, and his discontent came pouring out in an April 9 letter: "I find I must constantly ask the Lord to keep me from being dis-contented, and to give me the spirit of Paul, who said, 'I have learned that whatever state I am in, therewith to be content.' "[16] Although he recog-nized the value of his work and expressed no desire to disappoint Graham's expectations, Ferm became so discontented in England that he decided to take his problem directly to his boss; but the evangelist's predictable response, given his dependence on Ferm's daily sermons, was to insist that the homesick man stay with the crusade through the end of April. Ferm agreed, and it was at this point that Graham wired Stephen Paine, the pres-ident of Houghton College, with the request for an extension of Ferm's leave of absence. Ferm relayed this important news to his waiting family on April 12 and then added: "Today I am writing the Easter message, so you will know when you hear it."[17]

With the arrival of Easter Sunday, just days after he had learned that Graham also wanted ghostwriting services for sermons that he would preach on trips to Berlin, Paris, Stockholm, Oslo, and Copenhagen, Ferm found himself alone in his hotel room once again, writing yet another message for the evangelist. "I didn't go to church this morning, though it is Easter," he lamented to his family. "I had to finish a series of talks for Billy to go on B.B.C." Easter Sunday also brought the languorous Ferm a one-on-one meeting with Graham, who approved even more sermons to be ghostwritten. "I just had a meeting with Billy," he wrote. "Ruth called me to come up, and he gave approval of the series I am working on. Messages from the Beatitudes. He also told me what he wanted from the continent, and we knelt to pray for God's blessing on the trip. I have the feeling that I'm just in some strange way being carried along, not planning but following a plan."[18]

Twelve days later an airplane would carry an exhausted Ferm back to his family, but he felt touched by the afflatus of God and knew that he would not—could not—leave behind what he considered to be the divine plan for his life with Billy Graham. The omnicompetent researcher would eventually become a fulltime employee of the Billy Graham Evangelistic Association and travel with Graham throughout Europe and then the world. As director of research and special projects, he would continue to do research and writing for Graham, especially for his newspaper column titled "My Answer by Billy Graham," and would later direct major administrative duties associated with the planning and execution of Graham's worldwide crusades. But devoted to Graham and his ministry, Ferm, like other crusade associates and even Ruth Bell Graham, would never publicly disclose his sensitive role in ghostwriting the evangelistic sermons that Graham had preached in Harringay and across the globe. Ferm's complicity in keeping the secret even appears to be recorded in an interview conducted by his wife Lois on June 21, 1978, in which he obliquely referred to his special research during a cryptic exchange:

> *Lois Ferm:* "You did other types of research too."
> *Bob Ferm:* "Yes, many others."
> *Lois Ferm:* "Some of which are those things which are best known to Mr. Graham and they could be left there."
> *Bob Ferm:* "Well, the very first one, I think my breaking in, was in his book, *Peace with God*. I assisted in the preparation in that book."[19]

From this point on, the interview stutters and stops and stutters some more, addressing every major issue but Robert's ghostwriting of Graham's evangelistic sermons, presumably the research that Lois thought best to keep hidden from the public.

It is clear, then, that Graham and his associates have sought to keep the ghostwriting roles of Lee Fisher, Robert Ferm, and perhaps a number of other individuals in Graham's inner circle, including John Akers, from the

public eye. Also clear is that the role of the ghostwriters was simply indispensable for the success of Graham's public ministry, especially given the
evangelist's grueling schedule at the peak of his career. Like other major
public figures, Graham often faced daily schedules that were simply unbear-
able, fully packed with meetings, interviews, speeches, strategy sessions,
and even golf outings: there was very little time for Graham to study and
reflect on the Bible and biblical commentaries, let alone to complete an
entire sermon for every preaching date. In short, he was simply too busy to
write all of the sermons he preached during his crusades. Given this hectic
schedule, it should come as no surprise that he relied on ghostwriters for his
evangelistic sermons. Interestingly, however, Graham's biographers, in
addition to his critics and the worldwide media, have either missed or
ignored this practice, with the result that the contributions of Graham's
staff have yet to limn into public consciousness. The one exception is
William Martin, whose massive biography (rightly critiqued by Tom Wicker
for its sympathetic tone) notes Graham's reliance on ghostwriters in only
one sentence.[20]

One of the reasons for the oversight surely reflects the style and delivery
of the sermons: When Graham preached, it seemed that the words really did
flow from his own heart, mind, and soul. On the one hand, this is partly
because he was not actually borrowing words written by unknown others;
staff members who doubled as friends were writing words especially *for*
Billy Graham. On the other hand, the evangelist was simply masterful in his
presentation. His mellifluous and powerful delivery, able to quiet a stadium
with 60,000 worshippers, young and old, gave very little indication that he
was preaching sermons written by ghostwriters; rarely did he ever stumble
over the words before him, and rarely did he seem removed from the sermon text as he condemned and cajoled, swayed and persuaded. Perhaps
another reason for the oversight is the undeniable cultural expectation that
preachers, even famous ones, will devote significant parts of their work
schedule to preparing and writing their own sermons. While we expect
that politicians will openly rely on writers for their speeches—indeed, we
know that speechwriters are on the public payroll and occupy public
offices—we seem to hold our preachers to a different standard. We do not
expect them to have ghostwriters on the payroll but trust them to share
with us what they have personally discovered, in their daily study and practices, about faith in the God of everyday life.

Whatever the reasons for the oversight might have been, a stereoscopic
focus on Graham's ghostwriters would certainly sharpen the quality of
works on the making of Billy Graham. Graham biographer Grant Wacker
has rightly suggested that "what is needed . . . is a careful effort to see how an
array of historically specific personal ingredients—talent, ambition, charisma,
stamina and integrity—combined with an array of historically specific social
ingredients—militarization, suburbanization, internationalization, and
diversification—to create a man and a legacy of exceptional proportions."[21]
But Wacker's thesis is insufficient: Also of fundamental importance is

significant research into Graham's immediate sources—his ghostwriters—
and the various sources they adapted for encouraging millions of individuals
to surrender their lives to Jesus Christ. Careful questioning about the role
of ghostwriters could lead to the pinpointing of possible changes, subtle and
otherwise, in the substance and tone of Graham's evangelical theology: Did
the writers shape his theology of atonement? Did they help him evolve
from the alarmist stance he had adopted early in his career? Were they
driving forces behind his ecumenical appeal?

The task of pursuing these questions is necessary, not merely helpful, for fully
understanding the indisputable power of Billy Graham's ministry, but the pro-
tectiveness currently surrounding Graham's personal papers, as well as those of
his former associates, makes answering the questions virtually impossible at this
point in history. And so the making of Billy Graham is a story that remains
for Graham scholars to tell in years to come. Until we have full access to those
papers and begin studying Graham as the head of a research and writing staff,
we will not tell his story as well as we could. But this much is already
unassailable: The extraordinary ministry of Billy Graham was due in large
part to the hard work of ordinary researchers and writers who typed and
retyped manuscripts in rooms far from the Billy pulpit.

NOTES

Introduction: "Bowed in Prayer"—Resurrecting the Assassinated King

1. Billy Graham, *Just As I Am: The Autobiography of Billy Graham* (San Francisco, CA: HarperSanFransisco, 1997), 696.
2. Martin Luther King, Jr., "The Birth of a New Age," in *Papers 3*, 346.
3. Quoted in Marshall Frady, *Billy Graham: A Parable of American Righteousness* (Boston, MA: Little, Brown and Company, 1979), 416.
4. "Billy Graham Closes Brisbane Conference," April 7, 1968, News Release, Crusade Information Service, Billy Graham Team Office, collection 345, box 55, no. 5, BGCA.
5. The *Hour of Decision* was the Billy Graham Evangelistic Association's weekly radio program. Inaugurated in 1950, the program usually included Christian music, announcements about Graham's ministry, prayers, and a sermon by Graham or a guest.
6. Graham, no title, April 7, 1968, collection 191, tape 952, BGCA.
7. See Segment for McNeil/Lehrer News Hour, Public Broadcasting System, April 7, 1992, collection 74, V42, BGCA; Graham, *Just As I Am*, 426.
8. David L. Chappell, *A Stone of Hope: Prophetic Religion and the Death of Jim Crow* (Chapel Hill, NC: The University of North Carolina Press, 2004), 140–144.
9. Chris Rice laments that "King and Graham exemplify probably the greatest partnership that never happened: two ministers of the gospel, representing two streams that truly need each other but have never combined in a massive, interracial movement" ("An Unrealized Dream—Billy Graham and Martin King: The Road Not Traveled," *Sojourners* [January 27, 1998]: 14). My study explores some of the reasons behind the divergent streams of King and Graham, but unlike Rice, I believe that the convergence of their streams would have meant the dominance of one or the other. By their very nature, the different streams, at least as they existed in the public ministries of Graham and King, sought to overtake each other.
10. I say "credible" because there is also a corpus of vitriolic and academically unhelpful writings against Graham, especially from rabid fundamentalists. For a credible book-length critique, see the overlooked Joe E. Barnhart, *The Billy Graham Religion* (Philadelphia, PA: Pilgrim Press, 1971). Although often hyperbolic, the sharpest analysis and criticism of Graham continues to be William McLoughlin, *Billy Graham: Revivalist in a Secular Age* (New York, NY: Ronald Press, 1960); a far less substantive and mostly unhelpful critique is Chuck Ashman, *The Gospel According to Billy* (Secaucus, NJ: Lyle Stuart, 1977). The best biography by far is William Martin, *A Prophet with Honor: The Billy Graham Story* (New York, NY: William Morrow & Company, 1991); although Tom Wicker has accused Martin of being unduly sympathetic, all other biographies come nowhere near the critical analysis that he offers. Among the few critical articles, the best are those written by Richard Pierard on the evangelist's presidential and war politics. Unfortunately, the hagiographic, or at least relatively uncritical, literature on Graham is simply enormous. For example, see David Aikman, *Great Souls: Six Who Changed the Century* (Nashville, TN: Word, 1998); Mary Bishop, *Billy Graham, The Man and His Ministry* (New York, NY: Grosset & Dunlap, 1978); Lois Blewett, *20 Years Under God: Proclaiming the Gospel of Jesus Christ to the World* (Minneapolis, MN: World

Wide Publications, 1970); George Burnham, *Billy Graham: A Mission Accomplished* (Westwood, NJ: Revell, 1955); George Burnham and Lee Fisher, *Billy Graham: Man of God* (Westchester, IL: Christian Readers Club, 1958); Russ Busby, *Billy Graham, God's Ambassador: A Lifelong Mission of Giving Hope to the World* (Alexandria, VA: Time-Life Books, 1999); Charles T. Cook, *The Billy Graham Story: "One Thing I Do"* (London: Marshall, Morgan & Scott, 1954); Glenn Daniels, *Billy Graham: The Man Who Walks with God* (New York, NY: Paperback Library, 1961); Lewis A. Drummond, *The Evangelist* (Nashville, TN: Word Publishers, 2001); *The Canvas Cathedral* (Nashville, TN: Thomas Nelson Publishers, 2003); *The Early Billy Graham: Sermon and Revival Accounts* ed. Joel A. Carpenter (Grand Rapids, MI: Zondervan, 1947); Robert O. Ferm, *Cooperative Evangelism: Is Billy Graham Right or Wrong?* (Grand Rapids, MI: Zondervan, 1958); John French, *My Fight with Billy Graham* (Memphis, TN: C. Goodman, 1959); David Frost, *Billy Graham: Personal Thoughts of a Public Man—30 Years of Conversations* (Colorado Springs, CO: Chariot Victor, 1997); Lewis William Gillenson, *Billy Graham and Seven Who Were Saved* (New York, NY: Trident Press, 1967); Stanley High, *Billy Graham: The Personal Story of the Man, His Message, and His Mission* (New York, NY: McGraw-Hill, 1956); Helen Kooiman Hosier, *Transformed: Behind the Scenes with Billy Graham* (Wheaton, IL: Tyndale House Publishers, 1970); Bill Jefferson, *Billy Graham, Footprints of Conscience* (Minneapolis, MN: World Wide Publications, 1991); David Lockard, *The Unheard Billy Graham* (Waco, TX: Word Books, 1971); Curtis Mitchell, *Billy Graham: The Making of a Crusader* (Philadelphia, PA: Chilton Books, 1966); *Billy Graham, Saint or Sinner?* (Old Tappan, NJ: Revell, 1979); Ronald Paul, *Billy Graham: Prophet of Hope* (New York, NY: Ballantine Books, 1978); David Poling, *Why Billy Graham?* (Grand Rapids, MI: Zondervan Publishing, 1977); John Charles Pollock, *Billy Graham: The Authorized Biography* (Grand Rapids, MI: Zondervan, 1967); *Billy Graham, Evangelist to the World: An Authorized Biography of the Decisive Years* (San Francisco, CA: Harper & Row, 1979); *Billy Graham: Highlights of the Story* (Basingstoke: Marshalls, 1984); *The Billy Graham Story* (Grand Rapids, MI: Zondervan, 2003); *Crusades, 20 Years with Billy Graham* (Minneapolis, MN: World Wide Publications, 1969); *To All the Nations: The Billy Graham Story* (San Francisco, CA: Harper & Row, 1985); Maurice Rowlandson, *Life with Billy: An Autobiography* (London: Hodder & Stoughton, 1992); Gerald S. Strober, *Graham: A Day in Billy's Life* (Old Tappan, NJ: Spire Books, 1977); *Billy Graham, His Life and Faith* (Nashville, TN: Word Books, 1977); Jay Walker, *Billy Graham: A Life in Word and Deed* (New York: Avon Books, 1998); Sam Wellman, *Billy Graham: The Great Evangelist* (Ulrichsville, OH: Barbour and Company, 1996); Terry Whalin, *Billy Graham* (Minneapolis, MN: Bethany House Publishers, 2002); Grady Wilson, *Billy Graham as a Teenager* (Wheaton, IL: Miracle Books, 1957); Jean Wilson, *Crusader for Christ: The Story of Billy Graham* (Fort Washington, PA: Christian Literature Crusade, 1973); Sherwood Eliot Wirt, *Billy: A Personal Look at the World's Best-Loved Evangelist* (Wheaton, IL: Crossway Books, 1997).

11. William F. Buckley, Jr., *Miles Gone By: A Literary Autobiography* (Washington, DC: Regnery Publishing, Inc., 2004), 326.

12. See *Billy Graham: A Tribute from Friends*, compiled by Vernon McLellan (New York, NY: Warner Books, 2002), 71–72.

13. Mark A. Noll, "The Innocence of Billy Graham," *First Things* (January 1998): 34.

Chapter One   "The Bible Says": Heart

Problems and the Divine Cure

1. "Here Is Text of Graham's Saturday Night Sermon," *The Charlotte Observer*, September 28, 1958, 10-A. The BGCA, which holds this text in collection 74, box 7, folder 3, lists the sermon title as "What's Wrong with the World?" Subsequent references to this sermon will cite the BGCA title. The chapter will focus on this sermon because it offers a clear example of Graham's lifelong under-standing of social problems and their remedy.

2. King, Jr., "To Billy Graham," *Papers 4*, 265.

3. Christian Smith, with Michael Emerson, Sally Gallagher, Paul Kennedy, and David Sikkink, *American Evangelicalism: Embattled and Thriving* (Chicago, IL: University of Chicago Press, 1998), 10. My brief explanation of the emergence of the neo-evangelicals is deeply indebted to Smith's outstanding study. Beyond Smith's work, the literature on American evangelicalism is substantial. Other particularly help-ful studies include Randall Herbert Balmer, *Blessed Assurance: A History of Evangelicalism in America*

(Boston, MA: Beacon Press, 1999); and *Mine Eyes Have Seen the Glory: A Journey into the Evangelical Subculture in America* (New York, NY: Oxford University Press, 2000); Donald Bloesch, *The Evangelical Renaissance* (Grand Rapids, MI: Eerdmans, 1973); Donald Dayton and Robert Johnson, *The Variety of American Evangelicalism* (Knoxville, TN: University of Tennessee Press, 1991); D.G. Hart, *Deconstructing Evangelicalism: Conservative Protestantism in the Age of Billy Graham* (Grand Rapids, MI: Baker Academic, 2004); James Davison Hunter, *American Evangelicalism: Conservative Religion and the Quandary of Modernity* (New Brunswick, NJ: Rutgers University Press, 1983); George Marsden, *Evangelicalism and Modern America* (Grand Rapids, MI: Eerdmans, 1984); *Reforming Fundamentalism: Fuller Seminary and the New Evangelicalism* (Grand Rapids, MI: Eerdmans, 1987); Steven Miller, "Billy Graham, Evangelicalism, and the Changing Postwar South (M.A. thesis, Vanderbilt, 2002); Mark Noll, *American Evangelical Christianity: An Introduction* (Oxford: Blackwell Publishers, 2001); and J. Christopher Soper, *Evangelical Christianity in the United States and Great Britain* (New York, NY: New York University Press, 1994). For more on Billy Graham's split from fundamentalism, see Butler Farley Porter, "Billy Graham and the End of Evangelical Unity" (Ph.D. diss., University of Florida, 1976).

4. Smith, *American Evangelicalism*, 14. Fundamentalists continue to harangue Graham for his "accommodationism." See, for example, Brad K. Gsell, *The Legacy of Billy Graham: The Accommodation of Truth to Error in the Evangelical Church* (Charlotte, NC: Fundamental Presbyterian Publications, 1998).

5. For a helpful sketch of the founding of *Christianity Today*, including the neo-evangelicalism that spurred the founding, see Martin, *A Prophet with Honor*, 211–217. See also Dennis Hollinger's interesting "American Individualism and Evangelical Social Ethics: A Study of Christianity Today" (Ph.D. dissertation, Drew University, 1981). The complete history of *Christianity Today* is yet to be published, but significant papers related to the topic exist in collection 8 (*Christianity Today, Inc.,* 1956–) at BGCA.

6. Chappell has rightly argued that "King recognized the huge benefit of Graham's soft-pedaled but persistent initiatives" (*A Stone of Hope*, 144).

7. King, Jr., "To Billy Graham," *Papers 4*, 265.

8. Graham, *Just As I Am*, xv.

9. I have decided not to focus on the making of Billy Graham, let alone the making of Martin Luther King, Jr., but I do wish to suggest that we cannot fully understand and appreciate these two personalities until we set them within the histories of their respective ecclesial contexts. These contexts—the white Baptist Church and the black Baptist Church—were radically different in many ways, and there is no better source to begin tracing these differences, and then connecting them to Graham and King, than Andrew Michael Manis, *Southern Civil Religions in Conflict: Black and White Baptists and Civil Rights, 1947–1957* (Athens, GA: University of Georgia Press, 1987). One of my undeveloped theses is that the eventual conflicts between Graham and King were but microcosmic replications of the larger battles fought between their respective conventions—the Southern Baptist Convention and the National Baptist Convention. On a related note, the differences between the revivialist traditions of the two figures is surveyed in Edward Lee Moore, "Billy Graham and Martin Luther King, Jr." (Ph.D. diss., Vanderbilt University, 1979).

10. In an October 17, 1940 speech, King, Sr. had argued that in the historic life of Jesus, "we find we are to do something about the broken-hearted, poor, unemployed, the captive, the blind, and the bruised. . . . God hasten the day when every minister will become a registered voter and a part of every movement for the betterment of our people" (see "Introduction," in *Papers 1*, 34; the manuscript of the address is in the Christine King Farris Collection [in private hands]). Other clergy members of the black Baptist Church, for example, William Holmes Borders and Benjamin Mays, also taught King, Jr. that social-justice ministries are an integral part of ordained ministry.

11. Graham, *Just As I Am*, 426.

12. Lowell D. Streiker and Gerald S. Strober, *Religion and the New Majority: Billy Graham, Middle America, and the Politics of the 70s* (New York, NY: Association Press, 1972), understate the point: "It cannot be stressed too strongly that Graham's social thought is grounded in his theological presuppositions" (39). Graham's social thought is a species of his evangelical theology.

13. With increased attention to individuals beyond King, as well as social forces that assisted and complicated his leadership, the ever-expanding studies of the civil rights era are finally acknowledging that the movement, though partly grounded in King's person and work, was much larger than King himself. Although I assume the proper distinction between King and the civil rights movement, my study closely connects the civil rights leader and the movement on issues of deep convergence—for example, the major premises of both King and the movement regarding social action.

14. King's social focus is especially visible in his typical characterization of the nonviolence of the civil rights movement: "There is something else: that one seeks to defeat the unjust system, rather than the individuals who are caught in that system. . . . The thing to do is to get rid of the system and thereby create a moral balance within society" ("Love, Law, and Civil Disobedience," in *A Testament of Hope: The Essential Writings and Speeches of Martin Luther King, Jr.*, ed. James M. Washington [San Francisco, CA: HarperSanFrancisco, 1986], 47). On the tactical strategy he eventually termed "nonviolent direct action," see Martin Luther King, Jr., *Where Do We Go from Here: Chaos or Community?* (New York, NY: Harper & Row, 1967).

15. Reinhold Niebuhr, "A Theologian Says Evangelist Is Oversimplifying the Issues of Life," *Life* (July 1, 1957): 92; and Mark A. Noll, "The Innocence of Billy Graham," *First Things*, no. 79 (January 1998): 36.

16. Martin E. Marty, *Religion and Republic: The American Circumstance* (Boston, MA: Beacon Press, 1987), 24. For more on Graham's homiletics, see John E. Baird, "The Preaching of Billy Graham" (Ph.D. diss., Columbia University, 1959).

17. Interview with Dr. Dan M. Potter, December 11, 1970, collection 141, box 10, folder 49, p. 9, BGCA. Graham's own comments are also worth remembering here: "One newspaper article said that in my next sermon I would hold the Bible in one hand and the newspaper in the other, I don't know whether that was literally true, but it did symbolize my constant effort to show the timeliness of God's eternal truths. In preaching the Gospel, I could also comment on everything current—the Communist threat, moral and social issues in the newspaper, Judgment Day" (*Just As I Am*, 126).

18. The following sections in the text will suggest that Graham's answer to the question of cause, stated in Charlotte and elsewhere, consistently included all of the doctrines that James Davison Hunter has identified as characteristic of "the evangelical meaning system"—the final authority of the Bible, the deity of Jesus Christ, eternal salvation through personal acceptance of Christ as Savior, the significance of evangelism, and the Second Coming of Christ (*American Evangelicalism: Conservative Religion and the Quandary of Modernity* [New Brunswick, NJ: Rutgers University Press, 1983], 47). The heart of Graham's social ethics, as we will see, was nothing if not evangelical.

19. A major academic study of Mordecai Ham, whose papers are found in collection 118 at BGCA, has yet to be published in book form. Minor related works include *Battle Front Messages: Sermons That Brought Revival*, ed. Edward E. Ham (Louisville, KY: Old Kentucky Home Revivalist, 1950); Edward Everett Ham, *50 Years on the Battle Front with Christ: A Biography of Mordecai F. Ham* (Louisville, KY: Old Kentucky Home Revivalist, 1960); and Edward Reese, *The Life and Ministry of Mordecai Ham, 1877–1961* (Glenwood, IL: Fundamental Publishers, 1975).

20. Graham, *Just As I Am*, 139.

21. See King, Jr., "Contemporary Continental Theology," *Papers 2*, 137–138. Of special note here is that Graham cited Karl Barth as one of the theologians whose works had forced him to "struggle with concepts that had been ingrained in me since childhood," including fundamentalist convictions about the absolute authority of scriptures (*Just As I Am*, 135).

22. In addition, it is important to note that Graham was not biblicist in the sense of rejecting all of the theological tenets that emerged in post-biblical history, for example, tenets in trinitarian theology. I am reminded here of Eric Gritsch, *Martin—God's Court Jester: Luther in Retrospect* (Philadelphia, PA: Fortress Press, 1983), who claims that Luther's embrace of *sola scriptura* "did not lead Luther to embrace a biblicism rejecting the authority of Christian tradition in post-biblical history. Rather, he wanted tradition to be tested by Scripture" (103). Graham, I believe, adopted a similar approach, although he never explicated this approach in detail. For more on Graham and scripture, see Larry Davis, "Interpretation of Scripture in the Evangelistic Preaching of William Franklin 'Billy' Graham" (Ph.D. diss., Southern Baptist Theological Seminary, 1986).

23. Graham, "What's Wrong with the World?" 10-A.

24. Niebuhr, "A Theologian Says Evangelist Is Oversimplifying the Issues of Life," 92. Niebuhr's snobbishness especially came to expression in his undocumented claim that because Graham did not address social issues, few city residents attended the crusade. "The bulk of his nightly audience," Niebuhr wrote, "comes from out of town" (92).

25. Reinhold Niebuhr, "Literalism, Individualism, and Billy Graham," *Christian Century* (May 23, 1956): 64.

26. Pheme Perkins, "Mark," in vol. 8 of *The New Interpreter's Bible: A Commentary in Twelve Volumes*, ed. Leander Keck (Nashville, TN: Abingdon, 1995), 608.

27. Graham, "What's Wrong with the World?" 10-A.

28. For more on King's appeal to the individual heart, see King, Jr., "Unfulfilled Dreams," *A Knock at Midnight: Inspiration from the Great Sermons of Reverend Martin Luther King, Jr.*, ed. Clayborne Carson and Peter Holloran (New York, NY: Warner Books, 1998), 191–200.

29. Graham, *The Seven Deadly Sins* (London: Marshall, Morgan & Scott, 1956), 21.

30. Quoted in McLoughlin, *Billy* Graham, 91.

31. Graham, *Revival—Or the Spirit of the Age* (Minneapolis, MN: The Billy Graham Evangelistic Association, 1952), 3.

32. Graham, "Jesus, the Great Revolutionist," March 12, 1961, collection 191, tape 583, BGCA.

33. Graham, "The Great Reconciliation," *Decision* (June 1964): 2.

34. Graham, "The Needed Revolution," January 14, 1968, collection 191, tape 940, BGCA. The references to the heart are staggering in number. For a few more examples, see Graham, *The Signs of the Times* (Minneapolis, MN: The Billy Graham Evangelistic Association, 1957), 3–4; *Billy Graham Answers Your Questions* (Minneapolis, MN: World Wide Publications, 1960), 118; "Jesus, the Great Revolutionist," tape 583, BGCA; "The Human Heart," *Decision* (July 1962): 14; Press Conference Transcript, Columbus, Ohio, July 9, 1964, collection 24, box 4, folder 14, p. 6, BGCA; "A Cause to Fight," August 13, 1967, collection 191, tape 918, BGCA; and "False Prophets in the Church," *Christianity Today* (January 19, 1968): 5.

35. Graham, *Christ's Marching Orders* (Minneapolis, MN: The Billy Graham Evangelistic Association, 1955), 3.

36. See Graham, *World Aflame* (Garden City, NY: Doubleday & Company, 1965), 71.

37. Ibid., 67–68.

38. Ibid., 73.

39. Graham, "The Quiet Revolution," December 29, 1967, collection 345, box 43, folder 4, p. 8, BGCA.

40. Graham, "What's Wrong with the World?" 10-A. For more on Graham's understanding of sin, see Howell Burkhead, "The Development of the Concept of Sin" (Ph.D. diss., Southwestern Baptist Theological Seminary, 1998). For a more general thesis on Graham's theology, see Thomas Paul Johnson, "The Work of an Evangelist" (Ph.D. diss., Southern Baptist Theological Seminary, 2001).

41. Smith, *American Evangelicalism*, provides the best concise summary on this point: "And individualism in evangelicalism runs deep, with roots extending back to most of the historical wellsprings of the modern evangelical tradition: the sixteenth-century Reformation, English and American Puritanism, much of the Free Church tradition, frontier awakening and revivalism, movements of spiritual pietism, and anti-Social Gospel fundamentalism" (189). On a related note, Marc Ellingsen, *The Evangelical Movement: Growth, Impact, Controversy, Dialog* (Minneapolis, MN: Augsburg Publishing House, 1988), is far too general when claiming that in evangelical social thought, "concern for structural change is always combined with, and yet distinct from, a concern with individual personal redemption" (275). For Graham, concern for structural change was rarely separated from concern for individual conversion.

42. Graham, "What's Wrong with the World?" 11-A.

43. King, Jr., "MIA Mass Meeting at Holt Street Baptist Church," *Papers 3:* 74.

44. Graham, *Christ's Marching Orders*, 3.

45. Ibid.

46. The insufficiency of law was a key emphasis in Graham's thought throughout the King years, and it came to clearest expression during the school integration crisis in Little Rock, when Graham announced that it is impossible to legislate morality, and during the Watts riots, when he called for additional laws to safeguard society. For more on this, as well as King's reaction, see the following chapters.

47. See Press Conference Transcript, San Diego, California, April 30, 1964, collection 24, box 4, folder 13, p. 3, BGCA.

48. Graham, "What's Wrong with the World?" 11-A.

49. The different depictions of Jesus are from James Gustafson, *Christ and the Moral Life* (Chicago, IL: University of Chicago Press, 1968).

50. Graham, *World Aflame*, 116.

51. Graham, of course, pointed to the Bible when offering his Anselmian argument. In Charlotte, for example, he preached: "The Bible says, 'He hath made him to be sin for us, who knew no sin.' The Bible says, 'The Lord hath laid on him the iniquity of us all.' The Bible says, He 'his own self bears our sins in his own body on the tree.' The Bible says, 'Christ also hath once suffered for sins, the just for the unjust' " ("What's Wrong with the World?" 11-A).

52. King, Jr., "A View of the Cross Possessing Biblical and Spiritual Justification," *Papers 1*, 266.

53. For a critical study of Graham's view of salvation, see William D. Apel, "The Understanding of Salvation in the Evangelistic Message of Billy Graham: A Historical-Theological Evaluation" (Ph.D. diss., Northwestern University, 1977).

54. Graham, "What's Wrong with the World?" 11-A.

55. Graham, *World Aflame*, 140.

56. Ibid., 167.

57. Press Conference Transcript, Zagreb, Yugoslavia, July 1967, collection 24, box 1, folder 4, p. 2, BGCA.

58. Graham, "The Risen Christ—Adequate for the World's Greatest Problem," March 29, 1964, collection 191, tape 742, BGCA.

59. The phrase "personal influence strategy" comes from Christian Smith, *American Evangelicalism*, 187. "American evangelicals," Smith writes, "are resolutely committed to a social-change strategy which maintains that the only truly effective way to change the world is one-individual-at-a-time through the influence of interpersonal relationships" (187).

60. Graham was greatly disturbed by the tendency in the 1960s to identify evangelism with social action. In 1967, for example, he stated: "I think social activism is good, but I don't think it belongs in the category of evangelism as some people are saying. They say, 'You're not evangelizing unless you get in a picket line. You're not evangelizing unless you're protesting something.' Well, this is fine if people feel led to do this. But that is not evangelism." Graham not only wanted to distinguish evangelism from social action, of course, but to identify the former as the more fundamental practice of the two. "Evangelism," he continued, "is winning people to a commitment to Jesus Christ. Then after the commitment, then tell them, 'You've got a responsibility in social action'" (Press Conference Transcript, Atlanta, Georgia, December 29, 1967, collection 24, box 1, folder 7, p. 10, BGCA). For an excellent account of these arguments during the King years, see Thomas C. Berg, "Proclaiming Together? Convergence and Divergence in Mainline and Evangelical Evangelism, 1945–1967," *Religion and American Culture: A Journal of Interpretation* 5 (Winter 1995): 49–76.

61. Graham, "The Proper Balance of the Church," June 12, 1964, collection 191, tape 757, BGCA. The references to the proper sequence of social transformation are substantial in the Graham corpus. For an additional example, see Press Conference, San Diego, April 30, 1964, 3.

62. Graham, "Marching for Christ in Montgomery," June 20, 1965, collection 191, tape 806, BGCA. See also Press Conference Transcript, Tokyo, Japan, October 16, 1967, collection 24, box 1, folder 6, p. 10, BGCA; and Graham, *The Signs of the Times*, 4.

63. "Graham Endorses "Social Gospel" as Part of the Biblical Gospel," Religious News Service Press Release, collection 345, box 44, folder 5, BGCA.

64. Graham, untitled sermon, July 18, 1957, collection 26, tape 495, BGCA.

65. Graham, *Peace with God* (Garden City, KS: Doubleday, 1953), 169.

66. Graham's advice regarding "wholesome living" reflects the lifestyle of middle-class America in the 1950s: "You are to be radiant. You should be chivalrous, courteous, clean of body, pure of mind, poised and gracious. . . . Your appearance should be neat, clean, attractive, and as much as possible in style, with good taste. . . . You should strive to be the ideal gentleman or the ideal lady. Your life and appearance should commend the gospel and make it attractive to others" (Ibid., 171).

67. Graham, "The Needed Revolution," *Decision*, May 1968.

68. Graham, "A Cause to Fight," tape 918.

69. Letter from Billy Graham to Dwight D. Eisenhower, March 26, 1955, DDEL.

70. Niebuhr, "A Theologian says Evangelist Is Oversimplifying the Issues of Life," 92. In his optimistic moments, Graham liked to cite one of the most optimistic U.S. presidents. "Franklin Roosevelt," Graham preached in 1956, "once said, 'I doubt if there is any problem, social, moral or political that would not melt away before the fire of spiritual awakening'" (Graham, *The Revival We Need* [Minneapolis, MN: The Billy Graham Evangelistic Association, 1956], 7).

71. The expression "miracle motif" comes from Rodney Stark, Bruce D. Foster, Charles Y. Glock, Harold E. Quinley, *Wayward Shepherds: Prejudice and the Protestant Clergy* (New York: Harper & Row, 1971), 103.

72. Graham, *God and the Nations* (Minneapolis, MN: The Billy Graham Evangelistic Association, 1964), 10.

73. Graham, *World Aflame*, 178. See also Press Conference Transcript, Tokyo, October 16, 1967, 9.

74. Graham, "What's Wrong with the World?" 11-A.

75. "Billy Graham Discounts Human Efforts at Racial Harmony," *Los Angeles Times*, August 3 and 10, 1963, quoted in Martin, *A Prophet with Honor*, 296.

76. McLoughlin, *Billy Graham*, 71.

77. See Press Conference Transcript, Tokyo, October 16, 1967, 9; and Graham, *World Aflame*, 178.

78. See C.H. Dodd, *The Parables of the Kingdom* (New York, NY: Scribner, 1961).

79. Graham, *World Aflame*, 193. See also Graham, "The Soviet Threat to Life on Earth," *Decision* (October 1961): 14–15.

80. "This Is Text of Graham's Sunday Afternoon Sermon," *The Charlotte Observer*, Monday, October 6, 1958, 12-A. BGCA, which holds this text in collection 74, box 7, folder 3, lists the title of the sermon as "The Second Coming of Christ." Subsequent references to the sermon will cite the BGCA title.

81. King, Jr., "The Christian Pertinence of Eschatological Hope," *Papers 1*, 269.

82. Graham, *God's D-Day* (Minneapolis, MN: The Billy Graham Evangelistic Association), 6.

83. Press Conference Transcript, Tokyo, October 16, 1967, 8. With Graham's deep pessimism in mind, I disagree with Martin's claim that the evangelist's theology was "essentially optimistic" (*A Prophet with Honor*, 155). Martin is usually accurate in his critical interpretation of Graham, but on this point, he is far from accurate.

84. Graham, "The Second Coming," 13-A.

85. Graham, *That Day* (Minneapolis, MN: The Billy Graham Evangelistic Association, 1955), 8–9.

86. Graham, *The Kingdom Society* (Minneapolis, MN: The Billy Graham Evangelistic Association, 1965); and "The Kingdom Society," *Decision* (September 1965): 1, 14–15.

87. Graham, *World Aflame*, 191.

88. Press Conference Transcript, San Diego, April 30, 1964, 14.

89. Press Conference Transcript, Atlanta, December 29, 1967, 2.

90. Graham, *World Aflame*, 191.

91. Ibid., 192.

92. Ibid., 193.

93. Graham, "Wars and Rumors of Wars," April 29, 1962, collection 191, tape 642, BGCA. See also Graham, *Needed! Strong Men* (Minneapolis, MN: The Billy Graham Evangelistic Association, 1960), 3–4.

94. Graham devoted no sustained attention to his claim about the restructuring of social institutions during the thousand-year reign.

95. Graham, "The Second Coming of Christ," 13-A.

96. I agree with McLoughlin: "That [Graham's Gospel] differs little from the stereotype of fundamentalism is apparent (*Billy Graham*, 79).

97. Lee Nash, "Evangelism and Social Concern," *The Cross and the Flag*, ed. Robert G. Clouse, Robert D. Linder, and Richard V. Pierard (Carol Stream, IL: Creation House, 1972), 144.

Chapter Two   "Preaching Nothing but the Bible": Against a Political Church

1. Press Conference Transcript, Phoenix, Arizona, April 23, 1964, collection 24, box 4, folder 11, p. 6, BGCA.

2. King, Jr., *Strength to Love* (Philadelphia, PA: Fortress Press, 1981), 62.

3. King, Jr., "Revolution and Redemption," 9, MLKJP, GAMK.

4. King, Jr., *Strength to Love*, 61.

5. Graham, *Peace with God*, 175.

6. "Here Is Text of Graham's Friday Night Sermon," *The Charlotte Observer*, October 25, 1958, 11-A. All subsequent references will list this sermon as "The Church," the title listed by BGCA.

7. Graham, "The Risen Christ—Adequate for the World's Greatest Problem," tape 742, BGCA. And thus Ralph Reed, *Active Faith: How Christians Are Changing the Soul of American Politics* (New York, NY: The Free Press, 1996), misunderstands Graham when he argues that King, unlike the evangelist, "considered his duties as proselytizer and political player inseparable" (60).

8. Graham, *My Answer* (Garden City, KS: Doubleday & Company, 1960; repr., 1967), 180.

9. Press Conference Transcript, Columbus, Ohio, January 28, 1963, collection 24, box 4, folder 9, p. 11, BGCA.

10. Graham, *My Answer*, 180–181.

11. Graham, "The Church," 11-A.

12. King, Jr., Interview by Hugh Downs, *Today Show*, NBC, April 18, 1966, p. 2, MLKJP, GAMK.

13. Graham, "The Risen Christ," tape 742.

14. Graham, *World Aflame*, 187. For a common but faulty spiritualization of Graham's theology, see Charles W. Dullea, *A Catholic Looks at Billy Graham* (New York, NY: Paulist Press, 1973): "As for what is called 'the social Gospel,' Graham's position is clear: Taking this term to mean that the church should concern itself with . . . the temporal lot of man, he wants none of it" (30). Dullea is terribly wrong; though never a traditional social gospeler, Graham was an advocate of church-driven charity to improve the material lot of humanity.

15. King, Jr., "Guidelines for a Constructive Church," *Knock*, 114–115; and *The Autobiography of Martin Luther King, Jr.*, ed. Clayborne Carson (New York, NY: Warner Books, 1998), 354.

16. Graham, *Peace with God*, 184.

17. Ibid.

18. Graham, "The Church," 11-A.

19. A. James Reichley, *Faith in Politics* (Washington, DC: Brookings Institution Press, 2002), 292.

20. Graham, *Peace with God*, 184.

21. Graham, "The Proper Balance of the Church," tape 757.

22. Graham, "The Real Role of the Church," November 26, 1967, collection 191, tape 933, BGCA.

23. Graham, *World Aflame*, 182.

24. Press Conference Transcript, Columbus, July 9, 1964, 8–9.

25. Graham, *World Aflame*, 181.

26. Ibid.

27. Press Conference Transcript, Los Angeles, California, May 13, 1968, collection 24, box 1, folder 10, p. 12, BGCA.

28. Graham, "The Proper Balance of the Church," tape 757.

29. Graham, "Alarming Trends within the Church," June 21, 1964, collection 191, tape 754, BGCA.

30. Graham, *World Aflame*, 180.

31. Graham, "The Real Role of the Church," tape 933.

32. The BGA transcript actually reads this way: "But I don't think the church should assert their authority of the state." That statement makes no sense, and in light of Graham's other comments in the press conference, I am convinced that the transcriber did not transcribe Graham's comments correctly—hence, my changing of the word "of" to "over." See Press Conference Transcript, collection 24, Sydney, Australia,1968, collection 24, box 1, folder 9, p. 5, BGCA.

33. Graham, untitled sermon, May 8, 1966, box 9, folder 26, BGCA.

34. Press Conference, San Juan, Puerto Rico, March 17, 1967, collection 24, tape 17, BGCA. See also Press Conference, Tokyo, Japan, October 16, 1967, 7.

35. Press Conference, Tokyo, Japan, October 16, 1967, 7.

36. Press Conference, San Juan, March 17, 1967, 7.

37. This argument is also recounted in Graham, *World Aflame*, 182–183.

38. For more on the evangelical appeal to the two-kingdoms approach, see Dennis P. Hollinger, *Individualism and Social Ethics: An Evangelical Syncretism* (Lanham, MD: University Press of America, 1983), 111–113.

39. Martin Luther, "On Secular Authority," in *Luther and Calvin on Secular Authority*, trans. and ed. Harro Hopfl (Cambridge: Cambridge University Press, 1991), 9.

40. Ibid., 11.

41. Ibid., 12.

42. Press Conference, Sydney, 1968, 6.

43. Graham, "Proper Balance of the Church," tape 757.

44. Graham, "A Cause to Fight," tape 918.

45. Press Conference Transcript, Washington, DC, December 22, 1964, collection 24, box 4, folder 6, p. 6, BGCA.

46. Graham, "Alarming Trends within the Church," tape 754.

47. Luther, "On Secular Authority," 11–12.

48. Graham, "The Real Role of the Church," tape 933.

49. Graham, "False Prophets in the Church," *Christianity Today* (January 19, 1968): 5. See also *World Aflame*, 184.
50. Press Conference Transcript, Washington, DC, December 22, 1964, 4.
51. Graham, *Just As I Am*, 568.
52. King, Jr., *Autobiography*, 200.
53. Ibid., 201.
54. Ibid.
55. See Hollinger, *Individualism and Social Ethics*, 103.
56. Graham, *My Answer*, 177.
57. Walter Pilgrim, *Uneasy Neighbors: Church and State in the New Testament* (Minneapolis, MN: Augsburg Fortress Press, 1999), 64.
58. Ibid., 66.
59. Press Conference, Columbus, January 28, 1963, 10.
60. Graham, *My Answer*, 177.
61. Ibid., 178–179.
62. Graham, "Cast Your Vote for Christ," November 4, 1956, collection 191, tape 356, BGCA.
63. Graham, "Cast Your Vote for Christ," November 6, 1960, collection 191, tape 565, BGCA.
64. Graham, *Billy Graham Answers Your Questions*, 58.
65. See Ibid., 57–58; and Graham, *My Answer*, 177.
66. Graham, *My Answer*, 177.
67. Press Conference Transcript, Atlanta, November 5, 1964, p. 3, collection 24, box 4, folder 15, BGCA.
68. Mark Noll, "The Innocence of Billy Graham," *First Things* (January 1998): 35.
69. See Segment for McNeil/Lehrer News Hour, Public Broadcasting System, April 7, 1992, collection 74, video 42, BGCA.
70. The phrase "strategy of access" is from Mark A. Noll, *American Evangelical Christianity*, 49. For more on Graham and the public square, see Eric J. Paddon, "Modern Mordecai: Billy Graham in the Political Arena" (Ph.D. diss., Ohio University, 1999).
71. Press Conference Transcript, Columbus, July 9, 1964, 8. For more on Graham's relationship with U.S. presidents, see Elizabeth Earl, "A Comparison of Billy Graham and Jerry Falwell" (Ph.D. diss., Ohio University, 1991); Danny Day, "The Political Billy Graham" (M.A. thesis, Wheaton College, 1996); and, most importantly, Richard V. Pierard, "Billy Graham and the U.S. Presidency," *Journal of Church and State*, vol. 22, no. 1 (1980): 107–127.
72. Graham to Truman, July 18, 1950, HSTL.
73. Graham to Eisenhower, May 10. 1954, DDEL.
74. Graham to Johnson, July 11, 1965, LBJL.
75. Graham to Johnson, June 21, 1968, LBJL.
76. Graham, "Nations, Repent!" March 8, 1964, collection 191, tape 739, BGCA.
77. Graham, *My Answer*, 177.
78. Graham to Eisenhower, August 19, 1955, DDEL.
79. Graham to Eisenhower, August 4, 1960, DDEL.
80. Graham to Nixon, September 1, 1960, Series 320, Vice Presidential General Correspondence, Dr. Billy Graham Folder, RMNPMP.
81. Graham to Nixon, August 23, 1960, RMNPMP.
82. Graham to Nixon, June 21, 1960, 1–2, RMNPMP.
83. Press Conference Transcript, Atlanta, November 5, 1964, 2, BGCA.
84. Graham to Nixon, May 27, 1960, RMNPMP.
85. See Press Conference Transcript, Columbus, July 9, 1964, 8.
86. Ibid., 4.
87. King, Jr., "Advice for Living," in *Papers 4*, 280.
88. Ibid., 281.
89. King, Jr., *Stride Toward Freedom: The Montgomery Story* (New York, NY: Harper & Row, 1958), 117.
90. Graham, "Love and Little Rock," September 29, 1957, collection 191, tape 403, BGCA.
91. Graham to Truman, February 17, 1949, HSTL.
92. Graham to Eisenhower, August 19, 1955, DDEL.
93. Graham, "Love and Little Rock," tape 403.

94. King, Jr., *Autobiography*, 193–194.
95. Graham, "Love and Little Rock," tape 403.
96. Graham, "Facing the Anti-God Colossus," *Christianity Today* (December 21, 1962): 8.
97. Graham, "Jesus, the Great Revolutionist," tape 583.
98. Graham, "The Proper Balance of the Church," tape 757.
99. Press Conference Transcript, Atlanta, November 5, 1964, 2–3.
100. Pilgrim, *Uneasy Neighbors*, 7.
101. Ibid.
102. Press Conference Transcript, May 13, 1968, Los Angeles, 4.
103. Press Conference Transcript, Atlanta, November 5, 1964, 3.
104. Graham, "Love and Little Rock," tape 403.
105. For more on Shadrach, Meschach, and Abednego, see Graham, "God with Us," *Decision* (December 1961): 14.
106. Graham, *Billy Graham Answers Your Questions*, 57.
107. Press Conference Transcript, Columbus, July 9, 1964, 7 (emphasis mine).

Chapter Three   "True Christian Loyalty in

Our Hearts": A Christian Defense of

American Patriotism

1. Graham, *Labor, Christ, and the Cross* (Minneapolis, MN: The Billy Graham Evangelistic Association, 1953), 5.
2. Ibid.
3. Graham, *The Ultimate Weapon* (Minneapolis, MN: The Billy Graham Evangelistic Association, 1961), 6.
4. Graham, *Labor, Christ, and the Cross*, 5. For more on Graham's anti-communist rhetoric, see Starla Drum, "The Anti-Communism Rhetoric of Billy Graham in the Early 1950s" (M.A. thesis, University of Oregon, 1970); and Christopher Trotta, "The Communist Threat and a Preacher's Ambition: Billy Graham and the Use of Political Anti-Communist Rhetoric during the Truman and Eisenhower Administrations" (M.A. thesis, Miami University, 2002).
5. Robert Bellah, "Civil Religion in America," *Daedalus*, vol. 96, no. 1 (Winter 1967): 14.
6. See Graham, "The Quiet Revolution," collection 345.
7. Noll, *American Evangelical Christianity*, 48.
8. Roderick P. Hart, *The Political Pulpit* (West Lafayette, IN: Purdue University Press, 1977), 69. Edwin Scott Gaustad, *A Religious History of America* (New York, NY: Harper & Row, 1990), describes Graham as "a kind of patriarch of what Benjamin Franklin had called 'public religion' " (367). And William McLoughlin, "Pietism and the American Character," *American Quarterly* (Summer 1965): 163–186, has described Graham's sermons as a "blatant equation of Christianity with American patriotism and the free enterprise system." I agree with all three characterizations.
9. Graham, "Thanksgiving," November 18, 1956, collection 191, tape 358, BGCA.
10. Graham, "Here Is Text of Billy Graham's First Sermon," *The Charlotte Observer*, September 22, 1958, 6-A. Subsequent notes will refer to this text as "Christ's Answer to the World," the title supplied by BGCA. See also Graham, "Here Is Text of Graham's Friday Night Sermon," *The Charlotte Observer*, October 11, 1958, 6-A. "Escapism" is the title given by BGCA.
11. Ibid.
12. Graham, *God and Crime* (Minneapolis, MN: The Billy Graham Evangelistic Association, 1956), 6.
13. Ibid., 11.
14. Graham, "Thanksgiving," tape 358.
15. Graham, "The Cost of Freedom," January 15, 1961, collection 191, tape 575, BGCA.
16. Graham, *Labor, Christ, and the Cross*, 4.
17. Graham, *The Kingdom Society*, 8.
18. Graham, *Billy Graham Answers Your Questions*, 58.
19. King, Jr., "The Ethical Demands for Integration," in *A Testament of Hope*, 117.
20. King, Jr., *Stride Toward Freedom*, 190.

21. King, Jr., Remarks to the NAACP-Sponsored Mass Rally for Civil Rights, 1, MLKJP, GAMK.
22. Graham, *Four Great Crises* (Minneapolis, MN: The Billy Graham Evangelistic Association, 1957), 2.
23. Ibid., 4.
24. Graham, *The Revival We Need*, 4.
25. Ibid., 5–6.
26. Graham, *Four Great Crises*, 5–6.
27. Graham, *The Revival We Need*, 7.
28. Quoted in Edwin Gaustad, *Faith of Our Fathers: Religion and the New Nation* (San Francisco, CA: Harper & Row, 1987), 65.
29. Quoted in Ibid., 77.
30. King, Jr., "The Birth of a New Age," *Papers 3*, 341.
31. Ibid.
32. King, Jr., Remarks to the NAACP-Sponsored Mass Rally for Civil Rights, 1.
33. See King, Jr., *Strength to Love*, 52–53.
34. Transcript of "My Answer," author marked as "Ferm," March 20, 1957, collection 19, box 9, folder 1, BGCA. Given Ferm's authorship, it seems likely that he was the theological catalyst behind the shift in Graham's thought.
35. Press Conference Transcript, Tokyo, October 16, 1967, 4.
36. Ibid., 9.
37. Graham, *The Revival We Need*, 10.
38. Ibid., 11.
39. King, Jr., "Who Is Their God?" *The Nation* (October 13, 1963): 209.
40. Graham, *The Revival We Need*, 7.
41. *Christianity Today* (January 19, 1973): 416, quoted in Richard V. Pierard, "Billy Graham—Preacher of the Gospel or Mentor of Middle America," *Fides et Historia*, vol. 5, nos. 1–2 (Fall 1972–Spring 1973): 130.
42. Pierard, "Billy Graham—Preacher of the Gospel or Mentor of Middle America," 130.
43. Graham, *The Seven Deadly Sins*, 52.
44. Ibid., 94.
45. Graham, *Americanism* (Minneapolis, MN: The Billy Graham Evangelistic Association, 1956), 5.
46. Graham, *Labor, Christ, and the Cross*, 4.
47. Graham, *Christ's Marching Orders*, 10.
48. Press Conference Transcript, San Diego, April 30, 1964, 15.
49. Graham, *Four Great Crises*, 11.
50. Graham, *America at the Crossroads* (Minneapolis, MN: The Billy Graham Evangelistic Association, 1958), 5–6.
51. *Engel v. Vitale*, 370 US 421 (1962), quoted in Steven K. Green, "Evangelicals and the Becker Amendment," *Journal of Church and State*, vol. 33 (Summer 1991): 547.
52. *Christianity Today* (July 5, 1963); 47, quoted in Green, "Evangelicals and the Becker Amendment," 555.
53. "The Becker Amendment," *Christian Century*, vol. 81 (April 15, 1964): 475.
54. Press Conference Transcript, Phoenix, April 23, 1964, 3.
55. Ibid.
56. Press Conference Transcript, San Diego, April 30, 1964, 18.
57. *Playboy* Interview: Martin Luther King, Jr., in *A Testament of Hope*, 373.
58. Graham, "The World's Bestseller," 1962, collection 74, tape 4, BGCA.
59. Hearings on School Prayers before the Committee on the Judiciary, House of Representatives, 88th Congress., 2nd Sess. (1964), quoted in Green, "Evangelicals and the Becker Amendment," 559, fn. 112.
60. Press Conference Transcript, Atlanta, November 5, 1964, 5.
61. Green, "Evangelicals and the Becker Amendment," 551.
62. Press Conference Transcript, Columbus, July 9, 1964, 7.
63. Graham, "My Answer—Individuals Make Nation Christian," *The Atlanta Constitution*, August 3, 1966, 5.
64. King, Jr., "MIA Mass Meeting at Holt Street Baptist Church," *Papers 3*, 73–74.
65. King, Jr., *Autobiography*, 354.
66. See Martin, *A Prophet with Honor*, 269–285. See also Randall Balmer and Lauren F. Winner, *Protestantism in America* (New York, NY: Columbia University Press, 2002). "During the 1960

presidential campaign," they write, "Graham met in Montreaux, Switzerland, with Norman Vincent Peale and other Protestant leaders to devise a way to derail the campaign of John F. Kennedy, the Democratic nominee, thereby assisting Nixon's electoral chances" (228). On this point, A. James Reichley is wrong when he writes that Graham "skirted the anti-Catholic enthusiasm that galvanized most evangelicals against John Kennedy" *Faith in Politics* (Washington, DC: Brookings Institution Press, 2002), 292.

67. There is a paucity of material on Graham and nationalism. For one study, see Barry Hankins, "Billy Graham and American Nationalism" (M.A. thesis, Baylor University, 1983).
68. Michael Eric Dyson, *I May Not Get There with You: The True Martin Luther King, Jr.* (New York: The Free Press, 2000).
69. News Release Transcript, Crusade Information Service, Billy Graham Team Office, November 17, 1965, Houston, Texas, collection 345, box 55, no. 5, p. 1, BGCA.
70. Press Conference Transcript, March 12, 1968, Black Mountain, North Carolina, collection 24, box 1, folder 8, pp. 8–9, BGCA.
71. Press Conference Transcript, Zagreb, July 1967, 1.
72. Press Conference Transcript, Atlanta, November 5, 1964, 3.
73. Graham, "Turn Back, America," July 26, 1964, collection 191, tape 759, BGCA.
74. Graham, *America at the Crossroads*, 10.
75. Graham, *Americanism*, 9.
76. Graham, *America at the Crossroads*, 10.
77. Ibid.
78. Graham, "The Sword of Damocles," *Decision* (May 1963): 14.
79. Graham, "The One Way Out," *Decision* (April 1964): 14–15.
80. Graham, *God and the Nations*, 9–10.

Chapter Four   "He Belonged to All the Races":

The Evolution of Graham's Race Ethics

1. Graham, "Why Don't Churches Practice Brotherhood?" *Reader's Digest* (August 1960): 55.
2. Graham, *Just As I Am*, 425.
3. Quoted in Marshall Frady, *Billy Graham*, 68. Frady's lively account here is of one of Graham's childhood friends.
4. Graham, *Just As I Am*, 12.
5. Quoted in Jerry Beryl Hopkins, "Billy Graham and the Race Problem, 1949–1969" (Ph.D. diss., University of Kentucky, 1986), 15. Although I disagree with some of his interpretations, I am greatly indebted to Hopkins's excellent and carefully documented dissertation. For more on the topic, see James French, "Billy Graham's Role in the Civil Rights Movement" (M.A. thesis, California State University, 1975); and Michael D. Hammond, "Conscience in Conflict: Neo-Evangelicals and Race in the 1950s" (M.A. thesis, Wheaton College Graduate School, 2002).
6. Graham, *Just as I Am*, 425.
7. Graham, "Why Don't Churches Practice Brotherhood?" 55.
8. Graham, *Just As I Am*, 63.
9. Ibid., 426.
10. Earnest Albert Hooten, *Up from the Apes* (New York, NY: Macmillan, 1931), 592–593, quoted in Hopkins, "Billy Graham and the Race Problem," 19.
11. Hopkins, "Billy Graham and the Race Problem," 36.
12. Graham, "Why Don't Churches Practice Brotherhood?" 55.
13. Ibid.
14. See Hopkins, "Billy Graham and the Race Problem," 41–42.
15. Quoted in Ibid., 42–43. Hopkins sources include *The Clarion-Ledger*, June 3, 1952 and July 19, 1952; and *Jackson Daily News*, June 25, 1952.
16. Graham, *Just as I Am*, 426.
17. "Southern-born Evangelist Declares War on Bigotry," *Ebony* (September 1957): 100.
18. Interview of Billy Graham by F. Lee Bailey, "Good Company," ca. 1960, collection 74, film 9, BGCA.

19. Graham, "Why Don't Our Churches Practice Brotherhood?" 55.

20. Press Conference Transcript, Washington, DC, December 22, 1964, 5.

21. Untitled Tape, April 1, 1970, Dortmund, Germany, collection 24, tape 18, BGCA.

22. *One Body, One Spirit* (Minneapolis, MN: The Billy Graham Evangelistic Association), collection 19, box 10, folder 2, BGCA.

23. Graham, *Peace with God*, 195.

24. "Southern-born Evangelist Declares War on Bigotry," 104.

25. Ibid.

26. Graham to Eisenhower, August 19, 1955, DDEL.

27. See, for example, Press Conference Comments, San Juan, Puerto Rico, March 17, 1967, tape 17, collection 24, BGCA.

28. "Southern-born Evangelist Declares War on Bigotry," 99.

29. Graham, "Billy Graham Makes Plea for an End to Intolerance," *Life* (October 1, 1957): 140–141.

30. Ibid., 143.

31. Graham, "No Solution to Race Problem 'at the Point of Bayonets,' " *U.S. News and World Report* (April 25, 1960): 94.

32. Graham, "Billy Graham Makes Plea to End Intolerance," 143.

33. Graham, "Racial Prejudice: The Answer," *Report* (December 1965): 11.

34. Graham, *Billy Graham Answers Your Questions*, 127.

35. For the most cogent articulation of this position, see James Cone, *Black Theology & Black Power* (New York, NY: Seabury Press, 1969).

36. Press Conference Transcript, Black Mountain, March 12, 1968, 11.

37. "Southern-born Evangelist Declares War on Bigotry," 100.

38. Ibid., 102.

39. Graham, "Love and Little Rock," tape 403.

40. Graham, "Solving Our Race Problems through Love," July 25, 1963, collection 191, tape 711, BGCA.

41. "Southern-born Evangelist Declares War on Poverty," 102.

42. Graham, "The Human Heart," 15.

43. Graham, "Billy Graham Makes Plea for an End to Intolerance," 143.

44. Graham, "God and the Color of a Man's Skin," *Decision* (August 1965): 1; see also Graham, *Billy Graham Answers Your Questions*, 125–126.

45. Graham, "The Only Hope for the Race Problem," March 28, 1965, collection 191, tape 794, BGCA.

46. "Press Conference," *Decision* (September 1962): 14; see also Graham, *Billy Graham Answers Your Questions*, 127.

47. Graham, "Billy Graham Makes a Plea for an End to Intolerance," 143.

48. Graham, "God and the Color of a Man's Skin," 15.

49. Graham, "The Great Reconciliation," *Decision* (June 1964): 2.

50. Graham, "God and the Color of a Man's Skin," 15.

51. Graham, *World Aflame*, 7.

52. Graham, "Billy Graham Makes a Plea for an End to Intolerance," 140; see also Graham, "No Solution to Race Problem 'at the Point of Bayonets,' " 94.

53. Graham, *Four Great Crises*, 8.

54. "Southern-born Evangelist Declares War on Poverty," 102.

55. Graham, "Christ, the Answer to the Race Problem," May 19, 1963, collection 191, tape 697, BGCA.

56. Graham, "Why Don't Our Churches Practice Brotherhood?" 53.

57. Graham, "No Solution to Race Problem," 94.

58. Ibid., 95.

59. Graham, "Memo to the Team: Statement by Billy Graham on Selma Situation from His Hospital Bed at St. Francis Hospital, Honolulu, Hawaii," no date, collection 345, box 44, no. 1, BGCA.

60. Letter from Billy Graham to President Dwight D. Eisenhower, March 27, 1956, DDEL.

61. Graham to Eisenhower, June 4, 1956, DDEL.

62. Graham, *Just as I Am*, 201.

63. Press Conference Transcript, Columbus, July 9, 1964, 5.

64. "Southern-born Evangelist Declares War on Bigotry," 102.

65. Graham, "Racial Prejudice," 10.

66. Ibid., 11.

67. Martin, *A Prophet with Honor*, 262.
68. Quoted in Ibid., 262.
69. Graham, *Just As I Am*, 338.
70. Quoted in Martin, *A Prophet with Honor*, 263.
71. Press Conference Transcript, San Diego, April 30, 1964, 10. See also Press Conference Transcript, Phoenix, April 23, 1964, 12.
72. "Statement by Billy Graham Released Following President Johnson's Civil Rights Address," no date, collection 345, box 44, folder 1, BGCA.
73. See Max Goldberg, Transcript of "Billy Graham Gives Frank Views on War in Viet Nam, Race Riots," September 25, 1965, North America Newspaper Alliance, 2, LBJL.
74. Quoted in Hopkins, "Billy Graham and the Race Problem," 95.
75. Graham, "The Great Reconciliation," 2.
76. Graham to Johnson, July 6, 1964, LBJL.
77. Graham, "Racial Prejudice," 10.
78. Graham, untitled sermon, July 18, 1957, collection 26, tape 495, BGCA.
79. Graham, *Just As I Am*, 360.
80. Press Conference Transcript, Washington, DC, December 22, 1964, 4.
81. See Letter from Chauncey Eskridge to Martin Luther King, Jr., June 13, 1962; Letter from Wyatt Tee Walker to Robert S. Denny, November 14, 1962; and Letter from Wyatt Tee Walker to Robert S. Denny, November 21, 1962. All these letters are on file with the Martin Luther King, Jr. Papers Project.
82. Dullea, *A Catholic Looks at Billy Graham*, 31.
83. Richard V. Pierard, "Billy Graham—Preacher of the Gospel or Mentor of Middle America?" 130.
84. Mark Silk, *Spiritual Politics: Religion and America Since World War II* (New York, NY: Simon and Schuster, 1988), 64.
85. Grant Wacker, "Uneasy in Zion: Evangelicals in Postmodern Society," in *Evangelicalism and Modern America*, ed. George Marsden (Grand Rapids, MI: William B. Eerdmans Publishing Company, 1984), 27.
86. Religious News Service, March 3, 1965, quoted in Streiker and Strober, *Religion and the New Majority*, 53.

Chapter Five   "This Is Freedom Out of Control!":

Graham's Dissent from the Civil Rights Movement

1. Graham, "The Only Hope for the Race Problem," tape 794.
2. Ibid.
3. Chuck Stone, "Silly Billy Graham Magnificent Phony," *Chicago Defender*, April 18–24, 1964, collection 19, box 4, folder 34, BGCA. Seven years later, the highly regarded Joseph A. Johnson, Jr. delivered equally pointed criticism by connecting plantation religion with Billy Graham. "The white church establishment," Johnson wrote, "presented to the black people a religion carefully tailored to fit the purposes of the white oppressor, corrupted in language, interpretation and application by the conscious and unconscious racism of white Christians from the first plantation missionary down to Billy Graham." See *The Soul of the Black Preacher* (Philadelphia, PA: Pilgrim Press, 1971), 90.
4. King, Jr., "To Billy Graham," *Papers 4*, 265.
5. Untitled Tape, Dortmund, Germany, April 1, 1970, collection 24, tape 18, BGCA.
6. Hopkins, "Billy Graham and the Race Problem," 61.
7. Graham to Eisenhower, March 27, 1956, 1, DDEL.
8. Graham to Eisenhower, June 4, 1956, 1, DDEL.
9. King, Jr., "To Billy Graham," *Papers 4*, 457–458.
10. Branch, *Parting the Waters*, 227–228.
11. I have taken this quote from Martin, *A Prophet with Honor*, 235. Martin quotes Howard O. Jones's recollection of the pre-crusade meeting.
12. Branch, *Parting the Waters*, 227–228.
13. "From Grady Wilson," *Papers 4*, 458.

14. News Release, Crusade Information Service, Billy Graham Team Office, Atlanta, Georgia, April 5, 1965, collection 345, box 55, no. 5.

15. Graham, "Love and Little Rock," tape 403.

16. Graham, "Here Is Text of Graham's Thursday Night Sermon," *The Charlotte Observer*, October 17, 1958, 8B. The title for this sermon at BGCA is "Youth Aflame."

17. Graham, "Why Don't Our Churches Practice Brotherhood?" 52.

18. Graham, "Christ, the Answer to the Race Problem," tape 697.

19. Graham, "Let's Keep God's Moral Standards," September 22, 1963, collection 191, tape 715, BGCA.

20. Graham, "Billy Graham Makes Plea for End to Intolerance," 138. On Africans enslaving Africans, Graham also added: "However, it must be remembered that they did not have the Christian concept of the Golden Rule."

21. Ibid., 144.

22. Graham, "Solving Our Race Problems through Love," tape 711; see also Graham, "No Solution to Race Problem 'at the Point of Bayonets,' " 95.

23. Graham, "Racial Prejudice," 10.

24. Graham, *World Aflame*, 5.

25. Graham, "Solving Our Race Problems through Love," tape 711. Here we would do well to remember James Cone's take on Billy Graham and Norman Vincent Peale. "Of course," Cone writes, "their view of the gospel is not arrived at through an open encounter with the biblical message, but is determined by the continued social and political dominance of whites over blacks. They are the best examples that religious conservativism and white racism are often two sides of the same reality." See *God of the Oppressed* (Seabury Press; repr., Maryknoll, NY: Orbis Books, 1997), 46.

26. Ibid.

27. Press Conference Transcript, December 22, 1964, Washington, DC, 6.

28. We will see that Charles Dullea is terribly wrong in his argument that Graham took a "firm stand for integration" (*A Catholic Looks at Billy Graham*, 120).

29. "Issues and Answers," ABC, New York, 1969, collection 74, tape 17, BGCA.

30. Press Conference Transcript, July 29, 1968, New York City, collection 24, box 1, folder 13, BGCA.

31. Graham, "Billy Graham Makes Plea for End to Intolerance," 143.

32. Graham, "No Solution to Race Problem," 94.

33. Graham, "Solving Our Race Problems through Love," tape 711.

34. Letter from Nelson Bell to Mrs. R.H. Peake, Norfolk, Virginia, August 7, 1956, collection 318, box 41, folder 11, BGCA.

35. Graham, "No Solution to Race Problem," 94.

36. King, Jr., "The Ethical Demands for Integration," *A Testament of Hope*, 118.

37. Ibid., 123.

38. Ibid.

39. Graham, "Billy Graham Makes Plea for an End to Intolerance," 138.

40. Graham, *World Aflame*, 7. See also Press Conference Transcript, Washington, DC, December 22, 1964, 2; and Graham, "Racial Prejudice," 10.

41. Graham, "Love and Little Rock," tape 403. It is grossly inaccurate of W. David Lockard, *The Unheard Billy Graham* (Waco, TX: Word Books, 1971) to write, unqualifiedly, that "Graham knows that gradualism may amount to a virtual stagnation of social and racial conditions as they are. He underscores the imperative role of vital legislation" (124–125). Graham was a gradualist who opposed using legislation as a tool for achieving "forced integration."

42. King, Jr., "The 'New Negro' of the South: Behind the Montgomery Story," *Papers 3*, 284.

43. King described legislation as a tool of justice in his first MIA speech. See King Jr., "MIA Mass Meeting at Holt Street," *Papers 3*, 74. King increasingly realized, in light of various obstructionist tactics, that passing legislation, issuing executive orders, and ruling in court cases were necessary but insufficient measures for establishing justice in society. He thus began to stress that the state must enforce compliance with its just laws. Justice, for King, became exactly that—enforced compliance with the just laws of the state.

44. King, Jr., "The 'New Negro,' " *Papers 3*, 284.

45. Graham, "Prayer, the Solution to the Race Problem," June 23, 1963, collection 191, tape 702, BGCA.

46. Press Conference Transcript, Columbus, July 9, 1964, 5.

47. Graham, "Statement by Billy Graham Following President Johnson's Civil Rights Address," collection 345.
48. Graham, "God and the Color of a Man's Skin," 14.
49. Graham, "Racial Prejudice," 10.
50. Press Conference Transcript, Phoenix, April 23, 1964, 3.
51. Press Conference Transcript, San Diego, April 30, 1964, 17.
52. Press Conference Transcript, Black Mountain, March 12, 1968, 12.
53. Press Conference Transcript, Columbus, July 9, 1964, 5.
54. Boykin to Eisenhower, March 19, 1956, 2, DDEL.
55. Graham to Eisenhower, June 4, 1956, DDEL.
56. Graham, "Billy Graham Makes Plea," 151.
57. Graham, "Why Don't Churches Practice Brotherhood?" 54.
58. Press Conference Transcript, Miami, Florida, December 5, 1963, collection 24, tape 4, BGCA.
59. King, Jr., "Letter from Birmingham Jail," *Why We Can't Wait*, 81.
60. S. Jonathan Bass, *Blessed Are the Peacemakers: Martin Luther King, Jr., Eight White Religious Leaders, and the 'Letter from Birmingham Jail'* (Baton Rouge, LA: Louisiana State University Press, 2001), 148.
61. See *New York Times*, April 17, 1963; quoted in Bass, *Blessed Are the Peacemakers*, 104; and Branch, *Parting the Waters*, 737.
62. Graham, "Statement by Billy Graham Following President Johnson's Civil Rights Address," collection 345; see also Graham, "Racial Prejudice," 11.
63. Graham, "Special Memo to the Team: Statement by Billy Graham on Selma Situation from his Hospital Bed at St. Francis Hospital, Honolulu, Hawaii," no date, collection 345, box 44, folder 1, BGCA.
64. King, "Letter from Birmingham Jail."
65. Graham, "Racial Prejudice," 10.
66. Quoted in Frady, *Billy Graham*, 416.
67. Graham, "Prayer, the Solution to the Race Problem," tape 702.
68. Ibid.
69. King, Jr., "Walk for Freedom," *Papers 2*, 279.
70. King, Jr., "Who Speaks for the South?" *A Testament of Hope*, 92.
71. King, Jr., "The Answer to a Perplexing Question," *Strength to Love*, 131–132.
72. King, Jr., "Nonviolence and Social Change," *The Trumpet of Conscience*, 59.
73. Press Conference Transcript, San Diego, April 30, 1964, 10.
74. Graham, "To Keep Our Flags Waving," July 4, 1965, collection 191, tape 808, BGCA.
75. Graham, "Christ's Answer to the World," 6-A.
76. Graham, "America Is in Trouble," August 6, 1967, collection 191, tape 917, BGCA.
77. Press Conference Transcript, May 13, 1966, Los Angeles, 5.
78. Graham, "Racial Progress in Alabama," *The Christian* (July 2, 1965): 1, collection 345, box 44, BGCA.
79. Graham, "Turn Back, America," tape 759.
80. See Stokely Carmichael and Charles V. Hamilton, *Black Power: The Politics of Liberation in America* (New York: Random House, 1967).
81. King, Jr., *Autobiography*, 323.
82. King, Jr., *Where Do We Go from Here: Chaos or Community?*, 32–44.
83. King, Jr., *Autobiography*, 325. On King's advances toward the black separatist position, see James Cone, *Martin & Malcolm & America* (Maryknoll, NY: Orbis Books, 1991), 226–227.
84. See King, Jr., "To Charter Our Course," Frogmore, South Carolina, May 1967, 9, MLKJP, GAMK.
85. "Issues and Answers," ABC, New York, 1969, BGCA.
86. Press Conference Transcript, Atlanta, December 29, 1967,12.
87. Press Conference Transcript, Black Mountain, North Carolina, March 12, 1968, 4.
88. Press Conference Transcript, March 17, 1967, San Juan, Puerto Rico, collection 24, tape 17, BGCA.
89. Graham, "The Quiet Revolution," 3, collection 345.
90. King, Jr., "Why We Must Go to Washington," Atlanta, January 15, 1968, 3, MLKJP, GAMK.
91. Ibid., 4.
92. Ibid., 8.
93. Ibid., 9.

94. James Cone, *Black Theology & Black Power*, 136.
95. Graham, "The Quiet Revolution," 9.
96. Graham, "Marching for Christ in Montgomery," tape 806.
97. Ibid.
98. Graham, "Billy Graham Makes Plea for an End to Intolerance," 151.
99. Ibid.

Chapter Six   "The Tramp, Tramp, Tramp of the Little Man": Graham's Conversion to the War on Poverty

1. Graham, *Just As I Am*, 5.
2. McLoughlin, *Billy Graham*, 99.
3. Graham, *Organized Labor and the Church* (Minneapolis, MN: The Billy Graham Evangelistic Association, 1952), 2.
4. McLoughlin, *Billy Graham*, 99.
5. Graham, *Organized Labor*, 2.
6. Graham, "My Answer" (manuscript), December 24, 1958, collection 19, box 9, folder 1, BGCA.
7. Graham, "Labor Day Message," September 9, 1959, collection 191, tape 504, BGCA.
8. Graham, "Thanksgiving," tape 358. Sara Diamond, *Not By Politics Alone: The Enduring Influence of the Christian Right* (New York, NY: The Guilford Press, 1998) understates the point when she argues that "Graham's message was explicitly anticommunist, and implicitly supportive of capitalism and all its attendant inequalities" (60). Graham was explicitly supportive of capitalism, too. But, as we will see in the text, he also became critical of the inequalities that capitalism generated.
9. Graham, "Labor Day Message," tape 504.
10. See Graham, *My Answer*, 101.
11. Graham, *World Aflame*, 186.
12. Graham, *Billy Graham Answers Your Questions,* 104.
13. Ibid.
14. Graham, *My Answer*, 106.
15. Graham, *Billy Graham Answers Your Questions*, 108–109.
16. Ibid., 109.
17. Ibid., 102.
18. Graham, *The Economics of the Apocalypse* (Minneapolis, MN: The Billy Graham Evangelistic Association, 1975), 9.
19. Graham, *Organized Labor*, 5.
20. Graham, "Christ's Message to the Laboring Man," August 31, 1958, collection 191, tape 451, BGCA.
21. Graham, "Labor Day Message," tape 504.
22. Stewart Burns, *To the Mountaintop: Martin Luther King, Jr.'s Sacred Mission to Save America: 1955–1968* (San Francisco, CA: HarperSanFrancisco, 2004), 67.
23. King, Jr., *Stride Toward Freedom*, 203.
24. King, Jr., *Why We Can't Wait*, 135.
25. King, Jr., "The Negro and the Constitution," *Papers 1*, 110.
26. King, Jr., "The 'New Negro' of the South," *Papers 3*, 286.
27. King, Jr., *Stride Toward Freedom*, 205.
28. Ibid., 204.
29. King, Jr., "If the Negro Wins, Labor Wins," in *A Testament of Hope*, 203.
30. Ibid., 204.
31. Graham, "The Love of Money," December 11, 1960, collection 19, tape 570, BGCA.
32. Graham, *The Seven Deadly Sins*, 95.
33. Graham, *Peace with God*, 197.
34. Graham, *Billy Graham Answers Your Questions*, 102.
35. Theodore Weber, *Politics in the Order of Salvation: Transforming Wesleyan Political Ethics* (Nashville, TN: Abingdon Press, 2001).

36. Graham, *Peace with God*, 197.

37. Graham, "The Love of Money," tape 570.

38. Graham, *Billy Graham Answers Your Questions*, 105.

39. Graham, *Peace with God*, 197.

40. Graham, *Billy Graham Answers Your Questions*, 105.

41. Graham, *Peace with God*, 197.

42. Graham, *Billy Graham Answers Your Questions*, 105.

43. "Here Is Text of Graham's Wednesday Night Sermon," *The Charlotte Observer*, September 24, 1958, 6-A. BGCA, which holds this text in collection 74, box 7, folder 3, lists the sermon title as "America's Greatest Sin." Subsequent references to this sermon will cite the BGCA title.

44. Ibid.

45. Graham, *America at the Crossroads*, 4.

46. Graham, *The Seven Deadly Sins*, 69.

47. Graham, *The Seven Deadly Sins*, 96.

48. King, Jr., "The Burning Truth in the South," in *A Testament of Hope*, 96.

49. Graham, "America's Greatest Sin," 6-A.

50. Ibid.

51. See, for example, Graham, "Love of Money," tape 570.

52. Graham, *America at the Crossroads*, 6–7.

53. Graham, "The Quiet Revolution," 5, collection 345.

54. Graham, *Needed! Strong Men*, 7.

55. Graham, *America at the Crossroads*, 6.

56. Graham, *Needed! Strong Men*, 7.

57. Graham, "Why Communism Is Gaining," November 17, 1963, collection 191, tape 723, BGCA.

58. Graham, *My Answer*, 184.

59. Graham, "Why Communism Is Gaining," tape 723.

60. Graham, *The Ultimate Weapon*, 1961.

61. Graham, *Three Dimensional Love of God* (Minneapolis, MN: The Billy Graham Evangelistic Association, 1959), 1.

62. Ibid., 3.

63. Ibid., 10.

64. Graham, *World Aflame*, 34.

65. Ibid., 10–11.

66. See Graham, *The Seven Deadly Sins*, 69.

67. Ibid., 68.

68. Graham, "A Look at 1956," January 1, 1956, collection 191, tape 312, BGCA.

69. Graham, "Sleeping through a World Revolution," collection 191, tape 637, March 25, 1962, BGCA. See also Graham, *World Aflame*, 223.

70. Press Conference Transcript, April 30, 1964, San Diego, 13–14.

71. Ibid., 14.

72. King, Jr., "Paul's Letter to American Christians," *Papers 3*, 416.

73. King, Jr., *Stride Toward Freedom*, 93.

74. Ibid., 94.

75. King, Jr., *Trumpet of Conscience*, 62.

76. King, Jr., *Where Do We Go from Here?* 180.

77. King, Jr., *Autobiography*, 301.

78. Press Conference Transcript, July 9, 1964, Columbus, 10.

79. "Get Tough Policy Urged by Graham," *The Atlanta Journal and Constitution*, August 15, 1965, 2.

80. "Probe of Religious Influence Expected in Aftermath of Los Angeles Riots," Religious News Service Transcript, August 16, 1965, 17, BGCA.

81. Ibid.

82. "King Favors Use of Police in Riot," UPI News Story, August 14, 1965, BGCA.

83. "Probe of Religious Influence Expected in Aftermath of Los Angeles Riots," Religious News Service Transcript, August 16, 1965, 16, BGCA.

84. "Billy Graham Says Riots a Symptom of the Revolt of Man against God," Religious News Service Transcript, August 27, 1965, BGCA. King was not the only one to offer a public rebuttal to Graham. The Fellowship of Reconciliation (FOR), a nonviolent organization closely aligned with King and the civil rights movement, also took issue. "It has become the favorite American myth,"

stated the FOR, "that every situation we do not like may be attributed to the machinations of 'sinister forces.' " If there were such forces present in Watts, they were "incidental to the underlying frustration and bitterness that permeate so much of the Negro population of our country, and that grow from the slowness with which Negroes are realizing the full participation in American life to which they are entitled" (see "Physical, Spiritual Rehabilitation Efforts Get Underway in Los Angeles," *Religious News Service Transcript*, August 18, 1965, BGCA, 2).

85. "Graham Asks LBJ, FBI Bare Race Agitators," *The Atlanta Journal*, July 19, 1966, BGCA, 3.

86. Ibid.

87. Graham, *World Aflame*, xiv–xv.

88. Graham, "Text of Remarks Prepared for Delivery by the Reverend Billy Graham: Presidential Prayer Breakfast," Washington, DC, February 17, 1966, BGCA, 6. For a concise and helpful look at Graham's role in the prayer breakfasts, see Nicole H. Miller, "The Political-Religious Discourse of Billy Graham at the Presidential Prayer Breakfasts of the 1960s" (M.A. thesis, Colorado State University, 1998).

89. Graham, *Our God Is Marching On* (Minneapolis, MN: The Billy Graham Evangelistic Association, 1966), 7.

90. Graham, *Rioting or Righteousness* (Minneapolis, MN: The Billy Graham Evangelistic Association, 1967), 3–4.

91. Graham, "America Is in Trouble," tape 917.

92. Ibid.

93. "Graham Slaps at Great Society," April 12, 1967, *Atlanta Journal*, 17, collection 345, box 44, no. 5.

94. For Graham's embrace of this passage, see "My Answer" (transcript), October 30, 1958, collection 19, box 6, folder 8, BGCA.

95. "Graham Slaps at Great Society," April 12, 1967, *Atlanta Journal*, 17.

96. Graham, *The Kingdom Society*, 7.

97. Ibid., 2.

98. King, Jr., *Why We Can't Wait*, 135.

99. King, Jr., Statement before the Platform Committee of the Republican National Convention, San Francisco, July 7, 1964, 9, MLKJP, GAMK.

100. King, Jr., Statement before the Platform Committee of the Democratic National Convention, Atlantic City, August 1964, 9, MLKJP, GAMK.

101. King, Jr., "Revolution and Redemption," 3, MLKJP, GAMK.

102. King, Jr., Remarks by King at the Convocation on Equal Justice under Law of the NAACP Legal Defense Fund, May 28, 1964, 3, MLKJP, GAMK.

103. Graham to Johnson, March 7, 1967, LBJL.

104. "Billy Graham: Only Government Action Can Win Poverty War," *Religious News Service Transcript*, June 16, 1967, box 44, no. 13, BGCA.

105. *Beyond These Hills: A Rural Community Action Film with Billy Graham* (Washington, DC: Office of Economic Opportunity, Community Action Program, 1967), collection 345, film 15, BGCA.

106. *Beyond These Hills: A Rural Community Action Film with Billy Graham* (Washington, DC: Office of Economic Opportunity, Community Action Program, 1967), collection 345, film 16, BGCA.

107. *Beyond These Hills*, film 15.

108. "Billy Graham: Only Government Action Can Win Poverty War," collection 345, BGCA.

109. Graham Says He's Been Converted on Poverty War," June 15, 1967, Baptist Press Release, collection 345, box 44, no. 13, BGCA.

110. *Beyond These Hills*, films 15 and 16.

111. *Beyond These Hills*, film 15.

112. *Beyond These Hills*, film 16.

113. *Beyond These Hills*, films 15 and 16.

114. Press Conference Transcript, Columbus, Ohio, January 28, 1963, collection 19, box 4, folder 9, BGCA.

115. "Graham Says He's Been Converted on Poverty War," collection 345, BGCA.

116. *Beyond These Hills*, film 16.

117. *Beyond These Hills*, film 15.

118. Ibid.

119. Ibid.

120. *Beyond These Hills*, film 16.

121. Graham to Johnson, June 30, 1967, LBJL.

122. *Report of the National Advisory Commission on Civil Disorders* (New York, NY: Bantam, 1968), quoted at http://web.mit.edu/gtmarx/www/kerner/html.
123. Press Conference Transcript, March 12, 1968, Black Mountain, 4.
124. Ibid.
125. Ibid., 5.
126. Ibid., 10.
127. Press Conference, May 13, 1968, Los Angeles, collection 24, tape 8, BGCA.
128. Ibid.
129. Ibid. Graham had criticized the Peace Corps in earlier years. In 1963, for example, he depicted it as "almost completely materialistic in its aims. Without God at its center, it cannot possibly accomplish all that we might hope for it" (Religious News Service, August 30, 1963, quoted in Streiker and Strober, *Religion and the New Majority*, 62.
130. King, Jr., Speech to Staff Retreat, Frogmore, November 14, 1966, 18.
131. Ibid., 20.
132. Graham, "This Violent Hour," May 12, 1968, collection 191, tape 957, BGCA.
133. Ibid.
134. In the early 1970s Richard Pierard wondered whether Graham would backtrack on the poverty question, given Nixon's dismantling of the War on Poverty. But Pierard could have posed his question much earlier than he had, primarily because Graham was backtracking long before the 1960s came to an end. See Pierard, "Billy Graham—Preacher of the Gospel or Mentor of Middle America?" 130.

Chapter Seven   "I'm Not a Pacifist": On Militarists, Pacifists, and Vietnam

1. Telegram from Graham to Truman, June 26, 1950, HSTL.
2. Graham to Truman, July 18, 1950, HSTL.
3. Graham, *America's Decision* (Minneapolis, MN: Billy Graham Evangelistic Association, 1953), 2.
4. Ibid., 4. In addition to preaching a number of sermons on Korea, Graham also wrote a small book on his personal reflections of a trip he had taken to Korea. See *I Saw Your Sons at War: The Korean Diary of Billy Graham* (Minneapolis, MN: The Billy Graham Evangelistic Association, 1953).
5. Graham, *America's Decision*, 3.
6. Graham to Eisenhower, May 10, 1954, DDEL.
7. Graham, *The Signs of the Times* (Minneapolis, MN: The Billy Graham Evangelistic Association, 1957), 1.
8. Ibid., 3.
9. Graham, *Needed! Strong Men*, 2.
10. Ibid., 3. Mark A. Noll, *The Scandal of the Evangelical Mind* (Grand Rapids, MI: William B. Eerdmans Publishing Company, 1994), has argued that because of Graham's example, "other American evangelicals began to overcome fundamentalist Manichaeism" (214). Noll's point, that Graham empowered the evangelical community to begin cooperating with other Christians, is certainly well-taken. But throughout the King years, the evangelist also encouraged his followers to adopt a Manichaeism in terms of their interpretation of global politics. Manichaeism, that is, did not disappear from Graham's thought.
11. Graham, *The Signs of the Times*, 2.
12. Graham, *Needed! Strong Men*, 6.
13. Graham, "The Cause of War Is Spiritual," March 17, 1957, collection 191, tape 375, BGCA.
14. Ibid.
15. Ibid.
16. Graham, *World Aflame*, 68.
17. Graham, "The Cause of War Is Spiritual," tape 375.
18. Graham, *The Signs of the Times*, 3.
19. Graham, "God With Us," *Decision* (December 1961): 14–15.
20. Graham, "Wars and Rumors of Wars," tape 642.
21. Graham, *The Secret of Happiness: Jesus' Teaching on Happiness as Expressed in the Beattitudes* (Garden City, KS: Doubleday & Company, 1955), 72.

22. Graham, "War and World Peace," June 4, 1967, collection 191, tape 908, BGCA.

23. Graham, *The Signs of the Times*, 4.

24. Ibid.

25. Graham, "The Cause of War Is Spiritual," tape 375.

26. Graham, *Needed! Strong Men*, 4.

27. Ibid.

28. Ibid., 5.

29. Ibid.

30. Ibid., 8.

31. Ibid., 10.

32. Graham, "The Quiet Revolution," 7.

33. "Modern History Sourcebook: Khrushchev and Eisenhower: Summit Statements, May 16, 1960," fordham.edu/halsall/mod/1960summit-statements1.

34. Graham, "Peace with God," May 15, 1960, collection 191, tape 540, BGCA.

35. Ibid.

36. "Press Conference," *Decision* (September 1962): 14.

37. Address by Billy Graham, July 30, 1965, Asheville, North Carolina, Crusade Information Service, collection 345, box 44, folder 6, p. 8, BGCA.

38. Graham, "The Quiet Revolution," 7.

39. Graham, "Christian Attitudes Toward World Crisis," February 4, 1968, collection 191, tape 943, BGCA.

40. Graham, *World Aflame*, 224.

41. Graham, "Flames of Revolution," June 25, 1967, collection 191, tape 911.

42. Graham, *The Signs of the Times*, 7.

43. Graham, *World Aflame*, 237.

44. "This Is Text of Graham's Sunday Afternoon Service," *The Charlotte Observer*, October 20, 1957, 5-B. BGCA, which holds this sermon in collection 74, box 7, folder 2, lists the title of this sermon as "The Great Judgment."

45. Graham, *World Aflame*, 236.

46. Ibid., 237.

47. Press Conference Transcript, Atlanta, December 29, 1967, 2.

48. Graham, *Peace with God*, 214.

49. Ibid., 215.

50. Graham, *World Aflame*, 216–224.

51. Ibid., 226.

52. Graham, "The Way for World Peace," December 3, 1967, collection 191, tape 934, BGCA.

53. Ibid.

54. For a pathetic reaction to Graham's relationship with Rome, see Ian R.K. Paisley, *Billy Graham and the Church of Rome* (Belfast: Martyrs Memorial Free Presbyterian Church, 1970).

55. Graham, *World Aflame*, 228.

56. Graham, "The Way for World Peace," tape 934.

57. "The 'Great Society' Will Be God-Made, Not Man-Made, Billy Graham Tells Congress," *The Maryland Baptist*, Baltimore, Maryland, July 8, 1965, 3, collection 345, box 42, folder 4.

58. Graham, "Peace with God," tape 540.

59. Graham, "The Way for World Peace," tape 934.

60. Graham, "Peace with God," tape 540.

61. Graham, "Christian Attitudes Toward World Crisis," tape 943, February 4, 1968.

62. "Press Conference," *Decision*, 16.

63. Ibid., 15.

64. Graham, *World Aflame*, 197.

65. Ibid., xiv.

66. Ibid., 197.

67. Ibid., 198. See also Graham, "Flames of Revolution," tape 911.

68. Graham, *Billy Graham Answers Your Questions*, 121.

69. Ibid.

70. Graham, *World Aflame*, 209.

71. Graham, *My Answer*, 181.

72. "5,000 Hear Evangelist at Pentagon Building," December 13, 1965, Religious News Service, collection 345, box 42, folder 23, BGCA.

73. Graham, "My Answer: Bible Hints Defensive War Is Just," *The Atlanta Constitution*, May 11, 1966, 5, collection 345, box 43, folder 19.

74. See Text of Remarks Prepared for Delivery by the Reverend Billy Graham, February 17, 1966, collection 345, 1. See also Graham, *Our God Is Marching On*.

75. Text of Remarks, February 17, 1966, 2.

76. Ibid., 2–3.

77. Ibid., 4.

78. Ibid.

79. Ibid., 4–5.

80. Ibid., 5.

81. Ibid., 6.

82. Ibid., 5.

83. Ibid., 6.

84. Press Conference Tape, San Juan, Puerto Rico, March 17, 1967, collection 24, tape 17, BGCA. One Graham interpreter, Charles Dullea, accepted Graham's thoughts here uncritically. "Graham," Dullea writes, "has avoided taking sides on certain political-moral questions, notably the Vietnam War, and this has caused criticism" (*A Catholic Looks at Billy Graham*, 116). As we will see, Dullea could not be more deceived than he is.

85. Graham, *Prepare for the Storm* (Minneapolis, MN: The Billy Graham Evangelistic Association, 1961), 2.

86. Ibid., 1. As noted.

87. Graham, *The Ultimate Weapon*, 2.

88. See Graham, "Facing the Anti-God Colossus," 6.

89. Graham, *God and the Nations*, 8.

90. Graham, "Why Communism Is Gaining," tape 723. The previous chapter addressed the economic dimension of this definition.

91. Max Goldberg, Transcript of "Billy Graham Gives Frank Views on War in Vietnam, Race Riots," September 25, 1965, 1, LBJL.

92. Graham to Johnson, July 11, 1965, LBJL (emphasis mine).

93. I am interested here in expanding a thesis set forth by Richard T. Hughes in his excellent study titled *Myths America Lives By* (Urbana, IL: University of Illinois Press, 2003). Hughes argues that because of his anti-communism preaching "Graham perhaps did as much as any other American in the 1950s to divide the world into good versus evil" (172). I would expand this in two ways. One, because of his sky-high profile in the 1950s, Graham was one of the primary movers in shaping American public opinion about communism. Two, as the text suggests, Graham divided the world into goodness versus evil in the 1950s and the 1960s.

94. See *Christian Century* (March 29, 1967): 410–411, quoted in Pierard, "Billy Graham and Vietnam," 47.

95. Graham, *World Aflame*, 12.

96. Graham, "The Real Cause of War," May 30, 1965, collection 191, tape 803, BGCA.

97. Graham, *When Silence Is Yellow* (Minneapolis, MN: The Billy Graham Evangelistic Association, 1965), 1.

98. Ibid., 2.

99. Ibid., 5–6.

100. Ibid., 6.

101. Ibid., 9. I strongly disagree with Richard Pierard's sense that Graham was "quite circumspect in public statements about Vietnam and careful not to affirm it as a crusade for righteousness in Southeast Asia" ("Billy Graham and Vietnam: From Cold Warrior to Peacemaker," *Christian Scholars Review* [1980]: 41). As the text above shows, Graham used the language of holy war in private and public.

102. Transcript of "Billy Graham Gives Frank Views on War in Vietnam, Race Riots," 1.

103. "Billy Graham to Servicemen: 'Millions Pray for You,'" Religion News Service, December 13, 1965, collection 345, box 43, folder 27, BGCA.

104. Graham, "Christmas in Vietnam," December 25, 1966, collection 191, tape 885, BGCA.

105. Graham, "Vietnam Impressions," January 1, 1967, collection 191, tape 886, BGCA.

106. Graham to Johnson, March 7, 1967, 2, LBJL.

107. King, Jr., "War and Pacifism," *Papers 1*, 435.

108. King, Jr., Address at the Conference on Religion and Race, Chicago, Illinois, Edgewater Beach Hotel, January 17, 1963, 13, MLKJP, GAMK.

109. King, Jr., *Strength to Love*, 36.
110. King, Jr., "Who Is Their God?" 210. King was responding here to the use of troops to safeguard the admission of James Meredith to the University of Mississippi.
111. King, Jr., "Pilgrimage to Nonviolence," in *A Testament of Hope*, 39.
112. King, Jr., *Where Do We Go from Here?* 181.
113. King, Jr., "Revolution and Redemption," 10, MLKJP, GAMK.
114. King, Jr., *A Trumpet of Conscience*, 72.
115. King, Jr., "Nobel Prize Acceptance Speech, Oslo, Norway, December 10, 1964, MLKJP, GAMK.
116. King, Jr., "Brighter Day," copy of article for *Ebony*, March 1965, 5, MLKJP, GAMK.
117. *Redbook* transcript of interview with King, Jr., November 5, 1964, question 2, MLKJP, GAMK.
118. King, Jr., "A Time to Break Silence," in *A Testament of Hope*, 233.
119. Ibid., 234.
120. See Henry E. Darby and Margaret N. Rowley, "King on Vietnam and Beyond," *Phylon* vol. 47 (Spring 1986): 49.
121. "Graham Criticizes Dr. King," *New York Times*, April 26, 1967, collection 345, box 44, folder 1, BGCA.
122. "Demonstrations Prolong War, Billy Graham Charges," Religion News Service, April 27, 1967, collection 345, box 44, folder 12, BGCA.
123. King, Jr., "To Charter Our Course," 26, MLKJP, GAMK.
124. King, Jr., "The Drum Major Instinct," *A Testament of Hope*, 265.
125. King, Jr., "Remaining Awake through a Great Revolution," *A Testament of Hope*, 275.
126. Graham to Johnson, June 30, 1967, LBJL.
127. Ibid.
128. Press Conference Transcript, Atlanta, December 29, 1967, 2.
129. Ibid., 2–3.
130. Ibid., 3. Again, I disagree with Pierard, who states that Graham "stood behind the president" throughout 1967 ("Billy Graham and Vietnam," 45). Graham had begun to side with the president's critics by the end of 1967. More fundamentally, Pierard makes a misstep when he claims in another article that "unlike many other prominent clergymen Graham refused to criticize the manner in which Lyndon B. Johnson and Nixon pursued the war or to call for American withdrawal" ("Billy Graham and the U.S. Presidency," *Journal of Church and State* 22, no. 1 (1980): 107–127. Graham did not call for withdrawal, but he did openly criticize Johnson's handling of the war.
131. Ibid., 4.
132. Ibid., 3.
133. Ibid.
134. Ibid., 3–4.
135. Press Conference Transcript, Black Mountain, March 12, 1968, 7.
136. Ibid., 8.
137. Ibid.
138. Ibid.
139. Ibid.
140. Graham, "Jesus, the Great Revolutionist," tape 583.
141. Ibid.
142. Ibid.
143. Ibid.
144. Graham, "Racial Prejudice," 10.
145. Graham, "Love and Little Rock," tape 403.
146. Ibid.
147. Ibid.
148. Graham, "Rioting, Looting, and Crime," July 30, 1967, collection 191, tape 916, BGCA.
149. Graham, "The Real Role of the Church," tape 933.
150. Graham, "A Cause to Fight," tape 918.
151. Graham, *World Aflame*, 12.
152. Ibid., 78.
153. Ibid., 12.
154. In light of Billy Graham's advocacy for disarmament talks in the 1980s, Donald G. Bloesch, *The Future of Evangelical Christianity: A Call for Unity Amid Diversity* (Garden City, KS: Doubleday & Company, Inc., 1983) argued that "Billy Graham has become one of the leading voices on behalf

of peace" (6). (For more on Bloesch's take on Graham, see his "Billy Graham: A Theological Appraisal," *Theology and Life* [May 3, 1960]: 136–143.) Richard Pierard responded to Graham's call for nuclear disarmament in a much more reasonable way—by asking whether the evangelist would "stay the course for peace." Given Graham's quick baptism of the wars against Iraq, the answer to that question is a resounding "no." See Richard V. Pierard, "Billy Graham: Will He Stay the Course for Peace?" *Covenant Quarterly* (February 1984): 17–29.

Conclusion: "We Are Now in the Violent Society"—A Question of Legacy

1. Graham, no title, April 7, 1968, collection 191, tape 952, BGCA.
2. Ibid.
3. King, Jr., "The Drum Major Instinct," *A Knock at Midnight*, 185–186.
4. Drew D. Hansen, *The Dream: Martin Luther King, Jr. and the Speech that Inspired a Nation* (New York: Ecco, 2003), 228.
5. The recently revealed derogatory comments he made about Jews in Nixon's Oval Office suggest that the ignominy did not stop with the King years. For news story on item, as well as its context, see http://www.beliefnet.com/story/101/story_10193_1.html.
6. Martin Marty, *Religion and Republic: The American Circumstance* (Boston, MA: Beacon Press, 1987), accurately claims that Graham's premillenialism "says in effect that churches cannot do much about the nagging issues of their day. The only substantial change in history will occur with the Second Coming of Christ . . ."(256). McLoughlin, *Billy Graham*, made a similar point, though using a different interpretive hermeneutic. "Graham," McLoughlin wrote, "is giving voice to that strong perfectionist streak in American pietism which, by refusing to be satisfied with anything less than a perfect social order, leads to a refusal to make any effort to alter the status quo" (91). McLoughlin's comment is enlightening but not as helpful as tracing Graham's politics of resignation to his premillenialism.
7. Streiker and Strober, *Religion and the New Majority*, rightly argue that "any analysis which conceives Billy Graham to be either the greatest revivalist of all time or White House 'chaplain' falls short of defining his actual place in American society." Writing in 1972, the authors attempt to define his role as "the leader of the politically decisive majority, the man who more consistently than anyone else articulates the aspirations and fears of the bulk of his fellow citizens" (189). By contrast, my thesis defines his role during the King years as two-fold—as the twentieth century's greatest evangelist, and as the major Protestant obstructionist to the beloved community. On a related note, Joel Carpenter, *Revive Us Again: The Reawakening of American Fundamentalism* (Oxford: Oxford University Press, 1997), refers to Graham as the "evangelist to the nation"—hence my "world's best trumpeter for personal salvation."
8. For more on Graham's rhetoric, see Wayne Bond, "The Rhetoric of Billy Graham: A Description, Analysis, and Evaluation" (Ph.D. diss., University of Southern Illinois, 1979); and Billy Edward Vaughn, "Billy Graham: A Rhetorical Study in Adaptation" (Ph.D. diss., University of Kansas, 1972). Perhaps the most creative subject in this field can be found in Hubert Coleman, "A Comparative Rhetorical Analysis of Speeches of Stokely Carmichael and Billy Graham" (M.A. thesis, Bowling Green State University, 1970). And for more on Graham's consistent popularity during part of the King years, see Jon P. Alston, "Popularity of Billy Graham, 1963–1969: Review of the Polls," *Journal for the Scientific Study of Religion* (June 1973): 227–230.

Appendix: Behind the Billy Pulpit

1. Letter from Robert O. Ferm to Family, April 12, 1954, collection 19, box 13, folder 3, BGCA. The Ferm letters cited in this appendix are all from this same collection, box, and folder.
2. Telegram from Billy Graham to Lois Ferm, no date, collection 19, box 13, folder 3, BGCA.
3. Interview of Lee Fisher, January 1976, Oral History 70, collection 141, box 7, folder 17, BGCA, 4.
4. Ibid.

5. Letter from Lee Fisher to Lois Ferm, December 21, 1975, collection 171, box 7, folder 17.
6. Graham, *Just As I Am*, 283.
7. Letter from Robert O. Ferm to Family, March 18, 1954, BGCA.
8. Ferm to Family, March 23, 1954, BGCA.
9. Ferm to Family, March 27, 1954, BGCA.
10. Ferm to Family, March 28, 1954, BGCA.
11. Ferm to Family, undated, BGCA.
12. Ferm to Lois Ferm, April 9, 1954, BGCA.
13. Ferm to Family, postmarked April 9, 1954, BGCA.
14. Ferm to Family, April 12, 1954, BGCA.
15. Ferm to Family, April 10, 1954, BGCA.
16. Ferm to Family, April 9, BGCA.
17. Ferm to Family, April 12, 1954, BGCA.
18. Ferm to Lois Ferm, April 18, 1954, BGCA.
19. Interview of Dr. Robert O. Ferm, June 21, 1978 and January 10, 1979, collection 141, box 7, folder 15, BGCA, 14.
20. Martin, *A Prophet with Honor*, 138.
21. Grant Wacker, "The Billy Pulpit," *The Christian Century* (November 15, 2003): 26.

INDEX